Evolution, Gender, and Rape

Evolution, Gender, and Rape

edited by Cheryl Brown Travis

A Bradford Book
The MIT Press
Cambridge, Massachusetts
London, England

Chapter 8, "Evolutionary Models of Why Men Rape: Acknowledging the Complexities," by Mary P. Koss, was originally published in 2000 in *Trauma, Violence, and Abuse,* vol. 1: 182–190. Reprinted by permission of the author. Chapter 12, "The Origins of Sex Differences in Human Behavior: Evolved Dispositions versus Social Roles," by Alice H. Eagly and Wendy Wood, was previously published in 1999 in *American Psychologist,* vol. 54 (6): 408–423. Reprinted by permission of the author and APA Press.

The index was prepared by Celeste Newbrough.

This book was set in Sabon by Graphic Composition, Inc.

Printed and bound in the United States of America.

Library of Congress Cataloging-in-Publication Data
Evolution, gender, and rape / edited by Cheryl Brown Travis.
    p. cm.
"A Bradford book."
Includes bibliographical references and index.
ISBN 978-0-262-20143-8 (hc. : alk. paper) — ISBN 978-0-262-70090-0 (pb.)
1. Thornhill, Randy. Natural history of rape. 2. Rape. 3. Men — Sexual behavior.
4. Human evolution. I. Travis, Cheryl Brown, 1944–.
HV6558 .E92   2003   2002071892
364.15'32—dc21

10 9 8 7 6 5 4 3 2

Contents

Evolutionary Models and Gender

1

Talking Evolution and Selling Difference

Cheryl Brown Travis

Are women and men bipolar opposites in perpetual discord over conflicting interests? Did we evolve to be this way? Does this reach the extent of an evolutionary, genetic basis for sexual aggression? The publication of *A Natural History of Rape: Biological Bases of Sexual Coercion* by Thornhill and Palmer (2000) answered these questions largely in the affirmative and vaulted the debate into national prominence. This volume offers consideration of these questions from the perspective of a variety of scientific and scholarly disciplines and highlights the complex issues about gender, sexuality, evolution, and violence involved in understanding the intersection of evolution, gender, and rape. The account of rape as evolutionary offered by Thornhill and Palmer (2000) is given detailed analysis.

Gender politics are nowhere more profound than in the area of sexual aggression. The significance of rape was first brought to widespread public attention by the defining work of Susan Brownmiller (1975). A key feature of her analysis was to point out that sexual aggression was sustained by differential status and power and that it carries social meanings that express issues beyond sexuality. These ideas were elaborated and affirmed by other scholars (e.g., Holmstrom and Burgess 1980). Careful, quantitative field studies validated the perspective that status (i.e., the ability to access resources and to exert choice) is a basic feature of sexual violence (Baron and Strauss 1989). These works challenged the common myth that rape was a rare event perpetrated by mentally weak sociopaths on careless victims and suggested instead that dynamics of power and status might touch the lives of ordinary women and men. Indeed, it was found that ordinary cultural discourse included commonly held beliefs and rape myths that foster and help sustain sexual aggression (Burt 1980). It was a shocking discovery that rape might be much more frequent than supposed and that it might invade ostensibly normal dating relationships (Koss et al. 1987). Understanding the acquisition and development of sexually aggressive behavior and the factors that are likely to elicit and to sustain it have been topics of extensive and careful study (Crowell and Burgess 1996; Hall 1996; Heise 1998; Malamuth 1983; Malamuth and Check 1981; Malamuth, Haber, and Feshbach 1980).

If one hopes to make use of evolutionary theory to understand gender differences and to understand sexual aggression in particular, it is necessary to take a considered look at basic principles of evolution and it is necessary to examine assumptions about gender in general. Far from being "anti-evolution," this volume illustrates the care that must be taken in making use of evolutionary theory and includes some attention to how evolutionary theory might guide empirical research. Evolutionary theory is not sexist. The basic principles of evolutionary theory have helped to organize information, to understand some phenomena, and to generate hypotheses. The number of scholarly disciplines, such as evolutionary anthropology, evolutionary biology, evolutionary ecology, and evolutionary psychology, that have emerged evidences the appeal and usefulness of the theory. Because applications of evolutionary principles to human relationships are frequently characterized by grandiose overgeneralization and by political philosophy thinly disguised as evolutionary science, this chapter begins with a short primer of basic concepts. Later chapters introduce more complex questions of theory and methodology.

However, the overgeneralization and grandiosity that has characterized popularized and simplistic accounts of gender and sexuality cannot be dismantled merely by clarifying the tenets of evolutionary theory. One must recognize the cultural context that supports and invites such accounts. Therefore, a second section in this chapter entitled "Media, Culture, and Science" discusses the reciprocal and mutual influences of culture and science as these are played out in the media. The reciprocal link between a cultural predilection for dichotomies and a gender science that supports this predilection can be seen in the media attention given not only to *A Natural History of Rape: Biological Bases of Sexual Coercion,* but to a number of studies focused on biological gender differences. I argue that there should be a broad understanding of gender and of sexuality as phenomena that are as much social as biological.

A final section of this chapter offers the reader a brief overview of the entire volume and serves as an introduction to the major parts of the book. These parts offer useful discussions of some of the more difficult problems one must solve in order to make productive use of evolutionary theory. The second part is focused particularly on the proposal that rape is best understood in terms of evolution, and the final third part of the volume offers a range of other perspectives and models.

A Short Primer

The persistent misapplication and misuse of evolutionary principles has generated an understanding of human maleness and femaleness as categorically opposite, universal, and invariant. Early political renderings of evolutionary theory by politically conservative philosophers resulted in a social Darwinism that served as an account of the disease and poverty of worker classes. Other, pop sociobiology, accounts of human psychology and culture were also loosely formulated in the language of evolution. The pop sociobiology accounts of gender difference based on evolution are often what Stephen Jay Gould (Gould and Lewontin 1970) called "just-so stories," because things *might* have happened as hypothesized. Ethel Tobach and Rachel Reed in this volume point out that simplistic evolutionary models of human behavior are sometimes advanced zoomorphizing (the inappropriate interpretation of human behavior in terms of animal models). Jerry Coyne in this volume makes it clear that the misuse of evolutionary principles invokes the resentment of evolutionary biologists who do work carefully to meet exacting standards. I have elaborated elsewhere (Moore and Travis 2000; Travis and Yeager 1991) on problems of sociobiological approaches that emphasize inherent gender-based conflict as a key to sexuality.

In these "just so stories," sexuality is cast in a one-dimensional and somewhat problematic light. In this popularized view, sex is almost exclusively a matter of reproduction and is fraught with conflict and danger. However, others suggest quite different perspectives and propose that much of what is understood about sex and sexuality is socially constructed (Boyle 1994; Tiefer 1995; Travis and White 2000). Scholars from a variety of disciplines have developed this idea of knowledge as socially constructed; it is not simply an antiscience philosophy promulgated strictly within feminism (Gergen 1985; Lewontin 1992; Parker and Shotter 1990; Simon 1996). The history of sexology research (Tiefer 2000) illustrates the changeable nature of the facts of sexuality and how these are understood among scientists. In studies involving a wide range of animal species, biologist David Crews (1994) has demonstrated a wide range of permutations in reproductive anatomy, physiology, and behavior. Whether sex among primates is largely about reproduction can be questioned. For example, primatologist Frans de Waal (with F. Lanting, 1998) offers a quite different picture of sexuality from field observations of one of our nearest evolutionary neighbors, the bonobo chimpanzee, for whom sexual encounters are largely a form of social exchange and a basis for cohesion rather than reproduction.

When evolutionary theorizing is used to inform a general audience about the nature of sexuality, as well as many other phenomena, there are a lot of references to natural selection, fitness, and environment. But often the connection between these terms and the conclusions about sexual behavior are accomplished only by linguistic fiat. Basic assumptions and corollaries often remain implicit and without empirical corroboration. To read these accounts with a critical eye, a very short primer may be helpful.

Principles of evolution rest on three tenets and involve the ideas that: individuals vary; some variations are more favorable for survival and reproduction than others; some of this variation is genetically based and therefore can be inherited. Most evolution (i.e., differing gene frequencies in successive generations) is due to differential reproductive success as a function of these variations. It is also possible for evolution to occur through genetic drift and other mechanisms that might seem almost to be matters of happenstance. Evolution does not ensure that only adaptive or beneficial traits will occur; nor does it result in an ever-upward move toward perfection. From a biological perspective, the process should be viewed as the elimination of the grossly unfit and those who have met with an unlucky moment. Individuals who are marginally fit may continue to reproduce as long as they do not meet with an unlucky moment. Fitness and natural selection are important conceptual ideas of evolutionary theory that must be understood in terms of gene-environment interaction.

Fitness   The unit for evaluating evolutionary "success" is genetic fitness. Specifically, the bottom line of fitness is the representation of genes in successive generations of offspring that themselves reproduce. Contrary to popular notions, fitness does not necessarily mean that the individual will have a long or prosperous life of ease. Mutualism in the immediate instance can result in greater general and inclusive fitness than immediate exploitation. In some cases, the increased representation of an individual's genes in successive generations may actually be enhanced by what appears to be altruism. W. D. Hamilton (1964) first described this seeming anomaly, whereby individual fitness may be enhanced because genetic relatives in future generations carry an increased frequency of genes carried in the altruistic individual. Thus, fitness is measured not only in the number of direct offspring, but also in the offspring of genetic relatives, what is known as *inclusive fitness*. The process by which these altruistic behaviors are retained in successive generations is termed *kin selection*. Any argument about the evolutionary fitness derived directly from a behavior or trait must show that the behavior or trait results in an increased gene frequency in several succeeding generations. That is, there must be grandchildren and great grandchildren that reproduce these genes. Fitness is always shaped by environmental, ecological, and social context as well as genetic factors. Natural selection is the process by which this interaction may evolve differing gene frequencies. Patty Gowaty in this volume emphasizes that natural selection should be understood as consisting of many components and elaborates on a "components-of-fitness" model in her chapter.

Natural selection   Natural selection operates to increase (or diminish) characteristics or behaviors that result in greater reproductive success among *future* generations. Only those traits having genetic components and some implication for reproductive success are subject to natural selection. Natural selection may operate on a wide range of adaptive patterns, such as offspring behaviors, foraging behaviors, predator defense, social behavior within a group, mate selection, reproductive and gestation patterns, parenting behaviors, and so on. If a behavior, no matter how beneficial, has no genetic component, it is not subject to natural selection. Further, those genetic characteristics likely to be expressed in life stages *after* reproductive effort and parenting are less likely to be subject to natural selection. This explains in part why, after thousands of years of evolution, humans continue to suffer from heart disease and cancer. They are conditions that for the most part express themselves after reproduction and child rearing, when the relevant genes have already been transmitted to the next generation.

Although new genes can be introduced by mutation or by the inward migration of new individuals, adaptations largely reflect the range and limits of the initial gene pool. Thus, in some ways it is better to think of adaptations as ways of "making do" rather than as expressions of increasingly refined solutions. Whether one or another adaptation persists in being expressed depends on its effectiveness relative to other competing permutations. However, in circumstances of reproductive isolation with weak or no competition, less than optimal patterns may be sustained. In these circumstances, entire populations may carry forward a less than optimal genetic condition, sometimes referred to as *founder effects*. These founder effects can accrue merely by entering a certain ecological niche first when there are no competitors and not necessarily because the trait has unique adaptive benefits.

Gene-environment interaction   In every case, natural selection occurs in a gene-environment context. That is, the benefit (if any) of a genetic component for a characteristic depends on the environment. Environment includes not only physical ecology, but also the behavior patterns of conspecifics and other species. (If the termite changed its behavior what would happen to the aardvark?) In many cases, whether a behavior pattern is adaptive or not may depend on the frequency of the behavior relative to similar but competing strategies that might be displayed by peers. Maynard Smith (1977; Maynard Smith and Price 1973) has referred to this balancing of relative frequencies among different solutions to a similar problem as an *evolutionarily stable strategy* (ESS). For example, whether or not cooperation or competition will accrue benefits to the individual depends on the behavioral strategies of other members of the group. Being cooperative in a group of similarly inclined individuals is likely to produce benefits for the individual and related kin. Reciprocal altruism can best evolve where there is opportunity for repeated interactions over time and where helpful acts can be repaid, either directly to the original helper individual or to the helper's related kin. Similarly, the fitness associated with a given reproductive strategy may depend in part on the strategies of other members of the group. Thus, where the reproductive norm is that of bonded, genetically invested adults, strategies that depend on deception and manipulation are not likely to be associated with long-term success.

Environment is a complex that includes not only the surrounding physical ecology, but also the interactive, social ecology. This is particularly important for species that live in groups. The expectations, beliefs, and habits of one's peers and partners constitute a social environment that can elicit and sustain, or extinguish, certain behaviors as well as the feelings and rationale that support such behaviors. For humans, group living has facilitated foraging, predator defense, and care of offspring. Indeed, one may argue that the survival of humans depended on the ability to sustain group integration. Among other things, the recognition of individuals and memory for their past behavior and personal traits would have been key to the formation and maintenance of group living among early humans. It would be functional to be able to sort other individuals in terms of privilege and hierarchy with respect to the self. But the ability to recognize dominance and power would be only one way of mentally marking other individuals in one's group. It also would be functional to remember who was generous and who stingy, who trustworthy and who nefarious.[1] Rogues who were disruptive to group welfare were probably excluded from most beneficial social exchanges, and they and their offspring would have suffered the consequences of such exclusion. One might suppose that this winnowing process would have produced a predilection for affiliation and an emotional desire to belong to a group, even if it involved restraint on immediate self-interests.

Other chapters in this volume discuss additional complexities of evolutionary theory, gender, and sexuality. Despite this complexity, discussions of genetics in human ability and behavior can take on a remarkably simplistic tone. These discussions do not reduce simply to matters of confirmed or unconfirmed fact. The same errors of exaggeration, oversimplification, and overgeneralization are repeated over a wide range of topics. Part of the reason lies in not only in casual misuse of evolutionary concepts, but also in cultural bias about gender and difference.

Media, Culture, and Science

Grandiosity in the misuse of evolutionary theory does not occur simply because someone forgot basic evolutionary principles. There is a cultural readiness to locate causes for human events in biology and a cultural receptivity for the idea that gender roles are the product of orderly laws. Scientific reports consistent with this cultural bias receive high-profile coverage in the media. *A Natural History of Rape* is part of this cultural phenomenon. It is not simply an explication of an idea. Although it is couched in scientific terms, it can be understood as a product not of science but of culture. The emphasis on a supposedly "natural" link between sexuality, danger, and violence might in fact reflect less about scientific empiricism and more about cultural beliefs that emerge from Western Christianity linking sex with sin (Pagels 1999, Ruth 1987) and the more recent moralizing by conservative religious leaders that HIV/AIDS is punishment for sexual sin (John 1995).

The fundamental ideas of biological determinism and categorical sex differences resonate with long-standing cultural biases. There are ongoing tensions about the study of gender differences: how big are they; how consistent are they; how significant are they; how amenable are they to change; and what implications do they have for social politics? Similar tensions also exist in studies of racial politics and IQ (Gould 1981). Gender differences in math, verbal, spatial, and other cognitive functions, even when small by scientific standards, remain topics of extensive study and continue to be reported as important news. Gender differences in psychological qualities such as anxiety, depression, intuition, and aggression are of similar interest. There is, in addition, a general predilection to see differences as located within individuals and thus "natural," uniform, and invariant. The framing of such questions in terms of a homogeneous group difference simultaneously reflects and contributes to a cultural understanding of the genders as dichotomous and categorically opposite. When explanations for these different qualities and roles invoke brain function, hormones, or evolution they are made to seem even more "natural," more invariant, and more permanent.

Western, occidental views of sex and sexuality are built around categorical dichotomies, where the creation and celebration of sex differences are understood to be crucial to social order. One gains the impression from this dichotomous view that society would pretty nearly collapse without the orderliness derived from these differences. Such differences are extolled, as if orderliness in the presumed "natural" social arrangements were a completely value-neutral condition.

Stereotypic notions of gender roles are by and large cherished in American culture. Popular books trade quite successfully on the same notion of inherent, fixed gender differences. The idea that women and men are effectively from different planets was such a successful marketing idea that it was reiterated in a book series and even became the basis for a one-man

Broadway show. Such books provide reassurance about the natural, and therefore rightful, divisions of labor. They also offer reassurance about the natural basis for unequal political privilege[2] that goes along with these gender differences.

In harmony with this cultural value system, much of the research on sex and gender has focused on difference. This is despite the fact that an extensive body of research based on statistical techniques of meta-analysis, developed by Eagly, Hyde, and others (Eagly and Steffen 1986; Hyde 1984), has shown that, compared to individual variability *within* a gender, many of the presumed differences between genders fall in the moderate, small, or nonexistent range. Jacob Cohen (1994) argued that the ritualized testing of difference is flawed by numerous logical errors. As an alternative, he advocated an emphasis on estimating effect sizes and the use of confidence intervals. This approach is important because it prompts us to question not only whether there is a difference between groups, but to ask about the practical size of differences.

The focus on difference carries with it a number of implications and value judgments outlined by Dale Miller (Miller, Taylor, and Buck 1991). The first point is that research on difference begins with an implicit normative case and tacitly seeks to explain differences from this norm. The thing that needs explaining is, by implication, abnormal, difficult, or puzzling. Exceptions to the norm are seen as problematic, and explanations of the problem tend to target internal, person-based causes while ignoring interactive, contextual factors. This tradition of looking for differences is related to the fact that science occurs in a cultural context and is in part a product of that cultural context. The history of science is replete with instances where flawed and highly improbable ideas have been advanced as science, a science that just happened to be congruous with cultural beliefs of the time. The influence is reciprocal, and culture in turn is informed and perpetuated by confirmatory distillations of science. The penchant for conceptualizing male and female gender as opposites continues to characterize popular culture as well as scholarly publications. This is especially apparent in renderings of research results for public consumption in news media.

These cultural biases are normalized and reinforced by selective reporting of findings, overgeneralization, and social constructions found in news stories. In this framework, it makes cultural sense that groups with such categorically and uniformly different qualities should have different social roles, obligations, and privileges. It follows that men and women frequently will find themselves with conflicting interests and that what benefits one may be anathema to the other. The phenomenon is not specific to ideas about rape and is illustrated here by the media treatment of three other studies of sex differences.

Gender Science in the News

Dozens of news stories covered discussions of *A Natural History of Rape: Biological Bases of Sexual Coercion,* in part because sex sells and ideas about inherently conflicted roles for men and women are of considerable interest. But the book is only one example of this cultural interest. Nowhere has cultural and scientific bias been more evident than in research on gender and brain function. There's a long history of efforts to use brain size and function as a basis for prejudicial discrimination, not only involving gender but also involving color and race (Gould 1981). Research selected for high media coverage is interpreted as validating common stereotypes about femininity and masculinity. The media chooses to highlight scientific findings that confirm stereotypes because they think people will attend to them. People do attend to these stories, because they are easily integrated with preexisting concepts (stereotypes).

In particular, significant media attention is paid to science studies that lend themselves to a discussion of brain differences between women and men. Brain differences seem to be an especially favored topic in these representations on the natural and universal aspects of gender differences. News stories seem to promote the idea that women and men are different and have the brains to prove it. Common flaws in these news stories include distortion and exaggeration of differences, pejorative labeling, and overgeneralization. Findings are extrapolated by the media to aptitudes and abilities not relevant in the least to the study being reported. Labels, meaning, and interpretations are regularly presented in judgmental terms that focus on women's deficits and limitations. Further, the news stories often locate the origins of these differences in deterministic genes and evolution. Three examples illustrate this reciprocal and confirmatory relationship between culture and science.

Listening with Half a Brain   A good example of this reciprocal relationship can be seen in a study presented at the radiological meetings at Chicago in fall of 2000, by Dr. Joseph Lurito and his colleagues at Indiana University medical school. They used functional magnetic resonance imaging to track blood flow in the brains of ten women and ten men as they listened to a voice reading passages from a John Grisham thriller. Both men and women had the greatest increase in blood flow on the left side of the brain. Both men and women also showed some increase in blood flow on the right side. Differences between left and right brain activity were relatively larger for men who showed significantly more increase in the left-brain. The left-right hemisphere differences for women were less striking and suggested a more even pattern of blood flow and activation. The authors suggested that this even pattern of activation might allow women to more readily recover language functions following a stroke.

Thirteen news stories depicted the differences between women and men as more categorical than in fact they were reported in the original study. In these stories, the difference in blood flow while listening to the Grisham thriller was extrapolated to mean something about quality of thinking style, about general reasoning, and about emotion. A flippant analysis might lead one to suggest that men listen with only half a brain. However, a number of stories took care to protect male worthiness. Lurito was quoted in several stories as stating that the observed difference did *not* indicate that women were better listeners. He additionally was quoted in several of the news stories as suggesting that women might even find listening more difficult. He suggested that this might be so because women used more of their brain to accomplish the same task. The implications of the study for potential deficits in women and their brains were reiterated in several stories. The general implication was that listening is difficult for women. That is, women try harder to achieve the same result that men accomplish with relative ease.

Navigating with Half a Brain   The journal *Nature Neuroscience* published a research study conducted by Mathias Riepe and his colleagues at the University of Ulm in Germany (Groen et al 2000) that used MRI methodology similar to that of the paper by Lurito on listening. This study presented 12 women and 12 men with 3 computerized virtual 3-D mazes, each maze containing several potentially successful pathways. This task is

not unlike computer games in video arcades, a recreational setting fre-
quented by boys more often than by girls. The study found that the average score for the 12 men to complete a maze was 54 seconds faster than
the average score required for the 12 women. Functional magnetic resonance imaging was used to measure activity in a number of different brain
regions in both the left and right hemispheres and *multiple comparisons*
were later conducted to assess sex differences. In four regions, women and
men both showed bilateral activation. In two brain regions men showed
bilateral activation and women unilateral, and in one region women
showed bilateral activation while men had unilateral activation. In three
other regions one gender showed unilateral activation while the other
showed no elevated activation at all. If you're counting, that's at least ten
comparisons.

Out of these similarities and differences, only the differences were
noted, namely that men had higher activation for the hippocampal regions
in both left and right hemispheres, whereas women showed higher activation in only the right hippocampal regions. Men showed more bilateral
activation while women showed more unilateral activation. This is a situation similar, but in reverse, to that reported by Lurito in the listening
study, that is, ostensibly women were using half their brain to accomplish
the task, while men needed to work hard with both sides of their brain.

Reports on the Riepe study credited men's 54-second superiority in part
to the fact that compared to women they were using more of their brain.
For example, one headline read "Men really don't need to ask for directions: Men's brains specially wired for navigation, new research suggests,"
while another headline reassured readers that "You Know Where You Are
With a Man." Yet another made a more direct allusion to the battle of
the sexes by proclaiming that "Maps of the Mind Reveal Why Women
Navigators Drive Men Round The Bend." Most of the stories distorted the
findings and overgeneralized findings from the computerized maze to
statements about men's superior ability to read and understand maps and
to find their way in unfamiliar settings—though the study did not assess
map-reading skills or navigational skills in natural settings.

Gray Matter and Computer Science   In May of 1999, Ruben Gur[3] and
several co-authors published an article in the journal *Neuroscience* reporting that a study of 40 women and 40 men found that compared to

men, women have proportionately more gray matter (GM). The men not only had a lower percentage of GM, their GM was distributed asymmetrically, with relatively more GM in the left than the right hemisphere. Women showed no asymmetries. Women and men in the study were of comparable age and education and had equivalent IQ test scores. Participants were administered verbal subtests from the revised WAIS adult intelligence scale and a vocabulary test from the California Verbal Learning Tests. They also received two spatial tests, a block design subtest from the WAIS and a Judgment of Line Orientation test, which requires subjects to identify the true vertical or horizontal of a stimulus line. Percentage of gray matter and white matter were moderately correlated with verbal and spatial performance for both women and men, that is, the more GM the better the score. Women and men had similar scores in verbal performance. Men did have higher scores on the block design test and on judging vertical and horizontal orientation of lines. However, the higher test scores on spatial tasks reported for the men were not associated with the lateral variation in GM. Men with more uneven lateral distribution of GM than other men (or women) did not score better on these spatial-perception tasks. Nor was laterality of GM associated with any of the verbal measures. Thus, the distribution of GM was not associated with any of the performance measures, any more, say, than a study of gender difference in pickle eating and in cognitive measures. Gur and his colleagues conservatively and appropriately noted that "These conclusions should be considered tentative because these correlations could be spurious, pending replication in other samples and across a wider range of cognitive measures" (Gur et al. 1999, p. 4070). Nevertheless, media accounts distorted, exaggerated, misinterpreted, and overgeneralized the findings. Media coverage forgot to mention there was no association between the distribution of gray matter and any of the measures, but instead supported a vague notion that differences in cognitive function were produced by differences in gray matter. Not only did these errors occur in the press, Gur himself eventually repeated them.

Press representations of the study and later press interviews with Gur expanded significantly on the implications and the "facts." The *Independent,* a London-based paper, reported that women have smaller brains than men, but use what they have more efficiently, thus accounting for why women and men perform equally well on IQ tests. Two days later the same story was picked up by the *London Guardian,* and the results were said to explain why women perform better on verbal tasks while men perform better on spatial tasks, though Gur found no gender differences in verbal test scores.

A week or so later the story moved to the United States, and the *Washington Post, Buffalo News,* and *Pittsburgh Gazette* ran virtually identical stories reporting sex differences in gray matter and white matter. These stories incorrectly noted that gray matter is used for communication and white matter is used for computation.[4] This is a case where prevailing gender stereotypes, not the facts, become the basis for allocating meaning to the findings. Since stereotypes are that women are better than men in language skills, if women have more gray matter it must be associated with language and communication. Since men are thought to be better at math, then brain differences in white matter are interpreted as the anatomical basis for a math propensity. In these stories gray matter is associated specifically with communication, a stereotypic feminine quality, rather than with general intelligence, thinking, logic, or problem solving; these "tough-minded" qualities are not part of the feminine stereotype.

One might ignore these extrapolations and overgeneralizations as simply sloppy writing by reporters who understand little about science. However, in July of 2000, a full year later, the *Ottawa Citizen* carried excerpts of an interview with Gur where he elaborated on the possible social and educational implications. He noted that women's brains are structured in a way that can put them at a disadvantage when it comes to learning computer skills, despite the fact that Gur did not assess women's ability to learn computer skills. In the interview Gur further suggested that the difference in brain tissue could provide a biological reason for why so few women in North America take an interest in computer science. What the news stories imply is that having more gray matter and having it relatively evenly available in the brain makes it harder for people, or at least women, to think systematically.

Despite the flaws in such logic, there is a ready home for such "expert" reports of stereotypic gender in the general culture. The cultural desire for ordered gender differences sets a context for the formulation of research questions and for the interpretation of research findings. What passes for science is often merely a reiteration of cultural myth. The same desire provides an impetus for the media attention that gives added significance to group differences. In some cases differences are reported where none were found. The Thornhill and Palmer thesis on rape as a product of evolution was partly granted a flurry of media attention because it is a story that easily can be seen as part of this larger cultural context. It was welcomed in a cultural context where ideas about the biological and fixed nature of sex differences are already widely accepted.

Theory, Research, and Alternative Models: An Introduction to the Rest of the Volume

Remaining chapters in this volume are organized in three major parts and address the evolutionary account of rape from the perspectives of animal behavior, ecology, evolutionary biology, cultural anthropology, philosophy, primatology, psychology, and sociology. Contributors reflect varying academic backgrounds, different research traditions, and a range of personal philosophies. None finds the evolutionary account of rape to be in any way compelling.

The first part offers a collection of additional chapters that elaborate and greatly extend the consideration of evolutionary theory. Discussion includes problems of methodology, as well as nosology and logic that plague efforts to apply evolutionary theory to human social behavior. The second part of the volume gives specific and detailed attention to the ideas, reasoning, and data relevant to the proposition that rape is the product, or by-product, of evolution as these were presented in *A Natural History of Rape: Biological Bases of Sexual Coercion*. The final part of the volume offers alternative models and frameworks that include evolutionary, psychological, and cross-cultural perspectives.

I   Evolutionary Theory and Sociobiology Theory

Initial chapters raise a variety of theoretical and methodological issues for evolutionary models and pop sociobiology. Chapters 2 and 3 point to ways in which evolutionary theory can be useful to feminist analysis. Christine Drea and Kim Wallen unveil the widespread androcentric focus of much theorizing about gender relations. Using primate data, they demonstrate the significant role that females play in reproductive decisions. Females are vested with significant sexual control. They not only are active agents with respect to their own sexual behavior, but it may be argued from empirical data that female interests and strategies also have an significant role in shaping and controlling male sexual behavior. This analysis is consistent with the observation of Patricia Gowaty in chapter 3 that feminists and evolutionary biologists have interesting things to say to each other. Gowaty points to the concepts of the environment of evolutionary adaptation (EEA) as one such fruitful area of discussion. Rather than seeing a categorical divide between "nature" and "nurture" positions, she observes that most ideas in evolutionary ecology assume that the mechanisms of heredity are not just genes, but environments, cultures, and development.

Chapters 4 and 5 address methodological concerns and the ways in which methodology is linked to theory. Stephanie Shields and Pamela Steinke discuss the distinction between proximate and ultimate explanations and the use of self-report data. For example, sociobiological explanations often make inferences about human feelings and motivations and rely on self-report data to confirm hypotheses about ultimate evolutionary causes. Shields and Steinke argue that investigations of "ultimate explanations" need to rely on data that can differentiate proximate from ultimate. Investigatory techniques or data, such as self-report, that are derived from proximate variables do not qualify as valid for testing ultimate explanations.

Tobach and Reed elaborate on these methodological problems. They point out that in retrospective "what if" accounts, much theorizing and data analysis is characterized by anthropomorphic interpretations wherein human expectations, motives, and feelings are imposed arbitrarily on animal behaviors. There also is a reciprocal phenomenon of zoomorphizing, whereby the apparent causes and effects of the behavior of other animals is taken as sufficient for the understanding of human behavior. Specific considerations are raised with respect to violence, including a review of the diverse sources of information, definitions, and data concerning rape.

Vicker and Kitcher conclude the first section and point out that behavioral and mathematical ecology have pursued evolutionary questions about behavior in nonhuman animals. They contrast this careful and painstaking work with the casual storytelling of pop sociobiology and the putative evolutionary advantages claimed for certain forms of human behavior. Vicker and Kitcher argue, along with others, that model building requires attention to the details, and mathematical modeling uncovers and refines hidden presuppositions. They further discuss the importance of intraspecific variability and the role of cultural transmission, especially in discussions of human behavior.

II Research Data and Rape

The second part contains a collection of short papers that directly address the data and theory relevant to the thesis that rape evolved as a result of natural selection and that rape therefore has a genetic component. Jerry Coyne, an evolutionary biologist, offers a no-holds-barred critique. He points out that most of the media coverage has pitted Thornhill and Palmer against feminists as science vs. politics. Coyne, instead, focuses on the science that lies behind, or does not lie behind, the evolutionary account of rape. Coyne argues that the scientific errors in this evolution-rape thesis are far more inflammatory than are its ideological implications.

Mary Koss, whose work is challenged by Thornhill and Palmer, raises points about the social construction of science and inherent flaws of measurement in every study. She focuses on the question of who exactly suffers emotionally from rape and sexual aggression. This is a key piece of scientific data, because an important source of reasoning for the rape-evolution account is that victims of rape suffer distress in accord with the degree to which rape diminishes their reproductive interests. The rape-evolution account rests to a large extent on the secondary analysis of data initially published by McCahill, Meyer, and Fishman (1979) on responses of rape survivors who made use of a Philadelphia hospital emergency room. Koss questions the relevance of this data for assessing constructs developed in the rape-evolution proposal long after the original data were collected. She further notes that the respondents of the original study represented probably only 5 percent of rape victims. She directly challenges the assessment of distress and long-lasting impact of rape as most serious among women of reproductive age with a number of empirical sources documenting distress, fear, and long-lasting impact among other groups of women.

I have indulged myself with a second chapter in this volume to give detailed consideration to the data and logistics relevant to scientifically evaluating the rape-evolution hypothesis. I first consider the hypothesis that rape is a by-product of selection for oversexed males and discuss the unexamined concepts of sexuality and gender underlying this proposition. I next consider the proposal that rape is itself an adaptation subject to natural selection. Among other key data, pregnancy rates associated with rape are reviewed, and I offer some observations on the evolutionary (social and ecological) environment where this behavior supposedly evolved. In addition, for rape to be an evolutionarily based adaptation, rapists should differ genetically from the nonrapists *in the same category*, that is, the category of youths or of misfits *assumed* by Thornhill and Palmer to be the most likely characters to perpetrate rape.

Michael Kimmel concurs that the account of rape as the product of evolution constitutes bad science. He notes that the supposed natural conflict between males and females is based on assumptions that females, especially female primates, are coy and careful in their sexual behavior. However, primatologist Sarah Blaffer Hrdy (1977) has effectively refuted this notion. She observed that females often exhibit a natural propensity toward promiscuity, while it is males who may work hard to ensure monogamy and parental certainty for themselves. Kimmel additionally observes that the hypothesized male propensity for rape is an unacknowledged form of male bashing where all men are painted with a common brush as violent, rapacious predators.

In the final chapter of this part Elisabeth Lloyd takes issue with the public discussions of Thornhill and Palmer regarding the conflict between their position, construed by them as science, and that of feminist criticisms, construed as antiscience politics. This is the "Galileo Defense," the claim that their true conclusions are the result of excellent science, and that most critics, and especially feminists, are ignorant and politically motivated. Lloyd chooses to argue the merits of the rape-evolution proposal by carefully examining the necessary assumptions. For example, necessary assumptions would require that men have special psychological adaptations for recognizing female vulnerability, a preference for raping women of peak fertility, and a psychological adaptation to be sexually aroused by gaining physical control over an unwilling sexual partner. Further assumptions are that men have a psychological adaptation to rape wives and girlfriends if they believe their women are cheating on them and an evolved psychological tendency to be paranoid about women's claims of being raped.

All the chapters in this part are critical of the shallow and limited treatment given to the reduction of rape in Thornhill and Palmer's proposal. The rape reduction programs are trivial, and this is in itself a problem because the authors purport to be motivated by a desire to reduce this heinous act and the grief and suffering that follow from it. They offer five pages about educational programs for young men and two pages on barriers to rape, such as keeping women from any social situation that might permit rape. Nothing in the book suggests that something needs to be done about the sense of entitlement derived from being male in a patriarchal society. Nothing suggests that it might be useful to challenge the common cultural understanding of rape as sex and of sex as overwhelming biological desire. Nothing offers a way for women to feel a greater sense of agency and entitlement. Nothing addresses the construction and limitations of traditional gender roles.

III   Alternative Models

The challenge is to go beyond discussing, yet again, the limits of sociobiological storytelling and to offer ways to think about the problem that can suggest useful questions, other methodologies, and different theoretical models. Recognizing variability among individuals and among cultures is a starting point. For example, not all men engage in rape behavior, even when in positions that would permit rape. Thus, there are different developmental outcomes and variation among individuals. Some of this variation may be cultural context and learning.

Alice Eagly and Wendy Wood argue that the status of women's roles within varying cultures and contemporaneous social conditions accounts for a significant amount of variance in individual behavior patterns, romance, attraction, and gender relationships. They further argue that forms of sexual control emerge along with the development of particular socioeconomic structures and that these structures have had particular utility for men. For example, men's concern with paternity and the associated sexual jealousy is strongest under conditions of intensive agriculture, ownership of private property, patrilineal inheritance, and community stratification (Schlegel and Barry 1986; Whyte 1978). Eagly and Wood offer a re-analysis of data on mate preferences from 37 countries initially presented by David Buss and find significant cross-cultural variation in the understanding of gender and women's status. These cultural factors support a social structural account of sex differences in mate preferences. From this perspective, sex differences in behavior reflect the greater power and status associated with men's roles and from the sex-typed division of labor and of gender.

Wade Mackey argues directly against the assumption that men are less emotionally invested in the outcomes of their sexual encounters than are women. Instead he offers cross-cultural analyses supporting the contention that men do have affiliative, nurturing orientations toward their own children and that this is a key element in the well-being of children. Absence of this supporting and affiliative connection harms the child and the community, and offers no genetic advantage to men. Mackey provides evidence from physical as well as cultural anthropology. For example, he notes that among species where there is active paternal involvement and dual provisioning of young, there is also limited physical sexual dimorphism. Notably, human evolution shows a pattern whereby sexual dimorphism decreased significantly. As dimorphism declined, it is likely that the roles of males and females were beginning to converge. He further argues that psychological traits among men (potential fathers), such as honesty, reliability, and trustworthiness, would have become increasingly salient. These traits would have been desirable not only from the perspective of the individual woman, but would have increasingly become of interest to her genetic relatives, the kin group, and eventually her larger cultural group.

Emily Martin and Peggy Reeves Sanday argue for a cross-cultural, sociological, and anthropological understanding of rape. Martin proposes that rape can be understood only in a cultural context. She reminds us that human behavior is complex, context-dependant, and often changes through time and across space. Intentional actions, such as rape, cannot be separated from the contexts in which they occur. The understanding, meaning, and significance accorded actions are derived not from biological features, but from society and culture. She points out that rape is not simply a physical "thing in the world," such as an eye with a fixed anatomy. It can be understood only as it is constructed in social discourse. Martin suggests that the "thick description" used in qualitative research is more appropriate than relying on questionable sociobiology.

In her field studies, Peggy Sanday has found that the incidence of rape varies across 95 band and tribal societies. She and other researchers have reported that rape is absent or rare in 50 to 60 percent of these groups. This finding directly undermines at least some of the support for the proposal that rape evolved among men more or less universally. Findings from these societies collectively point out an inverse correlation between the incidence of rape and the social status of women. Societies where rape is rare are characterized by significant roles of authority and power for women as managers not only of their immediate families but also as personages of consequence in society at large. Rape-prone societies are characterized by interpersonal violence in general and by an emphasis on male dominance as part of the natural way of things and on beliefs that male dominance is important for the existence of an orderly society. Where cultural beliefs call for men to be dominant, it additionally becomes important for men to "stick together." Her accounts of gang rapes in the context of American college fraternities additionally point out that sexual gratification (if any)[5] was secondary to the celebration of fraternity bonding and group pride in the conquest of the young woman's body. Sanday's extensive and ongoing work with the Minangkabau of West Sumatra, where rape is extremely rare, has further clarified the cultural belief structures that foster peaceable relationships.

Jackie White and Lori Post offer a multivariate model of rape. Their chapter builds on White and Kowalski's (1998) integrative contextual developmental model of violence against women. The model focuses on social development and argues for the study of behavior in context. Data on violence against women, and rape in particular, are conceptualized as a function of five interacting factors proposed by the model: sociocultural (including historical, cultural, and community traditions and values); social networks (including the family and peer group); dyadic; situational; and intrapersonal. Results of the analysis support the proposition that sociocultural, socialization, and socioemotional experiences of men provide a compelling and comprehensive account of variations in men's violence toward women.

Notes

1. Kin recognition is relevant for altruism and for exploitation and has been found to be important in many other species, including other primates, squirrels, bees, and wasps.

2. It *is* unequal; it *is* political; and privilege to some at the expense of others *is* one of the consequences.

3. The news stories that referenced Gur's study include the following: Connor, S. (1999, May 18), "In brains, size doesn't matter," *Independent (London)*, p. 5; (1999, May 31), "How men's and women's brains differ," *Pittsburgh Post-Gazette*, Sooner edition, p. A10; Quan, D. (2000, July 13), "Women's brains aren't wired for computer work," *Ottawa Citizen*, final edition, p. A1; (1999, May 20), Science Update: "How to pack a thinking cap: Men have bigger heads," Science Page, *Guardian (London)*, p. 103; (1999, May 30), "Shades of gray and white," Science section, *Buffalo News*, final edition, p. 6H.

4. White matter is most likely to reflect (almost literally) the myelin sheath surrounding axons. It functions in part to prevent the equivalent of electrical interference when impulses are discharged along the axon. There is likely to be no functional or specific cognitive process performed in this tissue.

5. Some of the participants reported later that they could not "get it up."

References

Altmann, J. (1980). *Baboon Mothers and Infants.* Cambridge, Mass.: Harvard University.

Barron, L. and M. A. Straus (1989). *Four Theories of Rape in American Society.* New Haven, Conn.: Yale University Press.

Bownes, I. T. and E. C. O'Gorman (1991). Assailants' sexual dysfunction during rape reported by their victims. *Medical Science Law* 31, no. 4: 322–328.

Boyle, M. (1994). Gender, science, and sexual dysfunction. In T. R. Sarbin and J. I. Kitsuse, eds., *Constructing the Social,* pp. 101–118. Thousand Oaks, Calif.: Sage.

Brownmiller, S. (1975). *Against our Will: Men, Women, and Rape.* New York: Simon and Schuster.

Buffalo News (1999). Shades of gray and white. May 30, Science section (final ed.), p. 6H.

Burt, M. (1980). Cultural myths and supports for rape. *Journal of Personality and Social Psychology* 38 (2): 217–230.

Casebolt, D. B., R. V. Henrickson, and D. W. Hird (1985). Factors associated with birth rate and live birth rate in multi-male breeding groups of rhesus monkeys. *American Journal of Primatology* 8: 289–297.

Chapais, B. (1983). Matriline membership and male rhesus reaching high ranks in natal troops. In R. A. Hinde, ed., *Primate Social Relationships: An Integrated Approach,* pp. 171–175. Sunderland, Mass.: Sinauer.

Cohen, Jacob (1994). The earth is round. *American Psychologist* 49 (12): 997–1003.

Connor, S. (1999). In brains, size doesn't matter. *Independent (London),* May 18, p. 5.

Crews, D. (1994). Animal sexuality. *Scientific American* 270 (1): 108–114.

Crowell, N. A. and A. W. Burgess, eds. (1996). *Understanding Violence against Women.* Panel on Research on Violence Against Women, National Research Council. Washington, D.C.: National Academy Press.

Dawkins, Richard (1976). *The Selfish Gene.* New York: Oxford University Press.

de Waal, F. B. M. and F. Lanting (1998). *Bonobo: The Forgotten Ape.* Los Angeles: University of California Press.

Eagly, Alice and Valerie J. Steffen (1986). Gender and aggressive behavior: A meta-analytic review of the social psychological literature. *Psychological Bulletin* 100: 309–330.

FBI (1998). *Uniform Crime Report.* http://www.FBI.gov.

Ferris, L. E. and J. Sandercock (1998). The sensitivity of forensic tests for rape. *Medicine and Law* 17 (3): 333–350.

Gergen, Kenneth J. (1985). The social constructionist movement in modern psychology. *American Psychologist* 40 (3): 266–275.

Gould, S. J. and R. Lewontin (1970). The spandrels of San Marco and the Panglossian paradigm: A critique of the adaptationist programme. *Proceedings of the Royal Society of London* 205: 581–598.

Gould, S. J. (1981). *The Mismeasure of Man.* New York: W. W. Norton.

Groen, George, Arthur P. Wunderlich, Manfred Spitzer, Reinhard Tomczak and Matthias W. Riepe (2000). Brain activation during human navigation: Gender-different neural networks as substrate of performance. *Nature Neuroscience* 3 (4): 404–408.

Groth, A. N. and A. W. Burgess (1977). Sexual dysfunction during rape. *New England Journal of Medicine* 297 (14): 764–766.

Guardian (London) (1999). Science Update: How to pack a thinking cap: Men have bigger heads. May 20, p. 103.

Gur, Ruben C., Bruce I. Turetsky, Mie Matsui, Michelle Yan, Warren Bilker, Paul Hughett, and Raquel E. Gur (1999). Sex differences in brain gray and white matter in healthy young adults correlations with cognitive performance. *Journal of Neuroscience* 19 (10): 4065–4072.

Hall, G. N. (1996). *Theory-Based Assessment, Treatment, and Prevention of Sexual Aggression.* New York: Oxford University Press.

Hamilton, W. D. (1964). The genetical evolution of social behavior, I, II. *Journal of Theoretical Biology* 7: 1–52.

Heise, L. L. (1998). Violence against women: An integrated, ecological framework. *Violence against Women* 4: 262–290.

Hook, S. M., D. A. Elliot, and S. A. Harbison (1992). Penetration and ejaculation: Forensic aspects of rape. *New Zealand Medical Journal* 105 (929): 87–89.

Holmstrom, L. L. and A. W. Burgess (1980). Sexual behavior of assailants during reported rapes. *Archives of Sexual Behavior* 9 (5): 427–439.

Hrdy, S. B. (1977). *The Langurs of Abu.* Cambridge, Mass: Harvard University.

Hyde, Janet (1984). How large are gender differences in aggression? A developmental meta-analysis. *Developmental Psychology* 20: 722–736.

John, T. J. (1995). Sexuality, sin and disease: Theological and ethical issues posed by AIDS to the churches; reflections by a physician. *Ecumenical Review* 47: 373–384.

Lee, R. B. and I. DeVore, eds. (1976). *Kalahari Hunter-Gatherers.* Cambridge, Mass.: Harvard University Press.

Lewontin, R. C. (1992). *Biology as Ideology: The Doctrine of DNA.* New York: Harper Collins.

Koss, M. P., C. A. Gidycz, and N. Wisniewski (1987). The scope of rape: Incidence and prevalence of sexual aggression and victimization in a national sample of higher education students. *Journal of Consulting and Clinical Psychology* 55 (2): 162–170.

Malamuth, N. M. (1983). Factors associated with rape as predictors of laboratory aggression against women. *Journal of Personality and Social Psychology* 45 (2): 432–442.

Malamuth, N. M. and J. V. Check (1981). The effects of mass media exposure on acceptance of violence against women: A field experiment. *Journal of Research-in-Personality* 15 (4): 436–446.

Malamuth, N. M., S. Haber, and S. Feshbach (1980). Testing hypotheses regarding rape: Exposure to sexual violence, sex differences, and the "normality" of rapists. *Journal of Research-in-Personality* 14 (1): 121–137.

Maynard Smith, J. (1977). Parental investment, a prospective analysis. *Animal Behaviour* 25: 1–9.

Maynard Smith, J. and G. R. Price (1973). The logic of animal conflict. *Nature* 246: 15–18.

McCahill, T. W., L. C. Meyer, and A. M. Fischman (1979). *The Aftermath of Rape*. Lexington, Mass.: D. C. Heath.

Miller, Dale T., Brian L. Taylor, and Michelle L. Buck (1991). Gender gaps: Who needs to be explained? *Journal of Personality and Social Psychology* 61: 5–12.

Moore, D. S. and C. B. Travis (2000). Biological models and sexual politics. In J. G. White and C. B. Travis, eds., *Sexuality, Society, and Feminism*, pp. 35–56. Washington, D.C.: American Psychological Association.

Pagels, E. H. (1999). Exegesis of Genesis 1 in the gospels of Thomas and John. *Journal of Biblical Literature* 118: 477–496.

Parker, I. and J. Shotter, eds. (1990). *Deconstructing Social Psychology*. New York: Routledge.

Pittsburgh Post-Gazette (1999). How men's and women's brains differ. May 31 (Sooner ed.), p. A10.

Quan, D. 2000. Women's brains aren't wired for computer work. *Ottawa Citizen*, July 13 (final), p. A1.

Rand, M. R. and K. Strom (1997). Violence-related injuries treated in hospital emergency departments. *Bureau of Justice Statistics: Special Report*. August 1997, NCJ-156921.

Riger, Stephanie. (1992). Epistemological debates, feminist voices. *American Psychologist* 47: 730–740.

Ruth, S. (1987). Bodies and souls/sex, sin and the senses of patriarchy: A study in applied dualism. *Hypatia* 2: 149–163.

Schlegel, A. and H. Barry III. (1986). The cultural consequences of female contribution to subsistence. *American Anthropologist* 88: 142–150.

Simon, W. (1996). *Postmodern Sexualities*. New York: Routledge.

Smuts, B. B. (1985). *Sex and Friendship in Baboons.* New York: Aldine.

Thornhill, R. and C. T. Palmer (2000). *A Natural History of Rape: Biological Bases of Sexual Coercion.* Cambridge, Mass.: MIT Press.

Tiefer, L. (1995). *Sex Is Not a Natural Act and Other Essays.* Boulder, Colo.: Westview.

Tiefer, L. (2000). The social construction and social effects of sex research: The sexological model of sexuality. In C. B. Travis and J. W. White, eds., *Sexuality, Society, and Feminism,* pp. 79–108. Washington, D.C.: American Psychological Association.

Travis, C. B. and J. W. White, eds. (2000). *Sexuality, Society, and Feminism.* Washington, D.C.: American Psychological Association.

Travis, C. B. and C. P. Yeager (1991). Sexual selection, parental investment, and sexism. *Journal of Social Issues* 47 (3): 117–129.

Trivers, R. L. (1972). Parental investment and sexual selection. In B. Campbell (ed.), *Sexual Selection and the Descent of Man 1871–1971,* pp. 136–179. Chicago: Aldine Publishing.

White, J. W., B. Bondurant, and C. B. Travis (2000). Social constructions of sexuality: Unpacking hidden meanings. In C. B. Travis and J. W. White, eds., *Sexuality, Society, and Feminism,* pp. 11–34. Washington, D.C.: American Psychological Association.

White, J. W. and R. M. Kowalski (1998). Male violence toward women: An integrated perspective. In Russell Green and Edward Donnerstein, eds., *Human Aggression: Theories, Research, and Implications for Social Policy.* New York: Academic Press.

Whyte, M. K. (1978). *The Status of Women in Preindustrial Societies.* Princeton, NJ: Princeton University Press.

2

Female Sexuality and the Myth of Male Control

Christine M. Drea and Kim Wallen

In *A Natural History of Rape: Biological Bases of Sexual Coercion* (MIT Press, 2000), Randy Thornhill and Craig T. Palmer propose that rape has been evolutionarily selected as a human male mating strategy. Their conceptualization emphasizes male control of reproduction and ignores the significant role that females play in reproductive decisions. Our chapter illustrates the inadequacy of this male-centric view of reproduction by demonstrating the female's active role in controlling sexual behavior, reflecting not only her own sexuality, but her control over male sexual behavior. We draw primarily from the primate literature, but also examine other mammalian species to illustrate the variety of female control mechanisms. We begin with a discussion of specialized physical, structural, and behavioral female "barriers" to forced copulation, then present examples of more subtle relationships between mating strategies, social structure, reproductive cycles, and sexual behavior that emphasize female sexual desire and mate choice. We argue that even in simians and humans where forced copulation occurs, it is minimally effective as a means of reproduction. Last we discuss postcopulatory mechanisms that allow females control of their reproductive output. We suggest that, through behavioral, structural, physiological, and social mechanisms, females are vested with significant sexual control that limits the reproductive benefits of sexual coercion.

An Emerging Discipline

Historically, the study of human sexual behavior has been hindered by religious and societal taboos, especially against viewing females as libidinous. Because women were expected to be sexually meek and obedient

(Darwin 1871), their active participation in courtship or mating decisions was deemed inappropriate and, therefore, went unconsidered. Similarly, the early study of animal sexual behavior, particularly in nonhuman primates, centered on males. All eyes were focused on the larger, brightly colored, sexy and pugnacious male, the perceived solicitor and initiator of behavior, whereas smaller, drab females were seen as passive recipients of the male's advances (Zuckerman 1932). Thus, the female primate's primary function in sexual activity was believed to be limited to attracting and accommodating the male's sexual interest (Keverne 1976; Michael 1972; Michael and Keverne 1968).

Beyond the influence of traditional cultural norms, we believe that female stereotypes probably also reflected the fact that, within the arena of sexual selection (Darwin 1871), female choice is far less obvious than intermale competition. Despite its active connotation, female "choice" can be responsive, cryptic (Eberhard 1996), and quite distinct from sexual assertiveness (Small 1993). By contrast, male sexual displays are typically showy, specifically designed to attract attention. Similarly, but more to the point of this chapter, mechanisms by which females regulate sexuality are more subtle and less easily recognized than is male sexual coercion.

It was not until the 1970s that sex researchers began to rethink these biases and recognized females as initiators of sexual behavior (Beach 1976; Goy and Resko 1972). This change required new terms to describe components of the female's sexual repertoire (Beach 1976). The concept of female "attractivity" was already firmly entrenched in the literature to describe the female's stimulus value or sexual appeal to the male. Similarly, "receptivity" referred to the female's psychological willingness and physiological preparedness to engage in sexual behavior. But no term described the interest of a female (or male for that matter) to initiate sexual interactions. Beach corrected this omission by coining the term *proceptivity* to characterize the appetitive behavior used in sexual initiation by either males or females. However, Beach primarily applied the term proceptivity to females, advancing the revolutionary idea that females played an *active* and crucial role in soliciting sexual behavior from males.

Beach's semantic contribution radically changed the course of research on reproductive behavior, permanently altering our view of male and female sex roles in the process. Consequently, today, the distinction between simply accepting a male's advances and proactive solicitation is obvious.

Similar trends were evident in other areas of animal behavior, such as sexual selection theory, in which the contribution of female choice was being increasingly emphasized (Hrdy 1981, 1997; Small 1989, 1993). As a result, the myth of the sexually passive female (Hrdy 1981) was discarded in favor of viewing females as selective, dynamic, and responsible agents of their own sexuality. Or was it?

Current Misconceptions

Although we now understand more completely the range of mechanisms by which females regulate sexuality and shape reproductive behavior, preconceptions and misconceptions linger. Thornhill and Palmer's (2000) proposal of human rape as an evolutionarily adaptive reproductive strategy for males is a case in point. Aside from the paucity of empirical evidence to support such a claim, their theory has other striking flaws that have rightfully attracted attention and criticism (Cartmill 2000). In keeping with the theme of our chapter, however, we address a less obvious flaw, namely that it places reproductive control or power entirely in the hands of the male. By ignoring the significant role that females play in reproductive decision-making, their treatise returns to the Victorian age of coy maidens and blushing brides. It is time to hammer a final nail into the coffin of the sexually passive female. Toward that end, we highlight female control of sexuality and use the term *gynarchy* to refer to female physical barriers, physiological defenses, behavioral strategies, and individual choices (the majority of which do not imply a conscious mechanism).

A growing body of evidence shows that, except with cases of forced copulation, mating requires or is facilitated by cooperation of the female. We present some of that literature in this review, drawing our examples of female sexuality primarily from our closest relatives—other primates. Nonhuman primates are traditional subjects for the study of human behavioral evolution (Small 1989), but because there is no typical primate (Strier 1994) that most closely embodies human characteristics, we de-emphasize any particular species. We focus instead on the diversity of mechanisms available to females within this order. Examples of similar strategies in other mammals are interspersed to remind us of the pervasiveness of female reproductive control: Gynarchy is the rule rather than the exception. Nevertheless, the diversity of control mechanisms represented in female mammals also suggests that no clear pattern of reproduction can be correlated with taxonomy (Weir and Rowlands 1973). If generalizing from primate to primate is fraught with difficulty, what can be said of attempts to generalize from insects to humans?

Before presenting evidence of gynarchy, however, we offer both a caveat and a disclaimer. First, it is critical to note that patterns of sexual behavior and sexual aggression do not necessarily serve a reproductive function. The variety of animal sexual behavior expressed in nonreproductive contexts is staggering (Bagemihl 1999). Thus, motor patterns that are normally associated with mating behavior can be incorporated into different social contexts to take on new meaning. Genital inspection can serve as a social greeting (East, Hofer, and Wickler 1993; Kruuk 1972), and presentation of hindquarters or mounting can reinforce rank relations, deter aggression, reduce tension, or repair social bonds (de Waal 1988). Likewise, sexual aggression and rape in humans is frequently described as sexuality in the service of nonsexual needs, such as dominance (Cohen et al. 1971; Groth, Burgess, and Holmstrom 1977).

Second, our discussion of "forced copulation," "sexual coercion," or "resisted mating" (Estep and Bruce 1981; Smuts and Smuts 1993) in nonhuman primates does not imply that we view these events as necessarily similar to (or having the same underlying mechanisms as) rape in humans. On the contrary, the term rape has connotations far beyond its dictionary or diagnostic definitions that should limit its usage to human behavior (Gowaty 1982). Moreover, even if applied solely to humans, the term *rape* is problematical in that it subsumes behavior similar in form, but not in function or etiology (Berlin 1988; Rada 1978). For the purposes of our discussion we will consider only the potential reproductive consequences of rape, not the myriad motivational or psychological factors influencing both its occurrence and its outcome.

To consider rape a reproductive strategy, one must first discount the majority of reported cases that fail to provide any reproductive potential (Baron 1985). Rapists who target males, prepubescent girls, pregnant and postmenopausal women clearly are not doing so for reproductive gain. Likewise, rapists who fail to ejaculate or ejaculate outside the vagina, insert objects rather than their penis into the woman's vagina, engage in sodomy or oral sex rather than vaginal penetration, and severely injure or kill their victim, are not expecting progeny. Thus, only a small subset of rape cases, namely those involving females of reproductive age who have been inseminated vaginally, is relevant to substantiating Thornhill and Palmer's argument. This subset includes many cases in which the perpetrator is related to the victim (Holmes et al. 1996). If incestuous rapes result in pregnancy, there is a decreased likelihood of producing a healthy infant.

The suggestion that rape (even narrowly defined) has been evolutionarily selected as a facultative male reproductive strategy is premature, at best. We develop our critique in primates using a definition of sexual coercion that incorporates both structural and functional components. Accordingly, sexual coercion is "use by a male of force, or threat of force, that functions to increase the chances that a female will mate with him at a time when she is likely to be fertile, and to decrease the chances that she will mate with other males, at some cost to the female" (Smuts and Smuts 1993, p. 2). We argue that observed behavior might meet the physical properties of this definition without necessarily satisfying the functional criteria.

Without empirical assessment of a female's sexual status, it can be only assumed, most likely falsely, that "she is likely to be fertile." Similarly, the condition that females are less likely to "mate with other males" following forced copulation is not only rarely ascertained, but of dubious relevance for evaluating the reproductive success of the act in question. Theoretically, sperm competition would reduce a male's chances of insemination, but the relationship between mating with multiple males and paternity has not been established in any nonhuman primate. Mating behavior is a necessary but insufficient condition for reproduction. For sexual coercion to be a male reproductive strategy it must result in the production of offspring; yet, definitive paternity data are generally unavailable. Forced copulation in nonhuman primates is rare, and most of the relevant research concentrates on the overt behavior without providing information about its reproductive consequences—information that is prerequisite to any discourse on functionality.

Preventative Measures: Specialized Physical, Structural, and Behavioral Barriers

As a high-risk behavior, rape implies haste. An offender typically performs the act quickly to reduce the potential cost of injury or avoid retaliation. However, mating in many species is not a simple act that can be performed with great speed: Copulation can be an intricate ballet in which successful choreography demands an investment of time and necessitates careful coordination between the actors. Even if one excludes the rituals of courtship, the act itself can require a certain finesse. The following are examples of female-imposed structural, physical, and behavioral barriers that constrain male mating behavior and highlight the fact that it takes two to tango.

Because female genital details are typically cryptic, they generally have been ignored in accounts of sexual behavior. Again, the extravagance and species diversity of the male genitalia has garnered most of the attention (Austin 1984; Dixson 1998; Eberhard 1985). Careful consideration of female reproductive anatomy, however, reveals structural incompatibilities between the sexes, with remarkable implications for copulatory activity. Female mammals show extensive species variation in external genital morphology (Hill 1953; Ioannou 1971; Short 1979), including physical obstacles that limit or complicate mating.

Highly specialized physical barriers are displayed by the female guinea pig, for example, whose vagina is sealed by a membrane that only disappears temporarily under appropriate hormonal stimulation (Young 1937). Similarly, various female prosimians are imperforate most of the year: Their vaginal orifice is not discernible during sexually quiescent periods of the seasonal cycle. This condition has been described for bushbabies (Eaton, Slob, and Resko 1973), mouse lemurs, dwarf lemurs (Petter-Rousseaux 1964), ruffed lemurs (Foerg 1982), and tarsiers (see Hrdy and Whitten 1987) but may prove to be more widespread with further study. In females of these species, estrus occurs only during certain months of the year and is accompanied by modification of the external genitalia. A vaginal aperture appears for as little as 1 to 3 days per cycle before completely disappearing again, and sexual receptivity can last for as little as four hours (Foerg 1982; Petter-Rousseaux 1964).

The old adage "timing is everything" is particularly germane for these primates. Obviously vaginal closure limits the possibility of forced copulation to the extremely brief period when the vagina is open. No one is arguing that forced copulation could be a fruitful mating strategy in these animals. The relevant point is that females of "primitive" primate species exert significant control over the timing and opportunity for mating. Under such conditions the only reproductive tactic that works for males is to be attendant and await invitational cues (Foerg 1982). By opening and closing the orifice necessary for reproduction, females control sexual activity. Moreover, by assuring male investment, females realign male strategies to coincide with their own needs.

The most extreme example of vaginal closure of any female mammal belongs to the spotted hyena. In this species, female external genitalia are "masculinized": The labia are permanently fused to form a pseudoscrotum and the clitoris, or pseudopenis, is elongated and fully erectile, traversed to its tip by a central urogenital canal (Matthews 1939; Watson 1877). Thus, the female hyena must urinate, copulate, and give birth through the small opening in her clitoris. To the untrained eye, the two sexes are virtually indistinguishable (Drea et al. 1998; Frank, Glickman, and Powch 1990). Because of the female's unusual external anatomy, males have considerable difficulty locating the elusive clitoral opening and achieving intromission (Drea, Coscia, and Glickman 1999; Kruuk 1972). Consequently, successful mating behavior requires extraordinary cooperation and the utmost patience. Not only must the female stand exceptionally still while the male performs his necessary acrobatics, but she must retract her clitoris into the abdomen to allow penetration (Drea et al. 1999; Neaves, Griffin, and Wilson 1980). In addition, females are socially dominant to hyena males (Frank 1986; Kruuk 1972), and thus misdirected sexual advances are quite risky for the male. The technical challenges of mating with a socially dominant partner through a peniform clitoris can be overcome only by a high degree of male motivation combined with the female's willing consent.

There has been a long-standing debate about the evolutionary origins and functional significance of female genital virilization. Because the mechanics of mating with a female spotted hyena would thwart any unwanted reproductive advances, some researchers have argued that genital masculinization is a defense against forced copulation (East et al. 1993). Nevertheless, others disagree with this adaptationist argument (Gould and Lewontin 1979) and suggest that female morphology is merely a byproduct of the selection for hormonal masculinization (Gould 1981). Hormonal masculinization (Racey and Skinner 1979; Glickman et al. 1987) would produce female advantage through increased size and social dominance over males (Gould 1981) or through increased aggressiveness in exceptionally competitive feeding situations (Frank 1997; Hamilton, Tilson, and Frank 1986). We might never resolve the dilemma of reconstructing the most parsimonious evolutionary explanation for why female spotted hyenas have inconvenient genitalia or for why they are larger, more aggressive, and higher ranking than males. The implication pertinent to this discourse is that female spotted hyenas have several highly effective means of reproductive control over males. More attention to variation among females will no doubt reveal additional mechanisms of female agency.

So far, our discussion has focused on exceptional models, but postural constraints on mating or even various forms of behavioral accommodation are evident in numerous mammalian species. For instance, the vagina of the female Asiatic elephant is situated far enough forward that the male has difficulty reaching the urogenital sinus opening to achieve penetration (Eisenberg, McKay, and Jainudeen 1971). The awkwardness of this situation is exacerbated for the male by his reduced hind limb and sacral joint mobility. Thus, one tiny step forward is sufficient for the comparatively petite female to foil the bull's sexual advances. Moreover, ejaculation appears to be reflexive, such that any false move can cause the male to ejaculate prematurely outside his partner's body. Successful penetration and internal discharge therefore require complete cooperation on the part of the female.

Likewise, but on a much smaller scale, the vagina of rodents (Pfaff 1980) and certain prosimians, for example, ring-tailed (Evans and Goy 1968) and ruffed lemurs (Shideler, Lindburg, and Lasley 1983), points downward. Consequently, vaginal penetration by the male is unlikely without the female's assistance. In the rat, and probably in all of these species, female sexual receptivity involves assuming the lordosis posture. Accordingly, the female, crouches, arches her spine to elevate her hindquarters, rotates her pelvis so that her vagina is easily accessible by the male (Diakow 1974; Pfaff et al. 1978), and becomes physically immobilized (Smith et al. 1985). This postural shift or pelvic realignment denotes reproductive readiness, but involves a spinal reflex that is not under female cognitive control. Hormonally modulated brain processes disinhibit this spinal reflex and behavioral interactions with potential mates can initiate or facilitate the neuroendocrine events required for the display of lordosis (Pfaff 1980). Thus, successful copulation requires physiological and behavioral coordination between the sexes.

In higher primates, female sexual receptivity (her ability to engage in sex) does not rely on the release of spinal reflexes and appears to be independent of hormonal control (Wallen 1990). Nevertheless, postures that accommodate and facilitate sexual intercourse are common among anthropoid primates and are an integral part of mating behavior. In many Old World monkeys (e.g., macaques, baboons, mangabeys, and talapoins), the male uses a "double foot clasp mount" to achieve vaginal penetration (Dixson 1998; Goy and Wallen 1979). He grasps the female's ankles with his feet and she supports his entire weight while standing on all fours. An accommodating female will spontaneously present her hindquarters to the male, and often move her tail aside, but an unwilling female need merely sit down to prevent the male from copulating with her. The latter is a simple solution, maybe, but nonetheless an effective one—sufficient for a female savannah baboon to thwart the unwanted advances of a male nearly twice her size. Unlike in rodents and prosimians, where much of female control results from hormonal input, in anthropoid primates female control results from behavioral ingenuity reflecting her motivation.

The disappearance of hormonal control over mating capability in anthropoid primates would seem to increase the success of males in forcing copulation on females. This does not appear to be the case, however, as very few incidences of forced copulation have been observed in these species. Even in the most often cited case, the orangutan, female behavioral strategies combined with the male orangutan's sexual anatomy are sufficient to prevent successful insemination: "Due to the small size of the male penis and the difficulty of arboreal suspended copulation it is probable that only when the female co-operates in the mating can successful intromission be achieved. In one of the observed instances of rape the female continued to struggle throughout and the male's penis could be seen thrusting on her back" (MacKinnon 1974, p. 57). Through the power of words, readers remember that the author termed the event "rape," but readily overlook the fact that this passage illustrates a completely failed reproductive act.

Lastly, the reproductive ritual can be a complex and time-consuming endeavor. For instance, in the jargon of sex research, male rhesus monkeys are "multiple intromitters" who must perform a sequence of repetitious copulatory elements to eventually achieve ejaculation. At the height of the breeding season, lustful females typically hound potential suitors, soliciting their sexual attention by slapping the ground repeatedly. Fruitful seductions result in ventro-dorsal "pair sits." These consortships can last for hours, even days, and are only briefly interrupted by the female presenting her hindquarters to the male. The male may inspect the female and then respond by grasping her hips with his hands ("hip-touch") followed by a double foot clasp mount, pelvic thrusting, and if the male and female are compatible, an intromission with more thrusting, and finally a dismount. This sequence may be repeated as many as 50 times, although 10 to 12 repetitions are the norm. It may take anywhere from 15 minutes to 3 hours before the male ejaculates. This is not to say that mating is always such a leisurely affair. When conditions require rapid mating, a well-synchronized male and female can copulate in less than a minute, with a single intromission. However, such rapidity requires the active cooperation of the female. As in so many other species, female adjustment, compensation, and assistance reflect "much more than immobile acquiescence" (Beach 1976, p. 126).

Turning the Tables: Reverse Sexual Size Dimorphism and Female Dominance

Typically, mammalian males are larger, stronger, and more aggressive than females. In light of male fighting advantages (including weaponry) in sexually dimorphic species, females generally fare poorly in intersexual contests of strength or domination. Therefore, the simplest proximate explanation for why males might force copulation on females is because they *can* (sexual or reproductive motivation need not even be a consideration).

By this line of reasoning, any species in which females are stronger than, more aggressive than, or socially dominant over males will show a reverse asymmetry of physical power or social leverage. In such species, a physical contest with a female could escalate and involve risk of serious injury to both parties. Therefore, selection pressures would operate against male use of force during copulation. We use size as an estimate of strength (acknowledging that it is not a perfect match) and adopt Rowell's (1974) definition of social dominance, whereby one sex is considered dominant if it usually wins intersexual agonistic encounters. Size advantage is often correlated with enhanced dominance, and dominance often covaries with aggression, but these characteristics are not necessarily linked (Ralls 1976). Consequently, we address size and dominance separately.

Females are larger than males in many species of invertebrates, fish, amphibians, reptiles, and birds, but reversed sexual size dimorphism also occurs in some mammalian species (Ralls 1976). In mammals, female size advantage is displayed in (or even characteristic of) a broad range of taxonomic groups, from shrews to whales. Female bats, in particular, dwarf their male counterparts. Among primates, only in marmosets and possibly tamarins are females larger than males. However, many species display sexual size monomorphism, including most prosimians and generally all of the monogamous species (Dixson 1998). Even females of size monomorphic species would gain more equal footing in intersexual encounters. The reversed sexual size dimorphism of various species undoubtedly reflects different selective pressures on males and females, but in some cases the sexual "arms race" may be driven by the benefits of increasing female sexual control.

In any discussion of size differences between the sexes, it is important to note that categorizations are often based on gross generalizations. A species may be labeled dimorphic even if there is only a small percentage difference between average male size and average female size. The label fails to reflect the range of individual variation. Thus, even in humans, one cannot deny the significant overlap in male and female weight or height distribution patterns (Harrison, Tanner, and Pilbeam 1988). If rape were a reproductive strategy, it theoretically would be reflected in increased sexual dimorphism because larger males should be more likely to succeed in their forced attempts against females. Nevertheless, the pattern of evolutionary change in modern humans is toward moderate dimorphism, compared to the apparently extreme sexual dimorphism of our extinct ancestors (McHenry 1994). The increased overlap in size range of modern humans is inconsistent with the selection for rape as a reproductive strategy.

Turning now to social dominance, we find that the general mammalian pattern is again one in which the male is the more aggressive and more dominant sex. As before, however, there are many exceptions. Species in which females are unambiguously dominant over their male counterparts include shrews (Romanow, Poduschka, and Deutsch 1996), hamsters, duikers, otters, beavers, nutria, dwarf mongooses, and spotted hyenas (Ralls 1976). Female social dominance is also fairly common in primates as it describes most of the Malagasy lemurs (Jolly 1966; Richard 1987). Particularly bellicose female primates include the ring-tailed, ruffed, and black lemurs (Digby and Kahlenberg 1999; Kappeler 1990; Meyer, Gallo, and Schultz 1999; Raps and White 1995). The driving selective force behind the evolution of female dominance may well be ecological, in that dominance over males assures females access to higher quality resources in times of greater energetic demands; nevertheless, female reproductive control becomes an obvious bonus of such a social system.

Female dominance also characterizes some New and Old World primates (Hrdy 1981; Smuts 1987); however, definitional issues remain unresolved. Although dominance can be enforced aggressively or gained through deference (Rowell 1974), it is a term typically reserved for the ability to elicit submissive signals (Bernstein 1981). Thus, in the strictest sense, *all* females must "consistently evoke submissive behavior from all males in dyadic agonistic interactions" for females to be considered the dominant sex (Kappeler 1993, p. 143). The fact that the reverse condition is hardly always met in species traditionally considered to be male dominant suggests a double standard. We hesitate to accord dominant status to females if they gain priority of access to resources without a show of muscle (e.g., some lemurs), if only certain females hold high positions (e.g., squirrel monkeys, talapoins, cebus, vervets, macaques), if males fail to display submissive gestures (e.g., patas), if dominance relations change seasonally (e.g., chimpanzees), or if the sexes are codominant (e.g., gibbons) (Kappeler 1993; Ralls 1976; Smuts 1987). Moreover, although the requirement for the relationship to be judged in a dyadic context enables human observers to rank their subjects, dyadic interactions are not necessarily natural or ecologically relevant for the animal's behavior. More often than not, social networks involving coalitions and alliances are more critical determinants of social interactions than are the dominance relationships between two individuals.

Strength in Numbers: Social Networking and the Politics of Sex

Social context influences the sexual behavior of primates. In female-bonded species the matrilineal social organization is characterized by female philopatry and male dispersal (Wrangham 1980). Whereas females remain in their natal group, males leave around puberty to join new groups. As a consequence, females have a lifetime in which to establish, maintain, and benefit from social bonds with kin and nonkin. Although some males may be socially dominant over many females, females form the core of the group and maintain the social structure through alliances and coalitions based on kinship and social history. In conflict situations, individual members profit from the support available through their complex network of social relationships.

In numerous species in which a male may outrank a female in dyadic conflicts, females win in group conflicts. In patas monkeys, females may attack males individually or in coalitions (Hall and Mayer 1967; Kaplan and Zucker 1980). Similarly, rhesus macaques display sexual size dimorphism, males possess impressive canine weaponry, and yet their societies include many females that outrank males because of their kinship structure and female allies. Because some of the first terrestrial primates to be studied in detail had social structures with dominant males and extreme sexual dimorphism, such as the baboon, the focus has been almost exclusively on male control of females (DeVore 1965). This bias has carried over even to female-bonded species where male sexual coercion, despite its rarity, has been seen as an important part of the sexual life of rhesus monkeys (Smuts and Smuts 1993). Nevertheless, others stress female participation, noting that females can overcome male dominance through social alliances (Bercovitch 1991).

The bonobo (or pygmy chimpanzee) aptly illustrates the importance of female social relations. Although females are the dispersing sex in this species, they develop strong bonds in their new group and their coalitions play a critical role in all aspects of behavior (Furuichi 1989; Kano 1982; Kuroda 1979, 1980; White 1992). Male harassment of females is tempered by female alliances, which allow females to counter males who may be individually stronger. Thus, female bonobos, without the benefit of kinship ties, can maintain a female dominance structure through social coalitions.

Sexual relations between males and females are not simply the result of size and power differences between individuals, but are strongly affected by the current social context, social history, and alliances. In considering rape as a reproductive strategy in humans, the social context of women's lives is as important a consideration as is the capacity of males to physically force copulation. Whether social structures that facilitate female alliances have evolved in some human societies to protect women from rape is a matter of speculation. Our primate relatives, however, demonstrate how effectively female coalitions increase female control of mating and reproduction.

Female Sexuality: Desire and Reproductive Choice

It is a striking characteristic of many primate species that the capacity to engage in sex has become uncoupled from gonadal hormones. Miller (1931) noted this characteristic of human and nonhuman primates and concluded that humans are uniquely capable of rape because sex could be forced on females at any time. Although his view of forced sexual intercourse as uniquely human is inaccurate, the capacity to engage in sex without hormonal input is a hallmark of most nonhuman primates, certainly of anthropoid primates as well as humans. More than fifty years ago it was suggested that sexual mechanisms regulated by hormones in "lower" species are, in primates, emancipated from hormonal control and are controlled instead by higher, probably cortical, brain areas (Beach 1947). Whereas some prosimians have hormonally controlled barriers to sexual activity, such physical barriers have not evolved (or have disappeared) in other primates. Thus, in anthropoids, mating has become decoupled from fertility, as these primates are capable of mating at any time without regard to their hormonal state (Wallen 1990, 1995).

Historically, this primate capacity for continual mating has been seen as evidence of continual sexual receptivity (Lovejoy 1981). Although these females can mate at any time, they certainly are not continually sexually interested. As Beach (1974, p. 354) stated many years ago: "No human female is constantly receptive (Any male who entertains this illusion must be a very old man with a short memory or a very young man due for bitter disappointment)." The same applies to our anthropoid relatives; interest in mating, that is, "sexual desire," and not sexual capability, is under strong hormonal control (Wallen 1990, 1995, 2000, in press; Wallen et al. 1984; Zehr, Maestripieri, and Wallen 1998). Hormonal modulation of sexual desire plays a particularly important role in primates because of their capacity to mate at any time and the nature of sexual behavior in complex societies.

Sexual intercourse is inherently risky behavior that can have negative social consequences, result in the transmission of fatal infections, and, in humans, produce unwanted pregnancies. In many primate species, females are harassed and threatened by other group members when they sexually consort with males (Niemeyer and Anderson 1983; Wallen and Tannenbaum 1997), making one wonder why they would take such risks. Sexual motivation minimizes the perceived risks and encourages females to seek sexual opportunities and initiate sex, even when there could be immediate negative consequences. By using the hormones regulating female fertility to also increase female sexual desire, fertility and sexual desire can be tightly linked (Wallen 2000; Wallen et al. 1984; Wilson, Gordon, and Collins 1982). This linkage increases the female's sexual initiation when she is fertile, assuring her reproductive success even in the face of sexual disincentives (Wallen 1995, 2000). Because this hormonal system does not also regulate mating capability, the degree of linkage between fertility and sexual behavior varies in anthropoid primates according to the specific social conditions. Current social context, life history, and, in humans, the type of contraceptive used and the desire to avoid pregnancy, can break this link, decoupling sex from fertility (Wallen 2000, in press). Thus, there are many circumstances when the occurrence of sex bears little relationship to female fertility (Wallen 1990, 1995), rape being an excellent example of one such circumstance.

Continuous ability to mate would seem to provide ideal conditions for the evolution of rape as a successful reproductive strategy in some primates. It has exactly the opposite effect, however, making the reproductive payoff from rape exceedingly unlikely. When gonadal hormones control mating capability and fertility simultaneously, a male cannot force mating on an infertile female because she is physically incapable of mating, consensually or otherwise. In prosimian primates that display cyclic vaginal closure, forced mating with an unwilling female could be successful only when the female is fertile because her physical ability to mate always coincides with her fertility. In anthropoid primates, because they lack similar hormonally regulated physical barriers, forced mating would be randomly distributed across the female's ovarian cycle. Thus, the probability that an individual mating is a fertile mating would be accordingly small.

Although males may succeed in forcing some females to mate some of the time, in a variety of primate species including humans (Clutton-Brock and Parker 1995; Smuts and Smuts 1993) these matings are unlikely to be fertile matings unless they are initiated by the female. For example, despite reports of sexual coercion in chimpanzees, several long-term studies demonstrate female control and emphasize that females copulate promiscuously, but not randomly, consenting to or rejecting courtship depending on male traits (Matsumoto-Oda 1999; Nishida 1997). Mating during the peri-ovulatory period, when the likelihood of conception is greatest, was reserved for high-ranking adult males. Females indicated preference by performing a "penis erection check," initiating courtship, or by showing strong reluctance to mate with particular males. Female recalcitrance may have driven rejected males to violence, but aggression proved futile as more dominant males came to the female's rescue. Thus, the sexual behavior of female chimpanzees is tightly linked to their web of social relations with males. In the wild, females exercise control through their choice of copulation partners as well as their choice of male social partners, as has been shown in captivity (Nadler et al. 1994).

The constant ability of anthropoid primate females to mate reduces the information males obtain about female fertility. Paradoxically, many primate females advertise their fertility through sexual skin surrounding the genitals, or the genitals themselves become flushed (dramatically changing color) or swollen (Hrdy and Whitten 1987). Although true sexual skin is absent in prosimians and is generally rare in New World primates (Ioannou 1971), it is prominent among Old World monkeys and some apes (Hrdy and Whitten 1987; Nunn 1999). In these latter species, cues that advertise the female's fertility correlate (albeit imprecisely) with her sexual receptivity.

In theory, such advertisement increases the female's vulnerability to relinquishing reproductive control to forced copulation by males. However, most of the female primates with pronounced genital swelling live in multimale social groups, and it has been suggested that "sexual advertisements" function to incite male competition, thereby increasing the likelihood that females will mate with the fittest males (Clutton-Brock and Harvey 1976). Alternatively, conspicuous swellings combined with an interest in copulating with multiple males (another characteristic of primate females with conspicuous sexual signals) encourage many copulations with different males during the short period of fertility. According to the latter scenario, females accrue potential genetic and paternity confusion benefits (Hrdy 1981, 1997). Whenever sexual skin swellings are imprecise signals for the timing of ovulation, male confusion should increase. It may also be that sexual swellings advertise female quality as a means of attracting males (Pagel 1994). Whatever the explanation, the presence of sexual signals by females suggests that intersexual competition has been resolved in favor of female interests.

Concealed Ovulation: A Cryptic Method of Female Control

Women do not have such sexual advertisements, reflecting that fertility has become physically concealed ("concealed ovulation," Alexander and Noonan 1979). Concealed ovulation is thought to confuse paternity, as a male cannot know whether a female is fertile when she engages in sex or if paternity attribution is honestly assigned. In certain populations, men have attempted to prevent female deception by mandating honest advertisement of menstruation (Strassmann 1992).

One view is that paternity uncertainty benefits the female by reducing possible male infanticide and increasing male investment in offspring that he suspects might be his (Alexander and Noonan 1979). Others have suggested that concealed ovulation prevents females themselves from knowing when they ovulate, thus limiting their ability to avoid pregnancy and, thus, indirectly increasing their reproductive output (Burley 1979). Although this notion is intriguing, it is apparent that ovulation is not necessarily concealed from women. Many women can detect the slight pain that accompanies the bursting follicle, "mittelschmertz," and thus are aware of when they ovulate (Adams, Gold, and Burt 1978), whereas others use different cues, such as increased sexual interest or genital changes (Small 1996). It appears that only males lack information in this regard, unless their female companion lets them in on the secret (Small 1996). By physically concealing ovulation from males while being able to detect it themselves, females increase their control of sexuality such that they effectively counter rape as a reproductive strategy.

The orangutan is often cited as an example of a primate species in which forced copulation may be a mating strategy adopted by younger, less powerful males. However, female orangutans also conceal ovulation and, even in this species, we find that consort formation is crucial to male reproductive success. Orangutans display extreme sexual dimorphism, with males being approximately twice the size of females (Rodman and Mitani 1987). Whereas some adult males ("flanged" males) develop full secondary sexual characteristics, such as cheek flanges, crowns, long hair, throat pouches, and larger size, others ("unflanged" males) remain in a state of arrested development, reaching reproductive maturity but lacking these secondary sexual characteristics (MacKinnon 1974). In addition to pronounced physical differences, flanged and unflanged males may differ in their mating strategies. Flanged males hold territories and advertise their presence by "long" calls, which may function in intrasexual communication to increase spacing between rival males (Rodman and Mitani 1987) or in intersexual communication to attract mates. Female orangutans often approach flanged males and initiate consortships for periods of up to several days, indicating female preference and control of the sexual interactions (Rodman and Mitani 1987). By contrast, unflanged males are not territorial and are less successful at forming consortships. Females typically resist the sexual advances of unflanged males and thus mating behavior of these males is more opportunistic and sexually coercive (Galdikas 1985; Mitani 1985).

Such coercive mating tactics have been offered as evidence of "rape" in nonhuman primates, but the behavior is not a successful reproductive strategy unless it produces viable offspring. The general consensus has been that there is negligible reproductive output from forced copulation in orangutans (Fox 1998; Galdikas 1985). One study determined paternity in 11 Sumatran orangutans (Utami 2000) and found that unflanged males sired as many offspring as did flanged males, *but* they formed consortships in order to do so. As other studies have shown (MacKinnon 1974), sub-adult males often engage in consortships with females, implying that the dichotomy between unflanged "rapists" and flanged consorts may not be as clear as previously suggested.

Behavioral studies have shown that association patterns between orangutans are driven by the reproductive states of adult females (Mitani et al. 1991). If the female plays a key role in these association patterns (Delgado and van Schaik 2000), we suggest that females retain control over the paternity of their offspring by preferentially associating with certain males during their maximally fertile period. Therefore, sexually coercive males are unsuccessful sires because they (1) lose in intermale competitions and are excluded from accessing fertile females (Fox 1998; Galdikas 1985) and/or (2) lack information about female fecundity.

The latter interpretation is supported by reproductive studies in captive orangutans. By manipulating housing conditions, a male and female pair either were forced to cohabitate or the female controlled her access to the male (Nadler 1982). When a consort was confined to a restricted space and the female was unable to avoid or escape from the male, the male initiated or forced copulation on the female. Forced copulations were associated with an increase in mating frequency, but did not result in pregnancy. By contrast, when the female could regulate her access to the male, she initiated sexual activity, determined when copulation occurred, and became pregnant. Female control of the sexual interaction reduced the frequency of copulations, but directly increased the likelihood of conception. These findings show that female choice is a more effective reproductive strategy than is forced copulation.

Turning now to human rape, we recognize the lamentable fact that women meeting our more stringent "reproductive" criteria are victims of forced copulation. The question is not if rape sometimes results in the production of offspring. Although the incidence of rape varies cross-culturally (Sanday 1981), according to one count, the national rape-related pregnancy rate was 5 percent per rape among victims of reproductive age (Holmes et al. 1996). Instead, the question is if rape is a sufficiently effective means of reproduction when weighed against the potential costs. We argue that it is not.

Costs associated with the commission of rape include the risk of injury, infection, and possible death. Female resistance alone can prove injurious, but the potential costs escalate if the act is detected by others. Moreover, a male opting for rape runs an increased risk of contracting a sexually transmitted disease through intercourse with a stranger. Certain infections could reduce the male's reproductive potential. Moreover, as humans possess memory and language, there are potential retributive costs following identification of the rapist. Retaliation from family members or punishment from society can include castration, incarceration, and even death. Such severe costs are presumed to outweigh the benefits of producing very few progeny.

We propose that rape has minimal reproductive benefits because human females (1) conceal ovulation and (2) are notoriously infertile (Short 1976).

Therefore, a rapist lacks information about the reproductive state of the intended mother of his children and has minimal prospects of fertilizing her even under the most opportune conditions (Einon 1998). If rape is to have evolved as a reproductive strategy it must have done so prior to modern times. Thus, we shall ignore modern day concerns, such as various forms of birth control and hysterectomy, and consider the merits of Thornhill and Palmer's theory only in relation to cycling, noncontracepted women. Obviously this population is not a perfect match for the ancestral population of potential rape victims, as the latter were likely to include a majority of woman who were either already pregnant or lactating, and therefore naturally "contracepted." According to some estimates, primitive women would have experienced fifteen years of lactation amenorrhea, four years of pregnancy, and four years of menstrual cycles (Short 1976), leaving few reproductive opportunities for an ancestral rapist.

Returning to more modern times, let us first consider the implications of concealed ovulation. The timing of sexual intercourse in relation to ovulation strongly influences the likelihood of conception, but the actual number of fertile days in a woman's menstrual cycle is uncertain. Ovulation occurs on a single day, but sperm may be viable for up to six days, with low probability of conception if sperm are older than three days (Wilcox, Weinberg, and Baird 1995). More conservative estimates place survival times for sperm and the ovum at 1.4 days and 0.7 days, respectively (Ferreira-Poblete 1997). Moreover, the ovum remains fertilizable longer than it can produce a normal embryo (Ferreira-Poblete 1997). Within the limited population of cycling women, a rapist's chances of targeting a fertile female are somewhere between 1 in 5 and 1 in 28, if we assume that women have cycles of average length. Cycle length can be influenced by many factors, including women's contact with males. Sexually inactive women, for example, have longer cycles (Einon 1998), which would decrease a rapist's probability of targeting their fertile days.

Nevertheless, gamete life expectancy and cycle length are not the only factors affecting peak fertility. Our second consideration is that the maximum fecundability estimate for women aged 20 to 29 is only 23 percent (Short 1976). Women have low fecundity because ovulation is a rare event: About 50 percent of menstrual cycles in women are anovular or infertile (Baker and Bellis 1995; Döring 1969). Sexually inactive women show an additional drop in ovulation, sometimes by as much as 40 percent (Pollard 1994). We discounted surgical sterilization as a modern concern, but about 8 percent of women are involuntarily sterile (Einon 1998). If anovulatory or infertile cycles are taken into consideration, the rapist's odds of targeting a fertile female drop dramatically, presenting little incentive for a man to engage in such high-risk behavior as rape. As we shall see in the next section, a rapist's chances decrease even further when additional factors, such as a 38 percent embryonic mortality rate (Short 1976), are taken into consideration.

In humans and certain apes, female fertility has been decoupled from the capacity to engage in sex. We propose that this independence of fertility and sexual behavior serves as a mechanism that gives females control of their sexuality and, in particular, their reproduction. Thus, although males can force sex on these females, they are more likely than not to "rape" an infertile female. In contrast, females, whose sexual desire is coupled with fertility, can initiate sex at the most propitious time and influence their reproduction in a way unavailable to males.

Copulatory, Postcopulatory, and Postfertilization Mechanisms of Female Control

As we have seen throughout this chapter, female mammals show great diversity in the reproductive mechanisms and behavioral strategies they use to promote or prevent mating. Female control over reproduction (gynarchy), however, does not stop after the behavioral act of mating. We now address female control mechanisms, by and large cryptic to the male partner (Eberhard 1996), operating internally during copulation, after ejaculation but before fertilization, and after conception.

One factor complicating fertilization is that females often copulate with more than one male during a single reproductive cycle. Female promiscuity is common among mammals (including humans) and can lead to the spermatozoa of several males "competing" to fertilize the ova (Ginsberg and Huck 1989). Traditional models of sperm competition have viewed the female reproductive tract as "a passive receptacle in which males play out their sperm competition games" (Baker and Bellis 1993, p. 887), but growing evidence suggests that females affect the outcome in several ways and at various stages (Birkhead and Møller 1993; Dixson 1998). It is unclear what mechanisms are operating in humans; nonetheless, the likelihood that a man will inseminate a woman should be inversely proportional to the number of partners she has in a single reproductive cycle (Einon 1998).

During mating, female behavior can influence the amount of vaginal stimulation the female receives, which can affect her fecundity (Ginsberg and Huck 1989) or whether or not ejaculation by the male occurs at all. If ejaculation does occur, sperm selection, sperm transport, and the manipulation of ejaculate can be important avenues of female choice or flexibility throughout the animal kingdom. For instance, in several mammalian species, including humans, females can eject sperm immediately after copulation (Baker and Bellis 1993; Birkhead, Møller, and Sutherland 1993; Ginsberg and Huck 1989).

Sperm that are retained rather than flushed must survive in the female internal reproductive tract, which is a veritable obstacle course and remarkably hostile to sperm. As sperm is a "highly perishable commodity" (Ginsberg and Huck 1989, p. 76), anything that delays its transport affects the likelihood of fertilization. The female's reproductive anatomy and physiology impose numerous constraints on males after the deposition of semen (Dixson 1998). For instance, low vaginal pH reduces sperm survival and uterine contractions affect the rapidity of sperm transport (Baker and Bellis 1993). The cervix acts as a physical barrier, with cervical crypts that function as sperm reservoirs. The cervix is also a source for antisperm antibodies, and the chemical properties of cervical mucus affect sperm viability. Moreover, filtering of sperm can occur in the uterotubule junction, and oviductal stimulation is involved in sperm capacitation (Dixson 1998). Thus, the structure, chemical composition, and immune response of the female genital tract prevent most sperm from ever reaching the ova, let alone achieving fertilization (Birkhead et al. 1993; Eberhard 1985).

If fertilization occurs, the zygote typically enters the uterus, implants, and develops into an embryo that is nurtured until parturition, but not always. Female mammals have control mechanisms to manipulate pregnancy. For instance, they can avoid or abandon investment in an undesirable pregnancy by selective resorption (Raju, Rao, and Reddy 2000; Westlin et al. 1995) or spontaneous abortion of the fetus (Bruce 1959; Gosling 1986). In some species, the female may selectively invest in certain embryos within a litter by differentially channeling the nutrients (Gosling 1986). Both fetal resorption and expulsion can be caused by a variety of physical and environmental stressors that effectively create a hostile environment, including food shortage or vitamin deficiency (Wellik and Deluca 1995). Primates may even ingest plants that induce abortion (Garey 1997; Page et al. 1992). In humans, a woman may conceive but not implant the conceptus or carry the embryo to term: 90 percent of fertilized eggs fail to reach the uterus, only 58 percent implant, 42 percent survive to day 12 (Baker and Bellis 1995), and 11 percent to 20 percent are aborted or miscarried (Holmes et al. 1996; Pollard 1994). Additional losses come from stillborn infants, premature infants, and perinatal mortality (Einon 1998). Among healthy women trying to conceive, only two thirds of pregnancies end in live births (Wilcox, Weinberg, and Baird 1995).

The picture that emerges is that few copulatory acts translate into paternity (Eberhard 1996) and those that do may not necessarily result in viable offspring (Cunningham and Birkhead 1998). Obviously, mechanisms for preventing pregnancy and increasing fetal mortality needn't involve conscious female decision making. Moreover, the extent to which humans can unconsciously "control" unwanted pregnancies is yet unknown. The incidence of spontaneous abortions in rape-related pregnancies is nearly 12 percent (Holmes et al. 1996). Nevertheless, women have ultimate voluntary control. The "morning-after" pill and planned abortions are deliberate mechanisms available to human victims of rape that merit more than cursory mention (50 percent of rape-related pregnancies end in elected abortion, Holmes et al. 1996), but modern technology is beyond the scope of our evolutionary argument. Such reproductive control mechanisms are unlikely to have shaped the pattern of behavior that Thornhill and Palmer argue evolved to benefit males. The best that can be said is that if there were ever a time when rape would have been a successful reproductive strategy, which we strongly doubt, that time is not today.

Concluding Remarks

The mechanisms of female control that we have described encompass a broad range of species, including those in which forced copulation has neither been observed nor invoked as a reproductive strategy. We have included them to illustrate the underlying theme that females have evolved a variety of mechanisms (for various and perhaps unrelated reasons) that nevertheless function to limit male control of reproduction. "Since the female has the greatest energy investment in reproduction and human societies tend to be polygynous, the woman is the limiting resource; therefore Nature has concentrated on female mechanisms for the natural regulation of fertility" (Short 1976, p. 5).

To preempt critics who may accuse us of swinging the pendulum too far in the opposite direction, let us emphasize that we are not casting males in a passive role or denying them any say in reproduction, far from it. Instead the evidence points toward very powerful mechanisms that give females control of their own reproductive output. Males who form social relationships with females, attend to female social and sexual signals, and are assimilated into female social structures readily share in mutual reproductive success. Females are as much a product of evolutionary biology as are males and have evolved even more effective mechanisms to control reproduction than have males. How could it be otherwise in internally gestating species, where only females truly know which offspring are their own?

It is undoubtedly true that there are males who may try rape as a reproductive strategy, just as there are, apparently, academics who promote the idea as an academic strategy. The latter argue that as long as there is any nonzero probability that rape will produce an offspring it could be a viable reproductive strategy for males without other options. This argument is essentially unfalsifiable given the data currently available. However, in calculating the costs and benefits of rape, we assert that one must consider the effects of female sexual control. The rape strategy would pale in male intrasexual competition to one that produces even minimally functional social relationships with females. These relationships allow males to capitalize on some of the information that females have about their own fertility, as evidenced through their willingness to initiate sexual activity. It is our opinion that rape is unlikely to be a meaningful or widespread reproductive strategy or to be of much evolutionary consequence. The fact remains that, in this area, females have the final say. Although male control is a powerful myth reflecting male desire, control resides in the less flashy but more heavily invested female.

References

Adams, D. B., A. R. Gold, and A. D. Burt (1978). Rise in female-initiated sexual activity at ovulation and its suppression by oral contraceptives. *New England Journal of Medicine* 299: 1145–1150.

Alexander, R. D. and K. Noonan (1979). Concealment of ovulation, parental care, and human social evolution. In N. A. Chagnon and W. Irons, eds., *Evolutionary Biology and Human Social Behavior*, pp. 436–453. North Scituate, Mass.: Duxbury Press.

Austin, C. R. (1984). Evolution of the copulatory apparatus. *Bollettino di Zoologia* 51: 249–269.

Bagemihl, B. (1999). *Biological Exuberance: Animal Homosexuality and Natural Diversity*. New York: St. Martin's Press.

Baker, R. R. and M. A. Bellis (1993). Human sperm competition: Ejaculate manipulation by females and a function for the female orgasm. *Animal Behaviour* 46: 887–909.

Baker, R. R. and M. A. Bellis (1995). *Human Sperm Competition: Copulation, Masturbation, and Infidelity*. London: Chapman Hall.

Baron, L. (1985). Does rape contribute to reproductive success? Evaluation of sociobiological views of rape. *International Journal of Women's Studies* 8: 266–277.

Beach, F. A. (1947). Evolutionary changes in the physiological control of mating behavior in mammals. *Psychological Review* 54: 297–315.

Beach, F. A. (1974). Human sexuality and evolution. In W. Montagna and W. A. Sadler, eds., *Reproductive Behavior*, pp. 333–366. New York: Plenum.

Beach, F. A. (1976). Sexual attractivity, proceptivity, and receptivity in female mammals. *Hormones and Behavior* 7: 105–138.

Bercovitch, F. B. (1991). Mate selection, consortship formation, and reproductive tactics in adult female savanna baboons. *Primates* 32: 437–452.

Berlin, F. S. (1988). Issues in the exploration of biological factors contributing to the etiology of the "sex offender," plus some ethical considerations. *Annals of the New York Academy of Science* 528: 183–192.

Bernstein, I. S. (1981). Dominance: The baby and the bathwater. *Behavioral and Brain Sciences* 4: 419–457.

Birkhead, T. and A. Møller (1993). Female control of paternity. *Trends in Ecology and Evolution* 8: 100–104.

Birkhead, T. R., A. P. Møller, and W. J. Sutherland (1993). Why do females make it so difficult for males to fertilize their eggs? *Journal of Theoretical Biology* 161: 51–60.

Bruce, H. M. (1959). An exteroceptive block to pregnancy in the mouse. *Nature* 184: 105.

Burley, N. (1979). The evolution of concealed ovulation. *American Naturalist* 114: 835–858.

Cartmill, M. (2000). Understanding the evil that men do. *Chronicle of Higher Education,* June 2, B4–B6.

Clutton-Brock, T. H. and P. H. Harvey (1976). Evolutionary rules and primate societies. In P. P. G. Bateson and R. A. Hinde, eds., *Growing Points in Ethology,* pp. 195–237. Cambridge: Cambridge University Press.

Clutton-Brock, T. H. and G. A. Parker (1995). Sexual coercion in animal societies. *Animal Behaviour* 49: 1345–1365.

Cohen, M. L., R. Garofalo, R. Boucher, and T. Seghorn (1971). The psychology of rapists. *Seminars in Psychiatry* 3: 307–327.

Cunningham, E. J. A. and T. R. Birkhead (1998). Sex roles and sexual selection. *Animal Behaviour* 56: 1311–1321.

Darwin, C. (1871). *The Descent of Man, and Selection in Relation to Sex.* London: John Murray.

Delgado, R. and C. P. van Schaik (2000). The behavioral ecology and conservation of the orangutan (*Pongo pygmaeus*): A tale of two islands. *Evolutionary Anthropology* 9: 201–218.

DeVore, I. (1965). *Primate Behavior: Field Studies of Monkeys and Apes.* New York: Holt, Rinehart and Winston.

de Waal, F. B. M. (1988). The communicative repertoire of captive bonobos (*Pan paniscus*) compared to that of chimpanzees. *Behaviour* 106: 183–251.

Diakow, C. (1974). Motion picture analysis of rat mating behavior. *Journal of Comparative and Physiological Psychology* 88: 318–335.

Digby, L. J. and S. M. Kahlenberg (1999). Female dominance in blue-eyed black lemurs (*Eulemur macaco flavifrons*) at the Duke University Primate Center. *American Journal of Physical Anthropology* 28 (Suppl.): 119.

Dixson, A. F. (1998). *Primate Sexuality: Comparative Studies of the Prosimians, Monkeys, Apes, and Human Beings.* Oxford: Oxford University Press.

Döring, G. K. (1969). The incidence of anovular cycles in women. *Journal of Reproduction and Fertility* (Suppl.) 6: 7–81.

Drea, C. M., E. M. Coscia, and S. E. Glickman (1999). Hyenas. In E. Knobil, J. Neill, and P. Licht, eds., *Encyclopedia of Reproduction,* vol. 2, pp. 718–725. San Diego: Academic Press.

Drea, C. M., M. L. Weldele, N. G. Forger, E. M. Coscia, L. G. Frank, P. Licht, and S. E. Glickman (1998). Androgens and masculinization of genitalia in the spotted hyaena (*Crocuta crocuta*). 2. Effects of prenatal anti-androgens. *Journal of Reproduction and Fertility* 113: 117–127.

East, M. L., H. Hofer, and W. Wickler (1993). The erect "penis" is a flag of submission in a female-dominated society: Greetings in Serengeti spotted hyenas. *Behavioral Ecology and Sociobiology* 33: 355–370.

Eaton, G. G., A. Slob, and J. A. Resko (1973). Cycles of mating behavior, oestrogen and progesteron in the thick-tailed bushbaby (*Galago crassicaudatus crassicaudatus*) under laboratory conditions. *Animal Behaviour* 21: 309–315.

Eberhard, W. G. (1985). *Sexual Selection and Animal Genitalia*. Cambridge, Mass.: Harvard University Press.

Eberhard, W. G. (1996). *Female Control: Sexual Selection by Cryptic Female Choice*. Princeton: Princeton University Press.

Einon, D. (1998). How many children can one man have? *Evolution and Human Behavior* 19: 413–426.

Eisenberg, J. F., G. M. McKay, and M. R. Jainudeen (1971). Reproductive behavior of the Asiatic elephant (*Elephas maximus maximus* L.). *Behaviour* 38: 193–225.

Estep, D. Q. and K. E. Bruce (1981). The concept of rape in non-humans: A critique. *Animal Behaviour* 29: 1272–1273.

Evans, C. S. and R. W. Goy (1968). Social behaviour and reproductive cycles in captive ring-tailed lemurs (*Lemur catta*). *Journal of Zoology, London* 156: 181–197.

Ferreira-Poblete, A. (1997). The probability of conception on different days of the cycle with respect to ovulation: An overview. *Advances in Contraception* 13: 83–95.

Foerg, R. (1982). Reproductive behavior in *Varecia variegata*. *Folia Primatologica* 38: 108–121.

Fox, E. A. (1998). *The function of female mate choice in the Sumatran orangutan* (*Pongo pygmaeus abelii*). Ph.D. thesis, Duke University.

Frank, L. G. (1986). Social organization of the spotted hyena *Crocuta crocuta*. II. Dominance and reproduction. *Animal Behaviour* 34: 1510–1527.

Frank, L. G. (1997). Evolution of genital masculinization: Why do female hyaenas have such a large "penis"? *Trends in Ecology and Evolution* 12: 58–62.

Frank, L. G., S. E. Glickman, and I. Powch (1990). Sexual dimorphism in the spotted hyaena (*Crocuta crocuta*). *Journal of Zoology, London* 221: 308–313.

Furuichi, T. (1989). Social interactions and the life history of female *Pan panicus* in Wamba, Zaire. *International Journal of Primatology* 10: 173–197.

Galdikas, B. M. F. (1985). Subadult male orangutan sociality and reproductive behavior at Tanjung Putting. *American Journal of Primatology* 8: 87–99.

Garey, J. D. (1997). The consumption of human medicinal plants, including abortifacients, by wild primates. *American Journal of Primatology* 42: 111.

Ginsberg, J. R. and U. W. Huck (1989). Sperm competition in mammals. *Trends in Ecology and Evolution* 4: 74–79.

Glickman, S. E., L. G. Frank, J. M. Davidson, E. R. Smith, and P. K. Siterii (1987). Androstenedione may organize or activate sex reversed traits in female spotted hyenas. *Proceedings of the National Academy of Sciences, U.S.A.* 84: 3444–3447.

Gosling, L. M. (1986). Selective abortion of entire litters in the coypu—adaptive-control of offspring production in relation to quality and sex. *American Naturalist* 127: 772–795.

Gould, S. J. (1981). Hyena myths and realities. *Natural History* 90: 16–24.

Gould, S. J. and R. C. Lewontin (1979). The spandrels of San Marco and the Panglossian paradigm: A critique of the adaptionist programme. *Proceedings of the Royal Society of London, Series B* 205: 581–598.

Gowaty, P. A. (1982). Sexual terms in sociobiology: Emotionally evocative and, paradoxically, jargon. *Animal Behaviour* 30: 630–631.

Goy, R. W. and J. A. Resko (1972). Gonadal hormones and behavior of normal and pseudohermaphroditic nonhuman female primates. *Recent Progress in Hormone Research* 28: 707–733.

Goy, R. W. and K. Wallen (1979). Experiential variables influencing play, footclasp mounting, and adult sexual competence in male rhesus monkeys. *Psychoneuroendocrinology* 4: 1–12.

Groth, A. N., A. W. Burgess, and L. L. Holmstrom (1977). Rape: Power, anger, and sexuality. *American Journal of Psychiatry* 134: 1239–1243.

Hall, K. R. L. and B. Mayer (1967). Social interactions in a group of captive patas monkeys (*Erythrocebus patas*). *Folia Primatologica* 5: 213–236.

Hamilton, W. J. III, R. L. Tilson, and L. G. Frank (1986). Sexual monomorphism in spotted hyaenas, *Crocuta crocuta*. *Ethology* 71: 63–73.

Harrison, G. A., J. M. Tanner, and D. R. Pilbeam (1988). *Human Biology: An Introduction to Human Evolution, Variation, Growth, and Adaptability,* third edition. Oxford: Oxford University Press.

Hill, W. C. O. (1953). *Primates: Comparative Anatomy and Taxonomy. I—Strepsirhini.* London: The Edinburgh University Press.

Holmes, M. M., H. S. Resnick, D. G. Kilpatrick, and C. L. Best (1996). Rape-related pregnancy: Estimates and descriptive characteristics from a national sample of women. *American Journal of Obstetrics and Gynecology* 175: 320–325.

Hrdy, S. B. (1981). *The Woman That Never Evolved.* Cambridge, Mass.: Harvard University Press.

Hrdy, S. B. (1997). Raising Darwin's consciousness—female sexuality and the prehominid origins of patriarchy. *Human Nature* 8: 1–49.

Hrdy, S. B. and P. L. Whitten (1987). Patterning of sexual activity. In B. B. Smuts, D. L. Cheney, R. M. Seyfarth, R. W. Wrangham, and T. T. Struhsaker, eds., *Primate Societies,* pp. 370–384. Chicago: University of Chicago Press.

Ioannou, J. M. (1971). Female reproductive organs. In E. S. E. Hafez, ed., *Comparative Reproduction of Nonhuman Primates,* pp. 131–159. Springfield, IL: Charles C. Thomas Publisher.

Jolly, A. (1966). *Lemur Behavior.* Chicago: University of Chicago Press.

Kano, T. (1982). The social group of the pygmy chimpanzees *Pan paniscus* of Wamba. *Primates* 23: 171–188.

Kaplan, J. R. and E. Zucker (1980). Social organization in a group of free-ranging patas monkeys. *Folia Primatologica* 34: 196–213.

Kappeler, P. (1990). Female dominance in *Lemur catta:* More than just female feeding priority? *Folia Primatologica* 55: 92–95.

Kappeler, P. (1993). Female dominance in primates and other mammals. In P. P. G. Bateson, P. H. Klopfer, and N. S. Thompson, eds., *Behavior and Evolution: Perspectives in Ethology*, vol. 10, pp. 143–158. New York: Plenum Press.

Keverne, E. B. (1976). Sexual receptivity and attractiveness in the female rhesus monkey. In R. A. H. D. S. Lehrman and E. Shaw, eds., *Advances in the Study of Behavior*, vol. 7, pp. 155–200. New York: Academic Press.

Kruuk, H. (1972). *The Spotted Hyena: A Study of Predation and Social Behavior*. Chicago: University of Chicago Press.

Kuroda, S. (1979). Grouping of pygmy chimpanzees. *Primates* 20: 161–183.

Kuroda, S. (1980). Social behavior of the pygmy chimpanzees. *Primates* 21: 181–197.

Lovejoy, C. O. (1981). The origin of man. *Science* 211: 341–350.

MacKinnon, J. (1974). The behaviour and ecology of wild orang-utans (*Pongo pygmaeus*). *Animal Behaviour* 22: 3–74.

Matsumoto-Oda, A. (1999). Female choice in the opportunistic mating of wild chimpanzees (*Pan troglodytes schweinfurthii*) at Mahale. *Behavioral Ecology and Sociobiology* 46: 258–266.

Matthews, L. H. (1939). Reproduction in the spotted hyena, *Crocuta crocuta* (Erxleben). *Philosophical Transactions of Royal Society London Series B* 230: 1–78.

McHenry, H. M. (1994). Behavioral ecological implications of early hominid body size. *Journal of Human Evolution* 27: 77–87.

Meyer, C., T. Gallo, and S. T. Schultz (1999). Female dominance in captive red ruffed lemurs, *Varecia variegata rubra* (Primates, Lemuridae). *Folia Primatologica* 70: 358–361.

Michael, R. P. (1972). Determinants of primate reproductive behaviour. *Acta Endocrinologica, Suppl.* 166: 322–361.

Michael, R. P. and E. B. Keverne (1968). Pheromones in the communication of sexual status in primates. *Nature* 218: 746–749.

Miller, G. S. (1931). The primate basis of human sexual behavior. *Quarterly Review of Biology* 6: 379–410.

Mitani, J. C. (1985). Mating behaviour of male orangutans in the Kutai Game Reserve, Indonesia. *Animal Behaviour* 33: 392–402.

Mitani, J. C., G. F. Grether, P. S. Rodman, and D. Priatna (1991). Associations among wild orang-utans: Sociality, passive aggregations, or chance? *Animal Behaviour* 42: 33–46.

Nadler, R. D. (1982). Laboratory research on sexual behavior and reproduction of gorillas and orang-utans. *American Journal of Primatology Supplement* 1: 57–66.

Nadler, R. D., J. F. Dahl, D. C. Collins, and K. G. Gould (1994). Sexual behavior of chimpanzees (*Pan troglodytes*): Male versus female regulation. *Journal of Comparative Psychology* 108: 58–67.

Neaves, W. B., J. E. Griffin, and J. D. Wilson. (1980). Sexual dimorphism of the phallus in spotted hyaena (*Crocuta crocuta*). *Journal of Reproduction and Fertility* 59: 509–513.

Niemeyer, C. L. and J. R. Anderson (1983). Primate harassment of matings. *Ethology and Sociobiology* 4: 205–220.

Nishida, T. (1997). Sexual behavior of adult male chimpanzees of the Mahale Mountains National Park, Tanzania. *Primates* 38: 379–398.

Nunn, C. L. (1999). The evolution of exaggerated sexual swellings in primates and the graded-signal hypothesis. *Animal Behaviour* 58: 229–246.

Page, J. E., F. F. Balza, T. Nishida, and G. H. N. Towers (1992). Biologically active diterpenes from *Aspilia mossambicensis,* a chimpanzee medicinal plant. *Phytochemistry* 31: 3437–3439.

Pagel, M. (1994). The evolution of conspicuous oestrous advertisement in Old World monkeys. *Animal Behaviour* 47: 1333–1341.

Petter-Rousseaux, A. (1964). Reproductive physiology and behavior of the lemuroidea. In J. Buettner-Janusch, ed., *Evolutionary and Genetic Biology of Primates,* vol. 2, pp. 91–132. New York: Academic Press.

Pfaff, D. W. (1980). *Estrogens and Brain Function.* New York: Springer.

Pfaff, D. W., C. Diakow, M. Montgomery, and F. A. Jenkins (1978). X-ray cinematographic analysis of lordosis in female rats. *Journal of Comparative and Physiological Psychology* 92: 937–941.

Pollard, I. (1994). *A Guide to Reproduction: Social Issues and Human Concerns.* Cambridge: Cambridge University Press.

Racey, P. A. and J. D. Skinner (1979). Endocrine aspects of sexual mimicry in spotted hyenas *Crocuta crocuta. Journal of Zoology, London* 187: 315–326.

Rada, R. T. (1978). *Clinical Aspects of the Rapist.* New York: Grune and Stratton.

Raju, K. G. S., K. S. Rao, and M. R. Reddy (2000). Fetal resorption in a deer. *Indian Veterinary Journal* 77: 444.

Ralls, K. (1976). Mammals in which females are larger than males. *Quarterly Review of Biology* 51: 245–276.

Raps, S. and F. J. White (1995). Female social dominance in semi-free-ranging ruffed lemurs (*Varecia variegata*). *Folia Primatologica* 65: 163–168.

Richard, A. F. (1987). Malagasy prosimians: Female dominance. In B. B. Smuts, D. L. Cheney, R. M. Seyfarth, R. W. Wrangham, and T. T. Struhsaker, eds., *Primate Societies,* pp. 25–33. Chicago: University of Chicago Press.

Rodman, P. S. and J. C. Mitani (1987). Orang-utans: sexual dimorphism in a solitary species. In B. B. Smuts, D. L. Cheney, R. M. Seyfarth, R. W. Wrangham, and T. T. Struhsaker, eds., *Primate Societies,* pp. 146–154. Chicago: University of Chicago Press.

Romanow, P., W. Poduschka, and W. Deutsch (1996). On intraspecific acoustic communication in the Russian *Desman Desmana moschata* (Linnaeus, 1758) (Insectivora: Talpidae: Desmaninae), with some notes on its social behaviour. *Contributions to Zoology* 66: 43–54.

Rowell, T. E. (1974). The concept of social dominance. *Behavioral Biology* 11: 131–154.

Sanday, P. R. (1981). The sociocultural context of rape—a cross-cultural-study. *Journal of Social Issues* 37: 5–27.

Shideler, S. E., D. G. Lindburg, and B. L. Lasley (1983). Estrogen-behavior correlates in the reproductive physiology and behavior of the ruffed lemur (*Lemur variegatus*). *Hormones and Behavior* 17: 249–263.

Short, R. V. (1976). Definition of the problem: The evolution of human reproduction. *Proceedings of the Royal Society of London, Series B* 195: 3–24.

Short, R. V. (1979). Sexual selection and its component parts, somatic and genital selection, as illustrated by man and the great apes. *Advances in the Study of Behavior* 9: 131–158.

Small, M. F. (1989). Female choice in nonhuman primates. *Yearbook of Physical Anthropology* 32: 103–127.

Small, M. F. (1993). *Female Choices: Sexual Behavior of Female Primates*. Ithaca, N.Y.: Cornell University Press.

Small, M. F. (1996). "Revealed" ovulation in humans? *Journal of Human Evolution* 30: 483–488.

Smith, R. L., D. G. Webster, C. Van Hartesveldt, and M. E. Meyer (1985). Effects of estrus, estrogen-progesterone priming, and vaginal stimulation on tonic immobility, dorsal immobility, and lordosis in the female rat. *Physiology and Behavior* 35: 577–581.

Smuts, B. B. (1987). Gender, aggression, and influence. In B. B. Smuts, D. L. Cheney, R. M. Seyfarth, R. W. Wrangham, and T. T. Struhsaker, eds., *Primate Societies*, pp. 400–412. Chicago: University of Chicago Press.

Smuts, B. B. and R. W. Smuts (1993). Male aggression and sexual coercion of females in nonhuman primates and other mammals: Evidence and theoretical implications. *Advances in the Study of Behavior* 22: 1–63.

Strassmann, B. I. (1992). The function of menstrual taboos among the Dogon: Defense against cuckoldry? *Human Nature* 3: 89–131.

Strier, K. B. (1994). Myth of the typical primate. *Yearbook of Physical Anthropology* 37: 233–271.

Thornhill, R. and C. T} Palmer (2000). *A Natural History of Rape: Biological Bases of Sexual Coercion*. Cambridge, Mass.: MIT Press.

Utami, S. S. (2000). *Bimaturism in Orang-utan Males: Reproductive and Ecological Strategies*. Ph.D. thesis, Utrecht University, the Netherlands.

Wallen, K. (1990). Desire and ability: Hormones and the regulation of female sexual. *Neuroscience and Biobehavioral Reviews* 14: 233–241.

Wallen, K. (1995). The evolution of female sexual desire. In P. Abramson and S. 60 Pinkerton, eds., *Sexual Nature, Sexual Culture*, pp. 57–79. Chicago: University of Chicago Press.

Wallen, K. (2000). Risky business: Social context and hormonal modulation of primate sexual desire. In K. Wallen and J. Schneider, eds., *Reproduction in Context*, pp. 289–323. Cambridge, Mass.: MIT Press.

Wallen, K. (2001). Sex and context: Hormones and primate sexual motivation. *Hormones and Behavior* 40: 339–357.

Wallen, K. and P. L. Tannenbaum (1997). Hormonal modulation of sexual behavior and affiliation in rhesus monkeys. *Annals of the New York Academy of Science* 807: 185–202.

Wallen, K., L. A. Winston, S. Gaventa, M. Davis-DaSilva, and D. C. Collins (1984). Periovulatory changes in female sexual behavior and patterns of ovarian steroid secretion in group-living rhesus monkeys. *Hormones and Behavior* 18: 431–450.

Watson, M. (1877). On the female generative organs of *Hyaena crocuta*. *Proceedings of the Zoological Society, London* 24: 369–379.

Weir, B. J. and I. W. Rowlands (1973). Reproductive strategies of mammals. *Annual Review of Ecology and Systematics* 4: 139–163.

Wellik, D. M. and H. F. Deluca (1995). Retinol in addition to retinoic acid is required for successful gestation in vitamin A-deficient rats. *Biology of Reproduction* 53: 1392–1397.

Westlin L. M., J. T. Soley, N. H. Van Der Merwe, and Y. J. Van Dyk (1995). Late fetal development and selective resorption in *Saccostomus campestris* (Cricetidae). *Reproduction, Fertility, and Development* 7: 1177–1184.

White, F. J. (1992). Pygmy chimpanzee social organization: variation with party size and between study sites. *American Journal of Primatology* 26: 215–223.

Wilcox, A. J., C. R. Weinberg, and D. D. Baird (1995). Timing of sexual intercourse in relation to ovulation—Effects on the probability of conception, survival of the pregnancy, and sex of the baby. *The New England Journal of Medicine* 333: 1517–1521.

Wilson, M. E., T. P. Gordon, and D. C. Collins (1982). Serum 17 beta-estradiol and progesterone associated with mating behavior during early pregnancy in female rhesus monkeys. *Hormones and Behavior* 16: 94–106.

Wrangham, R. W. (1980). An ecological model of female-bonded primate groups. *Behaviour* 75: 262–300.

Young, W. C. (1937). The vaginal smear picture, sexual receptivity, and the time of ovulation in the guinea pig. *Anatomical Record* 67: 305–325.

Zehr, J. L., D. Maestripieri, and K. Wallen (1998). Estradiol increases female sexual initiation independent of male responsiveness in rhesus monkeys. *Hormones and Behavior* 33: 95–103.

Zuckerman, S. (1932). *The Social Life of Monkeys and Apes*. New York: Harcourt Brace.

3

Power Asymmetries between the Sexes, Mate Preferences, and Components of Fitness

Patricia Adair Gowaty

Despite Thornhill and Palmer's rejection of feminist-inspired science, feminists and evolutionary biologists have productive and interesting things to say to one another. Sarah Hrdy (1981, 1986, 1997, 1999; Hrdy and Williams 1983) and others (Dickemann 1979a, b, 1981; Smuts 1992; Smuts and Smuts 1993; Smuts 1994) have been making this point for a long time. I hope this discussion of new Darwinian ideas about human mating systems illustrates the possibility of further productive dialogue.

Whereas Thornhill and Palmer focused on traits supposedly fixed in the human psyche during the Pleistocene, my focus is on dynamic selective pressures affecting natural and sexual selection of social behavior and phenotypic evolution in real time, ongoing, even now. Whereas Thornhill and Palmer implicitly retain a static view of the action of genes for rape, my view is that the mechanisms of heredity include genes, environments, culture, learning, and development. Whereas they focus almost exclusively on individual selection, my view is that many levels of selection contribute to dynamic interactions between the sexes. The most productive approach to understanding power asymmetries between the sexes explicitly uses concepts of multilevel selection. Whereas Thornhill and Palmer characterize women as victims, my view is that unless extraordinary ecological perturbations reduce the selective power of females, women are powerful selective forces, whether they "feel" it or not.

In the first section of the paper, I use parallels between an experiment on fruit flies and a futuristic novel to introduce the importance of the environments the sexes create for one another in shaping behavior, physiology, and morphology of opposite sexes. The juxtaposition of fictional story with experimental results anchors a discussion of the nature of Darwinism, essentialism, the mechanisms of heredity, and selection pressures.

The second section describes the hypothesis of sexually antagonistic selection pressures currently acting on the phenotypes of the sexes. If it is true, within-species variation among females in their abilities to remain in control of their own reproductive decisions and behavior may be the fulcrum on which depends much of the rest of sexual behavior. The hypothesis posits that male attempts to control females' reproductive behavior and female attempts to resist males' control efforts are universal or almost universal aspects of sexual behavior. Variation in offspring viability maintains control-and-resistance dynamics. Offspring viability—not limited to humans, but characteristic of sexually reproducing organisms—is another overlooked key to understanding sexual dialectics.

The third section introduces components of fitness analyses and the implications for understanding of within-individual fitness trade-offs in sexual species. It is unlikely that the often-assumed positive correlation between fitness components always exists.

The fourth section emphasizes predictions and potential tests of Darwinian politics. In these models, first drawn to predict behavior of ducks, the relative mating success variance among males, the relative fecundity of females, the viability of offspring, and the within-population variance in offspring viability are functions of female control of reproductive "decisions." In the model for humans, they are functions of women's reproductive autonomy. Based also on variation among women in reproductive autonomy, a model of institutionalized monogamous marriage predicts which women are most likely to have extramarital affairs. Brownmiller's (1975) controversial view of the functional significance of human monogamy inspired the testable avian model.

This paper shows again what Hrdy has shown repeatedly. Hypotheses sparked by feminist consciousness can be both completely consistent with Darwinian explanations of behavior and testable. I hope the paper contributes to consilience by showing that collaboration of social scientists, other humanists, and evolutionary biologists will hasten our understanding of human behavioral evolution.

1   Females and Males Are Equal Forces in Evolution

This section emphasizes the active and varied roles of females in the ongoing conflict between the sexes. The reproductive interests of females are selection pressures on males, and likewise the reproductive interests of males are selection pressures on females. To reproduce—and sometimes even to survive—each individual within a sex must solve the ecological (social) problems created for them by other individuals, including members of the opposite sex. If sexually antagonistic selection pressures are dynamic, there will seldom be a single, invariant solution; variability is more likely to result from the free interplay of male and female interests. When experimental manipulation allows one sex to dominate completely the interests of individuals of the other sex, there is catastrophe for individuals of one sex, as imagined in Burdekin's (1937) fiction and shown in Rice's (1996) momentous experiment.

From my perspectives (Gowaty 1992a; 1997b) the most important experiment of the twentieth century (Rice 1996) showed definitively that females are forces in evolution. It was also a female's worst nightmare, albeit in an experimental population of *Drosophila melanogaster*. Using exquisite knowledge of fly genomics, Rice manipulated and then removed the genetic influence of females through selectively allowing only those sons with no (i.e., almost no) genetic contributions from their mothers to breed. These manipulations allowed the males to experience only the females from the static, unselected lines of flies, so that males evolved in the absence of co-evolving female behavior and physiology. The males became "hyper males" with superior abilities to manipulate the reproductive capacities of the females from the unselected source population. Matings of hyper males to the females in the nonselected source lines resulted in increased female mortality and reduced abilities of females to manipulate the outcomes of competitive interactions among the males.

Rice did this experiment to understand the selective forces leading to nonrecombining sex chromosomes (the Y does not recombine with the X). He designed his experiment to see what happened when one made the entire genome like a nonrecombining Y (Rice 1998). His experimental results, however, exposed—as no previous experiment ever did—the power of traits in one sex to affect the evolution of traits in another. The experiment demonstrated the existence of "sexually antagonistic allelic coevolution," which Rice defined as occurring when alleles in one sex enhance their bearer's fitness, but simultaneously are deleterious to the fitness of the opposite sex. Rice's explanations focused on how the possession of an allele for, say, a long tail useful in male-male competitive displays could be deleterious to a female if she also had the exaggerated trait. Deleterious alleles in females would provide selection favoring their modification, not just in females, but also in males at a cost to males. This would lead to a back-and-forth of relative advantage and disadvantage between the sexes that would play out as an equilibrium trait value set by the costs and benefits to males and females, that is, through sexually antagonistic allelic co-evolution.

Among the things that fascinated me about this fly experiment was that there is another explanation of the results. Based not on alleles in males and females, the alternative explanation is about *selection pressures* favoring dynamic, ongoing, perhaps ubiquitous between-sex conflict. The conflict does not originate from within the genomes of males and females but from between-sex contests over the control of reproduction. The selective forces in these contests favor the creation by the sexes of "environmental," ecological problems that individuals of the opposite sexes must solve to reproduce and sometimes even survive. The environmental problems that the sexes create for one another can act on genes, on culture, through learning and development, and through interactions among all these mechanisms of heredity. Sexually antagonistic *selection pressures* (Gowaty 1992a; 1997b) may cause evolution of genes, individual phenotypes, development, culture, and their interactions. Unless ecological or social factors destabilize power symmetries between the sexes, sexually antagonistic selection should be dynamic. Evolution of countertraits in opposite sexes will oppose traits that advantage one sex at a cost to the other. The limitation on dynamical evolution is, as it is on all evolutionary processes, the existence of variation—in genes, in culture, or in developmental systems. Rice's experimental removal of female influence was a huge environmental perturbation that allowed hyper males to evolve in fewer than fifty generations. By creating the worst nightmare of a female fly, the experiment showed that the environments created by one sex for the other are profoundly powerful.

Rice claimed, and I agree with him, that the implications of his experiment for understanding evolutionary change are huge. He said, "Sexually antagonistic co-evolution may be far more extensive than adaptation to the physical environment" and may be an important engine of adaptation and speciation (Rice 1996). In the language of natural selection that I prefer, his experiments showed that the ecological problems created by one sex for the survival and reproductive success of the other are important—as important as Sarah Hrdy's (1977) observations of female counterstrategies to sexually selected infanticide by male langurs indicated in 1977. The ecological problems created by one sex for survival and reproduction of the other are as important as novelist Catharine Burdekin (1937) thought as long ago as 1930.

Catherine Burdekin created a female dystopia in her 1937 novel *Swastika Night*. Readers might consider her "futuristic" novel a thought experiment. The fictional dystopia was analogous to the experimental dystopia. The story was about a hyper masculinist world that developed during the first 800 years of the "Hitlerian millennium," when the "reduction of women" was completed.[1] In the opening of the novel, individual commitments to the cult of the masculine have come to completely determine men's lives. Nazi exterminations had resulted in a completely Aryan world. Rank-and-file men had similar access to wealth and resources; each had a wife. Women's lives were limited to their role as breeders. Women were captive, held under enforced monogamy in central holding facilities, where their "husbands" visited only for sex. Men took their sons as toddlers and raised them in crèches without further contact with their mothers. Male-only exposures fitted the boys into the "masculinist life way." Socialization and training rendered girls and women without self-esteem, seemingly complicit in their "reduction." Burdekin's fictional details explored how small incremental exaggerations in culturally mediated sexual power asymmetries similar to those extant in Europe during the mid-1930s might look after forty or fifty generations.

The similarities of the fly experiment to the futuristic fiction are remarkable, even though the fly geneticist interpreted his experimental results as due to genetic changes, and the futuristic novelist created her story on imagined cultural changes. Nevertheless, both were concerned with the creation of "hyper males" concomitant with the reductions in the abilities of females to control their reproduction. They are similar in that each examined how the ecological problems males create for females run amuck when females are stripped of social agency—whether they are stripped of their power through genes or culture. By removing female influence, by halting female evolution, Rice showed how significantly powerful is variation in females for phenotypic evolution. Burdekin did the same thing in her fictional thought experiment.

Both the experiment and the fiction were about the dialectical interplay of female resistance to male control of females' reproductive behavior. That is the most compelling lesson from the fly experiment and why I called it the most important of the twentieth century: *variation in females in their abilities to remain in control of their own reproductive decisions is critical to the evolutionary play between females and males.*

2   Offspring Viability and Mating Behavior

This section argues that when variation in offspring viability is the main selective pressure on reproduction, the absolute control of reproductive "decisions" by one sex is catastrophic not just for individuals of the controlled sex, but for most individuals—females and males—in a population. This section describes the theoretical significance of offspring viability to the dynamics of sexually antagonistic selection pressures and to a new view of the environment of evolutionary adaptiveness.

Contests over the Control of Reproduction and Sexually Antagonistic Selection Pressures

Sexually antagonistic selection pressures are set in motion when advantages to mating discrimination exist for individuals of both sexes, but males are more willing than females to mate with nonoptimal partners. This might happen whenever the encounter rates with potential mates and postmating latencies vary between the sexes (Hubbell and Johnson 1987). When this happens, females will reject some males as partners for copulation and reproduction. Female mate discrimination thereby creates a social (ecological) problem for rejected males, and selection then acts on them to "change females' minds" by persuasion, manipulation, or coercion. When males attempt to influence females' reproductive behavior, they create a social (ecological) problem for females. Females who are sold a bill of goods, tricked, or forced will experience detrimental fitness effects in comparison to females who resist the sales pitch, detect the trickery, or overcome the force. If variation in the viability of offspring favors the evolution of mating preferences, as I assumed (Gowaty 1997b), *among female variation in offspring viability also must favor female resistance to coercion and manipulation.* In other words, females who resist male influences on their reproductive behavior will more likely have offspring capable of surviving the deleterious forces of evolving pathogens.

Recent theories argue that mate preferences are for immune-complementary alleles (Wedekind 1999) or for general heterozygosity (Brown 1997). In contrast, classic sexual selection theories (Hamilton and Zuk 1982) argue that females prefer males with traits that advertise male health relative to other males in the population. Though all are often grouped under "good genes" explanations for female mate choice, these hypotheses are different. Hamilton and Zuk's idea assumes that health-enhancing alleles in fathers will enhance also the health of offspring who inherit them, so that there is often a best or a few best males that all females prefer. Wedekind's and Brown's hypotheses suggest that mate preferences must be self-referential, so that individual female mate preferences are relative to the alleles that a given female will contribute to her offspring, so that there is unlikely to be one best male that all females prefer. All of these "good genes" ideas focus attention on the traits that cue mating preferences.

If one changes perspective, focusing not on the cues mediating preference but instead on the fitness consequences of mating preferences, a new view of the evolution of social behavior emerges (Gowaty and Hubbell MSa; MSb). This new view posits that variation in offspring viability is a fundamental force acting on the evolution of social and reproductive behavior in sexual species. It emphasizes fitness consequences when choosers express preferences under constraints from sexually antagonistic selective pressures (Gowaty 1997b).

This view (Gowaty and Hubbell MSb) has implications that contrast with classical views about sex roles and sexual selection. These include: (1) Females *and males* who discriminate among potential mates should be favored, whether or not parental investment patterns vary and whether or not rates of reproduction by females and males differ; (2) within-population variation in females is the most important influence on the outcomes of other sexual selection modalities, even those acting among males; and (3) just as male attempts to influence females' reproductive decisions are mechanisms of male-male competition, mechanisms of female resistance to male attempts to control them are mechanisms of sexual selection among females (Smuts and Smuts 1993). All of this means that (4) the list of sexually selected mechanisms is larger than usually assumed. It includes not just male-male combat and female mate choice, but male mate choice, female resistance, and female-female competition.

(5) Within-population variation among females in their abilities to remain in control of their own reproductive capacities is a simple variable that predicts other important trait variation, including patterns of male parental investment (Gowaty 1996a, 1999). (6) If mate preferences arise because of variation in offspring viability and if constraints on females' reproductive decisions arise from attempts by males to control females, another under-appreciated evolutionary contest among females is the one over offspring viability. When offspring viability varies because of constraints on females' control of reproductive decisions, the among female variation in their abilities to resist constraints is due to sexual selection, not just natural selection, acting on females (Gowaty and Hubbell MSb). This view also has implications for our understanding of the environment of evolutionary adaptation (EEA).

Offspring Viability and the EEA

A widely accepted assumption among evolutionary psychologists and cultural anthropologists (Kaplan 1996, pp. 92–93) is that most natural selection on humans occurred in the context of hunting and gathering. This idea has stimulated controversy, because it is an unverifiable assumption (Foley 1996; Irons 1998) and its imagined selective consequences are impossible or extremely difficult to evaluate (Betzig 1998). Part of the problem is that our knowledge of social selective pressures during the Pleistocene are guesses at best. This is not a unique problem in the study of humans. It exists also in studies of social selection of nonhumans. The response of behavioral ecologists has been pragmatic. We study how selection works in contemporary populations. Sometimes this allows us to infer how selection pressures may have worked during the EEA of nonhuman animals such as flies, mallards, and mice. We do studies of experimental evolution that are obviously impossible with humans. These have revealed, as did the fly experiment, that the list of selection pressures acting on social behavior should include male control and female resistance. The fly experiment also demonstrated what others have suspected: It is difficult to capture the dynamic traces of sexually antagonistic selection in anything but a living population. This is the main reason that so many practicing biologists find unverifiable assumptions about the Pleistocene questionable sources of adaptive hypotheses, even when our studies are limited to nonhuman animals.

If offspring viability selection is as important as I think, there are other problems with the Pleistocene as the human EEA. The last 10 to 15 thousand years of human evolution, during the flowering of agriculture and subsequent settlement of people in large, sedentary groups, has been a critically important period in human evolution. During this period, selection through offspring viability variation is likely to have been particularly important. The force of pathogens is much stronger on sedentary human populations in close proximity to domesticated farm animals than on smaller populations of mobile hunter-gatherers (Diamond 1997). Human settlements with close interactions with farm animals are precisely the environments in which pathogens potentially most deleterious to humans evolve most rapidly. Therefore, the last 10,000 years would seem a better estimate of the human EEA than the Pleistocene. However, because offspring viability selection theoretically never goes away (because pathogens have faster generation times than their hosts), the selective force on mate preferences of offspring viability is likely to never end (Gowaty and Hubbell MSa). Thus, if offspring viability selection continues to operate on mating discrimination, an even better estimate of the human EEA might be our parent's generation or now.

Parker (1979) identified oscillatory cycles of sexual conflict as a potential mechanism of between-generation evolution. Oscillating selection may act even more rapidly from one bout of reproduction to the next in long-lived, iteroparous organisms such as humans in which learning and culture are central mechanisms of information transfer between the generations (Maynard Smith and Szathmary 1999). Modern-day cultural backlashes to women's control of reproduction, such as those pointed out by Faludi (1992), may represent within-culture oscillatory cycles of male responses to female gains in advantage. Certainly, the content of *Stiffed: The Betrayal of the American Man* (Faludi 1999) documents these most current swings and is consistent with continuously acting forces of between-sex contests over the control of reproduction in modern U.S. culture.

If the environment of evolutionary adaptation was our parent's generation or now, an answer to why human social-sexual behavior currently is so variable may lie in the dynamical sexually antagonistic interactions fueled by variation in offspring viability. Predictions of this idea (Gowaty and Hubbell MSb) mean that it is directly testable using experiments in nonhumans. Predictions include:

• offspring viability is higher when individuals reproduce with preferred rather than nonpreferred partners;

• individuals reproducing with nonpreferred partners attempt to compensate for lower offspring viability by increasing fertility, fecundity, parental care, or parental effects on the timing of offspring reproduction; and

• mechanisms of male control and female resistance are facultatively expressed and costly to breeders' survival.

One need not assume very much, in contrast to Thornhill and Palmer, about the selective environment. Rather if one can manipulate constraints, say by enforced reproduction with nonpreferred partners, one can measure selection differentials directly. Unlike hypotheses based on inferences about Pleistocene-era selective forces on human sex differences, hypotheses about the results of ongoing, real-time selection are quantifiable, directly observable, and, therefore, empirically vulnerable—for flies, mallards, mice, other nonhumans, and also for people. Furthermore, "adaptive responses to current environments" strikes me as a better null expectation than imaginary, guessed-at social environments of the Pleistocene.

The possibility that selection is ongoing in real-time presents a difficulty, however, to those defining evolutionary change only in terms of changes in gene frequencies. In organisms with life spans vastly longer than the life spans of their evolving pathogens or in organisms with iterated bouts of reproduction, selection for male control alleles and female resistance alleles would likely be too slow to outpace the force of evolving pathogens or counter male control or female resistance. This is the classic situation that favors learning and phenotypic plasticity (Levins 1968; Scheiner 1993; Dukas 1998). Because humans are long-lived and reproduce in bouts, gene for gene substitutions would seem inefficient as mechanisms of heredity (information transfer between generations) for control and resistance traits. Better that long-lived humans in dynamical social environments facultatively express changes through cultural variation and learning. Facultatively expressed and culturally mediated traits may serve survival and reproductive success more readily than fixed, genetic traits. Thus, the role of genes might be different from what Thornhill and Palmer assume. In this scenario, genes coding for mate preferences code for facultatively *varying* behavioral and physiological responses of individuals depending on the environments in which they find themselves. Genetic variation may be only for correlated traits.

In such a scenario, a fixed mate preference rule coding for flexible, facultative reproductive behavior might result. This rule might be to prefer a mate most dissimilar in immune function to one's self (Wedekind and Furi 1997), but to alter physiology or behavior (and psychology) when mating with a nonpreferred or less optimal mate (Gowaty and Hubbell MSb). In this case, the differences between individuals would be attributable not to genes, but to the environments in which individuals found themselves. And, therefore, the mechanism of information transfer (Maynard Smith and Szathmary 1999) on which differences between individuals would depend would be primarily social-environmental. This suggests that the "developmental systems" logic of Oyama (2000a, b) and Odling-Smee and colleagues (Leland et al. 2000, 2001) might be a far better way to characterize what it is that selection acts on than any partitioning of action on genes or on culture or on their interactions.

Phenotypic plasticity as a response to changing environments suggests that human psychology, flexibly adjusted to the problems at hand, might be powerfully affected by conscious or unconscious perceptions of the Darwinian success of other individuals. Has anyone investigated how the psychology of individuals varies with conscious or unconscious perceptions of their relative survival or reproductive success probabilities? It would seem a productive collaboration between social, clinical psychologists, and evolutionary biologists. How do perceptions of relative offspring viability affect individual desires for more or fewer children? Do such empirical examinations of people's *perceptions* of their own Darwinian status relative to others exist?

3   Components of Fitness

To test ideas about selection due to variation in offspring viability and sexual antagonism one needs to know about more than one component of fitness. This section is a brief introduction to components of fitness.

Selection occurs when there is within-sex variance in fitness. Measures of fitness include, but are not limited to, the probability that an individual survives to reproductive age (individual viability) and the subcomponents of "reproductive success": the number of mates an individual acquires (mating success or number of copulation partners), the number of bouts of reproduction (fertility), the number of offspring born per bout (fecundity), the number of offspring surviving to reproductive age (productivity), and the probability of survival of a given offspring from birth to reproductive age (offspring viability). The best measure of an individual breeder's lifetime fitness is the relative number of offspring that survive to reproductive age, which is the product of offspring viability, breeder fertility, and breeder fecundity. In practice, many evolutionists use only one fitness component as an estimate of fitness, and they often assume, unrealistically, a positive correlation among fitness components. When individuals trade off one fitness component for another, this assumption is often unlikely to be valid.

For example, the classic discussion (Andersson 1994) of the naturally selected costs of some sexually selected traits in males is about components of fitness. A big showy tail may increase the numbers-of-mates component, but at the same time make its possessor more vulnerable to predation, lower his probability of survival or his viability. Among-individual variance in survival is selection, which may act to dampen the expression of the trait, even while the among-individual variance in the numbers-of-mates component favors an increase in trait expression (Fisher 1958). What this means is that the on-average expression of the trait will result from within-individual trade-offs among sets of selection pressures, but it also shows that fitness indicators need not be positively correlated.

Selection pressures acting on components of fitness of individual females have important implications for our understanding of social behavior and social organization evolution, as well. Theorizing about fitness component trade-offs for females has only recently begun. For example, if variation among parents in offspring viability is the most important selection pressure favoring mate preferences (Gowaty 1998b; Gowaty and Hubbell MSa, MSb), choosers reproducing with preferred and nonpreferred mates will have offspring that differ significantly in viability. In turn, if females are often subject to reproduction with nonpreferred males, any declines in offspring viability compared to females mating with preferred males will be selection acting against reproduction with nonpreferred males. If females are so constrained that reproducing with a nonpreferred male is the best they can do, those who attempt to compensate potential fitness losses will be favored (Gowaty and Hubbell MSb). Compensation might be through a lowering of the age of her first reproduction, which would decrease the time to the next generation. This may increase the number of offspring a mother produces. It may act so that her daughters and sons reproduce more rapidly than others in the population. This could increase the offsprings' chances to make more optimal matches than their mother achieved. A decrease in generation time would be a mechanism that favors the mother's expectation of representation in future generations through her daughter's fitness. A decrease in the time between bouts of reproduction for individuals reproducing with nonpreferred, nonoptimal partners could work the same way. Or, compensation might be through compensatory shifts in a variety of fitness measures at once.

From my point of view, for between-sex contests over the control of reproduction to be a ubiquitous feature of the lives of sexual organisms, offspring viability selection must also be ubiquitous. Similar experiments in mice (Drickamer et al. 2000), mallards (Bluhm and Gowaty submitted), killifish (Downhower and Matsui MS), cockroaches (Moore et al. 2000; Moore et al. submitted), and flies (Anderson et al. MS) suggest that it is. In each of these species, greater offspring viability or adult survivorship resulted when females reproduced with males they preferred rather than males they did not. These species live in different places, have different types of macrosocial organizations, and shared common ancestors from 400 (insects and vertebrates) to 200 (birds and mammals) million years ago. Despite only distant phylogenetic relationships, variation in offspring viability continues to have effects.

It is difficult to know if human females also have offspring viability benefits from the free expression of mating preferences, because it is impossible to do the experiment. Indirect evidence (Gowaty and Hubbell MSa) from between-country comparisons suggests that offspring viability varied with the amount of social-political power mothers exercise relative to fathers. The proxy predictor variable we used was relative literacy of women and men. We assumed that when women's literacy was as high or almost as high as men's, women's reproductive autonomy was high and the likelihood that they were reproducing with preferred partners also high. We also assumed that when women's autonomy decreased, their probability of reproduction with nonpreferred partners increased. Our between-country test showed that offspring viability increased with women's autonomy. There exists a clear sexually antagonistic effect of literacy on fecundity: Controlling for variation in offspring viability and women's literacy, as men's literacy increases, fecundity increases. Controlling for offspring viability and men's literacy, fecundity declines. Thus, we suspect that free expression of mating preferences is as important to humans as it is in flies and mice.

One of the implications of within-population variation in females is that there are many ways males may attempt to manipulate females' reproductive behavior (Gowaty 1997b). Some are "nasty," like rape and aggression, in that they can decrease females' survival probabilities (individual viability). Some are "nice" in that they have a null or positive effect on female survival. Yet, even when males are "helpful," say by brokering essential resources to females, reproducing with them could simultaneously be costly in terms of offspring viability and favor female resistance to "helpful coercion."

No one has systematically applied to any species to my knowledge a components-of-fitness approach to dissecting the effects of all the different mechanisms of sexual selection on social behavior and social organization. Even partial studies are rare (Partridge 1980), though path analyses examining the contributions of different behavioral and ecological contributions to mating success of males have recently increased in number. It seems to me that analysis of the components of fitness is a necessary first step in our attempts to understand the Darwinian forces that may (or may not) shape existing variation in social behavior and psychology of humans. This method seems preferable to the often unsatisfying approach of attempting to find species-specific, unvarying sex differences in behavior in organisms like humans. Given how much within-sex variation in behavior exists, this essentialist approach doesn't make sense (Gowaty 1992b).

Far from increasing the divide between the biological and social sciences, the components of fitness approach brings the expertise of social scientists directly to bear on variables that are the usual private bailiwick of evolutionists. Social scientists and anthropologists cannot do the sorts of manipulative experiments that behavioral and evolutionary ecologists do on nonhuman animals. However, some correlation studies of causation would be informative, even though not definitive. Considered against results in nonhuman animals, such studies may be especially valuable. The next section presents operationally explicit models that might guide such research.

4   Gender Politics as Darwinian Process

The two models in this section are about how constraints act on females' reproductive decisions and affect the fitness of women, men, and their children. The first predicts between-population variation in fitness components when women vary in constraints. The second predicts within-population, between-individual variation in fitness components under institutionalized monogamous marriage.

A Bird Model Applied to Humans

I originally drew figure 3.1 (Gowaty 1996b) to explain social dynamics in polygynous, monogamous, and promiscuous birds. It says that offspring viability (figure 3.1a), variance among males in mating success (figure 3.1b), and fecundity (figure 3.1c) depend on variation among females in their abilities to remain in control of their reproductive decisions. Offspring viability (figure 3.1a) increases as the mother's reproductive autonomy increases (figure 3.1a). The percentage of men mating is relatively small when women's autonomy is least, so that variance among males (figure 3.1b) is high. On the assumption that populations are outbred, when women have complete reproductive autonomy most males mate so that variance in male mating success is low. When women have middling autonomy, as they may under social monogamy in birds and under institutionalized monogamous marriage in humans, the percentage of men mating is relatively high, so that variance is low. Additionally, fecundity (figure 3.1c) declines as women's autonomy increases.

Human societies vary in terms of their codified, legal proscriptions about the behavior of women (e.g., see Lerner 1986), and the mechanisms constraining the behavior of women (e.g., Rogers 1995). This model predicts that societies with the fewest codified, legal proscriptions for women's behavior will be those in which close to all men are able to (noncoercively) reproduce (not marry, but reproduce). In such a society, the variance among men in mating success will be very low. It also says that when women have high reproductive autonomy, the viability of men's children will be higher than when women have lower autonomy, and the among-women variance in the viability of children will be low.

Some data support these ideas, including data on sexual power asymmetries associated with differences in literacy of women and men (Gowaty

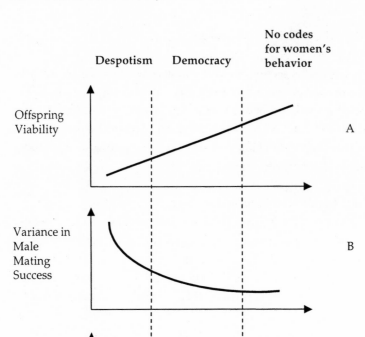

Despotism   Democracy

**No codes
for women's
behavior**

Offspring
Viability

A

Variance in
Male
Mating
Success

B

Women's
Fecundity

C

Women's Reproductive Autonomy

Figure 3.1
Theoretically, variation in women's reproductive autonomy predicts the components of fitness under different social-political systems. The components of fitness
are A. offspring viability (the percentage of offspring born that survive to reproductive age); B. variance in male mating success (the number of women with whom
a man copulates); and C. women's fecundity (the number of offspring born).

and Hubbell MSa). In addition, in societies where women have the lowest
autonomy, despots control their reproductive behavior (Betzig 1992a,b
1993, 1995). Women and many or most men are under the control of an
alpha male, or an elite male power coalition who exploit the productive labor of many men, while also inhibiting their reproduction. The theoretical
association between women's autonomy and among-male variance in mating success seems to correspond to contemporary, Western democracies.

This is not surprising, because social institutions based on "one man–one vote" ideologies go a long way toward equalization of power asymmetries among individual men. Is the power symmetry language of many democracies manipulative code that favors reproductive symmetries among men too? Is that, in fact, its main point? Evolutionary-minded psychologists might consider investigation of the Darwinian costs and benefits to signalers and receivers of the social rhetoric characterizing social change activists under despotism and more egalitarian societies.

Control by women of their reproductive capacity probably does indicate that many rules about reproductive behavior and sexuality have been relaxed or never instituted (Lerner 1986). In such systems, according to this model, the variance among men in mating success will be lower than under institutionalized "one man–one woman" systems, because the most important curbs on male mating success would be women's differential preferences. Assuming that offspring viability selectively shapes female preferences (Gowaty and Hubbell MSb), the model predicts that individual women's optimal preferences vary when there are relaxed rules about women's behavior. Likewise, it predicts that women's mate preferences are similar when male brokering constrains women's access to resources.

A related model of Darwinian costs and benefits (one that did not take women's reproductive autonomy into account) predicted that reproductive asymmetries between despots and subservient men stimulated "subservient men" to formulate ideologies fueling revolutions that deposed despots (e.g., the Scottish revolts). As far as I know, Richard Alexander (1979) first made this argument. Similarly, the new model based on women's reproductive autonomy predicts that the fitness differentials between the men women freely prefer and the men women do not prefer ultimately motivate the development of ideologies against women's freedom of choice, expression, right to education, right to work, and equal pay for equal work.

The model predicts that the ideologies arising against extreme male-male competition and the expression of free female mate preferences are different. The rhetoric motivating coalitions against despots will be about power among men and differential resource distribution among men, even when the precipitating events that may give hints to what all these revolutions are ultimately about is differential access to women. Male-male coalitions against despots will also attract many women, and women will be the acknowledged leaders of some of these. The coalition rhetoric will be against individual behavior and institutions that buttress women's behavioral control of own reproduction. Thus, these coalitions will truly be male-only institutions and they will specifically exclude women. These male-male coalitions will seem to be about "family values" and be against abortion, for example.

Women's Constraints in Institutionalized Monogamous Marriage

How do the components of fitness vary in institutionalized monogamous marriage? The hypothesized answer depends on variation among women in their vulnerability to manipulation of their reproductive decisions.

Like many passerine birds, most people live in social monogamy (Murdock 1967). Sociobiological explanations for monogamy usually focus on female requirements for male contributions to parental care. In birds (Gowaty 1996a, b) and in humans, females seem to vary in the level of help that they need in provisioning their offspring, so the question, What do women need and why do they need it? is critical to understanding institutionalized monogamous marriage. When a woman's access to essential resources for reproduction is constrained, she may be vulnerable to manipulation of her reproductive decisions via male brokering of resources. What constraints act on women?

Lack of inventive genius, courage, pugnacity, or energy may constrain women's access to essential resources (Darwin 1871). More likely, some women may be metabolically inefficient. Institutionalized gender inequalities in pay schedules may constrain some. Customs may make it unseemly or illegal for women to be out of their homes (Jehl 1999a, b). Customs may physically maim and mutilate in the interest of desirability or suitability for marriage. Systematic ideological and social assaults on girls' and women's self-esteem may constrain them. These sources of variation are the short list of mechanisms that may render women vulnerable to trades between men and women. These trades may not always serve what I assume to be women's most important fitness interest, the viability of their children.

In this view, what monogamous marriage institutionalizes (Lerner 1986) is a trade: In exchange for prescriptive paternity certainty (Dickemann 1979a, b, 1981), women gain access to male-brokered resources. However, even when the church sanctifies and the state legitimizes these trades, it is unlikely that every woman experiences the same degree of vulnerability to reproductive manipulation. This is because women vary;

they vary in their physiological efficiencies, in their abilities to access resources besides through male brokering; in the degree of their physical and mental mutilations. Women vary in how smart, savvy, aggressive, assertive, pugnacious, energetic, and adventurous they are. They vary in how well nourished they were as infants and children. They vary in developmental experiences that contribute to levels of athleticism or mathematical abilities. Women also vary in luck. This short list suggests that typical sociological indicators might provide insight into variation in vulnerability to manipulation of reproductive decisions, and that these are important to understanding fitness outcomes.

Figure 3.2 shows the number of offspring surviving to reproductive age as a function of variation in women's abilities to resist influences on their reproductive behavior via male resource brokering. The horizontal axis must indicate something operational about a woman's intrinsic ability to conserve energy for reproduction, the success of her own efforts to amass necessary external resources, and the luck of ecological circumstances in which she finds herself. The two lines in the graph in figure 3.2 indicate the

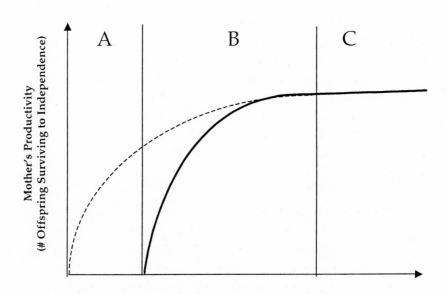

Women's Autonomy in Reproductive Behavior

Figure 3.2
Mother's productivity when she is helped by a male (dotted line) and when she is not helped by a male. The two lines converge as women's reproductive autonomy increases. Drawn after figure in Gowaty (1996b).

effect of the presence of male-brokered resources on the number of children surviving to reproductive age.

The figure illustrates three general conditions. Panel A women have no offspring surviving to reproductive age unless they have access to male-brokered resources. They are highly vulnerable to male control of their reproductive decisions because they will have no fitness without the resources men control. As figure 3.1a showed, these women will have offspring of lower viability than other women. But, without male-controlled resources, they will have no children. For panel B women, male-brokered resources enhance the number of surviving offspring but the degree of fitness enhancement varies among mothers. Some offspring survival is possible without male-brokered resources, but the number surviving is always higher with access to resources from males. These women will vary in how vulnerable they are to male manipulation of their reproductive decisions. For panel C women, the number of offspring surviving is the same with or without male-supplied resources. Panel C women are not vulnerable to male influence via resource brokering. Offspring viability will be highest for panel C mothers. All else equal, women in panel C will have affairs more often than women in panels A and B. Panel C women will have affairs with men with whom they are likely to have more highly viable offspring than they would with their husbands. Panel A women will be more likely to have affairs that increase their access to male-controlled resources. The viability of illegitimate offspring of panel A mothers will not be different from that of their legitimate children. Because the motivation for affairs of panel B women will vary, the variance in the difference scores between legitimate and illegitimate children will be greater than for either panel A or panel C mothers.

As is so for female birds, a woman's vulnerabilities to male influence are unlikely to be simply a function of her requirement for male-brokered resources (Gowaty and Buschhaus 1998). Brownmiller (1975) hypothesized that marriage may be favored because of women's fear of rape, which facilitates advantages for some men because some women need men for protection against "nearby dangerous solicitors." That quaint phrase came from a discussion of factors favoring social monogamy in ducks (Heinroth 1911). So, a modification of the model encapsulates another trade: Men get paternity certainty and women get protection, what Mesnick (1997) called the bodyguard advantage and what some have called "institutionalized extortion." These alternatives are (1) male exploitation of a pre-existing sensory bias, namely, women's fear; or (2) the perverse reciprocal altruistic creation by some men of fearful conditions for many women, favoring some women trading paternity certainty for protection. Though the arguments were originally about ducks (Gowaty and Buschhaus 1998), some apply to women, and many of the predictions are testable, because women vary in their vulnerability to reproductive control through male-brokered protection.

Women vary in their abilities to protect themselves against male aggression. They vary in intelligence, perception, balance, athletic ability, disciplined fighting skills, training. They vary in how quickly they think when under physical attack, in their willingness "to kick a guy in the balls," in how knowledgeable they are about their defensive abilities, whether they live near or far from blood-kin. They vary in how successful they are at building the female-female coalitions Barbara Smuts (1992, 1994) has argued are so important. They vary in whether or not they live near their mothers, grandmothers, and other older, helpful women (Hawkes et al. 1989, 1997, 1998).

Operational and repeatable characterizations of women's vulnerabilities to male control are essential to fair tests of this idea. Operational, repeatable, systematic ways to measure within-population variation in female autonomy in reproductive "decisions" is the major obstacle to testing the predictions. An especially robust test would hold husbands' economic resources constant.

Summary

A Natural History of Rape prematurely rejects insights and evolutionary hypotheses about the nature of coercive sexuality from the perspective of females. The assumptions Thornhill and Palmer share with other evolutionary psychologists about the selection pressures that shape(d) human behavior in the Pleistocene are likely to be incomplete or possibly wrong altogether. If offspring viability selection and sexually antagonistic selection interact, the selection pressures of most importance to social behavior variation are likely to be dynamical, ongoing, and constant. If so, contingent, environmental circumstances may more likely induce facultative behavior of individuals.

To understand the interplay of male attempts to control and female attempts to resist, one must include study of within-population variation among females. Variation among females in their abilities to remain in control of their reproductive decisions is critical to the evolutionary interplay between females and males. To understand sexually antagonistic selection pressures, one must evaluate the components of fitness of breeders and nonbreeders (both male and female) and the viability of their offspring. Variation in offspring viability is a ubiquitous selection pressure that favors female resistance to manipulation of reproductive decisions. These ideas suggest important fitness component trade-offs in individuals that should be included in studies of the evolution of social behavior of humans. I hope these ideas stimulate more collaborative research among evolutionary biologists and social scientists. I hope they lead to well-controlled descriptions of how variation in components of fitness affect what individuals in real-time populations do.

Acknowledgments

I thank Cheryl Travis for her many comments on a previous draft and her patience as I struggled to revise this paper during my mother's unexpected illness and death. I thank Steve Hubbell, Sarah Hrdy, and Mike Kaspari for comments on various drafts and many conversations that helped make my expression of these ideas clearer. For all they have taught me, I thank my collaborators in the "free female choice consortium," Wyatt Anderson, Cindy Bluhm, Lee Drickamer, Jerry Downhower, Yong-Kyu Kim, Steve Hubbell, and Allen Moore. For their persistence, creativity, and feminist consciousness, I thank Sarah Hrdy and Susan Brownmiller. Grants from the NIH and NSF helped support this work.

Note

1. The horror of real-life existence for women under Afghanistan's fundamentalist Islamic Taliban of which the world became aware after September 11, 2001 rendered the horror of Burdekin's fiction less fantastical.

References

Alexander, R. D. (1979). *Darwinism and Human Affairs*. Seattle: University of Washington Press.

Anderson, W. W., P. A. Gowaty, and Y.-K. Kim. (MS). Mate preferences and offspring viability. *Proc. Proceedings of the National Academy of Sciences (U.S.A.)* (forthcoming).

Andersson, M. (1994). *Sexual Selection.* Princeton: Princeton University Press.

Betzig, L. (1992a). Roman monogamy. *Ethology and Sociobiology* 13: 341–383.

Betzig. L. (1992b). Roman polygyny. *Ethology and Sociobiology* 13: 309–349.

Betzig, L. (1993). Sex, succession, and stratification in the first six civilizations: How powerful men reproduced, passed power on to their sons, and used power to defend their wealth, women, and children. In L. Ellis, ed., *Socioeconomic Inequality and Social Stratification,* pp. 37–74. New York: Praeger.

Betzig, L. (1995). Medieval monogamy. *Journal of Family History* 20 (2): 181–216.

Betzig, L. (1998). Not whether to count babies, but which. In C. Crawford and D. L. Krebs, eds., *Handbook of Evolutionary Psychology: Ideas, Issues, and Applications,* pp. 265–274. Mahwah, N.J.: Lawrence Erlbaum.

Bluhm, C. K. and P. A. Gowaty (submitted). Free Female Choice in Mallards, *Anas platyrhynchos,* Increases Mother's Productivity and Offspring Viability.

Brown, J. L. (1997). A theory of mate choice based on heterozygosity. *Behavioral Ecology* 8: 60–65.

Brownmiller, S. (1975). *Against Our Will: Men, Women, and Rape.* New York: Simon and Schuster.

Burdekin, K. (1985, c. 1937). *Swastika Night.* Old Westbury, N.Y.: Feminist Press.

Darwin, C. (1871). *The Descent of Man, and Selection in Relation to Sex.* London: Murray.

Diamond, J. (1997). *Guns, Germs, and Steel: The Fates of Human Societies.* New York: W. W. Norton.

Dickemann, M. (1979a). The ecology of mating systems in hypergynous dowry societies. *Social Science Information* 18: 163–195.

Dickemann, M. (1979b). Female infanticide, reproductive strategies, and social stratification: A preliminary model. In N. Chagnon and W. Irons, eds., *Evolutionary Biology and Human Social Behavior: An Anthropological Perspective,* pp. 321–367. North Scituate, Mass.: Duxbury Press.

Dickemann, M. (1981). Paternal confidence and dowry competition: A biocultural analysis of purdah. In R. D. Alexander and D. W. Tinkle, eds., *Natural Selection and Social Behavior: Recent Research and New Theory,* pp. 417–438. New York: Chiron.

Drickamer, L. C., P. A. Gowaty, and C. M. Holmes. (2000). Free female mate choice in house mice affects reproductive success, offspring viability, and performance. *Animal Behaviour* 59: 371–378.

Downhower, J. F. and M. L. Matsui (MS). Honest assessment: Female choice and offspring viability in medaka, Oryzias latipes.

Dukas, R. (1998). Evolutionary Ecology of Learning. In R. Dukas, ed., *Cognitive Ecology: The Evolutionary Ecology of Information Processing and Decision Making,* pp. 129–174. Chicago: University of Chicago Press.

Faludi, S. (1992). *Backlash: The Undeclared War against American Women.* New York: Crown.

Faludi, S. (1999). *Stiffed: The Betrayal of the American Man.* New York: William Morrow.

Fisher, R. A. (1958). *The Genetical Theory of Natural Selection,* second ed. New York: Dover Press.

Foley, R. (1996). The adaptive legacy of human evolution: A search for the environment of evolutionary adaptedness. *Evolutionary Anthropology* 4: 194–203.

Gowaty, P. A. (1992a). Evolutionary biology and feminism. *Human Nature* 3(3): 217–249.

Gowaty, P. A. (1992b). What if within-sex variation is greater than between-sex variation? Invited peer commentary of Thornhill, R. and N. W. Thornhill, "The evolutionary psychology of men's coercive sexuality." *Behavioral and Brain Sciences* 15: 393–394.

Gowaty, P. A. (1996a). Battles of the sexes and origins of monogamy. In J. L. Black, ed., *Black Partnerships in Birds,* pp. 21–52. Oxford: Oxford University Press.

Gowaty, P. A. (1996b). Field studies of parental care in birds: New data focus questions on variation in females. In C. T. Snowdon and J. S. Rosenblatt, eds., *Advances in the Study of Behaviour,* pp. 476–531. New York: Academic Press.

Gowaty, P. A. (1997a). Darwinian feminists and feminist evolutionists. In P. A. Gowaty, ed., *Feminism and Evolutionary Biology: Boundaries, Intersections, and Frontiers,* pp. 1–18. New York: Chapman Hall.

Gowaty, P. A. (1997b). Sexual dialectics, sexual selection, and variation in mating behavior. In P. A. Gowaty, ed., *Feminism and Evolutionary Biology: Boundaries, Intersections, and Frontiers,* pp. 351–384. New York: Chapman Hall.

Gowaty, P. A. (1999). Extra-pair paternity and paternal care: Differential male fitness via exploitation of variation among females. In N. Adams and R. Slotow, eds., *Proc. 22 Int. Ornitholog. Cong. Durban,* pp. 2639–2656. University of Natal.

Gowaty, P. A. and N. Buschhaus. (1998). Ultimate causation of aggressive and forced copulation in birds: Female resistance, the CODE hypothesis, and social monogamy. *American Zoologist* 38: 207–225.

Gowaty, P. A. and S. P. Hubbell. (MSa). Fertility variation, gender equity, and the Red Queen: The Women's Autonomy Hypothesis.

Gowaty, P. A. and S. P. Hubbell. (MSb). Social constraints on mate choice, offspring viability, and the hypotheses of reproductive compensation.

Hamilton, W. D. and M. Zuk. (1982). Heritable true fitness and bright birds: A role for parasites? *Science* 18: 384–387.

Hawkes, K., J. F. O'Connell, and N. G. Blurton-Jones. (1989). Hardworking Hadza grandmothers. In V. Standen and R. A. Foley, eds., *Comparative Socioecology: The Behavioral Ecology of Humans and Other Mammals,* pp. 341–366. London: Basil Blackwell.

Hawkes, K., J. F. O'Connell, and N. G. Blurton-Jones. (1997). Hadza women's time allocation, offspring provisioning and the evolution of long post-menopausal life spans. *Current Anthropology* 38: 551–577.

Hawkes, K, J. F. O'Connell, N. G. Blurton-Jones, H. Alvarez, and E. L. Charnov. (1998). Grandmothering, menopause, and the evolution of human life histories. *Proceedings of the National Academy of Sciences* 95: 1336–1339.

Heinroth, O. (1911). Beitrage zur Biologie, namenthlich Ethologie and Psychologie der anatiden. *Int. Orn. Kong. Verb.* 5: 589–702.

Hrdy, S. B. (1977). *The Langurs of Abu: Female and Male Strategies of Reproduction.* Cambridge, Mass.: Harvard University Press.

Hrdy, S. B. (1981). *The Woman That Never Evolved.* Cambridge, Mass.: Harvard University Press.

Hrdy, S. B. (1986). Empathy, polyandry, and the myth of the "coy" female. In R. Bleier, ed., *Approaches to Science,* pp. 119–146. New York: Pergamon.

Hrdy, S. B. (1997). Raising Darwin's consciousness: Female sexuality and the prehominid origins of patriarchy. *Human Nature* 8: 1–49.

Hrdy, S. B. (1999). *Mother Nature: A History of Mothers, Infants, and Natural Selection.* New York: Pantheon.

Hrdy, S. B. and G. C. Williams. (1983). Behavioral biology and the double standard. In S. K. Wasser, ed., *Behavioral Biology and the Double Standard,* pp. 3–17. New York: Academic Press.

Hubbell, S. P. and L. K. Johnson. (1987). Environmental variance in lifetime mating success, mate choice, and sexual selection. *American Naturalist* 130: 91–112.

Irons, W. (1998). Adaptively relevant environments versus the environment of evolutionary adaptedness. *Evolutionary Anthropology* 6: 194–204.

Jehl, D. (1999a). The fervor: Islam's teachings and chastity. *New York Times.* June 20.

Jehl, D. (1999b). Arab honor's price: A woman's blood. *New York Times.* June 20.

Kaplan, H. S. (1996). A theory of fertility and parental investment in traditional and modern human societies. *Yearbook Physical Anthropology* 39: 91–135.

Laland, K. N., J. Odling-Smee, and M. W. Feldman (2000). Niche construction, biological evolution, and cultural change. *Behavioral and Brain Sciences* 23 (1): 131ff.

Laland, K. N., J. Odling-Smee, and M. W. Feldman (2001). "Cultural niche construction and human evolution." *Journal of Evolutionary Biology* 14 (1): 22–33.

Lerner, G. (1986). *The Creation of Patriarchy.* New York, Oxford University Press.

Levins, R. (1968). *Evolution in a Changing Environment.* Princeton: Princeton University Press.

Maynard Smith, J. and E. Szathmary. (1999). *The Origins of Life: From the Birth of Life to the Origin of Language.* Oxford: Oxford University Press.

Mesnick, S. L. (1997). Sexual alliances: Evidence and evolutionary implications. In P. A. Gowaty, ed., *Feminism and Evolutionary Biology*, pp. 207–259. New York: Chapman and Hall.

Moore, A. J., P. A. Gowaty, and P. J. Moore (submitted). Females avoid manipulative males and live longer.

Moore, A. J., P. A. Gowaty, W. G. Wallin, and P. J. Moore (2000). Fitness costs of sexual conflict and the evolution of female mate choice and male dominance. *Proc. Royal Soc.* 268: 517–523.

Murdock, G. P. (1967). *Ethnographic Atlas*. Pittsburgh, Penna.: University of Pittsburgh Press.

Oyama, S. (2000). *The Ontogeny of Information: Developmental Systems and Evolution*. Durham, Duke University Press.

Oyama, S., P. E. Griffiths and R. D. Gray (2001). *Cycles of Contingency: Developmental Systems and Evolution*. Cambridge, Mass, MIT Press.

Parker, G. A. (1979). Sexual selection and sexual conflict. In M. S. Blum and N. A. Blum, eds., *Sexual Selection and Reproductive Competition in Insects*, pp. 123–166. New York: Academic Press.

Partridge, L. (1980). Mate choice increases a component of offspring fitness in fruit flies. *Nature* 283: 290–291.

Rice, W. (1996). Sexually antagonistic male adaptation triggered by experimental arrest of female evolution. *Nature* 381: 232–234.

Rice, W. R. (1998). Male fitness increases when females are eliminated from gene pool: Implications for the Y chromosome. *Proceedings of the National Academy of Sciences (U.S.A.)* (11): 6217–6221.

Rogers, W. (1995). Honor killings: A brutal tribal custom. *CNN*. Atlanta: December 7.

Scheiner, S. M. (1993). Genetics and evolution of phenotypic plasticity. *Annual Review of Ecology and Systematics* 24: 35–68.

Smuts, B. (1992). Male aggression against women: An evolutionary perspective. *Human Nature* 3: 1–44.

Smuts, B. (1995). The Evolutionary Origins of Patriarchy. *Human Nature—An Interdisciplinary Biosocial Perspective* 6 (1): 1–32.

Smuts, B. and R. W. Smuts. (1993). Male aggression and sexual coercion of females in nonhuman primates and other mammals: Evidence and theoretical implications. *Advances in the Study of Behavior* 22: 1–63.

Wedekind, C. (1999). Pathogen-driven sexual selection and the evolution of health. In S. C. Stearns, ed., *Evolution in Health and Disease*, pp. 102–107. Oxford: Oxford University Press.

Wedekind, C. and S. Furi. (1997). Body odour preferences in men and women: Do they aim for specific MHC combinations or simply heterozygosity? *Proceedings of the Royal Society of London (B)* 264: 1471–1479.

4

Does Self-Report Make Sense as an Investigative Method in Evolutionary Psychology?

Stephanie A. Shields and Pamela Steinke

Scientists aim to explain things, and most of what we try to explain has multiple causes. Randy Thornhill and Craig Palmer distinguish between *proximate* and *ultimate* explanations for rape (2000). They group together as proximate explanations a broad range of variables that sweep across a wide set of temporal, physical, and social features. They view factors of individual genetic and learning history, concurrent situational factors, and sociocultural institutions, values, and practices that sustain or promote a rape culture all as proximate explanations for rape. In bracketing these incommensurable variables within the single category of proximate explanation, they identify for themselves a higher goal. Their beat is ultimate explanation. They assert that "identifying ultimate causes . . . is important, because certain proximate explanations may be incompatible with certain ultimate explanations. This is because certain ultimate explanations specify the existence of certain types of proximate mechanisms" (p. 4). The power of ultimate explanation, they suggest, is that "an ultimate explanation of a biological phenomenon can account for all proximate causes influencing the phenomenon, whether the phenomenon is an adaptation or an incidental effect of an adaptation" (p. 12). They propose that the more inclusive causal model offered by the ultimate explanation gives it "enormous practical potential" because it should reveal the "best insights about proximate causes" (p. 12). The legitimacy of any and all proposed proximate explanations is thus weighed in terms of the specific circumstances that they name as the ultimate explanation.

Self-report data is among the evidence they marshal, and at several points it plays a critical role in building their case. At different points Thornhill and Palmer consider rapists' reports of their motives for rape, women's reports about their fear of rape, men's beliefs about influences on their sexuality and sexual behavior, and even devote an entire chapter to the experience of psychological pain and distress after rape. Self-report is not the only form of data on which Thornhill and Palmer rely, but self-report data at several points forms a crucial link in their reasoning. In this chapter we take a closer look at what self-report does and does not measure, how self-report has been used in creating an empirical foundation for their argument, and how well that self-report data actually fulfills the task. We focus specifically on a single type of data-gathering strategy in part because problems in their application of self-report data reveal a larger pattern of logical inconsistency in the arguments they put forward. The core of our claim is that investigation of putatively "ultimate explanations" needs to rely on data that can differentiate proximate from ultimate. Investigatory techniques or data derived from or otherwise dependent on proximate variables do not automatically qualify as equally valid for, much less relevant to, testing ultimate explanations.

Self-report, the linguistic representation of beliefs about the self, is a complex "output" of language, consciousness, culture, personal values, memory, and self-presentational concerns. Self-report, in the broadest sense, includes everything from responses to open-ended interviews designed for a single research study, to self-assessment on closed, objectively scored scales. Self-report relies on a panoply of cognitive capacities, and on a cultural construction of the *self* that ascribes legitimacy and credibility to individual memory. Self-report measures the individual's beliefs about her or his own behavior and experience. The self-report is not the literal description of a discrete event or attitude, but an amalgam, sharpened or leveled, of the many factors that might bear on the individual's interpretation of "experience." Lyons (1986) argues that even reports of occurrent states via introspection do not reflect a direct reading of one's own internal state, but a reconstruction of that experience, an account that interweaves memory, immediate bodily sensation, expectancies, and heuristics with the aim of predicting what "ought" to happen in the situation.

Thornhill and Palmer are not alone among evolutionary psychologists who use self-report data, nor is self-report just a small and optional part of the data on which evolutionary psychology's arguments are based. Other evolutionary psychologists who have used self-report data to investigate preferences regarding relationships and mating decision rules (see

Kenrick 2001 for a brief summary), purport gender differences in experience of emotion in general (Geary 1998), and in sexual and romantic jealousy in particular (e.g., Buss et al. 1992). Each of these has been met with criticism that supports alternate explanations equally well or better (e.g., Pratto and Hegarty 2000; Lott 1996) or reveals major flaws in the evidence brought forward to support the assertion and/or the execution of research (e.g., DeSteno and Salovey 1996).

Self-Report as Data in Evolutionary Psychology

The speculative and general nature of self-report questioning that characterizes its use in evolutionary psychology, combined with multiple competing influences on the content of reported behavior or beliefs about behavior and emotions, seriously compromises the validity of self-report for many investigations in evolutionary psychology. Here we outline three problems that seem to us especially central.

Inequivalence of Terminology

A number of critics have noted the tendency for broad and often perplexing anthropomorphism in evolutionary psychology's ascription of behavioral terms. Thornhill and Palmer define "rape" as "human copulation resisted by the victim to the best of her ability unless such resistance would probably result in death or serious injury to her or in death or injury to others she commonly protects" (p. 150). Although they aim to isolate rape from other forms of coercive sex and sexual aggression, they freely apply the term to other species: orangutans, ducks, and even insects. In addressing the topic of psychological distress they especially focus on insects such as waterstriders and dung flies—species for which notions of consent and coercion are at least questionable and at best problematic. As we discuss later in this chapter, "psychological distress," which they accord important evidentiary status, is neither easily nor unambiguously operationalized. Experience-based terms must be understood within the context of the experiencer and must be incorporated into explanatory structures very carefully. Words by themselves carry the freight of connotation and can too easily be credited with an unmerited equivalency across culture and historical time.

Asking People What They Do Not Know

The way the questions are framed inevitably influences the data that self-report yields. In studies concerned with identifying people's values, or their knowledge of cultural expectations and norms, or their beliefs about themselves, others, and the world, self-report is exactly the right method to use. If the investigator is trying to get through to something that operates outside of reflective self-awareness, the burden is on the investigator to demonstrate that asking people what they *can* know reveals something about which they *cannot* have direct knowledge. Because evolutionary psychologists try to probe ultimate explanations, which they assume to exert an effect on us without our explicit awareness of the mechanics of those effects, they have an especially heavy burden of proof.

Ineffective Methodological Triangulation

It is not enough to say that self-report is just one of several investigative tools and that the aggregate of "evidence" is what matters. Converging methods are persuasive only insofar as each method is a valid and reliable measure of the variable under study, and one that independently contributes to the explanation. Converging evidence is not inferred from the explanation. This may seem so obvious that it need not be stated, but the practice occurs with disappointing frequency in ultimate explanations like Thornhill and Palmer's.

What Self-Report Is, and What It Is Not

Self-report is an index of what people believe to be true about themselves. It is not a literal record of the individual's behavioral history nor is it necessarily a reliable predictor of future behavior. There are many important questions that can be profitably addressed with self-report methodologies, and there are ample and repeated demonstrations of the unique research insights that derive from the use of self-report data (e.g., King 2001; Seligman and Schulman 1986; Wylie 1974). Any legitimate use of self-report as data, however, must take into account the fact that self-report is always mediated. By "mediated" we mean that self-report is a self-aware construction of experience even as the self-report is generated. It is always therefore an interpretation of experience, not a "raw" throughput or readout of experience. The capacity to produce self-report, whether as narrative or as a response to a numerical rating scale, is shaped and constrained by language and expression via memory (e.g., heuristics), by the structure of language (e.g., implicit causality), by "layered experience" (i.e., the person's understanding of what ought to happen, what did happen, what is desired to happen, etc.), to name just a few features. One might even question when or even whether self-report is an appropriate index of processes theorized as *prior* to (unlinked from? independent of?) the capacity for reflective self-awareness, such as the impulses and attractions that Thornhill and Palmer hypothesize as the ultimate explanations for rape and reactions to it.

We want to emphasize that we are not implying that self-report is "spoiled data." Self-report has frequently been singled out for methodological criticism (Ericsson and Simon 1980), and it is not our intent to contribute to this bias. It is a great mistake, however, to assume that self-report is something that it is not. Three things need to be kept in mind when relying on self-report in any context: self-presentation, discrepancies, and interpretation. After a brief review of each, we turn to how Thornhill and Palmer inappropriately rely on self-report in trying to make a case for the ultimate explanation of rape as a male reproductive strategy.

Self-Presentation

Self-report is an account from the teller's perspective. Because self-report involves privileged access to beliefs, self-report cannot be "validated" in the same sense as can representations about others. That is, you may not view me the same way as I view myself, but your view does not negate the authenticity of my self-report, although it may question the report's accuracy. When reporting about the self, the research participant is presumed to have more at stake than when reporting about others. Setting aside the possibility of self-serving bias, other aspects of memory and self-report distortion are, as we described above, inevitably involved in telling about oneself.

On the other hand, the bulk of the evidence on subject dissembling shows that deliberate, malicious misrepresentation is rare (Christensen 1977). Researchers should have no reason to be overly suspicious of the majority of their research participants' willingness to be forthcoming, or to be overly concerned that otherwise well-socialized individuals will fail to follow certain general principles of cooperation inherent in interaction (e.g., being truthful; being relevant) within the research situation if they follow these principles systematically in other situations (Grice 1975). Usually a greater problem is the research participant's well-intentioned effort to cooperate with the aims of the investigator while maintaining or enhancing his or her own self-esteem, especially when discussing sensitive topics (e.g., Gargiulo and Yonker 1983). The situation is further complicated by the fact that even in the most innocuous testing situations research participants express concern about whether their responses show that they are "better than average" or at least "normal."

Standard strategies for minimizing the problem of self-presentation include disguising one's hypotheses; informing the participant that there are no "correct" or "incorrect" responses; reducing the salience of self-presentation concerns via extradesign strategies (e.g., making the experimenter's presence as unobtrusive as possible within the research setting). These are all important and useful; nevertheless, no adjustment in data collection or modification of the research context will transform reported beliefs into something they are not. Reports are influenced by subjects' concern with social desirability, but they are nevertheless statements of the phenomenal self, even if those beliefs about the self would not be corroborated by others' judgments (Wylie 1974).

Discrepancy between Behavior or Informant-report and Self-report
Even when self-report is used appropriately, as a measure of belief, it will not always correlate strongly with behavioral measures or informants' reports. When behavioral or informant-report and self-report measures are not strongly correlated, the discrepancy between measures is not inherently problematic. In fact, when the report is at odds with data obtained by other means, the discrepancy itself can be useful data. The discrepancy expresses which aspects of an individual's belief system operate in accord with his or her behavior or with others' perceptions and which aspects do not.

A number of factors can contribute to a low correlation between self-report and other measures. Low correlation is often due to the inappropriate use of self-report (White 1988). For example, people cannot predict their reactions to situations with which they have had no experience; even if a prediction is made on the basis of prior experience, people can only estimate what would be normative for themselves: "(I believe) I'd never fall in love with someone who is already married" or "(I believe) I would immediately help a child in need." Similarly, informants cannot report on others' subjective states, only on their inferences about those states. But just as discrepancy does not "invalidate" a self-report, agreement does not "validate" it. Agreement between self-report and other measures, like any other correlation, may indicate that the two measures tap the same construct, different manifestations of the same construct, or correlated constructs.

Discrepancy becomes useful data in a variety of areas concerned with people's understanding of what and how they know and feel, including studies of memory, values, attention, and motives. Discrepancies between expressed values and behavioral acts expressive of those values have been at the center of the attitude inconsistency literature since the 1930s (La Piere 1934). Discrepancies between self-report and other indices may be particularly informative in studies of values. "Inconsistencies" reveal the organization of the individual's system of beliefs about correct or important attributes of social relations or personal ethics. Individual belief systems, in turn, can then be contrasted with the individual's knowledge about cultural standards. Knowing what is important to or valued by individuals better enables researchers to predict the situations in which people will make efforts to align their actions with valued outcomes or social rules (e.g., Hunter 1984; Steinke 1992; Stokes and Hewitt 1976).

Interpretation of the Content of Self-Report

Ideally, questions are short, specific, simple, and unbiased. Yet in practice, researchers make common technical errors such as omission of anchors, asking people what they don't know or cannot say, and calling for finer distinctions than people can or want to make. As a consequence, response patterns may be influenced by factors above and beyond beliefs about the matter in question. When the research participant appears to be inconsistent, it may actually be the experimenter who has erred. The problem may be as simple as undue difficulty of individual words within questions. Apparent uninterpretability may also occur if the legitimacy of the research participant's beliefs are challenged by the content or wording of the instrument.

Self-reports must also be interpreted within a context that acknowledges the range of characteristics of the report itself. Self-report is encoded in language, takes the form of question answering or account giving, and is a structured discourse. Because self-reports are encoded in language, the data can be interpreted within a linguistic context (e.g., see Harré 1989). Self-report can be interpreted as the individual's attempt to provide a personal account or maintain a discourse. The most informative analysis may therefore come from examining the report's style or structure through use of an account or discourse analysis that involves studying the function of discourse in social situations (Potter and Wetherell 1987; van Dijk 1985). Linguistic units are also useful when viewing self-report as occurring within the context of question answering (Graesser and Murachver 1985; Lehnert 1978). Question answering presumes the respondent's implicit knowledge of interacting syntactic, semantic, and pragmatic information (Singer 1990). Viewing the self-report within this context allows the researcher to make important predictions about the report. For example, in any given question there is a focus to the question, which will determine which part of the question is answered (Clark and Haviland 1977; Graesser and Murachver 1985). Thus, the question "Did you feel anger when your father died?" may include a focus on "you," "anger," "father," or "died." The focus directs the respondent to the information that is new or not presupposed and therefore in need of a response. Identifying or marking the focus of the questions allows the researcher to make sure the scope of the response will include the desired information (e.g., "What was the felt emotion?"). seemingly minor changes in any linguistic or contextual factors may significantly alter the responses, and the investigator needs to be mindful of how these features affect comprehension so as to generate accurate interpretations of the data.

In summary, self-report measures beliefs, nothing more, nothing less. Beliefs tell us about values, about what people recall, about what they are attending to, about how they reconcile myriad conflicting pieces of information about themselves and others. Self-report can provide a rich source of data, but it cannot be taken as an unbiased indicator of probable behavior or beliefs uncontaminated by measurement context, personal history, demand characteristics, cultural mores, and so on. Schemas and stereotypes greatly influence what we attend to, what we remember, and the labels and meaning we give it. Take, for example, what is implied by identifying a person or that person's behavior as "emotional." Deeply embedded, culturally shared beliefs about the gendered nature of emotion color when and how we expect to see emotion. A similar kind of social construction goes on about jealousy and the naturalness of male social arrangements that control women. Although sociobiology often formulates an evolutionary fitness account of why men are commonly jealous about female behavior, it usually fails to recognize an equally reasonable evolutionary account for female jealousy, and often seems not even to acknowledge the commonly reported distress among women whose partners are philandering or flirting with other women.

How Thornhill and Palmer Misapply Self-Report

The Data

In the chapter entitled "The Pain and Anguish of Rape," Thornhill and Palmer focus on the emotional consequences of rape, particularly psychological pain. They define psychological pain as "the mental state of feeling distraught" (p. 85), which would seem to require a careful, well-operationalized method of measurement that has at least demonstrated face validity and a primary concern with the victim's perspective. In this chapter the authors do concern themselves with women victims, but broaden their description of distress to incorporate accounts of witnesses, mates, and close relatives of the victim. Indeed, Thornhill and Palmer examine psychological pain because of rape's hypothesized impact on the woman victim's relationship to her mate or other potential reproductive partners. Their version of the evolutionary hypothesis predicts that psychological pain will be cued or activated by (1) "events that lowered reproductive success in human evolutionary history" and (2) "the greater the negative effect of an event, the greater the psychological pain experienced," such that "more psychological pain is expected in a young and fertile woman than in a female of pre- or post-reproductive age" as a response to rape victimization (pp. 85–86). Their interest in subjective experience should require them to focus on first-person accounts, yet they pay scant attention to the subjectivity that is central to their definition of pain. Instead, their primary evidence pertaining to the severity of psychological pain comes from a secondary analysis of one data set comprised of a single interview within days following the assault. Thornhill and Palmer acknowledge some of the limitations of the sample (e.g., it is disproportionately poor and young), but they ignore those limitations as well as the fact that they insist on inferring causal linkages (proximate as well as ultimate) from correlational data.

The voluminous literature on psychological stress responses and coping has again and again demonstrated the multidimensionality of these constructs. But care to resist overgeneralizing or conflating discrete constructs is nowhere to be found in this chapter. Thornhill and Palmer do not distinguish between discrete manifestations of feeling distraught, and do not differentiate between feelings of fear, troubled relationships, or somatic symptoms. Nor do they consider the temporal dimension of distress responses. For example, they purport a link between "mateship status" and severity of psychological pain. They hypothesize that "the victims' pain *stems from* their mates' reduction or complete withdrawal of material support" (p. 90, emphasis added). They therefore predict that partnered women of childbearing age should experience greater distress than girls or other women, yet they seem to believe it irrelevant that half the questions in the distress interview concerned current relationships with men. Self-report data tends to be used to build the case rather than test the explanation, making reliance on it even more problematic. Nor are obvious incompatible alternate explanations ruled out. For example, physical or emotional rape trauma may generate fear or anxiousness with respect to men, that in turn mediates disruption in ongoing relationships.

Thornhill and Palmer's uninformed use of self-report can be contrasted with systematic and careful studies of the consequences of beliefs about rape. Bohner and Schwarz (1996) report a series of studies in which they investigated whether fear of rape, in fact, is causally linked to women's self-perceptions and the moderating role of beliefs about rape in women's and men's self-esteem after exposure to accounts of rape or assault. Their work is notable not only because it moves beyond correlational investigation, but because of its prudent interpretation of self-report as expressions of belief and values. They are careful to interpret their findings as reflecting the impact that rape threat has on women's self-perceptions, emphasizing that their possible impact on behavior must be explained in terms of the moderating effects of belief.

Underestimation of Self-Presentation
Thornhill and Palmer make much of rapists' reports of their sexual motivation for the crime. Thornhill and Palmer rightly point out that we need

to be cautious in taking those reports at face value; however, they err in fixing only on the possibility that the content of the report might be contaminated by rapists' self-presentation concerns about power and control. They assert that rapists' description of their actions in terms of power and control rather than sexual desire come primarily from studies of convicted rapists. This raises the question for Thornhill and Palmer: "Were these men truthfully reporting their motives, or were they giving the explanations desired by the researchers?" (p. 135). In setting two alternatives (either power and control *or* sexual motivation) as the only and oppositional explanations for rapists' explanation of their motives, Thornhill and Palmer sweepingly overlook other significant aspects of the context in which the reports are obtained and other self-presentation and non-self-presentation related motives for fashioning the report in a particular manner. Moreover, they fail to grasp the complex relation that will exist between *any* self-representation and "true" motives.

Failure to Look for Discrepancies in Data Sources

Thornhill and Palmer devote much of the discussion of the pain and anguish of rape to the emotional reactions of the woman's mate, and even consider it "highly possible" that selection "favored the outward manifestations of psychological pain because it communicated the female's strong negative attitude about the rapist to her husband and/or her relatives" (p. 88). Further, mate and kin themselves are hypothesized to guard their interests by being vigilant for rapists and judging some as more threatening than others. The woman's experience, then, is viewed as functioning *for* others, and the account of her experience is given through the effect it has on those others.

Placing the narratives of very different "stakeholders" on the same analytic plane obscures the differences among these groups. It shifts the emphasis of the data from what the narratives can tell us about the distinctive phenomenal experience of each group and what data might be provided by differences among these groups, to a least-common-denominator of interchangeability or equivalence. Some of the material in their discussion of the reactions of mate and kin to a woman's rape makes this plain. In support of their claim they cite the story of a woman assaulted by a captive male orangutan at a field research site in Borneo. The main point they wish to make by telling the story is that no permanent harm was done because the assailant was not human. What is interesting here, in relation to the question of report as evidence, however, is exactly how that point is made. Thornhill and Palmer summarize a second-party summary of the researcher's account of the husband's description of the incident. From the distance of a *fourth-hand account* they have no qualms in concluding that "neither the husband nor the victim seemed to suffer greatly" as a result of the attack (p. 87).

Problematic Interpretation of the Content of Self-Report: The Narrative

Griffiths (1997) identifies a major weakness in the general reasoning of evolutionary psychology. He notes that evolutionary psychology emphasizes that the adaptiveness of a biological trait is not equivalent to saying that the trait is an adaptation. Adaptiveness is a measure of a trait's current effect on an organism's reproductive fitness, whereas an adaptation is a trait explained as resulting from natural selection. "Adaptiveness is neither necessary nor sufficient for a trait to be an adaptation. . . . Evolutionary psychology claims that the human mind is a bundle of cognitive adaptations. It does not claim that these adaptations are currently adaptive" (p. 107)—because, of course, the environments of early evolutionary history are quite different from those inhabited by humans today. The distinction between adaptations and adaptiveness is a way for evolutionary psychologists to argue that their description of behaviors that may have once subserved adaptive functions in no way is an endorsement of the "rightness" or desirability of that behavior, trait, or preference for present-day human life. Thus, Thornhill and Palmer can argue that their description of rape as an adaptation can be presented as if it is a value-free description of the state of things.

One limitation of what Griffiths (1997) refers to as "the adaptationist program" stems from the fact that adaptationists suppose that selective problems are very strongly associated with particular solutions to those problems. On the one hand, adaptationists believe that they can infer the solution from the problem. That is, believing they know what adaptive problems an organism has faced, they infer what adaptations it will possess. Second, adaptationists think that they can infer the problem from the solution. They believe that by looking at the complex forms evolution has produced, they can infer the ecological interactions between ancestral organisms and the features of the environment that selected the forms taken by these organisms. Propensity to infer the problem from the solution, what Tang-Martinez (1997, p. 136) calls "adaptive storytelling," entails constructing an explanation as to why a trait is adaptive from the initial assumption that the trait is adaptive: "As long as the explanation is plausible and consistent with evolutionary theory, it is accepted as fact," and so "what is essentially a hypothetical postulate is accepted as evidence and elevated to the status of a conclusion." Even though most evolutionary psychologists would agree that solutions cannot simply be inferred from the problem, they nevertheless assume that nature, not nurture, is accountable, in the end, for complex behavior:

> Although nature gets the last word, the evolutionary psychologist thinks that the fact that a particular feature "makes evolutionary sense" is a reason for taking seriously even quite marginal data suggesting that it actually exists. If nature disagrees with the adaptationist about what should have evolved, then she has to shout. If she agrees, then she has only to whisper. (Griffiths 1997, pp. 109–110)

Does Self-report Make Sense for Evolutionary Psychology?

Self-report is embedded in a network of research variables all of which are potentially influenced by values of the investigators. What is an evolutionary psychologist to do? One possible solution is to modify the use of self-report to be less influenced by explicit personal experience. It might seem possible, for example, to adapt techniques from psychophysics in order to bypass the "mediated" quality of self-report. When self-report is modified to be apparently more free of the reporter's conscious intervention, however, the experimenter's selection of stimulus materials and presentation of the judgment task is not less crucial.

One example will make this point clear. Evolutionary psychologists have proposed the "waist-to-hip ratio" hypothesis as an explanation of why males will be attracted to certain females. The ideal ratio is purportedly the expression of attractiveness and fecundity that proves irresistible to human males. In an effort to be more objective through a kind of "social psychophysics" to test this proposition, researchers have tended to rely on a single set of line drawings that represent a range of waist-to-hip ratios and weight. Using this standard set, several researchers have reported verifying that a specific stimulus figure is reliably identified as optimizing attractiveness and perceived fecundity. Is the waist-to-hip ratio a truism not to be denied? It is if you use the same stimulus figures in study after study. Tassinary and Hansen (1998), however, showed that the apparent empirical demonstration of the validity of the hypothesis is simply an artifact of a confound among weight, waist size, and hip size in the standard stimulus figures. Using a wider range of ratios and unconfounding judgments of attractiveness and beliefs about fecundity, Tassinary and Hansen revealed the low correlation between the two judgments. As it turns out, then, the apparent robustness of judgments about the waist-to-hip ratio had been based more on the specifics of the stimulus set that served as a standard than on the hypothesized ratio itself.

Conclusion

Our critique has focused specifically on what is wrong with using self-report in evolutionary psychology rather than what is right (or wrong) about its use within other theoretical perspectives. The apparent scientific purity of evolution-framed models of social behavior gainsays the inevitable way in which systematic error may be encountered in theorizing and in conducting empirical research. As we have argued above, the research tools themselves are not the problem, but the use to which they are put may be. Wylie (1997) points out that because we can readily cite errors and biases in the application of a range of methods, it is important to think through what we can actually expect of those methods as independent indicators of fact. She emphasizes that the prevalence of error and bias reveals "systematic error made possible by a misplaced confidence in the powers of scientific method to neutralize, to counter or wash out, the effects of the standpoint-specific interests that we inevitably bring to the endeavour of science" (pp. 49–50). These are not errors of bad faith, but expressions of the pervasiveness of how the beliefs and practices that define sex and gender difference in contemporary society impinge on science so as to be transparent. Predominantly male science practitioners, Wylie says, simply do not see the need to test framework assumptions about gender structures and are not alert to ways in which their research design and results might be biased by gendered presuppositions.

It is ironic, too, that Thornhill and Palmer, on the one hand, take so literally self-representations of experience that appear to be consistent with their argument, yet do not similarly view as "data" their critics' discussion of motivation, belief, or values. Thornhill and Palmer perceive feminist views on rape as based in "ideology," but do not explain what is to be gained by proposing (as feminists are described as doing) that proximal, contingent, and contextual explanations are more germane to understanding the dynamics of rape (and coercive sexual behavior) than are so-called ultimate explanations. They do not explain why we should consider a developmental account that traces factors that promote or inhibit a propensity to rape necessarily less scientific or less descriptively accurate than the one they offer. Thornhill and Palmer argue that their adaptationist story buys more than proximate explanations do by way of rape prevention. As others in this volume point out, however, Thornhill and Palmer's recipe for prevention mixes the already proven (rape prevention education for men—which, because it aims to educate against coercive sex, does not actually fit Thornhill and Palmer's definition of rape), with the already demonstrated ineffective (chemical castration), with the reactionary blame-the-victim (women should take care against looking "too seductive"). Most important, none of the strategies they propose demonstrably curbs the occurrence of rape across contexts, victim profile, or perpetrator profile.

We also have to ask why the evolutionary psychology approach has gained a toehold in contemporary American psychology. Why is it so attractive to "explain" behavior by invoking hypothetical situations from tens of thousands of years ago over the proximate (and often apparently chaotic) causes that are so visible in recorded history? What is the attraction? We have been down this path before. Late nineteenth-century social applications of evolutionary theory routinely explained contemporary social fact as a manifestation of evolution pure and simple. For example, before tests of mental ability had been developed, "genius" was defined as achievement of social or professional eminence (Shields 1982). It surprised no one that, by this criterion, the proportion of men of genius far outnumbered women. After all, men were the judges and admirals and the successful inventors and artists. The point is that eminence, ostensibly an objective, behavioral index of mental superiority, is a fundamentally flawed indicator of natural "genius." It was only by ignoring the correlation between social eminence, economic privilege, and legal and de facto racial and gender barriers to achievement that eminence could be entertained as an index of genius.

To be sure, evolution manifests itself in many ways in human behavior—the "all overishness" that takes over as we stand at the edge of a cliff, our love affair with sweets, our capacity for language, to name just a few. Complex and vexed interpersonal relations, in contrast, take place within elaborately constructed and mutable social institutions. The evolutionary account goes awry when the assumption is made that "storytelling" about purported ultimate explanations constitutes a more useful and accurate account of proximal events than do the obvious, contemporaneous, material factors that have an already-demonstrated causal or correlational link to those events.

References

Bohner, G. and N. Schwarz (1996). The threat of rape: Its psychological impact on victimized women. In D. M. Buss and N. M. Malamuth, eds., *Sex, Power, Conflict: Evolutionary and Feminist Perspectives*, pp. 162–175. New York: Oxford University Press.

Buss, D. M., R. J. Larsen, D. Westen, and J. Semmelroth (1992). Sex differences in jealousy: Evolution, physiology, and psychology. *Psychological Science* 3: 251–255.

Christensen, L. (1977). The negative subject: Myth, reality, or a prior experimental experience effect? *Journal of Personality and Social Psychology* 35: 392–400.

Clark, H. H. and S. E. Haviland (1977). Comprehension and the given-new contract. In R. Freedle, ed., *Discourse Production and Comprehension*, pp. 1–40. Hillsdale, N.J.: Lawrence Erlbaum.

DeSteno, D. A. and P. Salovey (1996). Evolutionary origins of sex differences in jealousy? Questioning the "fitness" of the model. *Psychological Science* 7: 367–372.

Ericsson, K. A. and H. A. Simon (1980). Verbal reports as data. *Psychological Review* 87: 215–251.

Gargiulo, R. M. and R. J. Yonker (1983). Assessing teachers' attitude toward the handicapped: A methodological investigation. *Psychology in the Schools* 20: 229–233.

Geary, D. (1998). *Male, Female: The Evolution of Human Sex Differences*. Washington, D.C.: American Psychological Association.

Graesser, A. C. and T. Murachver (1985). Symbolic procedures of question answering. In A. Graesser and J. Black, eds., *The Psychology of Questions*, pp. 15–88. Hillsdale, N.J.: Lawrence Erlbaum.

Grice, H. P. (1975). Logic and conversation. In P. Cole and J. L. Morgan, eds., *Syntax and Semantics*, vol. 3, pp. 41–58. New York: Academic Press.

Griffiths, P. E. (1997). *What Emotions Really Are*. Chicago: University of Chicago Press.

Harré, R. (1989). Language and the science of psychology. *Journal of Social Behavior and Personality* 4: 165–188.

Hunter, C. H. (1984). Aligning actions: Types and social distribution. *Symbolic Interaction* 7: 155–174.

Kenrick, D. T. (2001). Evolutionary psychology, cognitive science, and dynamical systems: Building and integrative paradigms. *Current Directions in Psychological Science* 10: 13–17.

King, L. A. (2001). The health benefits of writing about life goals. *Personality and Social Psychology Bulletin* 27: 798–807.

La Piere, R. T. (1934). Attitudes vs. actions. *Social Forces* 13: 230–237.

Lehnert, W. (1978). *The Process of Question Answering*. Hillsdale, N.J.: Lawrence Erlbaum.

Lott, B. (1996). Politics or science? The question of gender sameness/difference. *American Psychologist* 51: 155–156.

Lyons, W. (1986). *The Disappearance of Introspection*. Cambridge, Mass.: MIT Press.

Potter, J. and M. Wetherell (1987). *Discourse and Social Psychology*. London: Sage.

Pratto, F. and P. Hegarty (2000). The political psychology of reproductive strategies. *Psychological Science* 11: 57–62.

Seligman, M. E. P. and P. Schulman (1986). Explanatory style as a predictor of productivity and quitting among life insurance sales agents. *Journal of Personality and Social Psychology* 50: 832–838.

Shields, S. A. (1982). The variability hypothesis: History of a biological model of sex differences in intelligence. *Signs: Journal of Women in Culture and Society* 7: 769–797.

Singer, M. (1990). The psychology of questions: Answering questions about discourse. *Discourse Processes* 13: 261–277.

Steinke, P. (1992). The effect of inmates' accounts on disciplinary penalties. *Journal of Social Psychology* 132: 475–485.

Stokes, R. and J. P. Hewitt (1976). Aligning actions. *American Sociological Review* 41: 838–849.

Tang-Martinez, Z. (1997). The curious courtship of sociobiology and feminism: A case of irreconcilable differences. In P. A. Gowaty, ed., *Feminism and Evolutionary Biology: Boundaries, Intersections, and Frontiers*, pp. 116–150. New York: Chapman and Hall.

Tassinary, L. G. and K. A. Hansen (1998). A critical test of the waist-to-hip-ratio hypothesis of female physical attractiveness. *Psychological Science* 9: 150–155.

Thornhill, R. and C. T. Palmer (2000). *A Natural History of Rape: Biological Bases of Sexual Coercion*. Cambridge, Mass.: MIT Press.

van Dijk, T. A. (ed.) (1985). *Handbook of Discourse Analysis,* vol. 2. London: Academic Press.

White, P. A. (1988). Knowing more about what we can tell: "Introspective access" and causal report accuracy 10 years later. *British Journal of Psychology* 79: 13–45.

Wylie, A. (1997). Good science, bad science, or science as usual? Feminist critiques of science. In L. D. Hager, ed., *Women in Evolution,* pp. 29–55. New York: Routledge.

Wylie, R. (1974). *The Self-Concept,* vol. 1, rev. ed. Lincoln, Neb.: University of Nebraska Press.

5

Understanding Rape

Ethel Tobach and Rachel Reed

Introduction

Several years ago, a group of well-intentioned biological and behavioral geneticists and psychologists met with a well-known advocate of a genetic base to so-called racial differences in IQ. They believed that if he were literate in genetics, he would abandon his formulation of group differences in IQ in terms of genetic processes. During that conference, I (Ethel Tobach) asked the participants to recognize the social/societal implications of the ideology that informed the racist formulation and warned that there was a conflagration pending if the scientific community did not actively refute that formulation. One of the behavior geneticists said, "Let them burn." And of course, this was just before the ghettos of the United States broke out in righteous outrage. And of course, the deep racism in USA society is still with us.

"[Sociobiology] went underground, where it has been eating away at the foundations of academic orthodoxy" (Thornhill and Palmer 2000 citing Wright on p. 107). They go on to say that "sociobiology is now re-emerging, primarily under the new label of 'evolutionary psychology.'" The possible effect of evolutionary psychology and human sociobiology on public policy is evidenced in the citations by Thornhill and Palmer of the work by Jones (1999) and Beckstrom (1993) in the application of those ideologies to law in the courts and rape.

Is there something inherent in the genetic determinism of ethology, sociobiology, and evolutionary psychology that attracts racists to psychologists who subscribe to those theories? For example, Rushton was invited to speak with Jared Taylor, of the New Century Foundation, which promotes white separatism (Staff, Southern Poverty Law Center 2000). Despite the avowals by sociobiologists and evolutionary psychologists that a nonsexist, nonracist evolutionary psychology and human sociobiology is possible, the continued expression of racist and sexist ideas about human behavior on the basis of evolutionary psychology and sociobiology continue to be featured in the media.

Scientific, critical examination of the activity called "rape" may help us formulate some program for prevention and justice for the victim. Scientific, societal responsibility calls on us to do this.

Plan for the Chapter

A key thesis of this chapter is that science and social responsibility should be critically linked and integrated. In this case, being a socially responsible scientist requires careful and detailed attention to the theory, principles, and data of evolutionary biology and population genetics. This is nowhere more true than when attempting to develop causal models of human social behavior, and it is especially appropriate when addressing issues of gender and violence. Being socially responsible in science demands thorough grounding in the assumptions, methodologies, and limitations of science and scientific inference. Thus, the chapter begins with a clarification of evolutionary principles and terminology, including acknowledgment of those areas of debate within evolutionary theory itself. The comparative method has been a basic approach to developing and testing hypotheses in evolutionary theory, and thus this method is given more detailed coverage. The epistemological debates of science in general are considered in the second section, including what constitutes compelling statistical evidence and the limits of causal inference based on such evidence. The nature of data, operational definitions, and databases are discussed in detail as these relate to rape. Finally, we examine how scientists can pursue a better and more relevant science in response to social issues, and the case of an evolutionary basis for rape in particular. Major sections are as follows:

I. Evolutionary Issues

II. Scientific Method

III. Conceptualizations of Science and Societal Responsibility of Scientists

I Evolutionary Issues

Ho and Saunders (1984) give us a picture of the present state of Darwinian and neo-Darwinian theory different from that given by sociobiology or evolutionary psychology:

It must not be supposed however, that there is anything approaching the "consensus" which is often claimed for the neo-Darwinian synthesis. Pluralism is a predominant feature of the emerging paradigm of evolution. . . . Evaluating is a complex phenomenon and . . . different kinds of explanations will be appropriate. . . . [H]igher level explanations cannot always be collapsed or reduced into lower level ones. . . .

Above all, however, our emphasis is on process. . . . The result is a transcendence of the predominantly Aristotelian framework of neo-Darwinism—in which organisms are explained in terms of essences or genes—to the post-Galilean world view in which relation and process [and change—ET] are primary. (Ho and Saunders 1984, p. 5)

People cannot be faulted for believing that what they believe is *the* truth and the only *right* way of thinking . . . the *scientific* way. We all do that. If we act on the premise that we are accountable to others for our beliefs and our actions, it is incumbent on us, nonetheless, to offer the basis for our beliefs and to demonstrate that we have considered other beliefs. It is important that when people disagree with us, we recognize the difference between the following two statements: 1. You don't understand me; that is why you disagree with me; and 2. You probably understand me; I don't know why you disagree with me.

The authors of this chapter profess to understand the evolutionary theory of the human sociobiologists; however, we do not accept their theory as *the* final truth; we do not accept any theory as *the* truth. We do find that other theories are compatible with our own work and research and our philosophy of science. We offer those other theories as possible candidates for developing an agenda for discussion and research, rather than providing a detailed response to the statements by Thornhill and Palmer.

A Agents of Evolution

Thornhill and Palmer list four agents of evolution: selection, drift, gene flow, and mutation (Thornhill and Palmer 2000, p. 6). In their discussion of rape, they also work with adaptation, natural selection, and sexual selection (Thornhill and Palmer 2000, pp. 5–15; 32 inter alia). Significant critical discussions have taken place in regard to all these processes (Lovtrup 1974, 1987), but most fundamental to the discussion about rape are the concepts of natural selection, sexual selection, and adaptation.

Two postulates from Darwin's theory have been elaborated by many evolutionary theorists: natural selection (including sexual selection) and adaptation (survival of the fittest). The two postulates explain speciation by descent of those individuals who survive by reason of their characteristics that distinguish them from other near and distant relatives and enable them to have viable offspring that have their characteristics and can successfully produce viable offspring that will also have those characteristics. The significant elaboration of these postulates was the development of genetics to produce the "new synthesis" of evolutionary theory.

1   Natural selection   Several questions have been raised about the concept of natural selection:

• Does selection take place on the behavioral level (as a function of the individual's or the group's activity in response to changes in the ecological setting in which the species acts)?
• Does selection take place on the genetic level (functional genes are retained by the successfully reproducing individuals; deleterious or dysfunctional genes are lost, either through activities of the nucleotides and proteins or by the fact that the individual does not survive or does not reproduce)?
• Is there a direction to the selection process, that is, is natural selection "progressive" (does it inherently lead to better characteristics to ensure survival and to greater complexity)?
• Is natural selection "determined" or random (are the successful reproducing organisms successful by chance or by preceding events that of necessity bring about natural selection)?
• Is the dominant or only process in natural selection the survival of some individuals until they are able to reproduce and the loss of others before they can reproduce?

The prevailing conceptualization of natural selection is that it is primarily based on individual survival as described in the fifth question above; the notion that selection takes place on a group level has been discarded by most evolutionary biologists. The evolutionary adaptiveness of rape would then depend on the individual's behavior being central to survival for reproduction of viable young that would themselves reproduce successfully. The data to support this are not yet available. Given that the survival of the species depends on the survival of the individual members of that species, the first two questions would appear to be in the affirmative: as life depends on functional nucleotides and proteins, and as the behavior of the individual is interdependent with the group's behavior if reproduction is to take place (animals that reproduce asexually are at one or another time in their life history related to other members of the species [Tobach and Schneirla 1968]).

The third and fourth questions are mentioned as examples of the complexity of the issues related to evolutionary theory. Recent authors (Camus 1997; Davies 1989; Fox 1984; Goodwin 1989; Ho 1984, 1987, 1989; Saunders 1984; Matsuno 1984; Wicken 1984) have discussed the concept of self-organization as a process described by Eigen (1971a, b) and Nicolis and Prigogine (1977) related to physical phenomena, but which may be applied to living organisms. The relationship among internal systems is developed in living organisms through self-organizational processes in dynamic change in the living organisms that are open systems. In effect, the second law of thermodynamics is modified by the special characteristics of living systems. This leads some evolutionary biologists to emphasize developmental processes as they are open systems (Ho 1987, 1989) rather than to focus on genetic processes, which are traditionally conceptualized as closed systems.

One of the consequences of these discussions is the recognition of the possibility that during evolution, change could take place on the genetic level as well as on all other levels. Recent discoveries in genetic processes have highlighted the dynamic possibility of change in genetic material, which may be related to processes of speciation (Steele et al. 1998; Steele 1979). Such possibilities cast some doubt on the evolutionary psychologists' claim that contemporary humans have the same genes as those that were present in the early stages of human evolution.

Because change may take place on all levels, the possibility of some random or chance process in evolution has been proposed (Lima-de-Faria 1988). Others believe that a historical, developmental approach suggests that as evolution is change in time, preceding events produce the processes that lead to the succeeding change in a type of "determinism" rather than by chance (Waddington 1957, 1959). This type of determinism is informed by the self-organizing principle in open living systems and is in

contrast to genetic determinist formulations that the burden of fundamental change is primarily on genes. The genetic process is one of a number of events that once having taken place on the biochemical level
(involving proteins, enzymes, etc.) are the predecessors of the next event in
time. This type of determinism is the integration of preceding events that
operate on more than one level. In that sense this is determinism, but it is
historical and developmental. A persevering theoretical presence in these
discussions is that of Waddington (1975). See also Thom (1989), whose
concept of the epigenetic landscape has been responsible for much of the
call to rethink neo-Darwinism. S. A. Kaufman (1989) has emphasized
that there are many targets of selection, as these act interdependently in
processes that organize other processes, such as the genetic process (epi-
genesis). These concepts suggest that the behavior of an individual is the
product of developmental experiences on many levels, including the internalization of externally generated experiences.

Mayr (1976) has written that group selection as a process has not been
supported by experimental data or observations for most species. But in
humans, group selection occurs because a human group is more than a
conglomeration of individual smaller groups (families). He attributes the
difference between humans and other animals to the special neuroanatomical evolution in humans. He finds that there are different kinds
of human groups and that the target of selection is the group, when it is a
founder group thus giving rise to many smaller groups that may respond
to selection pressure.

2   Adaptation   In a 1982 article, Gould and Vrba point out that the term
adaptation is used variously by biologists: as a process that is responsible
for variation; as an evolved structure; as a "state of being" (p. 5). None of
these usages reflects the structural and functional variations that take
place to bring about the diversity of species. They propose that the process
of adaptive variation that brings about evolutionary change is exaptation:
"characters that have evolved for other usages (or for no function at all)
and later 'coopted' for their current role" (p. 6). This process of expanding the function and development of existing structures that may have
evolved during earlier environmental challenges is responsible for the plasticity with which individuals respond to changes in the environment. For
example, the skin structures (feathers) that were present in the earliest an-

cestors of contemporary birds were primarily temperature-regulating systems. When environmentally challenged, these structures became involved in feeding, or flight. The feathers retained their temperature-regulating function as well. We suggest that such exaptations may be processes in behavioral evolution as well (see Tattersall 1998). These may be related to physiological, neuroanatomical evolution of structures that become involved in behavioral plasticity and diversity. This view of adaptation presents a challenge to static concepts of speciation and evolution through the subtraction of individuals who cannot reproduce successfully. It offers an alternative process of evolutionary change based on the interdependence and integration of the individual's internal and external experiences.

B   Continuities and Discontinuities in Evolution

The relationship among different species attests to the finding that there are activity patterns that are continuous throughout the animal world: interindividual activity, called *social behavior* (Tobach and Schneirla 1968). This continuity becomes discontinuous as the relationship between the individual and the environment changes, as the formation of different group relationships develop, and so on. The social activity of insects is discontinuous in the general pattern of social behavior. The similarities of all social behavior (interindividual activity) is subsumed in the dissimilarities in the social insect, in which the social behavior is based primarily on chemical experience during development. This type of social behavior is discontinuous when compared with human social behavior, in which the interindividual activity is interdependent with the societal setting in which the two or more individuals interact. A reliable and valid method of comparative studies involving different species recognizes the similarities and the differences, in order to define those activities that are continuous and those that are discontinuous (Albert, Walsh, and Jonik 1993).

The human sociobiologists tell us that their plan is to relate human behavior primarily to mammalian behavior, yet they refer to the behavior of invertebrates, as well as vertebrates other than mammals. The attempt to understand human behavior by extrapolating from the behavior of other animals to human behavior without recognizing the differences as well as the similarities results in the zoomorphism (attributing nonhuman animal characteristics to humans) that is the hallmark of sociobiology (Harding 1985).

Many scientists believe that it is easier to define behavior if zoomorphic or anthropomorphic terms are used. The language used frequently negates the evolutionary relationships among species and among their behavioral patterns. It also obscures differences among species and their behavior and leads to superficial analyses in which similarities are emphasized, and the significance of the differences is overlooked.

Thornhill and Palmer analyze human rape in zoomorphic terms. "Mate choice" involved in human woman/man relationships is assumed to be based on the same processes as those in animals, ignoring the sociosocietal processes underlying the development of the human relationship. In a similar confusion of an appropriate comparison, they attribute human characterics to the precopulatory activities of animals. This results in the presentation of a primarily anthropomorphic description of animal behavior and a zoomorphic description of human rape behavior.

Human reproductive behavior is continuous with the hormonal, enzymatic, and protein processes of other animals. However, the interconnectedness of societal processes with these biochemical and physiological processes results in activities that are discontinuous with those of the social behavior to which the reproductive behavior of mammals is related. An irritable husband's beating his wife whom he impregnated by rape bears little relationship to the reproductive behavior of other mammals, or primates. The production of "breeder women" (e.g., in slavery) to provide additional group members is equally discontinuous with the reproductive behavior of other animals.

Attention to such continuities and discontinuities can suggest appropriate levels of analysis for understanding human behavior. An attempt to understand human rape by consideration of different levels of function and of the continuities and discontinuities in evolved patterns can avoid the fallacies of zoomorphism and anthropomorphism.

1 Rape: A discontinuity in evolution of reproductive behavior   The hypothesis of Thornhill and Palmer is that rape is evolutionarily adaptive. If, in fact, it does not improve reproductive success, it is maladaptive. Until the data are in, the issue is unresolved.

If one were to approach the problem from a consideration of continuity and discontinuity of evolved patterns of behavior, the obvious continuity in reproductive behavior is that in all vertebrates (and especially in mammals and primates), the neuroanatomic pathways and neurotransmitter functions expressed in aggressive and reproductive behavior share many structural and biochemical features (Rauch et al. 1999; Yoshimura and Kimura 1991). In many species, aggressive behavior is part of the eventual conjugation of gametic material; aggression is in effect part of the process of sexual activity, that is, preconjugational activity. The complementary effect of the two processes, the facilitative effect of one on the other may have played a vital role in the evolution of some species (Tinbergen 1974). For example, aggressive activity promotes gonadal growth in some species. The complex interplay between the two behavioral patterns is distinctively different in different species, and the evolutionary processes that bring the diversity about are not clear. That their relationship may reflect the type of social organization of the species is possible.

Shared structural-functional relationships in aggression and sexual behavior are continuous in the evolution of many species. The relationship between shared structures and functions and the relative significance of aggression in sexual behavior differs among species. This is the discontinuity of the shared relationship. In other words, the facilitatory effect of aggression on the biochemistry (hormones, structures) of reproduction may be less in one species than in another, and this may be related to other factors, such as social organization, ecological processes, and so on.

2 Sociosocietal pathology expressed in an individual   The greatest discontinuity in the integration of aggression and copulation activity is seen on the human level when the two are integrated in a new way. Nonhuman animals can perform many activities before copulation, including: "gift" giving, touching, vocalization, "dances," and so on. (The seeming continuity of these activities with human activities is reflected in the anthropomorphic terms that biological behavioral scientists use to denote them.) The intersensory integration of sensorimotor pathways preliminary to actual copulation may be exapted as the species becomes more dependent on central neural systems in reproductive behavior (Rosenblatt 1974; Aronson 1974), so that the sensorimotor integrations in precopulatory behavior in animals other than humans becomes the fine art of presexual foreplay on the human level.

Although precopulatory behavior in humans is termed "foreplay," many elements of "playful aggression" may be involved (Pomeroy 1969; Foucault 1985). When the aggression ceases to be playful and becomes the preeminent activity required for sexual activity, some sort of behavioral dysfunction is involved.

That aggression and sexuality share many of the same hormonal and neural processes is not unusual, as other behavioral pathways are interdependent; for example, cognitive and emotional activities also overlap. However, in the case of aggression and sexuality, the significance of the interconnectedness of the two pathways is embedded in the psychosocial development of the individual in a way that has a direct bearing on the sociosocietal process in which women and men relate to each other. The literature frequently raises the issue of misogyny as a fundamental process in the rapist's behavior (Malamuth, Heavey, and Linz 1993; Sheffield 1997). This is not a necessary process in rape, as people may rape for many reasons, such as peer pressure, feelings about a particular person rather than a category of people. Misogyny may be sufficient to engender rape, however. The necessary process is the sociopathic inability to respond to the behavior of the victim in a way that is socially healthy for both individuals.

The psychopathology of sexual offenders has been studied by many (Milton 1997; Firestone et al. 2000); Groth and Birnbaum (1985) wrote that "Rape is always a symptom of some psychological dysfunction." The suggestion that rape is pathological does not necessarily place it in the rubric of individual psychopathology based on genetic, hormonal, or organismic variation. Rather, it reflects pathological conditions of society that become translated into an individual's pathology in which the patterns of aggression become dominant over the patterns of sexuality. The sociosocietal pathology is the relationship between women and men in which men are socialized to believe that they are "entitled" to satisfy their desire for sex, and that they are "entitled" to have and demonstrate control of women by engaging in aggressive activities (Hill and Fischer 2001).

Individuals growing up in this sociosocietal setting develop conceptualizations about societally derived acceptable behavioral patterns. How these concepts are expressed in individual behavior is a characteristic of ontogenic experience. The assumption that there is such a process of transition from a societal pattern to an individual pattern requires careful formulation and testing. There is always the possibility of individuals who are dysfunctional because of biochemical or neurophysiological disease and who are extremely aggressive both in and out of sexual activity.

Some believe that rape is psychopathology, on the basis of a Freudian analysis of the behavior. Rada (1978) writes that "Biological, psychological and social factors contribute to the commission of rape, but none, alone, is sufficient to a complete understanding of the cause of rape or the motivation of the rapist" (p. 22). Furthermore, Rada argues, "Rape is a crime of control, power, and dominance. . . . In this sense, the aggressive component appears to be more dominant in rape than the sexual component. In fact, for many rapists the sexual act itself appears to be less important than the ritual of the rape event, which is more often carefully planned than impulsive" (p. 24).

II Scientific Method

A Database

A critical examination of rape as derived from natural selection or other evolutionary processes requires valid and reliable information about the activity. We offer some material demonstrating the difficulty in obtaining such information.

1 Conceptualizing definitions As the data concerning rape are gathered by many different agents, the definition used becomes a significant factor in the information obtained. A definition that is generally accepted by individuals, agencies, governments, and legal instruments is a necessary tool. The fact that there is no universally accepted definition of rape requires investigation. It may be that the need for a single definition has not been clearly established, or that societal attitudes and values prevent establishing such a definition; in the United States, the disagreement about what constitutes state and federal rights may be involved.

Theoreticians formulate their own definitions. Thornhill and Palmer discuss the definition of rape as a societally based tool (pp. 150–152). As humans are elaborating the concept in a societal process (scientific research), it is important to identify the societal philosophy, the societal activity of the definers of the concept. Although Thornhill and Palmer decry the use of definition as a societal tool, it is clear that their definition is an expression of their philosophy concerning an activity that has a particular societal significance. They define rape in their glossary as "copulation resisted to the best of the victim's ability unless such resistance would probably result in death or injury to the victim or in death or injury to individuals the victim commonly protects" (p. 210). On p. 37, they add to the definition—the "production of an ejaculate" that is "place[d] in a female's vagina." The emphasis is on reproduction and on copulation that will have the benefit of producing offspring.

Recognizing that the activity of defining rape is indeed a societal process, we base our definition of rape on the concept of sexual autonomy (Schulhofer 1998) because the activity on which we are focusing is an activity of humans, a social activity, and a societal activity. It is societal because it is related to rules set down by the society in which it takes place. This differentiates it from the anthropomorphic definition of rape in nonhuman animals, a social process without any relationship to societal rules. The significance of the societal situation in which the sexual assault takes place is an important aspect of the definition of rape. In a study by Eigenberg (2000), the correctional officers' definitions were blurred by their views about homosexuality so that male rape was considered consensual sex, and the victim was blamed.

We, therefore, define rape as any action on the part of one person to violate the sexual autonomy of another by penetration, no matter the extent of penetration, of the penis, finger, tongue or foreign object into the vagina, anus, or mouth of the other. Violation of sexual autonomy denotes the act took place without mutual consent. Absence of consent is the necessary component of rape.

As the biologist (Thornhill) and the anthropologist (Palmer) (both human sociobiologists) base their evolutionary definition of rape on the reproductive success of the act, they narrow the human scope of the activity. In this way, they exclude all other activities that violate sexual autonomy, which signifies consent, such as unwanted touching, voyeurism, exposing genitalia, sexual harassment, stalking, obscene telephone calls, and so on. As these activities would be termed facultative responses (p. 18) leading to the achievement of the primary goal of preserving the offender's genes in the generation (reproductive success), the data necessary to support their view would require gathering information about whether an offender carrying out such activities was a "successful" rapist.

Not all rapists engage in all forms of sexual autonomy violation, but those who violate sexual autonomy in other ways are likely to become rapists (Saunders, Awad, and White 1986). Most theoreticians, including both genetic determinists and those who are not genetic determinists, would agree that the course of sexual crime is highly individualistic. The individuality of the behavior reflects the total experience of the individual: the biochemistry (genes and hormones) and the physiological/psychological developmental history. Studying the interdependency of these processes is a necessary research commitment that is given lip service by many theoreticians.

2   Definitions used in producing databases   As much of the data are obtained from societal agencies dealing with crime and law, we present tables 5.1 and 5.2, which give brief statements of legal statutes by state pertaining to force or consent, and to type of penetration, thus yielding different definitions of rape (National Sexual Violence Research Center 2000). The variations are clearly apparent. State rape laws may be divided into four general categories: forcible compulsion; against the victim's will; without consent I; and without consent II. (Definitions are given in the tables.)

Without consent II is the only criterion that does not rely on force or resistance, and comes closest to defining rape as "sex without consent." Unfortunately, this criterion is used in only seven of the fifty states as part of the definition of rape; in some states, sex without consent in which force or resistance is not demonstrated constitutes a crime of a lesser degree than rape. This variation means that the data on which any discussion is based are likely to be idiosyncratic. It is important to keep this caveat in mind in all discussions, including ours.

3   Some sources of data   Rape definitions vary not only among states, but among studies, some including only certain types of penetration committed against certain people (e.g., women).

The Uniform Crime Report (UCR), coordinated by the FBI, is an annual compilation of crime statistics voluntarily submitted by law enforcement agencies in each state (Federal Bureau of Investigation 1997). The UCR

Table 5.1
How State Statutes Define Rape

States	Forcible Compulsion	Against Will	Without Consent 1	Without Consent 2
Alabama	x			
Alaska			x	
Arizona			x	
Arkansas	x			
California	x	x		
Colorado	x	x		
Connecticut	x			
Delaware			x[1]	
Florida			x	
Georgia	x	x		
Hawaii	x			
Idaho	x[1]			
Illinois	x			
Indiana	x			
Iowa	x	x		
Kansas			x	
Kentucky	x			
Louisiana			x[1]	
Maine	x			
Maryland	x	x		
Massachusetts	x	x		
Michigan	x			
Minnesota	x			
Mississippi	*See below			
Missouri	x			
Montana			x	
Nebraska			x[1]	x
Nevada		x		
New Hampshire	x			x
New Jersey	x			
New Mexico	x			
New York			x	
North Carolina	x	x		
North Dakota	x[1]			
Ohio	x[1]			

Table 5.1 *continued*

States	Forcible Compulsion	Against Will	Without Consent 1	Without Consent 2
Oklahoma	x			
Oregon	x			
Pennsylvania	x**			
Rhode Island	x			
South Carolina	x			
South Dakota	x			
Tennessee	x			x
Texas			x	
US Code	x			
Utah	x			x
Vermont			x	
Virginia	x	x		
Washington, D.C.	x			x^2
Washington	x^1			x^2
West Virginia	x^1			
Wisconsin			x	x^2
Wyoming	x			

Forcible Compulsion   Physical force or threat of physical force, express or implied, that places a person in fear of death, physical injury to self or another person, fear of the kidnapping of self or another person, or fear of another criminal offense.

Against Will   "Against the victim's will" is typically accompanied by the use of force; however, it is not specifically defined.

Without Consent 1   Lack of consent in conjunction with the use or threat of force.

Without Consent 2   Lack of consent need not be accompanied by use or threat of force. The victim must demonstrate lack of consent with words or other conduct.

x^1 The statute mentions resistance, either to the utmost or a lesser degree, as a criterion necessary to prove lack of consent. The requirement of resistance may be waived if reasonable force or threat of force is present.

x^2 In these states, lack of consent not accompanied by force or threat of force constitutes a crime of lesser degree; a felony or a misdemeanor.

*   Mississippi, based on available information, does not appear to define sexual assault in terms similar to other states. The statute does, however, stress the importance of a victim's chaste character and requires corroborated testimony.

**   In defining forcible compulsion, the Pennsylvania statute includes physical, intellectual, moral, emotional, and psychological force, either express or implied.

Table 5.2
Types of Penetration in Rape Statutes

States	Penetration			Criteria — Type of Intercourse				Other		Not Given
	However Slight	All Types of	Penile Only	Semen Emission[1]	Vaginal Intercourse	Typical vs Deviate	Male to Female	Oral[2]	Objects[3]	
Alabama	x	x		x						
Arizona								x		
Alaska										x
Arkansas										x
California										x
Colorado										x
Connecticut	x	x		x						
Delaware	x			x					x	
Florida		x								
Georgia						x	x			
Hawaii	x									x
Idaho			x						x	
Illinois										x
Indiana										x
Iowa										x
Kansas	x				x	x				
Kentucky	x			x		x				

Table 5.2 *continued*

States	Penetration				Criteria Type of Intercourse			Other		Not Given
	However Slight	All Types of	Penile Only	Semen Emission[1]	Vaginal Intercourse	Typical vs Deviate	Male to Female	Oral[2]	Objects[3]	
Louisiana	x			x				x		
Maine		x								
Maryland	x	x		x	x					
Massachusetts										x
Michigan										x
Minnesota										x
Mississippi			x		x		x			
Missouri										x
Montana										x
Nebraska	x	x		x						
Nevada	x	x								
New Hampshire	x	x		x						
New Jersey	x	x								
New Mexico	x	x		x						
New York	x					x			x	
North Carolina	x	x			x	x				
North Dakota	x	x		x						
Ohio	x	x				x				

Table 5.2 continued

States	Penetration			Semen Emission[1]	Criteria — Type of Intercourse			Other		Not Given
	However Slight	All Types of	Penile Only		Vaginal Intercourse	Typical vs Deviate	Male to Female	Oral[2]	Objects[3]	
Oklahoma	x							x		
Oregon	x	x		x		x			x	
Pennsylvania	x	x		x		x				
Rhode Island	x	x		x						
South Carolina	x	x								
South Dakota	x	x								
Tennessee	x	x		x						
Texas	x	x				x	x			
US Code	x	x								
Utah										x
Vermont	x	x								
Virginia		x								
Washington, D.C.	x	x								
Washington	x	x								
West Virginia	x	x								
Wisconsin	x	x		x						
Wyoming	x	x		x						

1. Semen emission is not required for penetration
2. Oral penetration is not included in the statute
3. Penetration with an object is not included in the statute

uses only certain criteria: rapes against females; rapes of victims 18 years old or older; penile-vaginal penetration. As tables 5.1 and 5.2 show, all include penile-vaginal penetration as "rape," but the data they collect as "rape" include other activities.

The National Crime Victimization Survey (NCVS) is sponsored by the U.S. Department of Justice, Office of Justice Programs, Bureau of Justice Statistics (Greenfield 1997) and is an ongoing census that estimates the number of underreported serious crimes nationwide. They randomly select households (50,000) yielding more than 100,000 individual respondents to ask about sexual assaults. These include forced sexual intercourse where the victim may be either female or male; where the offender may be of the same sex or a different sex than the victim; unwanted sexual contact; and threats and attempts to commit such offenses.

The National Women's Study (NWS) funded by the National Institute of Drug Abuse (Kilpatrick et al. 2000) interviewed a national probability sample of 4,008 adult women in a three-year longitudinal study. They defined rape as "an event that occurred without the woman's consent, involved the use of force or threat of force, and involved sexual penetration of the victim's vagina, mouth or rectum." This study addresses the concerns of the victims and the demographics of the victim and the offender. They also report the effect of laws prohibiting disclosure of victims' names and the impact of this on rape reporting.

The National Violence against Women Survey (NVAWS) was funded by the National Institute of Justice and the Center for Disease Control, 1995 to 1999 (Tjaden and Thoennes 2000; Kilpatrick et al. 2000). This survey used the same screening questions as those in the NWS. This study addressed the psychological, emotional, physical, and financial effects of rape on the survivor, and the demographics of the victim and the offender.

The National Survey of Adolescents, funded by the National Institute of Justice, conducted interviews with a national household probability sample of teenagers aged 12 to 17. These interviews deal with sexual assaults and other crimes.

4 Reporting of rape   Accurate numbers are hard to come by for another reason: underreporting. Based on information from the UCR and the NCVS, the FBI stated that the incidence of rape is approximately 100,000 rapes a year, but only one in ten rapes is reported to the police (Federal Bureau of Investigation 1982). It should be noted that the FBI reported 96,122 rapes in 1997, a decrease that is being widely discussed today (Kilpatrick et al. 2000). The NCVS found that 32 percent of sexual assault cases were reported to police in 1994 (Kilpatrick and Saunders 1996). Koss (1990) reported that only 7 percent of rapes are reported to police. In a study done by the University of South Carolina (1992), 16 percent of rapes and sexual assaults were reported to the police (Kilpatrick et al. 1992).

The UCR report (1982) cautions that "forcible rape is still recognized as one of the most underreported of all index [UCR felony crimes] crimes. Victims' fear of their assailants and their embarrassment over the incident are just two factors that can affect their decisions to contact law enforcement."

Men who are raped are unlikely to report the event (Mitchell et al. 1999). These investigators cite the reasons for the reluctance of men to report being raped in the studies by Groth and Burgess (1980) and Kaufman et al. (1980): fear that they would not be believed; fear that their sexual orientation would be questioned; distress and embarrassment. In a 1999 report by Pino, men were found less likely to report rape victimization than women.

The nonexistence of laws that prohibit the reporting of victims' names is another factor that leads to the underreporting of data. Kilpatrick et al. (1992) report that "Half of rape victims surveyed (50%) stated that they would be a lot more likely to report rapes to the police if there was a law prohibiting news media from getting and disclosing their names and addresses" (p. 16).

Inexperience with sexual activity led 73 percent of college women whose sexual experience satisfied the definition of sexual assault (including rape) according to the Ohio Penal Code to consider themselves not victims of rape (Koss et al. 1987). As Donat and White (2000) point out cultural mores and myths may well affect the women's concept of rape or sexual assault, leading to denial of the event.

Self-blame and denial were responsible for only 5 percent of one sample reporting the incident to police, and for 42 percent not mentioning the incident to any other person (Warsaw 1998).

B   Rape and Human Sociobiology

1   Assumptions in human sociobiology's definition of rape   Understanding the act of rape as it involves the two sexes is sufficient to understanding all types of human rape. Acts in which (1) no penetration of any part of the body takes place, (2) no semen is produced, and (3) variations in the copulatory act occur would not be considered rape. Therefore, the evolutionary history or significance of those types of activity would not be examined.

In human sociobiology, rape is defined as passing the semen on to a potential mother. To test this assumption, relevant facts about the rape would have to be ascertained, that is, that semen was actually produced and transmitted. This is not always possible. Therefore, it may be necessary to infer the facts by indirection, as by resulting pregnancies and births. Such data are also difficult to obtain.

2   Issues of reproductive success and rape   The contribution of rape copulation to reproductive success, as evidenced by offspring that remain viable to the point of their being able to reproduce, would appear to be negligible. Thornhill and Palmer themselves propose that the rate of pregnancy after rape is probably 2 percent, far below the rate of pregnancy after planned and consensual copulation. Krueger in her article on pregnancy resulting from rape (1988) cites nine studies dating from 1970 to 1983. The listing in her report shows that the percentages of rapes resulting in pregnancy range from .6 percent (1971) to 10 percent (1978). The median percentage is 2 to 4 percent.

That pregnancy places women at higher risk for both physical and sexual abuse (including rape) by their partners who are presumably responsible for the pregnancy is described by Bergen (1999) in her article on marital rape. In a population of adolescents pregnant as a result of sexual assault, the women were physically traumatized by the boyfriend or spouse during the pregnancy in 80 percent of the cases (Berenson et al. 1992). Gessner and Perham-Hester (1999) working with a population of 200 women in Alaska reported that mothers less than 18 years of age were more likely to experience violence after pregnancy than women who were 18 to 19 years of age and that the percentage of women who reported experiencing violence each week increased following pregnancy.

The establishment of accurate data about the relationship between rape and pregnancy is further complicated by cultural factors. Koss et al. (1987) report that approximately 15 percent to 18 percent of rape victims become pregnant. In a more recent study, Stewart and Trussell (2000) report that in 1998, the estimated number of rapes was 333,000 with 25,000 pregnancies, or approximately 8 percent. Koss et al. (1987) contrast these figures with a finding of 5 percent of such cases in the United States. In this same chapter, Koss et al. report that in Lima, Peru, where abortions are illegal, 90 percent of young mothers 12 to 16 years of age delivered a child as a result of rape.

The practice of abortion in the course of human evolution and history should not be overlooked. However, it is not possible to write a history of rape, pregnancy, and abortion during early hominid evolution. The need for hands to assist in presedentation survival activities may have been a factor in such reproductive activity and control. Ancient agrarian societies probably promoted increases in population whether reproduction was consensual or not. With the establishment of philosophical and religious concepts, reproductive regulation in regard to procreation, birth control, rape, and legality or illegality of sexual activity became factors in measuring reproductive success. These historical issues are not featured in sociobiology or evolutionary psychology discussions of rape.

The possibility of abortion also affects the data of possible pregnancy and viability of offspring. In a review by Krueger in 1988, the number of reports of pregnancies after rape was affected by abortion laws, as many of the victims sought financial help in obtaining abortions. In the study carried out by Holmes et al. (1996) and cited by Thornhill and Palmer (p. 100), 62 percent of the pregnancies were aborted either spontaneously or medically, 32 percent of the offspring were kept by the mother, while 6 percent were placed for adoption. Access to abortion could very well affect the decision of the victim and the rapist about ensuing pregnancies. The need for such data is not considered in human sociobiology.

A historical phenomenon illustrates the significance of societal processes for the practice of rape. As documented by Susan Brownmiller (1975), during slavery in the United States, rape was practiced as an economic tool to increase the number of offspring that could be worked or sold ("breeder women," pp. 166–168). Slavery was a socioeconomic system in the sociobiological model of reproductive success.

3   Sociobiological discussions of rape and sexuality   Human sociobiologists use the term "sexuality" to denote an evolved activity pattern to advance the reproductive success of the organism. This activity pattern based on biochemistry (genes, hormones) and physiology differs in each organism so that feminine sexuality and masculine sexuality are expressed in different ways.

The use of the term "sexuality" or "sex" in connection with rape occasions debates. Human sociobiologists see sexuality, sex, at the root of rape. Some nonsociobiologists may also view sexuality as an evolved pattern based on biochemistry and physiology, and view the sexuality of women and men as being different. However, it is possible to view sexuality as a sociosocietal process that is not necessarily associated with producing offspring who will represent one's genes in ensuing generations. Sexuality, like other pleasures (activities sought out and engaged in for long periods of time and repeatedly) such as athletics, music, doing science, or dancing, are part of human sociosocietal behavior. The human sociobiologist sees such pleasures as having evolved for the purpose of ensuring progeny that will carry the genes into ensuing generations. However, here the fact that such activities frequently result in progeny does not give any evidence that they are related; to assume causality is to repeat the logical error of post hoc, ergo propter hoc. The "sexuality" of the nonsociobiologist relates to the concept of sexual autonomy, and anything that destroys or threatens that autonomy is nonpleasurable; that is, rape, which above all is nonconsensual. The debate between the two approaches to rape rests on this difference in viewing sexuality.

The automatic acceptance of the validity of the human sociobiological assumptions leads to a lack of data and discussion in the document produced by Thornhill and Palmer. There is no recognition of the changing societal practices in regard to homophilic sex activity, the lowering of the age at which sexual activity is undertaken by both sexes with the concomitant likelihood of nonreproductive sexual activity, and the increase in the occurrence of sexual activity without a reproductive base, stimulated by various cultural agencies, aided by the development of abortifacents and other means of birth control.

C   Causal Inference and Logical Fallacies

Despite the apparent difficulty in obtaining valid and reliable data about the incidence and demographics of rape in its many forms, it is apparent that some general characteristics, for example, age and sex of the offenders and the victims, are consonant in the reports of various agencies. The existence of such data does not provide information about the causal processes involved in the activity. To infer causality from such data is a logical error; that is, to say that if more men than women rape, it is something about the men that causes them to do that; or to say if more women are victims, it is something about the women that causes them to be victims. Assembling facts is insufficient. Relevant assumptions need to be stated, formulated, and tested. The formulation of the research questions should be patent. The methods by which the facts are obtained should be replicable. The questions asked about the data and how the answers are obtained need to be clear.

The problem with posing evolutionary processes as causal is that it is difficult to construct hypotheses that can be tested in the usual experimental fashion. Experiments based on Mendelian genetics, behavior genetics, molecular genetics—all work by inference: If change occurs concomitantly with an operation by the experimenter, a correlational statement may be made. Despite the fact that the limitations of such an analysis are well known, the lure of inferences about possible causes leads one to reify such correlations and make assumptions about their having demonstrated an agency (Nagel 1961).

As most of the data offered by the human sociobiologists are correlational in character, it is worthwhile reviewing what Cohen and Nagel (1934) say about other statistical errors that are frequently made in correlational thinking. Although Cohen and Nagel are writing about the actual calculation of correlational coefficients from quantitative measures, much of their warnings apply equally to the use of correlational data of a relatively quantitative/qualitative nature.

Another problem with sociobiological hypotheses is that observations of events, which are not necessarily set up as experiments, are seen as suggestive of causality, or some understanding of an agency in the observed results. This is a frequently seen logical fallacy, post hoc, ergo propter hoc: the assumption that whatever follows an event is therefore caused by it. Cohen and Nagel (1934, p. 379) describe "A material fallacy" as one that "denote[s] false claims or illusions of proof. Whether the A that follows event B is caused by it, is a question of fact and not merely of logic."

Thornhill and Palmer might consider these dangers in their readiness to place great confidence in correlations without further research to determine the processes of causal relationships among the characteristics they chose to correlate. This cannot be done by calling on the very criteria by which they chose the characteristics, that is, the criteria of the tenets of evolutionary psychology and sociobiology: "Coefficients of correlation . . . may be defined so generally that any two groups may be examined for their degree of correlation, even if we know on other grounds that the two groups are in fact independent of each other. [They] may be consistent with more than one hypothesis" (p. 317). Cohen and Nagel ask: Which correlation shall take precedence? Further, they claim that "It is very easy to commit an error in believing there is a significant connection between two types of events on the basis that they are frequently associated" (p. 318), and that "Obvious difficulties arise when we make comparisons on the basis of units or classifications which do not retain the same value or meaning for the different groups compared" (p. 320). This is another reason for not mixing comparisons of species without taking into account the differences between them. Finally, "Adding numbers of comparisons as bolstering the causal relations of correlations" (p. 317) is not recommended by Cohen and Nagel.

The problem with constructing narratives about evolutionary processes involved in the activities of individuals or species is the lack of information about events that have left no record useful for data analysis. Inferences may be made from environmental changes that have left a record in inanimate aspects of the planet, in fossils and so on, but these are open to debate based on other narratives and inferences. The reliance on molecular genetic relations among species available to us through fossil material still bases behavioral analysis on the assumption that the contemporary organisms are reliable substitutes for the extinct organisms. That DNA/RNA configurations are insufficient to provide a precise basis for behavioral analysis is evident in the newly emerging recognition that having the maps of nucleotide configurations tells us little about the relationship between them and the proteins (proteomics) that develop through their own and their nucleotide activities (Blattner et al. 1997).

The data from which the human sociobiologists construct their hypotheses about the relationship between contemporary human activity and the activity of earlier species is based primarily on correlation. Does this mean that there is no way to study the evolutionary processes that were involved in human behavioral evolution? For some the answer lies in seeking biochemical, physiological activity or other continuity between other species and the human species. Such continuities are helpful in understanding some of the evolutionary processes. However, a focus on continuities without an appreciation of the discontinuities obviates an understanding of the diversity of species, and the diversity among individuals within a species.

The comparative method examines the differences among individuals and species as well as the similarities. We have tried to illustrate this in our discussion of rape based on an evolutionary, developmental, and comparative approach by discussing the continuities and discontinuities of processes on biochemical, behavioral, and societal levels.

III   Conceptualizations of Science and Societal Responsibility of Scientists

A   War Rape: A Trial for Human Sociobiology

Rape is a psychosocial and societal process related to human history in many ways. In the development of the concept of war, possessions and societal stratification included the institution of slavery and the commodification of women, so that in the spoils of victory, not only land and objects but also women were the entitlement of the victors.

Thornhill and Palmer's discussion of war is in terms of cost-benefit analysis based on the human sociobiological hypothesis that masculine sexuality operates to guarantee that his genes will be preserved in ensuing generations. Thus, in wars, rape is an accepted activity organized by those in charge of the men, and for the individual soldier, rape represents an opportunity to engage in sexual activity without the woman's consent.

The human sociobiological approach to war rape attests to logical difficulties of defining rape under all circumstances as related to reproductive success. The military leaders in charge of organized rape as an "entitlement" for the soldiers are not concerned with the result of the rapes, in terms of increasing the population under their control. Rather they see their programs of rape as evidence of their power, their victory; they believe that men need to engage in sexual activity because of their drive (instinct), an expression of an ethological concept. Those in control of these inhuman programs are not necessarily aware of any theoretical base for their activity, but society has presented them with these ideas.

One is reminded of Klausewitz's definition of war as an extension of social policy. An article in the *New York Times* demonstrates this societal process (Simons 2001, p. 4). The arrangement was made for such activity to take place during the Bosnian war. The lawyers for the defense of the soldiers responsible for the enslavement of women not only for sexual activity but for housekeeping chores declared that the prosecution did not prove that the alleged victims of rape were exposed to any severe physical or psychological suffering. As a defense, these lawyers offered that this was so because some of the women had liked the soldiers. Chief defense counsel S. Prodanovic said that "The rape in itself is not an act that inflicts severe bodily pain." (p. 4) During the trial of the men accused of rape and enslavement, it was revealed that not only was the teenager in one family raped many times by many men, but her mother was also raped. In some cases the women were forced to give birth to the infants conceived as a result of the rape. There are no records of what happened to those children and whether the men responsible were concerned for the condition of the infants.

It is difficult to contemplate obtaining data about the cost-benefit analysis of the behavior of the men involved in such a situation. Reports of men being raped in war situations in El Salvador, Croatia, and Greece (Carlson 1997) present similar problems for testing any hypotheses that might be generated by human sociobiology.

The issue of reproductive success in those activities is equally problematic. In Algeria, abortions are prohibited, and the fate of the women and possible births that may have taken place as a result of the war is probably unrecorded. In Uganda, Liberia, and Myanmar, the acting out of the entitlement of soldiers to rape results in equally horrendous situations. The case of the "comfort women" maintained by Japanese soldiers has added to the impetus for the United Nations to seek justice and help for the people who have been victimized. Some sovereign nations still do not recognize war rape as a crime, and though various international commissions and instruments, including the Nuremberg and Tokyo Charters, list war rape as an international crime, action to control this behavior and render justice to the victims has been slow and incomplete.

B   Feminist Research

Thornhill and Palmer's discussion of feminist research and social science research requires consideration of the concepts of science and social responsibility of scientists. There is an honorable and ongoing history of the need for scientists to be conscious of the need to be accountable and responsible for their work (Tobach 1994). This is especially true because of the esteem with which they are generally held in contemporary society. This responsibility requires that we attempt to formally acknowledge the thinking that informs our activity in the scientific community and present it as part of that activity. For that reason, some thoughts about feminism, feminist science, sexism, and sexist science are presented here.

Feminism is a movement. Like other societal movements, it includes concerted, organized activities working toward or shaping some objective. That objective is to guarantee equity for women within a commitment to societal equity for all humans, regardless of race, ethnicity, sexual orientation, class, or religious belief. People of any gender or persuasion may participate in that movement.

A feminist is a participant in that movement. Participation is variable and diverse. A scientist, for example, a comparative psychologist, can integrate a commitment to that movement with activities in the scientific community (Tobach 1994).

Sexism is the practice of exclusionary, discriminatory, and exploitative activities designed to place women in a debased condition. Such activities are practiced in every aspect of human life, including scientific work. "Sexist" is the adjective describing such activities.

The significant term in the above narrative is "scientist." There is no contradiction between being a feminist and a scientist. The best scientist is societally and scientifically responsible for the work done in the name of science. Being societally responsible commits the scientist to a consciousness about equity for all humans.

Thornhill and Palmer discuss their views of the responses to their theory about rape in terms of "social science." The history of the acceptance of studies in social and societal activity as "science" reflects the rich, complex interdependence of societal processes and human knowledge. Evaluation of the scholarship and research of members of the scientific community requires attention to the publications, the available documentation of that thinking and research, no matter what the area of scholarship. Thornhill and Palmer dismiss critics as feminists or poor (social) scientists. However, their replies to them for the most part fall back on the initial assumptions of the theory of evolution they espouse.

Thornhill and Palmer say: "Science has nothing to say about what is right or wrong in the ethical sense. Biology provides understanding, not justification, of human behavior. . . . It is our hope that concerned people will . . . use . . . the knowledge that evolutionary biology provides . . . to reduce the incidence of rape and to better deal with this horrendous crime" (p. 199).

The people who hold to a human sociobiological ideology are very likely to be involved as citizens in attempts to solve these problems, as are nonsociobiologists. Perhaps the scientific work that we do should contribute to those efforts in some way.

Thornhill and Palmer are critical of the hypothesis that rape and other misogynist activities reflect the status of women in society. The testing of that hypothesis would be a worthwhile effort that could only have some beneficial results. If the experiment were to be conducted by providing women with equity in all phases of life, and if rapes were to continue, and if wars were to continue, at least the problem of exclusionary policies toward women would be ameliorated.

References

Albert, D. J., M. L. Walsh, and R. H. Jonik (1993). Aggression in humans: What is its biological foundation? *Neuroscience and Biobehavioral Reviews* 17 (4): 405–425.

Aronson, Lester R. (1974). Environmental stimuli altering the physiological condition of the individual among lower vertebrates. In Frank A. Beach, ed., *Sex and Behavior,* pp. 290–318. Huntington, N.Y.: Robert E. Krieger Publishing.

Beckstrom, J. (1993). *Darwinism Applied: Evolutionary Paths to Social Goals.* New York: Praeger.

Berenson, A. B., V. V. San Miguel, and G. S. Wilkinson. (1992). Prevalence of physical and sexual assault in pregnant adolescents. *Journal of Adolescent Health* 13 (6): 466–469.

Bergen, Raquel Kennedy (1999). Marital rape. Applied Research Forum. VAWnet. National Resource Center on Domestic Violence. Harrisburg, Pennsylvania, pp. 1–10.

Blattner, F. R., G. Plunkett III, C. A. Bloch, N. T. Perna, V. Burland, M. Riley, J. Collado-Vides, J. D. Glasner, C. K. Rode, G. F. Mayhew, J. Gregor, N. W. Davis, H. A. Kirkpatrick, M. A. Goeden, D. J. Rose, B. Mau, and Y. Shaol (1997). The complete genome sequence of Escherichia coli K-12. *Science* 277: 1453–1462.

Brownmiller, S. (1975). *Against Our Will: Men, Women, and Rape.* New York: Simon and Schuster.

Camus, Patricio A. (1997). Evolucion darwiniana y no darwiniana: hacia una "anti-sintesis" moderna? *Revista Chilena de Historia Natural* 70 (4): 459–464.

Carlson, Eric Stener (1997). Sexual assault on men in war. *Lancet* 349 (January 11): 129.

Cohen, Morris R. and Ernest Nagel (1934). *An Introduction to Logic and Scientific Method.* New York: Harcourt Brace.

Davies, P. C. W. (1989). The physics of complex organization. In Brian Goodwin and Peter Saunders, eds., *Theoretical Biology: Epigenetic and Evolutionary Order from Complex Systems,* pp. 101–111. Edinburgh: Edinburgh University Press.

Donat, Patricia L. N. and Jacquelyn W. White (2000). Re-examining the issue of nonconsent in acquaintance rape. In Cheryl Brown Travis and Jacquelyn W. White, eds., *Sexuality, Society, and Feminism,* pp. 355–376. Washington, D.C.: American Psychological Association.

Eigen, M. (1971a). Self-organization of matter and the evolution of biological macromolecules. *Naturwissenschaften* 58: 465–523.

Eigen, M. (1971b). Molecular self-organization and the early stages of evolution. *Quarterly Review of Biophysics* 4: 149–212.

Eigenberg, H. M. (2000). Correctional officers' definition of rape in male prisons. *Journal of Criminal Justice* 28 (5): 435–449.

Federal Bureau of Investigation (1982). *Uniform crime reports.* Washington, D.C.: U.S. Department of Justice.

Federal Bureau of Investigation (1997). Uniform crime reporting (UCR) Summary system: Frequently asked questions. Retrieved January 3, 2001 from <www.fbi.gov>.

Firestone, P., J. M. Bradford, D. M. Greenberg, and G. A. Serran (2000). The relationship of deviant sexual arousal and psychopathy in incest offenders, extrafamilial child molesters, and rapists. *Journal of the American Academy of Psychiatry and the Law* 28 (3): 303–308.

Foucault, Michel (1985). *The Use of Pleasure.* New York: Vintage Books.

Fox, Sidney W. (1984). Proteinoid experiments and evolutionary theory. In Mae-Wan Ho and Peter T. Saunders, eds., *Beyond Neo-Darwinism,* pp. 15–60. London: Academic Press.

Gessner, B. D. and K. A. Perham-Hester (1999). Experience of violence among teenage mothers in Alaska. *Journal of Adolescent Health* 22 (5): 383–388.

Goodwin, B. C. (1989). Evolution and the generative order. In Brian Goodwin and Peter Saunders, eds., *Theoretical Biology: Epigenetic and Evolutionary Order from Complex Systems*, pp. 89–100. Edinburgh: Edinburgh University Press.

Gould, S. J. and Elizabeth S. Vrba (1982). Exaptation: A missing term in the science of form. *Paleobiology* 8 (1): 4–15.

Greenfield, Lawrence A. (1997). Sex offenses and offenders: An analysis of data on rape and sexual assault. U.S. Department of Justice, February, NCJ-63392.

Groth, A. N. and H. J. Birnbaum (1979). *Men Who Rape: The Psychology of the Offender.* New York: Plenum Press.

Groth, A. Nicholas and Ann Wolpert Burgess (1980). Male rape: Offenders and victims. *American Journal of Psychiatry* 137 (7): 806–810.

Harding, Cheryl F. (1985). Sociobiological hypotheses about rape: A critical look at the data behind the hypotheses. In Suzanne R. Sunday and Ethel Tobach, eds., *Violence against Women: A Critique of the Sociobiology of Rape*, pp. 23–58. New York: Gordian Press.

Hill, M. S. and A. R. Fischer (2001). Does entitlement mediate the link between masculinity and rape-related violence? *Journal of Counseling Psychology* 48 (1): 39–50.

Ho, Mae-Wan (1984). Environment and heredity in development and evolution. In Mae-Wan Ho and Peter T. Saunders, eds., *Beyond Neo-Darwinism*, pp. 267–289. London: Academic Press.

Ho, Mae-Wan (1987). Evolution by process, not by consequence: Implications of the new molecular genetics on development and evolution. *International Journal of Comparative Psychology* 1 (1): 3–27.

Ho, Mae-Wan (1989). Coherent excitations and the physical foundations of life. In Brian Goodwin and Peter Saunders, eds., *Theoretical Biology: Epigenetic and Evolutionary Order from Complex Systems*, pp. 162–176. Edinburgh: Edinburgh University Press.

Ho, Mae-Wan and Peter T. Saunders (1984). Pluralism and convergence in evolutionary theory. In Mae-Wan Ho and Peter T. Saunders, eds., *Beyond Neo-Darwinism*, pp. 3–12. London: Academic Press.

Holmes, Melisa M., Heidi S. Resnick, Dean G. Kilpatrick and Connie L. Best (1996). Rape-related pregnancy: Estimates and descriptive characteristics from a national sample of women. *American Journal of Obstetrics and Gynecology* 175 (2): 32.

Jones, O. (1999). Sex, culture, and the biology of rape: Toward explanation and prevention. *California Law Review* 17: 827–942.

Kaufman, A., P. Divasto, R. Jackson, D. Voorhees, and J. Christy (1980). Male rape victims: Noninstitutionalized assault. *American Journal of Psychiatry* 137: 221–223.

Kaufman, Stuart A. (1989). Origins of order in evolution: self-organization and selection. In Brian Goodwin and Peter Saunders, eds., *Theoretical Biology: Epigenetic and Evolutionary Order from Complex Systems*, pp. 67–88. Edinburgh: Edinburgh University Press.

Kilpatrick, D. G., C. Edmunds, and A. Seymour (1992). *Rape in America: A Report to the Nation.* Charles, S.C.: National Victim Center and The Crime Victims Research and Treatment Center, Medical University of South Carolina.

Kilpatrick, D. G. and B. E. Saunders (1996). Prevalence and consequences of child victimization: Results from the National Survey of Adolescents. U.S. Department of Justice, Office of Justice Programs, National Institute of Justice, Grant No. 93-IJ-CX-0023.

Kilpatrick, D. G., R. Acierno, B. Saunders, H. Resnick, and C. Best (2000). Risk factors for adolescent substance abuse and dependence: Data from a national survey. *Journal of Consulting and Clinical Psychology* 68 (1): 19–30.

Koss, M. P. (1990). Violence against women. *American Psychologist* 45 (3): 374–380.

Koss, Mary P., Christine A Gidycz, and Nadine Wisniewski (1987). The scope of rape incidence and prevalence of sexual aggression and victimization in a national sample of higher education students. *Journal of Consulting and Clinical Psychology* 55 (2): 162–170.

Krueger, Mary M. (1988). Pregnancy as a result of rape. *Journal of Sex Education and Therapy* 14 (1): 23–27.

Lima-de-Faria, A. (1988). *Evolution without Selection.* Amsterdam: Elsevier.

Lovtrup, Soren (1974). *Epigenetics—A Treatise on Theoretical Biology.* London: John Wiley.

Lovtrup, Soren (1987). *Darwinism: The Refutation of a Myth.* London: Croom Helm.

Malamuth, N. M., Heavey, C. L., and D. Linz. (1993). Predicting men's antisocial behavior against women: The interaction model of sexual aggression. In G. C. H. Nagayama, J. R. Hall, and M. S. Zaragoza, eds., *Sexual Aggression: Issues in Etiology, Assessment, and Treatment,* pp. 63–91. Washington, D.C.: Taylor and Francis.

Matsuno, Koichiro (1989). Open systems and the origin of protoreproductive units. In Mae-Wan Ho and Peter T. Saunders, eds., *Beyond Neo-Darwinism,* pp. 61–88. London: Academic Press.

Mayr, Ernst (1976). *Toward a New Philosophy of Biology.* Cambridge, Mass.: Harvard University Press.

Milton, John (1997). Psychopathology of sexual offenders. *British Journal of Hospital Medicine* 57 (9): 448–450.

Mitchell, Damon, Richard Hirschman, and Gordon C. Nagayama Hall (1999). Attributions of victim responsibility, pleasure, and trauma in male rape. *Journal of Sex Research* 36: 369.

Nagel, Ernest (1961). *The Structure of Science.* New York: Harcourt, Brace, and World.

National Sexual Violence Research Center. (2000). *Catalog of state sexual violence statutes* (August). Enola, PA: National Sexual Violence Research Center.

Nicolis, G. and I. Prigogine (1977). *Self-organization in Non-equilibrium Systems.* New York: John Wiley and Sons.

Pomeroy, Wardell B. (1969). *Girls and Sex.* New York: Dell Publishing.

Rada, Richard T. (1978). *Clinical Aspects of the Rapist.* New York: Grune and Stratton.

Rauch, Scott L., Lisa M. Shin, Darin D. Dougherby, Nathaniel M. Alpert, Scott P. Orr, Mark Lasko, Mike L. Macklin, Alan J. Fischman, and Roger K. Pitman (1999). Neural activation during sexual and competitive arousal in healthy men. *Psychiatry Research* 91: 1–10.

Rosenblatt, Jay S. (1974). Effects of experience on sexual behavior in male cats. In Frank A. Beach, ed., *Sex and Behavior,* pp. 416–439. Huntington, N.Y.: Robert E. Krieger Publishing.

Saunders, Peter T. (1984). Development and evolution. In M.-W. Ho and Peter T. Saunders, eds., *Beyond Neo-Darwinism,* pp. 243–263. New York: Academic Press.

Saunders, E. B., G. A. Award, and G. White (1986). Male adolescent sexual offenders: The offender, and the offense. *Canadian Journal of Psychiatry* 31: 542–549.

Schulhofer, Stephen (1998). Unwanted sex. *Atlantic Monthly* (October): 55–66.

Sheffield, C. J. (1997). Sexual terrorism. In L. O'Toole and J. R. Schiffman, eds., *Gender Violence: Interdisciplinary Perspectives,* pp. 55–66. New York: New York University Press.

Simons, Marlise (2001). Bosnian war trial focuses on sex crimes. *New York Times* (February 18): 4.

Staff, Southern Poverty Law Center (2000). Coloring crime. *Intelligence Report* (summer): 37–39.

Steele, E. J. (1979). *Somatic Selection and Adaptive Evolution: On the Inheritance of Acquired Characters.* Chicago: University of Chicago Press.

Steele, Edward J., Steele, Robyn A. Lyndley, and Robert V. Blanden (1998). *Lamarck's Signature: How Retrogenes Are Changing Darwin's Natural Selection Paradigm.* Reading, Mass.: Perseus Books.

Stewart, F. H. and J. Trussell (2000). Prevention of pregnancy resulting from rape: A neglected preventive health measure. *American Journal of Preventive Medicine* 19 (4): 228–229.

Tattersall, Ian (1998). *Becoming Human: Evolution and Human Uniqueness.* New York: Harcourt Brace.

Thom, R. (1989). An inventory of Waddington's concepts. In Brian Goodwin and Peter Saunders, eds., *Theoretical Biology: Epipgenetic and Evolutionary Order from Complex Systems,* pp. 1–7. Edinburgh: Edinburgh University Press.

Thornhill, Randy and Craig T. Palmer (2000). *A Natural History of Rape: Biological Bases of Sexual Coercion.* Cambridge, Mass.: The MIT Press.

Tinbergen, N. (1974). Some recent studies of the evolution of sexual behavior. In Frank A. Beach, ed., *Sex and Behavior,* pp. 1–33. Huntington, N.Y.: Robert E. Krieger Publishing.

Tjaden, Patricia and Nancy Thoennes (2000). Full report of the prevalence, incidence, and consequences of violence against women: Findings from the National Violence Against Women Survey. Washington, D.C.: U.S. Department of Justice, NCJ 183781.

Tobach, E. (1994). Personal is political. *Journal of Social Issues* 50: 221–244.

Tobach, E. and Schneirla, T. C. (1968). The biopsychology of social behavior in animals. In R. E. Cooke, ed., *The Biologic Basis of Pediatric Practice*, pp. 68–82. New York: McGraw-Hill.

Waddington, C. H. (1957). *The Strategy of Genes.* London: Allen and Unwin.

Waddington, C. H. (1959). Behaviour as a product of evolution. *Science* 129: 203–204.

Waddington, C. H. (1975). *The Evolution of an Evolutionist.* Edinburgh: Edinburgh University Press.

Warsaw, I. L. (1998). *I Never Called It Rape: The MS Report on Recognizing, Fighting, and Surviving Date and Acquaintance Rape.* New York: Harper and Row.

Wicken, Jeffrey S. (1984). On the increase in complexity in evolution. In Mae-Wan Ho and Peter T. Saunders, eds., *Beyond Neo-Darwinism*, pp. 89–112. London: Academic Press.

Yoshimura, H. and N. Kimura (1991). Ethopharmacology of copulatory disorder induced by chronic social conflict in male mice. *Neurosciences and Biobehavioral Reviews* 15 (4): 497–500.

6

Pop Sociobiology Reborn: The Evolutionary Psychology of Sex and Violence

A. Leah Vickers and Philip Kitcher

1 Introduction: A Dismal History

Here's a recipe for winning fame and fortune as an architect of the new-and-improved human sciences. First, make a bundle of claims to the effect that certain features are universal among human beings, or among human males, or among human females. Next, couple each claim with a story of how the pertinent features were advantageous for primitive hominids, or males, or females, as they faced whatever challenges you take to have been prevalent in some lightly sketched savannah environment. (Don't worry that your knowledge of past environments is rather thin—be creative!) Finally, announce that each feature in the bundle has been shaped by natural selection and so corresponds to something very deep in human nature (male human nature, female human nature), something that may be overlain with a veneer of culture but that molds our behavior and the forms of our societies. Accompany everything with hymns to the genius of Darwin, broadsides against "blank slate" views of the human mind, and vigorous denunciations of the lack of rigor and clarity that has hitherto reigned in the human sciences.

In the second half of the twentieth century, three major movements tried to follow this recipe. First came animal ethology with stirring yarns about naked apes and territorial imperatives. These stories were recast by the second wave, as human sociobiology drew more systematically on the resources of contemporary evolutionary theory. In the 1960s and 1970s, the integration of mathematical models with field observations enabled students of animal behavior to advance, support, and refine detailed theories about caste structure in social insects (Oster and Wilson 1978), copulation in dungflies (Parker 1978), and the mating structures of red deer (Clutton-Brock et al. 1981). Successes like these inspired the ambitious to propose that kindred insights could be achieved with respect to our own species: They claimed that human beings are, by nature, xenophobic and "absurdly easy to indoctrinate," that human societies are inevitably stratified by relations of power and domination, that men are fated to be fickle and women to be coy, that human altruism is an illusion and that we can't hope to achieve genuine sexual equality (Wilson 1975, 1978; Barash 1979; van den Berghe 1979). Pop sociobiology was born.

By the middle of the 1980s, the movement had attracted a barrage of criticism. Skeptics pointed out that, in contrast with the careful studies of nonhuman animals, the suggestions about universals of human behavior (or male behavior, or female behavior) rested on anecdotal evidence. Furthermore, pop sociobiology contented itself with telling informal stories about advantages, instead of putting to work the mathematical tools of evolutionary theory, painstakingly deployed by workers on deer and dungflies. Careful work on the evolution of behavior had appreciated, from the beginning, the need to consider alternative hypotheses and to discriminate among them using data from evolutionary genetics, experiments, comparative observation or mathematical modeling, but no such pains were taken by the leading proponents of pop sociobiology (see, for critique, Lewontin, Rose, and Kamin 1984; Kitcher 1985). Nor was there, to begin with, any appreciation of the possibility that cultural transmission might affect the traits of human beings, and when, belatedly, pop sociobiology came to terms with this issue, its attempts to show that "the genes hold culture on a leash" depended on arbitrary assignments of values to crucial parameters (Lumsden and Wilson 1981; Maynard Smith and Warren 1982; Kitcher 1985, chap. 10).

Yet perhaps the most important defect lay in the conclusions, often announced with commendable regret, that certain unpleasant features were so deeply ingrained in human nature as to be unmodifiable. Critics noted that such conclusions cannot validly be derived from the kinds of evolutionary scenarios presented (Lewontin, Rose, and Kamin 1984; Kitcher 1985). The most those scenarios could reveal is that there are pieces of DNA that, in the particular environments encountered by our hominid ancestors, gave rise to characteristics—competitiveness, coyness, xenophobia, whatever—that proved beneficial in those environments; the scenarios have no bearing on whether, under different regimes of development, those traits would be bound to arise (nor whether they would be advantageous in these rival circumstances).

Would-be Darwinian reformers of the human sciences adopted a strategy for coping with these criticisms. "Indeed," they explained, "some sociobiologists have made unwarranted claims; but our approach should not be dismissed; we are aware of the criticisms; we have made them ourselves; we are reformed; we have abandoned the idea that genes are destiny; we are evolutionary psychologists, who aim to use Darwinian insights to fathom human tendencies." Some of them continued to insist on the importance of the enterprise in indicating to us how we might amend unwanted forms of behavior. In the late 1980s, when evolutionary psychology kept its claims modest and its head down, charity commended giving the new movement the benefit of the doubt. But the publication of a rousing revival of the pop favorites of the past (Thornhill and Thornhill 1992) made it apparent that the old mistakes haven't lost their allure. Evolutionary psychology turns out to be pop sociobiology with a fig leaf.

2   The Pop Sociobiology Revival: An Overview

We'll try to substantiate this last accusation by looking at two of the most prominent exhibits in the pop revival: David Buss's proposals about male and female sexual attractiveness and the hypotheses of Randy Thornhill and Craig Palmer on rape (Thornhill and Palmer—henceforth T and P—draw on Buss's efforts, so our critique of Buss will extend to their program). First, however, we'll offer a more general view of the evolutionary psychology movement.

The principal advance evolutionary psychologists take themselves to have made consists in recognizing that natural selection doesn't shape human behavior directly, but rather shapes the psychological mechanisms underlying behavior. Bad old pop sociobiology supposed that natural selection would favor males who were fickle and promiscuous. Thoroughly modern Darwinian analyses recognize the need to integrate biology with the right approach to psychology, to wit the view that the mind consists of lots of special-purpose devices (modules)[1] that prompt different forms of behavior. Evolutionary psychology reflects on the problems and challenges faced by our hominid ancestors, generating hypotheses about the kinds of psychological traits natural selection has bequeathed to us. These hypotheses are evaluated by collecting evidence from human subjects who report their feelings and preferences in actual or imagined situations, or by studying human behavior. Support for a psychological claim is supposed to come from juxtaposing contemporary data with an *independent* Darwinian expectation about what kinds of ancestral tendencies would have contributed to reproductive success.

If this is to be successful, then *both* the evidence collected and the Darwinian theorizing have to satisfy important constraints. Let's start with the evidence. Whether or not this consists of responses to questionnaires or statistical patterns of behavior, it will have probative force with respect to a hypothesis about a psychological mechanism only if that hypothesis can be integrated with other claims about the psychology of human subjects to generate expectations about what should be observed in the pertinent experimental or natural situations. When the mind is conceived as a bundle of psychological capacities and dispositions that interact with one another and that are causally affected by external cues, the psychological account has to tell us enough about the nature of the interactions and the responses to the cues so that we can derive specific claims about human actions. A claim about a single trait, in splendid isolation, leaves entirely open what sorts of behavior are to be expected—since the activity of other mechanisms could override, suppress, amplify, or redirect whatever tendency is hypothesized—and, in consequence, loose associations between hypothesized psychological tendencies and a pattern of behavior should impress nobody.

It would, of course, be unfair to ask any evolutionary psychologist to provide us with a complete, detailed psychology. Yet if the psychological account provided introduces a collection of capacities that might easily prompt an agent to incompatible forms of behavior—as for example when we're told that people are attracted to different characteristics that regularly turn up in different locations—then we can't tell much about what typical subjects will do. Consider preferences for various types of food. It's a familiar fact that someone's actual diet may not reflect her craving for a particular food, precisely because what she chooses to eat is a function of several underlying psychological dispositions. So we could "protect" an evolutionary story about universal gustatory yearnings by supposing that the underlying tendencies are inhibited by other mechanisms. Or, to put the point differently, the hypothesis that human beings have evolved to crave large hunks of red meat (say) issues no definite predictions about the frequency of carnivorous displays in any human population.

Turning now to the specifically Darwinian part of the enterprise, we should recognize an important point often made by John Maynard Smith: Model-building requires attention to the details, and mathematical modeling uncovers and refines hidden presuppositions. (Maynard Smith and W. D. Hamilton are pioneering figures in evolutionary theory, on whose work sociobiology has drawn; the illuminating work of people like Eric Charnov, Geoffrey Parker, Peter Harvey, John Krebs, and many others shows the salutary influence of Maynard Smith and Hamilton.) Mathematical models aren't always necessary in evolutionary work: Sometimes alternative hypotheses can be screened out by considerations drawn from genetics, or careful experiments, or detailed cross-species comparisons. In human sociobiology, however, where rival hypotheses can easily be multiplied, where genetic ignorance is the order of the day, where many of the experiments that might clear up controversy are rightly forbidden as unethical, and where cross-specific comparisons are vulnerable to worries about salient differences, it's crucial that the proposals about histories of natural selection should be formulated clearly and precisely. Pop sociobiology often substituted casual stories about selective advantages for rigorous models of selective pressures. To do better, one must know enough about the alleged environment in which the selection process occurred to be able to formulate defensible claims about reproductive costs and benefits.

In the human case (and, quite possibly, in investigations of other species), it's also important to recognize the possibility of cultural transmission. Since the important work of Robert Boyd and Peter Richerson (1985), everyone interested in Darwinizing the human sciences should have known that a population under the joint influence of natural selection and cultural transmission can exhibit characteristics different from those of a population under the influence of natural selection alone, and that the modes of cultural selection generating this type of deviation can themselves be sustained under natural selection.[2] Hence, even when one works out the precise details of a hypothesis about the *natural* selection of some trait, it will always be pertinent to wonder if that characteristic would have emerged under the *joint* influence of natural selection and cultural transmission. In short, then, the models that reformed pop sociobiologists are going to use have to be *more* elaborate than those used by their counterparts pursuing nonhuman studies.

There are two theoretical points that add further difficulties to pursuing a serious Darwinian psychology. As many leading Darwinians have declared repeatedly, Darwin replaced the notion of a species as a *type* with an emphasis on intraspecific variability. Perhaps, then, evolutionary psychology's commitment to a universal human nature is suspect. Even though there are surely some traits that are found (almost) universally across our species, it's important not to suppose that universal fixation is the norm. One can't reply that natural selection is a homogenizing force, for, although there are some circumstances—when the underlying genetics is free from well-known complications and there's an optimal from of a particular trait—in which natural selection would be expected to make one variant virtually universal, the necessary hedges can't be disregarded. Sometimes the genetic details make it impossible that the optimal form of a trait should be fixed (a simple example is when the optimal trait is coded by a heterozygote), and there are other instances in which natural selection is expected to generate a polymorphic equilibrium (a classic case is the hawk-dove polymorphism from elementary evolutionary game theory).

The idea of individually selected psychological capacities should also be carefully scrutinized. For all their shortcomings, earlier pop sociobiologists did recognize that evolution has something to do with genes, and they were frequently chastised for naive assumptions that there were genes available to direct females to be coy or human beings in general to be xenophobic. The error, here, as we've already remarked, was to introduce a form of genetic determinism: If the underlying genotype generated the pertinent trait in the ancestral environment, then, it was assumed, it would yield the trait in all environments. Recent pop sociobiologists, by contrast, don't like to talk about genes. For all their reticence, however, they can't avoid advancing genetic hypotheses. After all, without a genetic basis for a trait—that is, a tendency for the underlying genotype to yield a particular phenotype *in the selective environment*—there can be no natural selection. To suppose that there's a naturally selected psychological mechanism for this or that—cheater detection, say, or directing young women to swoon at the prospect of powerful older men—is to claim that there's been genetic variation in some ancestral population pertinent to the propensity to perform such narrowly defined tasks. Although they don't say as much, they must think that there are two alleles—call them A and B—associated in the primeval environment (or range of environments), with a greater or lesser ability to carry out the appointed task (detect cheats or swoon appropriately).

Let's take a deep breath at this point. It's worth reminding ourselves of what genes do. Genes encode proteins. So A and B encode different proteins, and, on a simple version, it seems that evolutionary psychologists are committed to saying that these differences amount to solely and precisely a difference in cheat-spotting-acuity or swoonability. We're prepared to concede that differences in proteins might show up in alternative forms of neural chemistry, evident in psychological changes—it's not incredible that a modified neural receptor protein might make a mouse, or a human, more or less good at remembering things, or slower or faster to learn. What's highly implausible is that changing a protein could leave all our psychological tendencies untouched while fine-tuning the talent for cheat-spotting or weakness at the knees at the thought of a mate with status, power, and wealth. Until we are offered some plausible idea about mechanisms, we ought to dismiss these suggestions as vague speculation. The overreaching is hidden only because the latest Darwinizers have learned from the demise of old-style pop sociobiology: Be cagey about genetic hypothesizing!

This is surely simplistic, and evolutionary psychologists ought to repudiate the words we've put into their mouths. A better suggestion would be that the pertinent proteins have lots of different phenotypic consequences, but *the one that matters* concerns the narrowly specified psychological disposition (spotting cheats, swooning appropriately). The claim, then, is that the rival genotypes give rise to phenotypes that differ in lots of ways, but *only the evolutionary psychologist's favorite disposition* makes a serious difference to reproductive success—the rest is a wash. The fitness contribution of the chosen trait swamps any correlated effects. But, lacking any hints about the underlying genotypes, how their differences might make neural—and therefore psychological—differences, and what impact such *overall* differences might have, there's just no reason to believe that claim. Why should a priori guesses about the nonexistence of correlations with selective significance serve as the basis for evolutionary analysis?

Let's put the point more positively. Forget the fine-grained psychological dispositions for the moment, and ask how natural selection might shape human psychology. Absent revolutionary proposals, the obvious answer is that different genotypes might encode proteins that participate differently in the reactions that underlie neural development, in the formation or pruning of synapses, in the sensitivity to various molecular signals, or in the speed of processes of transmission. It doesn't follow that selective modification of genotypes would affect all aspects of our psychology. But these considerations do suggest the real possibility that psychological phenomena are genetically linked in ways about which we're currently ignorant, so that a particular genetic modification would produce a spectrum of psychological responses, increasing some aspects of human performance and diminishing others. If so, then hunting for the ways in which selection has shaped such fine-grained psychological traits as a disposition to detect cheats is an unpromising strategy, and one can't do any serious Darwinian psychological analysis until there's much greater knowledge of the intricacies of neurodevelopment. Many evolutionary psychologists naively posit their favorite psychological atoms, each under individual selective control and thus each associated with some locus that affects nothing else. This is myth-making, not serious science.

We anticipate a response: "We have to start somewhere. Science must always begin from ignorance, so to demand knowledge at the beginning is anti-science" (see Thornhill and Thornhill 1992, p. 405). We acknowledge that no investigation begins from complete knowledge; so much is truism. But well-planned investigations recognize which forms of current ignorance matter and endeavor to ameliorate them, rather than whistling away the complications and hoping that they won't prove significant.

Our review of general issues is intended to highlight the mistakes that attend the recent pop sociobiology of sex and violence. We now turn to the details.

3   Savannah Yearnings: A Romance

The sun is setting, casting a soft bronze glow on the meadow. You, Primeval Pru, realize that you face the hardest decision of your life as a hunter-gatherer: It is time to choose your man. Two stand before you. On the left is a younger man whose deep-set eyes are framed by rich black lashes.

His body is unscarred, suggesting that he has not exerted himself much in close encounters with beast or man. But you find it hard to turn your gaze from his warm smile. On the right is an older, balding fellow with plain features and a commanding manner. He gestures to his impressive hut and his collection of animal skins. Whom should you pick?

David Buss knows. He has a theory of evolved mate selection in humans—his "Sexual Strategies Theory"—which informs us as to what Primeval Pru and her contemporary descendants will do (or, more exactly, what Primeval Pru would have done if she has a lot of contemporary descendants). This "theory" is best conceived as an amalgam of claims about mate selection, all of which rely on the same few fundamental tenets. The basic principle from which Buss generates his conclusions (as do T and P after him) is that "the sexes will differ in precisely those domains in which women and men have faced different sorts of adaptive problems" (Buss 1995, p. 164). The pertinent evolutionary pressures are supposed to have operated during the "environment of evolutionary adaptedness" (EEA), apparently the Pleistocene, when our ancestors lived in hunter-gatherer groups.

Here's the story. Men's and women's roles in reproduction are asymmetrical in three different ways. First, men, but not women, face "parental uncertainty." Second, women are fertile for a smaller portion of their lives than are men. Third, women invest considerably more in reproduction than do men. Following many other pop sociobiologists, Buss waxes lyrical about the contrast between the roughly 450 nutrient-loaded gametes that a woman will produce in a lifetime and the millions of tiny mobile gametes in a single male ejaculate (replenished, as he points out, at a rate of about twelve million an hour). After conception, a woman is also committed to nine months of pregnancy, and, after birth, only she can lactate and thus provide milk for the offspring.

These asymmetries create three adaptive problems for men and women. Men will need to increase the probability of paternity and to identify female reproductive value (which peaks in a woman's mid-teens when she has all of her fertile years before her [Buss 1989]). Women will need to find men who can provide them with resources, defend them and their children against predators and human aggressors. Natural selection will thus select for psychological dispositions that incline men to sexual jealousy, that will prompt them to take advantage of whatever opportunities they have for a quick copulation on the side, and that lead them to be attracted to women with the signs of peak reproductive value—full lips, clear eyes, lustrous hair, a bouncy gait (all these figure in Buss's catalog, as does a waist-hip ratio of roughly 0.7). Similarly, selection will favor women whose psychological dispositions lead them to be attracted to older men (men with power and resources) and that make them less inclined to wander.

So much for the Darwinian "expectations." Now for the data. To his credit, Buss has carried out an extensive survey in which questionnaires were administered to members of 37 cultures in 33 countries. Besides asking for biographical information (age, sex, religion, etc.) the questionnaires contain queries about mate preferences, first in the form of open-ended questions and then by means of rating and ranking tasks. The open-ended part requires the subject to state the age at which he or she wishes to marry, the age difference the subject would prefer to exist between the subject and the subject's spouse, and the number of children desired. The second part of the first instrument requires respondents to rate 18 characteristics (such as earning capacity, ambition/industriousness, youth, physical attractiveness, and chastity) based on how "important or desirable" each would be in choosing a mate (Buss 1989). The respondent must give a numerical rating on a scale from 0 to 3, ranging from "irrelevant or unimportant" (0) to indispensable (3). The second instrument asks subjects to rank 13 characteristics, based on their desirability in a mate. Ten thousand and forty-seven (10,047) subjects were included in the study.

Buss reports that the results accord with his Darwinian expectations. For 36 of 37 samples, there's a statistically significant difference showing that women rate "good financial prospect" higher than do men. In 29 of 37 samples, there's a statistically significant difference with respect to ambition/industriousness (women rating it more highly), and in 34 samples there's a statistically significant difference with respect to physical attractiveness (men rating it as more important). Averaged over all samples, women responded that they prefer men who are 3.42 years older than themselves, while men answered that they prefer women who are 2.66 years younger (Buss 1989).

Although his study is the centerpiece of his evidence, Buss defends his "Sexual Strategies Theory" with other considerations more squarely in the pop sociobiological tradition.

A comparison of the statistics derived from personal advertisements in newspapers reveals that a man's age has a strong effect on his preferences.

As men get older, they prefer as mates women who are increasingly younger than they are. Men in their thirties prefer women who are roughly five years younger, whereas men in their fifties prefer women ten to twenty years younger (Buss 1994, p. 52).

He also reminds us of the familiar male pride in "conquests" and "notches on the belt," which he views as signaling an adaptation to brief sexual encounters (Buss 1994, p. 77). A favorite tale of the differences in "short-term mating strategies" stems from an experiment conducted on a college campus: An "attractive person" approaches a member of the opposite sex and issues a sexual invitation; 100 percent of the women declined, 75 percent of the men accepted (Buss 1999, p. 161).[3]

So there's a clear message for Primeval Pru. Avert your gaze. Forget that smile. Snuggle down with the animal skins.

We disagree. We don't think we know enough to offer Pru any advice at all. In line with the general conclusions drawn in the previous section, we find Buss's claims about the operation of selection naive and his alleged empirical support questionable. Let's start with the data.

What exactly does Buss's questionnaire measure? Consider first the issue of whether the responses accord with respondents' preferences. Subjects may have beliefs about how they should respond to the questionnaire, or how those who distribute the questionnaire want them to respond. Although Buss notes that his research assistants did not know his hypotheses, any concordance between his predictions and the stereotypes prevalent in a culture will leave his results vulnerable to bias, whatever the ignorance of his subjects and those who administer the instruments. Furthermore, even if we neglect possibilities that responses will reflect widespread cultural values, Buss must assume that people have access to their own preferences. Interestingly, he emphasizes that "sexual strategies do not require conscious planning or awareness," so that his faith in the questionnaire has to rest on a nice distinction in typical human levels of awareness: We know our preferences but we don't recognize why we have them (see Buss 1992, p. 253). As we'll note shortly, inquiring what subjects would say in explaining their responses might well prove illuminating. An even more fundamental assumption is that there are such things as stable preferences that endure beyond the situation of answering the questionnaire into the contexts in which people actually make their decisions. A significant tradition of psychological research—pioneered by Walter Mischel over a period of three decades—has produced convincing evidence that many personality traits are situation-specific, and recent data suggest that the same may apply to preferences (Mischel 1968; Moore 1999).

Yet even if we grant that Buss is measuring genuine stable preferences, uncontaminated by cultural norms, the most important question concerns the *content* of these preferences. The connection between "mate choice"—the topic of the various questions and tasks—and sexual attraction needs scrutiny. Choosing a mate typically means more than picking a sexual partner (or even a reproductive partner), and, in many, if not all, of the cultures that figure in Buss's survey, the consequences of mate choice affect many dimensions of the parties' lives. Recall a point from the last section: Actual behavior results from the interaction among psychological mechanisms. Assuming that there are such mechanisms, it's only the most simplistic psychology that takes mate choice to reflect the pure operation of the "sexual attraction" mechanism(s). Can we seriously believe that, in societies in which virtually all of a woman's aspirations will be affected by the economic status of the man she marries, the response to questions about "mates" will be unaffected by nonsexual considerations? Buss's brief attempt to confront one instance of this point—his discussion of the hypothesis that women like men with resources because they are cut off from acquiring such resources for themselves—fails to appreciate both the force and the scope of the challenge. Data indicating that successful women have a strong preference for men with resources do not forestall the obvious concern that such women can attain their nonsexual goals, in the kinds of societies in which they live, only by following the culturally approved course for their less fortunate sisters and cousins. Furthermore, the general point is that in all cases libido may run one way and socioeconomic considerations quite another. Indeed, Buss might have found this out had he probed why his respondents gave the answers they did, for their explanations might have shown the various life dimensions along which they viewed mate choice. Perhaps, as Mae West unfortunately did not say, sex has nothing to do with it.

The point we've been developing extends to a broader criticism of Buss's "theory" by exposing its psychological poverty. As we noted above, in any attempt to link hypothetical psychological traits to behavior—even to the relatively special behavior of filling out a questionnaire—one must know how the traits interact and how they are affected by environmental cues. Imagine Buss's hero, Savannah Sam, with wonderfully refined dispositions to react to waist-hip ratio, hair luster, bounciness in gait, and so forth. If Primeval Pru sets all the sensitivities aquiver, then, provided that no non-sexual disposition interferes (a large assumption), we can expect Sam to court (if that's the right verb) Pru. Sam's alternatives are not likely to be Pru, on the one hand, and Geriatric Georgina on the other. Maybe one of the women Sam confronts is ahead on bounciness and fullness of lips, but another wins on hair luster and waist-hip ratio. What should the poor lad do? Buss doesn't tell us what the mate choice should be, and this is typical of the looseness of the amalgam of claims he offers. You can predict just about anything you want to from his hypotheses by adjusting the relative strength of the sexual attraction dispositions or by invoking interference from other parts of the psyche.

Does this matter? One might think that Buss has done enough by describing a bundle of psychological traits and that he can leave it to future researchers to decide how these traits interact to produce behavior. Recall, however, that the point of the enterprise was to connect human psychology with evolution under natural selection, and natural selection will presumably discriminate our primeval players on the basis of their behavior. Until we have some idea of how the traits posited will issue in behavior, we can't make any judgment about their selective impact.

The elasticity of the connection between claims and evidence can be illustrated by returning to the proposition-in-the-quad. On the face of it, there's a striking asymmetry in male and female responses to the opportunity for a spot of recreational sex. But what accounts for the difference? Just the firing of the "sexual attraction" disposition in the men and its inhibition in the women? We agree with Natalie Angier's suggestion that the evidence may have more to tell us about women's fears than about their sexual yearnings (Angier 1999, p. 367). Depending on how you adjust the relative strengths of the "attraction disposition" and the "fear disposition" you can predict the data from any hypothesis you choose about asymmetries in male-female sexual desire. Buss's favorite has no special privilege.

Even though we think that Buss's arguments from the data he assembles have the flaws to which we've pointed, we see his search for empirical evidence as an improvement in the customs of pop sociobiology. We can't be so positive about his Darwinizing. Consider his claim that "over a one-year period, an ancestral man who managed to have short-term sexual encounters with dozens of women would likely have caused many pregnancies" (Buss 1999, p. 162). A little sober physiology will show that there's a one to two percent chance of producing offspring per copulation. If Savannah Sam manages one-shot sex with one hundred different women, he may produce two offspring. His enduring evolutionary contribution will, of course, depend on whether these children survive (with whose support, exactly?). Even though one might wonder just what the expected reproductive success might be, it's important to recall that significant evolutionary change can occur when selection pressures are very small (of the order of 0.001, for example). So Sam's modest chances may make a crucial difference.

At just this point, however, the EEA fades into a rosy blur. Sam is supposed to be competing with other aggressive males for the chance to copulate. Some of his female targets may have long-term mates, primed (we recall) to be on the watch for lowered paternity certainty. The females themselves (we remember) are supposed to be less-than-completely interested in casual sex, so Sam is going to have to do a fair bit of talking before they go off with him for a romp in the bushes (but stay tuned! late-breaking news from T and P suggests that talk may not be needed!). So let's ask the obvious questions: How big is the population to which Sam belongs? To what extent is it possible for his rendezvous to go undetected by others? In what percentage of the pregnancies he brings about will the child receive biparental support? What's the chance of surviving to sexual maturity without biparental support? It may spoil the fun to raise these questions, but until they've been answered there's no way of telling whether Sam's ventures in sperm-spreading will prove selectively advantageous (or disastrous). To put it bluntly, we have to do some delicate accounting to decide if the expected increase in reproductive success is outweighed by the expected effects on Sam of the reactions of those around him to his activities. Any serious exploration of the operations of natural selection must make definite assumptions about what strategies are available to the organisms involved and what ecological constraints affect the reproductive payoffs.

One fundamental oversight of many misadventures in pop sociobiology (and its recent offshoots) is their neglect of within-group differences in strategies. Back to Primeval Pru. If (as Buss and others suggest) ancestral societies were pyramidal, with a few men in power and many more scrambling underneath, it's not entirely obvious that being attracted to the Big Man with the Resources is a good female strategy. Maybe there's too much competition there, and Pru would do better to latch on to Mid-Level Mel. (Similarly, if all the males are drooling over Pru, Sam may do better to respond to the maternal promise of Plain Jane across the watering hole.) Pru needs enough to support herself and the kids, but that doesn't mean she'll be at an advantage if she goes for power, age, and the big bucks. If she's good at spotting talent, then Energetic Ernie—nothing but promise but nothing but promise!—would be a better bet. These are only *possibilities*, but they are rival accounts of selection that must be explored, not simply neglected. We leave as exercises to the reader the construction of formal models that will yield any number of different "Darwinian expectations,"[4] although we're prepared to concede to Buss the banal point that in none of these will Pru find Doddering Dan the Deadbeat the lodestone of her life.

We'll close our critique of Buss by pointing out how his conclusions, allegedly generated from Darwinian analyses of life in the EEA are, in fact, used as premises in ameliorating his ignorance about ancestral environments and their demands. Consider the following claims that are typical of Buss's efforts in evolutionary analysis:

Women over evolutionary history could often garner far more resources for their children through a single spouse than through several temporary sex partners. (Buss 1994, p. 23)

A lone woman in ancestral environments may have been susceptible to food deprivation. She may also become a target for aggressive men. (Buss 1998, p. 416)

The second is cagey enough, but he quickly slides from the cautious "may" in order to argue that ancestral women would need the protection and support of mates. So in both instances we have definite pronouncements about the challenges of the EEA. Intriguing and informative pronouncements.

In fact, current researchers know very little about the EEA—or even whether there's some privileged time period on which we should concentrate in understanding the evolutionary origins of human psychological tendencies. Should we even be concerned with selection on our hunter-gatherer ancestors rather than considering primate evolution on the one hand, and more recent gene-culture coevolution on the other? But Buss has a simple way of overcoming his ignorance. Consider his defense of the idea that paternity uncertainty was a problem for ancestral men:

Behavioral, physiological, and psychological clues point powerfully to a human evolutionary history in which paternity uncertainty was an adaptive problem for men. (Buss 1996, p. 161)

So here's the argument. We know that current preferences and propensities are actually adaptations because we can identify them as selectively advantageous in the EEA. And we recognize the selective advantages by drawing conclusions about the EEA on the basis of our knowledge that those current preferences and propensities are really adaptations. The analysis is viciously circular.

4   The Slavering Beast Within: A Gothic Novella

The most substantial part of *A Natural History of Rape* (T and P 2000) is its second chapter, in which the authors draw on earlier pop sociobiological discussions of asymmetries in sexual strategies, particularly the work of David Buss. The authors aim to build on those discussions to advance an account of how natural selection underlies many aspects of rape. T and P are particularly interested in three main points, advanced in the writings we've just reviewed. First, the appropriate female strategy is to be choosy about potential mates. Second, the appropriate male strategy is to try to copulate as much as possible. Third, males have been selected to worry about issues of paternity. From these three points, T and P draw their central conclusions. Rape should be especially painful to females because their attempts to choose their mates have been subverted. Males should be more inclined to rape because they are primed to copulate even when females are not interested, and, of course, they should be especially tempted by those females who exhibit the signs of high reproductive value (the young with bouncy gait, lustrous hair, and so forth). Males have also evolved to be suspicious of female claims that they have been coerced into copulating (more specifically: Men have evolved to suspect the claims made by their mates), and that is why rape laws have taken the historical forms that they have.

So there we have it. An explanation of the principal features of rape by applying sound Darwinian principles. Add on a denunciation of that feminist canard that rape isn't a sexual act—what nonsense!—and we're done.

Well, not quite. What exactly are the Darwinian explanations supposed to be? Let's begin with the fundamental phenomenon. Some men rape women, and, sometimes, men rape other men. Why do these acts occur and why do they occur in the contexts they do with a certain distribution of types of victims? Critics of previous sociobiological stories about rape have pointed out that many instances of rape involve as victims girls who haven't yet reached menarche or women who are past menopause. T and P reply that "younger women are greatly overrepresented and that girls and older women greatly underrepresented in the data on victims of rape" (T and P 2000, p. 72, drawing on Thornhill and Thornhill 1983). Waiving some concerns that will occupy us later, we note that this evidence seems relevant only to the kinds of questions that occupy Buss: The most it can show is something about the women rapists find most attractive (and, of course, we don't think it shows much about that). The question has been subtly shifted. Given that some men rape—for whatever reasons—why do they tend to rape young women? Answer: Men are more likely to be attracted to young women, so whatever it is that impels them to sexual coercion, young women are more likely to be the victims.

We are concerned with two features of this answer. First, we want to note that there's a controversial assumption that the psychology of rape parallels that of consensual sex. The rapist's behavior is seen as the product of a disposition to be attracted toward certain kinds of people, whether or not they are willing, and a disposition to force sex on a particular occasion. There's an obvious alternative psychological hypothesis, one that not only corresponds to many people's introspective awareness but also seems to permeate the folk tales, poetry, dramas, and stories of almost every culture, that views reciprocity as a central feature of sexual attraction. If that alternative hypothesis is right, then the strategy of seeing the rapist as someone whose tendencies to sexual attraction are just like those of any one else of the same sex, with something extra added on, is misguided. We don't know that the hypothesis is true—indeed, we recommend psychological exploration of it—but we don't think it should simply be dismissed without careful consideration.

We'll spend more time on a second issue. In our view, the major question about rape concerns the causes of coercion. At risk of being pedantic, let's aim for maximal clarity on this point. Imagine two stylized situations. In the first, a man (Adam) is attracted to a woman (Eve) and makes her a sexual proposition. Eve demurely declines. Adam does not force her (he may try to persuade, but he doesn't coerce). In the second, another man

(Tarquin) is attracted to a different woman (Lucretia). Like Eve, Lucretia says "No." Tarquin presses on and eventually forces Lucretia to couple with him. Surely the centerpiece of a Darwinian account of rape should not be a story (a bad story, we've argued) about why Eve and Lucretia are found attractive, but rather an explanation of the difference between Adam and Tarquin. What is it about Adam that makes him hold back when Tarquin uses force?

T and P don't offer any clear answer to this question. Whether this is because they don't have the issues in focus or because they haven't made up their minds we don't presume to judge. They do tell their readers that there are two different ways to apply Darwinian ideas to the study of rape. The *direct* approach supposes that there are "psychological mechanisms designed specifically to influence males to rape in ways that would have produced a net reproductive benefit in the past" (T and P 2000, p. 59). The *by-product* approach proposes that there are a number of psychological mechanisms that have been shaped by natural selection that sometimes combine to trigger an act of rape. In a version of this approach that the authors draw from Donald Symons (1979, pp. 264–267), the mechanisms hypothesized are "the human male's greater visual sexual arousal, greater autonomous sex drive, reduced ability to abstain from sexual activity, much greater desire for sexual variety per se, greater willingness to engage in impersonal sex, and less discriminating criteria for sexual partners" (T and P 2000, p. 62). For reasons we've offered in earlier sections, we doubt that these hypothetical characteristics have been targets of natural selection, but the example does have the virtue of exposing T and P's intended contrast. On the by-product approach, there's no commitment to supposing that acts of rape enhance (or once enhanced) the reproductive success of the rapist. Maybe there are all these adapted psychological dispositions that sometimes combine in ways that are unfortunate for the rapist (as well as being terrible for the victim).

T and P don't advance any definite hypotheses about the Adam/Tarquin difference. We'll try to do better. Start with the direct approach. There are two possibilities. Either the adaptation is almost universal among human males or it isn't. On the former assumption, the rape disposition is present in just about every human being with a Y chromosome, and the fact that a lot of men don't engage in rape must be explained by invoking some combination of contextual cues and the inhibiting activity of other psychological dispositions. Plainly there's not going to be a lot of direct data to support this hypothesis until we've been told a lot more about possible cues and interactions. But maybe we can get some clues by thinking about the past action of natural selection.

Here's the simplest story. Males have been programmed to rape when they have a chance for copulating with a potentially fertile female and they can get away with it. If there were genetic variation in some savannah population with respect to the disposition to use force, so that most of the male population never engaged in sexual coercion while occasional mutants would rape fertile females only under conditions in which they incurred no costs, then the mutants would have slightly higher expected reproductive success (alternatively, we might suppose a disposition to use force only when the expected costs are lower than the expected reproductive benefits). At this point, everything depends on the details. As we noted in the last section, the chance that a copulation will lead to a birth is 1 to 2 percent (a figure with which T and P seem to agree; T and P 2000, p. 100), and this figure has to be discounted by the chance that the child will be abandoned, die before attaining puberty, or simply be ill prepared for a successful reproductive future. Equally, we need a sober evaluation of the potential costs of an act of rape. Under what conditions, if any, in the savannah environment, could a rapist be expected to recognize that the chances of physical injury from other hominids were sufficiently low that the small benefit of forcing a copulation outweighed the expected costs? Again, we leave to the reader the exercise of constructing formal models that show rampant rape, a low incidence of rape, or no possibilities for the aspiring rapist. Hint: It's simply a matter of adjusting group size, daily habits, social structures, and aggressive tendencies.

The natural selection of the rape disposition is, of course, mediated by that remarkable mutant genotype that expresses itself in just the tendency to coerce copulation in the face of female reluctance when the circumstances are right (or whose effects on fitness are only so mediated). We harbor doubts about that genotype just as we are doubtful that some (or all) of us carry a genotype that enabled our Pleistocene ancestors to stand firm and pick an extra berry or two just when a lion was sufficiently far off to let them garner a small nutritive benefit without cost.

As we acknowledged, the story we've been telling is the simplest version of the universal variant of the direct approach. One embarrassing feature of our tale is that it fails to account for the difference between Adam and Tarquin—there are many Adams who seem to pass up opportunities that Tarquins exploit. Plainly, we need some epicycles, another psychological disposition or two to explain Adam's undue reticence or Tarquin's lack of proper caution. We'll also have to face up to the fact that rape victims are sometimes young girls or older women, so there'll have to be other causal factors that make the tendency to rape misfire. Of course, as we build these in, we'll have to be very careful that we don't subvert whatever story we've been telling about the advantages in the ancestral environment; it will, for example, be disastrous if the sources of inhibition or excitation might have led our ancestors to actions that incurred great risks of injury (like the mythical Pleistocene berry-picker who tarries an instant too long).

Maybe we can do better by switching to the polymorphic variant of the direct approach. Now we suppose that some men develop the rape disposition and others don't. No problem now with explaining the difference between Adam and Tarquin: Tarquin has it, Adam doesn't. The challenge this time is to conjure up a plausible tale about the way in which natural selection on our ancestors produced this polymorphism. Here's one way to try. Suppose that all males share a conditional disposition: If one experiences one type of developmental environment the rape disposition develops, if one experiences a different type of developmental environment it doesn't. Back now to Savannah Sam, first bearer of the mutant allele associated with this conditional disposition. Sam is going to have to have some reproductive edge. If this fails to involve any act of rape on his part, then it's hard to see why the allele should persist in the population. But if Sam's Darwinian advantage is a consequence of his developing in the pertinent environment, acquiring the rape disposition, and going in for a rape or two, then it's hard to see why a *fixed* disposition to acquire the rape disposition, come what may, wouldn't have been equally good. Once again, we urge readers to be imaginative and to construct evolutionary models for their favorite outcomes.

Perhaps the indirect approach will fare better. Indeed, there's a reading of T and P on which the indirect approach must succeed if the direct approach fails. For, unfortunately, rape happens. The people who commit rape belong to a species that has evolved under natural selection. So, when an act of rape occurs, some combination of psychological features that humans have evolved to have must combine with environmental stimuli to prompt it. A triumph for the Darwinian approach to the human sciences?

Not really. The interpretation we've offered is banal, and would go through equally well whatever human activity—chopstick use or needle-point, say—we were to consider. If the indirect approach is to vindicate T and P's advertisement that evolutionary theory will guide "the scientific study of life in general and of humans in particular to fruitful ends of deep knowledge" (T and P 2000, p. 3), then it will have to provide something more substantive than the vacuous suggestion that human actions draw on evolved psychological mechanisms. Something more like the version T and P reconstruct from Symons, perhaps.

Let's assume for the time being that the asymmetries celebrated by Symons, Buss, and T and P are genuine: Males are more inclined to want casual sex than females and so forth (T and P 2000, p. 62). Somehow these differences are supposed to be parlayed into an account of why rape some-times occurs. So far as we can tell, there's just one option that will serve T and P's turn. From time to time, some men get so overstimulated that they just can't hold back, even though what they go on to do on some of these occasions may not enhance their reproductive success (as well, of course, as being traumatic for their victims).

It doesn't take much thought to see why so simple a proposal won't do. Without further elaborate psychological hypotheses, we have no reason to reject the apparent evidence that a fair number of men who are as sexually stimulated as those who rape manage to accept a woman's refusal. On the face of it, the difference between Adams and Tarquins isn't simply one of the strength of sexual desire. If T and P want to argue that appearances are deceptive, then they have a lot of work to do—they would have to show that there is some psychological (or neurophysiological) measure of level of sexual arousal that distinguishes all the rapists from all those men who accept rejection.

So what exactly is the difference between those males who behave like Tarquin and those, equally ardent, who emulate Adam? The obvious sug-gestion is that there are inhibitory mechanisms whose strength varies between the cases. Can we find any Darwinian clues about what such mech-anisms might be? T and P seem to believe we can. They cite work by "the evolutionary psychologist Neil Malamuth" on reduced sexual restraint. Malamuth, and others, have found that certain kinds of developmental experiences are correlated with an apparent "sexual impulsiveness and risk taking." Apparently, "reduced parental investment (resulting from poverty or the absence of the father)" leads to "a male's perception of rejection by potential mates." Allegedly, "[m]en emerge from this background with a perception of reduced ability to invest in women, an expectation of brief sexual relationships with women, a reduced ability to form enduring relationships, a coercive sexual attitude toward women, and an acceptance of aggression as a tactic for obtaining desired goals" (T and P 2000, p. 69; previous citations from pp. 68–69).

The Darwinian language in the passage from which we have quoted is entirely gratuitous. What the studies reveal is that boys who are brought up in poor environments without a father have a higher tendency to harbor certain attitudes toward women and toward sexual relationships, attitudes that increase the chances that they will force sex. There's no warrant whatsoever for suggesting that this has a lot to do with parental investment or the young men's investment in potential mates. You don't need an evolutionary perspective to discover these attitudes and you don't require an evolutionary perspective to interpret them. The basic point is that there do seem to be variations among males in the mechanisms that inhibit the expression of sexual desire in the face of female reluctance, and, by standard psychological studies of rapists, one can find correlations between the relative strength of the inhibitory mechanisms and characteristics of the developmental environment.

Once we've come this far, it's not hard to see that the insistent Darwinizing is at best irrelevant and at worst an obstacle. The fundamental question concerns the complex of psychological attitudes that inhibit, or fail to inhibit, the forcing of sex. If we consider the entire spectrum of rapes, including the rape of children and postmenopausal women, which T and P consistently downplay, we can reasonably conjecture that the rapist's attitude often fails to acknowledge the victim as a person and sometimes even embodies a deliberate intention to demonstrate that the victim is the object of hostility or contempt. Adam holds back, even in the grip of intense desire, because he acknowledges Eve's right to say "No." Tarquin, by contrast, sees Lucretia as less than fully human, or wishes to show his dominance of her, or intends that his rape will serve as an act of revenge. The critical task for a theory of rape is to be able to characterize these attitudes as precisely as possible, and to understand how they come about. We are prepared to believe that poverty can breed frustration, that a father's absence and the lack of parental affection can engender tendencies to see others as utensils rather than people. Exploring these psychological issues and the causal relationships they involve is not advanced by the speculative invocations of Darwin that T and P favor.

But wait! Don't T and P have a reply to the charges we've leveled? After all, they devote an entire chapter to attacking "the social science explanation of rape," in which they consider, and take themselves to demolish, arguments to the effect that rape is about hostility, dominance, punishment, and the desire for control. Consider the following typical passage.

> Brownmiller (1975) sees rape in large-scale war as stemming in part from the frenzied state of affairs and the great excitement of men who have just forcefully dominated the enemy. That hypothesis predicts that soldier rapists would be indiscriminate about the age of the victims. But they are not; they prefer young women. (T and P 2000, p. 134)

The second sentence we've quoted is, we believe, unwarranted. Brownmiller's position, as we would reconstruct it, can be developed as a pair of claims:

1. For whatever reasons (not necessarily the Darwinian tales T and P borrow from Buss), men are typically more attracted to young women.
2. The coercive expression of sexual desire is the result of a failure in an inhibitory mechanism that can be caused by hostility toward the victim.

So Brownmiller (at least on our reconstruction) would predict *both* that the frequency of rape would be greater in a situation of war, in which soldiers express hostility toward the victims (and, very probably, their desire to show dominance), *and* that the distribution of rape victims would be skewed toward younger women.

The logical mistake evident here is common to T and P's other discussions of social scientific hypotheses about rape in general and of feminist proposals in particular. They claim that all kinds of confusions flow from viewing rape "as an act of violence" (T and P 2000, pp. 136ff.). But the confusions are all T and P's. Rape is not just about violence: There's a difference between the rapist and the batterer. In our judgment, however, rape isn't just about sex either. If T and P had seen clearly that they need to account for the difference between Adam and Tarquin, they would have recognized that other psychological mechanisms and attitudes come into play and would have appreciated the obvious possibility that, in most instances of rape, motives of aggression and dominance are also present. Further, they might have seen that general characteristics of societies are pertinent to the attitudes that adult human beings have toward one another, and in particular to the attitudes that men have toward women. They might then have acknowledged that broad social tendencies can permeate psychological development and lead men to acknowledge women as full persons— or not. The feminist authors who have suggested that prevalent cultural images of women are relevant to how a woman's refusal is heard have a genuine point.[5]

We'll be completely explicit. When rape occurs, there's a sexual dimension to the event. When sexual intercourse is forced, there are typically nonsexual dimensions to the event. The attitudes that lead to the coercive sex often involve intentions to hurt, dominate, humiliate, and obtain revenge. Those attitudes are themselves often present because of a complex developmental history, one that may involve not just details of individual ontogenies (lack of parental affection, for example) but also more general cultural influences that lead men not to see women as full people (but, for example, as collections of salient body parts—genitals, breasts, buttocks, lustrous hair, full lips, and so on).

Let's sum up the discussion of this section. We've examined the two variants of the direct adaptation approach and found that the task of working out a coherent Darwinian model that will fit the evidence is, to say the least, challenging; the challenge is not taken up by T and P. The byproduct approach leads fairly quickly to the sensible proposal that rape occurs when certain inhibitory mechanisms are weakened. Despite their attempts to drag in Darwinian language, T and P fail to show how evolutionary psychology can illuminate the character of these inhibitory mechanisms. Further pursuit of the sensible proposal seems to require research in developmental psychology and, quite possibly, elaborations of the social science hypotheses that T and P deride.

We'll spare the reader an equally extensive treatment of T and P's two other major claims, the thesis that rape is especially hurtful to women because it subverts their preferred mating strategy and the idea that rape laws reflect male concern with paternity certainty. The analysis of these proposals would proceed on similar lines. Once again, we'd ask just what the selective advantage of intense female pain is supposed to be. Is this a psychological adaptation shared with other primates, or is it part of a female tactic for reassuring Mr. Big Bucks with his refined paternity uncertainties? We'd invite consideration of the hypothesis that people have a general tendencies to feel hurt when they have been used and to expect tenderness and the expression of affection in sexual contact. Similarly, it would be appropriate to ask exactly why attitudes of suspicion toward female testimony are supposed to be adaptive, and to consider the precise costs and benefits of reacting to rape in different ways.

We have offered only hints. Any serious evolutionary account is going to have to advance definite claims about the character of the adaptation, the set of available strategies, and the environment in which selection is alleged to have taken place. This, of course, is what evolutionary theorists do. But T and P do not live up to the standards of the discipline. Their identification of adaptations is entirely elusive, and there's not a shred of discussion of available strategies (let alone of potential genetic bases for them) or of the environmental details.

These are harsh words, and we anticipate protests. Surely T and P do appeal to broad and familiar features of evolution on sexual species, the sexual asymmetries, paternity worries, and so forth that they treat as cardinal dogmas of general evolutionary theory. Isn't it enough to rely on the work of others and to consider ways in which the challenges of natural and sexual selection might be met? No. To make progress in understanding the springs of human behavior, it's necessary to be far clearer about the nature of the selection pressures, the consequences of the allegedly favored strategy and the possible rivals. T and P tell us nothing specific about the problems that might be addressed by a tendency to rape or by a disposition to feel intense pain at being raped. All their readers get are vague gestures. Such insubstantial suggestions would not be taken seriously in other areas of evolutionary studies. Workers on social insects or sage grouse don't simply talk vaguely about the requirements of obtaining food or avoiding predators; they explore the ecological parameters they take to be significant; they engage in studies to discover the kinds of strategies their organisms can employ; they collect data on reproductive rates. We appreciate the difficulties of meeting such high standards in the study of our own species. But, when the gap between standards and practice is as vast as it is in T and P's discussion of human rape, it's simply false advertising to claim to be in the same business.

5 Conclusion: In Defense of Irreverence

We believe that the studies we have reviewed are scientifically shoddy. But there's surely a fair amount of bad work in the world. Why should people become so upset with the evolutionary psychology of sex and violence, as practiced by Buss, Thornhill, and Palmer? We'll close with a brief attempt at explanation.

It's not incumbent on scientific researchers to offer policy suggestions, but some recent pop sociobiologists—including T and P—have defended their proposals about human nature by declaring that they can help resolve urgent social issues. Even though we concede that they have good intentions, that they want to help decrease the incidence of rape, it's hard to avoid the judgment that T and P's suggestions, where not banal, will do little good. Given the speculative character of their Darwinizing and the elusiveness of their proposals, even their inability to recognize crucial issues, policies influenced by their text might well make matters worse.

Consider, for example, their suggestions about educational programs. They begin with a program for boys, agreeing "with social scientists that males should be educated not to use force or the threat of force to obtain sex" (T and P 2000, p. 171). No problem so far, but we didn't need any Darwinizing to arrive at this judgment. Keen to show the fecundity of their ideas, T and P continue with two disastrous further suggestions. First, they propose that educators should explain the differences between male and female sexuality. As we pointed out repeatedly in the last section, even granting the pop sociobiological claims about these differences, the crucial question is why some men (Adams) hold back from forcing women to their desires and others (Tarquins) don't. Any program based on stating "the evolutionary reasons why a young man can get an erection just by looking at a photo of a naked woman" (T and P 2000, p. 179) is pointing in the wrong direction and encouraging a view of the springs of rape that may encourage young men to downplay its importance ("Well it's only human nature after all!"). The critical part of the education, as so many feminists and their social scientific allies have insisted, should be to teach young men that "No" means No, and to help them overcome the kinds of hostility, dominance, and desires for power that are so frequently part of the psychological cause of rape.

A misguided program for boys is bad enough. But T and P also want a parallel program for girls, pointing out to them the True Nature of the Slavering Beasts with whom they are doomed to reproduce. Young women "should be made aware of the costs associated with attractiveness" (T and P 2000, p. 181). Not only is this vulnerable to just the criticisms we directed at T and P's tutorial for boys, but its social consequence is likely to be a continued perception that women are partly responsible for rape ("She was asking for it").[6] Any sensible approach to rape education should be freed from suggestions of female responsibility or complicity, directed toward correcting a problem in male attitudes, clearly demarcated from the expression of some hypothetically universal male sexuality and firmly linked to a failure in inhibiting mechanisms. T and P seem to be suggesting an educational program that will reinforce attitudes that ought to be extinguished.

No wonder, then, that they arouse such ire. But we still have told only part of the story. If, as many scholars believe, individual ontogenies are affected by stereotypes in the broader culture, so that male views of women are sometimes shaped by a widespread tendency to reduce them to sexual playthings, then pop sociobiologists don't just ignore crucial causal factors. In their style of analysis, their tendentious talk of "reproductive potential," "investment," "paternity certainty," and so forth, they dehumanize the complex activity of human courtship, love and marriage, embodying in their prose just those images of women as bundles of sexually pertinent body parts—genitals, breasts, lustrous hair and the rest—that are taken to contribute to the devaluation of women and the incidence of rape. Buss, T and P, and their colleagues give academic respectability to ways of regarding women and of viewing sexual relations that many people see as profoundly damaging, and they do so by using an idiom that portrays women as resources and sex as commerce.

There are self-pitying moments in *A Natural History of Rape* in which the authors wonder why their work inspires hostile reactions. No prizes for guessing their preferred explanation: They stand in a line of thinkers that extends back to Galileo, a line of fearless revolutionaries dedicated to science and truth. We offer a harsher alternative. They pretend to scientific rigor when they have none; they misunderstand the positions of those whom they lambast; they blunder into sensitive issues, self-righteously offering proposals that it's reasonable to fear will be counterproductive; and they employ language and images that reinforce just those social tenden-cies their opponents view as crucial factors in producing pain and humil-iation for women.

Just as we think the comparison with Galileo inappropriate, we don't recommend that pop sociobiologists be shown the instruments of torture. We think instead that what T and P and others of their ilk merit is a thor-ough irreverence, born of recognizing that the dignity of academic prose is not in order here. In short, the Bronx cheer.

Acknowledgments

We would like to thank Allan Gibbard for helpful conversations, although we are not persuaded by his more positive view of evolutionary psychol-ogy; we are also grateful to Patricia Kitcher for some extremely construc-tive advice about an earlier draft. Jerry Coyne and Richard Lewontin supplied extensive written comments on the penultimate version and have helped us to improve it in a large number of ways; we are deeply indebted to them.

Notes

1. A classic source of the modular approach to the mind is Fodor (1981). Whether Fodor would recognize the use that evolutionary psychologists make of his ideas is quite another matter. But many of the most influential writings in evolutionary psychology, particularly the articles of Leda Cosmides and John Tooby, do cham-pion the Fodorian notion of a module as an "informationally encapsulated psy-chological subsystem." The terminology is much less evident in the authors whose views we discuss here, although they share the common evolutionary psychologi-cal strategy of atomizing the mind into parts that are taken to be under indepen-dent selective control. We'll henceforth avoid the technical term "module."

2. In a rather uninformed discussion of culture and its impact on behavior, T and P show that they do not really understand the work of Boyd and Richerson (see T and P 2000, p. 27). They show a similar lack of comprehension in lumping the re-cent group selectionist proposals of Elliott Sober and David Sloan Wilson with older views that have been decisively discredited (T and P 2000, p. 6). It strikes us as odd that authors who are so keen to introduce an evolutionary perspective into the social sciences should be so superficially informed about theoretical issues per-taining to evolution.

3. The observant reader will note that there's a slight problem in Buss's co-opting this experiment for his own purposes, since the point of his investigations is to *dis-cover* what kinds of people men and women find attractive. The experiment was,

however, carried out (by Clarke and Hartfield) on the basis of a prior estimate of attractiveness. But we let this pass.

4. See Kitcher (1985, pp. 170–71) for some straightforward ways of replacing casual speculations about sexual strategies with the kinds of models that are constructed in competent evolutionary studies.

5. Perhaps there's a more charitable interpretation of T and P, one that sees them as recognizing the fact that rape isn't only about sex or only about aggression (power, dominance, etc.). Perhaps T and P and the feminists they criticize can agree on rejecting both polar positions (rape is a matter of sex alone, rape is a matter of aggression alone). We think that the constant emphasis on sexual strategies shaped by selection and the failure to distinguish the question of explaining the characteristics of rape victims from the question of distinguishing between Adam and Tarquin make any such interpretation unlikely. Authors with the more charitable interpretation clearly in view would have written a very different book.

6. As Dick Lewontin pointed out to us, this phrase needs careful consideration. Sometimes women do dress in ways that they hope will lead men to find them desirable. But surely these women do not want the male desires to lead to sexual coercion. Educational programs should surely be very clear about the difference between the desire to be desired and the desire to be attacked.

References

Angier, Natalie (1999). *Woman: An Intimate Geography.* Boston: Houghton Mifflin.

Barash, David (1979). *The Whisperings Within.* London: Penguin.

Boyd, Robert and Peter Richerson (1985). *Culture and the Evolutionary Process.* Chicago: University of Chicago Press.

Brownmiller, Susan (1975). *Against Our Will: Men, Women, and Rape.* New York: Simon and Schuster.

Buss, David (1989). Sex differences in human mate preferences: Evolutionary hypotheses tested in 37 cultures. *Behavioral and Brain Sciences* 12: 1–49.

Buss, David (1992). Mate preferences mechanisms: Consequences for partner choice and intrasexual competition. In J. Barkow et al., eds., *The Adapted Mind,* pp. 249–266. New York: Oxford University Press.

Buss, David (1994). *The Evolution of Desire.* New York: Basic Books.

Buss, David (1995). Psychological sex differences: Origins through sexual selection. *American Psychologist* 50: 164–168.

Buss, David (1996). Paternity uncertainty and the complex repertoire of human mating strategies. *American Psychologist* 51: 161–162.

Buss, David (1998). The psychology of human mate selection. In Charles Crawford and Dennis Krebs, eds., *Handbook of Evolutionary Psychology,* pp. 405–429. Mahwah, N.J.: Lawrence Erlbaum.

Buss, David (1999). *Evolutionary Psychology: The New Science of the Mind.* Boston: Allyn and Bacon.

Clutton-Brock, T., et al. (1981). *Red Deer.* Chicago: University of Chicago Press.

Fodor, Jerry (1981). *The Modularity of Mind.* Cambridge, Mass.: MIT Press.

Kitcher, Philip (1985). *Vaulting Ambition: Sociobiology and the Quest for Human Nature.* Cambridge, Mass.: MIT Press.

Lewontin, Richard, Steven Rose, and Leon Kamin (1984). *Not in Our Genes.* New York: Pantheon.

Lumsden, Charles and E. O. Wilson (1981). *Genes, Minds, and Culture.* Cambridge, Mass.: Harvard University Press.

Maynard Smith, John and N. Warren (1982). Review of *Genes, Minds, and Culture Evolution* 36: 620–627.

Mischel, Walter (1968). *Personality and Assessment.* New York: Wiley.

Moore, D. A. (1999). Order effects in preference judgments: Evidence for context dependence in the generation of preferences. *Organizational Behavior and Human Decision Processes* 78: 146–165.

Oster, G. and E. O. Wilson (1978). *Caste and Ecology in the Social Insects.* Princeton: Princeton University Press.

Parker, G. (1978). Searching for mates. In J. R. Krebs and N. Davies, eds., *Behavioral Ecology: An Evolutionary Approach.* Oxford: Blackwell.

Symons, Donald (1979). *The Evolution of Human Sexuality.* New York: Oxford University Press.

Thornhill, Randy and Craig Palmer (2000). *A Natural History of Rape: Biological Bases of Sexual Coercion.* Cambridge, Mass.: MIT Press.

Thornhill, Randy and Nancy Thornhill (1983). Human rape: An evolutionary analysis. *Ethology and Sociobiology* 4: 137–173.

Thornhill, Randy and Nancy Thornhill (1992). The evolutionary psychology of men's sexual coercion. *Behavioral and Brain Sciences* 15: 363–375.

van den Berghe, Pierre (1979). *Human Family Systems.* New York: Elsevier.

Wilson, E. O. (1975). *Sociobiology: The New Synthesis.* Cambridge, Mass.: Harvard University Press.

Wilson, E. O. (1978). *On Human Nature.* Cambridge, Mass.: Harvard University Press.

Critiquing Evolutionary Models of Rape

7

Of Vice and Men: A Case Study in Evolutionary Psychology

Jerry A. Coyne

1

In science's pecking order, evolutionary biology lurks somewhere near the bottom, far closer to phrenology than to physics. For evolutionary biology is a historical science, laden with history's inevitable imponderables. We evolutionary biologists cannot generate a Cretaceous Park to observe exactly what killed the dinosaurs; and, unlike "harder" scientists, we usually cannot resolve issues with a simple experiment, such as adding tube A to tube B and noting the color of the mixture.

The latest deadweight dragging us closer to phrenology is "evolutionary psychology," or the science formerly known as sociobiology, which studies the evolutionary origin of human behavior. There is nothing inherently wrong with this enterprise, and it has generated some intriguing theories, particularly concerning the evolution of language. The problem is that evolutionary psychology suffers from the scientific equivalent of megalomania. Many of its adherents are convinced that virtually every human action or feeling, including depression, homosexuality, religion, and consciousness, was put directly into our brains by natural selection. In this view, evolution becomes the key—the only key—that can unlock our humanity.

Unfortunately, evolutionary psychologists routinely confuse theory with idle speculation. Unlike bones, behavior does not fossilize, and understanding its evolution often involves concocting stories that sound plausible but are hard to test. Depression, for example, is seen as a trait favored by natural selection to enable us to solve our problems by withdrawing, reflecting, and thereby enhancing our future reproduction. Plausible? Maybe. Scientifically testable? Absolutely not. If evolutionary biology is a soft science, then evolutionary psychology is its flabby underbelly.

But the public can be forgiven for thinking that evolutionary biology is equivalent to evolutionary psychology. Books by Daniel Dennett, E. O. Wilson, and Steven Pinker have sold briskly, and evolutionary psychology dominates the media coverage of research on evolution. (It has also figured in the media's treatment of politics, as when evolutionary psychologists identified the lustful activity of Bill Clinton as the behavior of an "alpha male.") In view of the scientific shakiness of much of the work, its popularity must rest partly on some desire for a "scientific" explanation of human behavior. Evolutionary psychology satisfies our hunger for a comprehensive explanation of human existence, for a theory of inevitability that will remove the ambiguities and the uncertainties of emotional and moral life. Freud is no longer the preferred behavioral paradigm. Now Darwin is ascendant. Blame your genes, not your mother.

Hence the excitement—and the furor—that has greeted the publication of Randy Thornhill and Craig Palmer's (2000a) book, *A Natural History of Rape: Biological Bases of Sexual Coercion.*[1] Determined to show that human rape is a "natural, biological phenomenon that is a product of the human evolutionary heritage" (Thornhill and Palmer 2000b, p. 30), the authors take issue with social scientists and feminists (viewed as permanently conjoined Siamese twins), for whom rape represents men's deliberate attempt to subjugate and to humiliate women. In Thornhill and Palmer's account, the motive for rape is not just sexual, but reproductive. Rape, they argue, was favored by natural selection to give sexually dispossessed males the chance to have children, and to give males with mates the chance to have extra children.

Such a sexual strategy could operate in several ways. For example, men might resort to rape when they are socially disenfranchised and thus unable to gain access to women through looks, wealth, or status. Alternatively, men could have evolved to practice rape when the costs seem low— when, for instance, a woman is alone and unprotected (and thus retaliation seems unlikely), or when they have physical control over a woman (and so cannot be injured by her).

Thornhill and Palmer further claim that attempts to root out rape will not succeed until one accepts its evolutionary origin and uses this precious knowledge to make social policy:

Not only does an evolutionary approach generate new knowledge that could be used to decrease the incidence of rape; some of the proposals put forth by individuals uninformed by evolutionary theory may actually increase it. (2000b, p. x)

The media coverage of *A Natural History of Rape* has been critical, but largely devoted to pitting Thornhill and Palmer against feminists, who see the book as a misogynistic attempt to justify rape and to unravel the progress of recent decades. The results were predictable and largely unproductive: a lot of sound bites and shouting in television studios.[2] Meanwhile, the book has been warmly embraced by some evolutionary psychologists, notably Steven Pinker, who praised it as a "courageous, intelligent and eye-opening book with a noble goal." Nearly all of these public debates, however, have been fueled by ideology. What has been missing is a discussion of the science that lies behind, or does not lie behind, Thornhill and Palmer's assertions. After all, their book is only as good as their evidence.

Thornhill and Palmer have frequently invoked the authority of science to defend their evolutionary conception of rape. They insist that their detractors are motivated by ideology, while they are dispassionate scientists whose only priority is objective truth. In their media appearances, they have implied that their science is incontrovertible, and that any dissenter from their conclusions must be philosophically or politically blinkered. This is a grotesque misrepresentation of the book's science, which has by no means drawn unanimous approbation from the scientific community. Far from it: to a scientist, the scientific errors in this book are far more inflammatory than are its ideological implications.

Like much of evolutionary psychology, Thornhill and Palmer's book is utterly lacking in sound scientific grounding. Moreover, the authors use rhetorical tricks that mislead the general reader about their arguments. Once its scientific weaknesses are recognized, *A Natural History of Rape* becomes one more sociobiological "just-so" story—the kind of tale that evolutionists swap over a few beers at the faculty club. Such stories do not qualify as science, and they do not deserve the assent, or even the respect, of the public.

2

Thornhill and Palmer's thesis rests on current ideas about the evolution of sex differences. It is obvious that men and women show clear differences in many visible traits, ranging from body size to breasts. No biologist would deny that these differences resulted from natural selection acting on our ancestors. (The wider pelvis of the female, for example, is essential in childbirth.) And, given the agreement on the evolutionary basis of physical differences, it would seem foolish to deny a priori that evolution did not also produce some differences in behavior. It is true that human culture and learning may alter behavioral traits more readily than morphological ones, but there is convincing evidence that some behavioral differences evolved because they increased the reproductive success of our ancestors. Since rape is an act of sexual aggression, the pertinent question is whether males and females evolved to differ in aggression and in sexual behavior. Most evolutionists believe that they did.

In mammals, we see a fundamental asymmetry between the roles of the two sexes. Females must invest a great deal in their offspring (in the case of humans, nine months of metabolic trauma plus untold years of nursing and subsequent aggravation), while males can get away with investing very little (minimally one dose of sperm before moving on to the next female). This leads, in general, to a marked difference between the sexes in their strategies for selecting mates. For the female, it pays to be prudent and picky: She has relatively few shots at reproduction, and so must make each opportunity count by choosing the best possible father for her children. The male has a different approach: He wants to inseminate as many females as possible. He is interested in quantity, not quality.

For this reason, males inevitably compete for access to females. Darwin recognized that such competition occurs in two fundamentally different ways: males either try to impress the females (the peacock strategy) or they try to directly dominate the other males (the deer strategy). It is the latter course that seems most pertinent to the sexual behavior of humans, and this internecine male competition is assumed to have driven not only the evolution of increased male body size (on average, bigger is better in a physical contest), but also of hormonally mediated male aggression (there is no use being the biggest guy on the block if you are a wallflower).

Of course, there are aggressive and sexually promiscuous women as well as meek and monogamous men; but we are talking about averages here. Evolved differences need not be seen in every individual: many men are smaller than the average woman.

Whatever the role of culture—of "nurture" rather than "nature"—in determining human behavior, our evolutionary legacy is certainly alive and well in the size difference between males and females and in those aggression-promoting male hormones. It is no accident that most rapists, and most violent criminals, are men. Feminists are undoubtedly right to claim that culture reinforces sexual stereotypes, but there can be no adequate explanation of patriarchy that completely ignores evolution.

Thornhill and Palmer perform an ingenious trick by advancing two disparate theories to support the idea that rape is "natural and biological." The first is the "by-product hypothesis," which maintains simply that rape is a side effect of other evolved human traits. In other words, rape is "evolutionary" because it is performed by men whose brains, bodies, and behavior have evolved to a point where rape has become physically and emotionally possible. This is a reasonable view—indeed, a tautology— that few biologists will find objectionable. The second hypothesis, that of "direct adaptation," maintains that rape is much more than an evolutionary by-product: it is a direct adaptation installed by natural selection to allow sexually disenfranchised men to produce children.

This latter view is far more controversial but is clearly the centerpiece of *A Natural History of Rape*. Nearly all of the discussion and the cited evidence are directed at proving the truth of this second theory.

3

The "by-product hypothesis" views rape as a mere side effect of other adaptations that natural selection built into our ancestors. That is, natural selection favored not genes compelling men to rape, but genes producing aspects of human emotion and behavior that, in combination with human culture, allow the existence of rape. Thornhill and Palmer are not explicit about which evolved features yield rape as a side effect, but a good guess is a mixture of male promiscuity and aggression. This mixture, especially if combined with a male animus toward women, might readily explain rape. In this view, rape is an act of sexual violence—an outlet for rage and sexual release directed at a convenient target. It is an act of sex *and* violence, with one or the other predominating according to circumstances (date rape is more sexual, the violent rape of strangers more aggressive).

Given that in most reported cases rapists are sexually aroused, often reach orgasm, and sometimes admit to erotic motives, it is hard to disagree with Thornhill and Palmer's claim that rape is at least partly a sexual act. This claim is hardly new. Indeed, the sexual dimension of rape is painfully obvious. But Thornhill and Palmer note that "academic feminists and sociologists" have consistently denied any sexual motivation for rape, insisting instead that "rape is not about sex, but about violence and power." It is true that in recent decades the discussion of rape has been dominated by such notions, though one must remember that they originated not as scientific propositions but as political slogans deemed necessary to reverse popular misconceptions about rape.

The real problem with the by-product hypothesis is its banality. It explains everything about human beings. Since we have an evolutionary history, everything that we are and do can be furnished with an evolutionary explanation. There is no behavior, for example, that does not originate in our having a brain that is the product of natural selection. And this opens the evolutionary floodgates. Playing the violin? A by-product of creativity, manual dexterity, and the ability to learn. Collecting stamps? A by-product of our evolved desires to acquire resources and to categorize our environment.

But such explanations are crushingly trivial, as can be seen in Thornhill and Palmer's declaration:

> When one is considering any feature of living things, whether evolution applies is never a question. The only legitimate question is how to apply evolutionary principles. This is the case for all human behaviors—even for such by-products as cosmetic surgery, the content of movies, legal systems, and fashion trends. (p. 12)

Well, if Thornhill and Palmer want to lump rape together with tummy tucks and *Titanic* as "evolutionary" phenomena, then God (or Darwin) bless them. We might as well throw in adoption (a by-product of parental care), masturbation (a by-product of uncontrollable sexuality), bestiality (ditto), and priestly celibacy (a by-product of religion, which is itself a by-product of some evolved feature that nobody understands). Of course, the interesting thing about masturbation, adoption, bestiality, and celibacy is that they are *maladaptive* traits: they could never have been favored by natural selection because their practice reduces the chance of passing on one's genes. And we should not forget nonsexual crimes such as murder, assault, and robbery—all those other by-products of evolution.

The key phrase in the passage just discussed is "whether evolution applies is never a question." This is an explicit admission that the by-product hypothesis lacks the defining property of any scientific theory—*falsifiability*, that is, the ability to be disproven by some possible observation. An unfalsifiable theory is not a scientific theory. It is a tautology or an article of faith. The by-product theory may justify the view of rape as an evolutionary pathology, an indirect consequence of male sexuality and aggression; and the by-product theory may also justify the feminist view that rape is simply a way for males to dominate and humiliate females. We can thus dismiss the by-product hypothesis, because there is no conceivable observation that could disprove it.

4

After proposing the by-product hypothesis as their fallback position, Thornhill and Palmer introduce the centerpiece of their book: the direct-selection hypothesis. This theory holds that rape is not merely an aggressive or sexual act, but a reproductive act—that is, one based on genes that natural selection inserted into men's brains. As the story goes, men who lack committed relationships and are unable to find mates in the usual ways can produce offspring through acts of rape. The frequency of genes causing rape would then increase at the expense of genes carried by equally disenfranchised but nonraping males, who leave no offspring. This would eventually lead to the brain's acquisition of a "rape chip," a behavior as hardwired as our tendencies to sleep and eat.

In the direct-selection theory, all men are born as potential rapists, but they do not necessarily rape because the effect of the act on reproduction depends on external circumstances. For one thing, rape can be favored by natural selection only when it gives rapists a net reproductive gain. Thus, Thornhill and Palmer suggest that natural selection has also endowed men with the ability to perform a reproductive cost-benefit analysis before raping. The benefit is the likelihood that the act will produce a genetically related offspring. The cost is that the rapist might be caught and severely punished, depriving him of future offspring. Men will therefore rape only when they are most likely to get away with it. Moreover, the theory predicts that men are selected to evaluate not just circumstances but also victims, choosing those most likely to be fertile. As with all behavioral adaptations, the rapist need not be conscious of the evolutionary wellsprings of his actions, just as we do not ponder the need to stoke our metabolism when sitting down to dinner.

Viewing rape as a module of the male brain is provocative enough, but, as diehard evolutionary psychologists, Thornhill and Palmer go on to propose that many other aspects of rape are direct adaptations. While they see rape as adaptive for men, they concede that it is not so for women, who suffer physical violence, possible alienation of their partner, and loss of their own evolved ability to choose a good mate. Natural selection therefore gives women their own adaptation, the post-rape trauma:

Psychological pain is an adaptation that functions against such [reproductive] losses by focusing on the causes of the losses. The result is that attention is directed toward ways of dealing with current circumstances, given the loss, and of avoiding a repetition of events that caused the loss. (p. 85)

(As I have noted, others have proposed a similar explanation for the evolution of depression. I doubt, though, whether rape victims and depressives use their trauma so productively.) And since the partner of a raped woman may be unsure whether a subsequent child is his, Thornhill and Palmer propose yet another direct adaptation: male suspicion about their mate's claim that she was raped. That, too, is biologically mandated.

Finally, in a theory almost unbelievably grandiose, Thornhill and Palmer suggest that the *opposition* to their theories is itself based on evolution. Our brains, they say, are so much the product of evolution that they have been preprogrammed with a set of beliefs, one of which is a reluctance to believe explanations involving evolution: "Evolved psychological intuitions about behavioral causation can mislead individuals into believing that they know as much as experts do about proximate human motivation" (p. 114). Don't like the theory? Trust the "experts," who have painfully overcome their aversion to evolution. (This is one of the ways in which the new evolutionary psychologists resemble the old Marxists: There is no place to stand outside their system of meaning, except for the privileged place where they themselves stand.)

Although Palmer himself professes to favor the by-product hypothesis, the authors continuously push the mixture of directly adaptive theories that I have just described. The direct-selection theory first appears in the fourth chapter, and the remaining eight are devoted to discussing this theory alone and its implications for society. All of the supplied evidence is offered in support of the view that rape is a direct adaptation, not an evolutionary by-product. (The latter theory requires no evidence because it is true by definition.)

Thornhill and Palmer use three lines of evidence to support the direct-selection hypothesis. First, they maintain that rape is an adaptive act in other species and thus could have evolved by the same route in humans. In scorpion flies, Thornhill's own research organism, males have an abdominal clamp that apparently evolved to help them forcibly restrain females who resist their courtship. Several other species also seem to show forced copulation, although whether it increases the male's reproduction is not known. But surely it is absurd to assume that rape may be a reproductive strategy in humans because it is a reproductive strategy in flies or ducks. Flies and ducks do not create and inhabit a culture, as humans do; and our culture guarantees that there will be many meaningless parallels between the behavior of humans and of other species. Like dandelion seeds, we parachute, but we do so for recreational and not reproductive reasons. The simple-minded extrapolation from a handful of animal species is no proof that human rape is a direct adaptation.

The second test of the theory involves performing the actual reproductive calculus of a human rapist. Do rapists really have more children over the course of their lives than equally dispossessed but nonraping males? This calculation cannot be made in view of the large number of unreported rapes (figures range from 50 to 80 percent) and of rapists who are never caught. According to Thornhill and Palmer, a single rape in peacetime has about a two percent chance of producing pregnancy. The problem is that we will never know the reproductive *costs*. Does the chance of being caught lower a rapist's future reproductive output by more than two percent? Indeed, such a calculus, based on modern statistics, may be completely irrelevant to judging the costs and the benefits obtaining when rape really evolved. As the authors note, if natural selection built the human "rape module," this almost certainly occurred in our distant evolutionary past, when society differed from our own in unknown and unknowable ways. Human civilization, after all, arose in only the last one-tenth of one percent of the interval since we branched off from our primate ancestors.

All that we can say, therefore, is that the reproductive benefits of ancestral rapists may have been lower than those of modern rapists (because of a lack of contraception, it is possible that females were pregnant far more often than they are now, and subsequent nursing of a child usually suppresses ovulation); and the costs may well have been higher (given the lack of jails, punishments for rape were probably more severe, and the chances of getting caught higher in small social groups). But the important point is that all such speculations remain mere stories about our unrecoverable past. Thornhill and Palmer are right to note that current observations about rape may bear little relation to forces acting in our ancestors. But they then ignore their own warnings and proceed to buttress the direct-selection hypothesis with statistics from modern Western societies.

The highlight of Thornhill and Palmer's evidence—their third method of supporting the direct-selection hypothesis—is a series of "predictions" about what one would expect to see if rape had evolved as a direct adaptation. These predictions (all supposedly verified by the authors' research) are meant to confer the prestige of rigorous science on their argument. When examined closely, however, the scientific evidence fails on three counts.

First, it is hard to see from modern statistics that rape increases reproduction. Thornhill and Palmer make much of their verified prediction that women of reproductive age are overrepresented among rape victims, as one might expect if rapists prey on potential childbearers. But, looking closer, one sees that a significant number of rape victims are either too old or too young to reproduce. According to Thornhill and Palmer themselves, one cited study showed that 29 percent of victims were younger than eleven. (Given the frequency of unreported child molestation, the true percentage may be even higher.) Other studies concur; and, when one adds in postmenopausal women, at least a third of all rapes have no possibility of producing children. Also, roughly 20 percent of all rapes do not involve vaginal penetration, and 50 percent of all rapes do not include ejaculation in the vagina (see Thornhill and Thornhill 1983). So, although there is some overlap between these classes, these rapes must also be excluded from the "reproductive" category.

Thornhill and Palmer note that while few rapes in peacetime are accompanied by murder—as expected if rape is a reproductive act—more than 22 percent of rapes involve violence in excess of what is needed to force copulation. This rather plainly supports the view that at least some rapes involve anger and gratuitous violence and are not completely motivated by a desire to reproduce. Moreover, roughly 10 percent of all rapes in peacetime are gang rapes, and, insofar as they involve more males than are needed to overcome the victim, they must be considered less adaptive than individual rapes because competition between ejaculates lowers each rapist's chance to reproduce.

Although we lack hard statistics, anecdotal evidence also suggests that many wartime rapes involve large groups of soldiers and often culminate in the murder or sexual mutilation of the victim. These, of course, are acts of sexual violence, pure and simple, and cannot in any way be attributed to reproduction. And what about wartime sex prisons, such as those set up by occupying Japanese during World War II, in which kidnapped women were repeatedly raped by many different soldiers? Finally, same-sex prison rapes, which in most states are not even counted as rapes, cannot produce offspring, but involve the subjugation of victims for sex, power, and humiliation. There are thus a great many rapes that are nonreproductive.

5

Of course, not all biological adaptations are perfect, or apparent in every individual. Anorexics, for example, clearly contravene our evolutionary dictate to eat. Still, the large number of exceptions to what is proposed by Thornhill and Palmer as a direct adaptation is disturbing. The problem is that the authors never specify what percentage of rapes need be potentially reproductive to show that rape evolved. Fifty percent? Eighty percent? (Indeed, the vaginal-ejaculation data show that the proportion of "reproductive" rapes cannot exceed fifty percent; and this upper limit becomes even smaller if we include male victims.) As with most sociobiological arguments, apparently one need find only *some* level of concordance with prediction to consider a trait to be an evolutionary adaptation.

Faced with many clear cases of nonadaptive rapes, Thornhill and Palmer revert to their two fallback positions: the by-product hypothesis and special pleading about the different conditions of our evolutionary past. Thus, confronted by the annoying fact that some rapists have wealth and high status, the authors immediately invoke the by-product hypothesis: "Rape by men with high status and abundant resources may arise from a combination of impunity and the hypothetical adaptation pertaining to evaluation of a victim's vulnerability. If so, their raping must result from adaptations other than that suggested by the second hypothesis [direct adaptation]. . . ." (p. 68).

In this way, Thornhill and Palmer have constructed an airtight case, an argument that cannot be refuted. Aspects of rape that seem adaptive must have evolved by direct selection, while nonadaptive aspects are seen as evolutionary holdovers or by-products. Lawyers call this "arguing in the alternative." It is not science, but advocacy. And if many rapes can be written off as nonadaptive acts, why don't Thornhill and Palmer even consider the possibility that *all* rapes might be nonadaptive?

There is another difficulty that Thornhill and Palmer evade. For nearly all of their observations, there are reasonable alternative explanations that do not involve direct selection. As predicted by the direct-selection hypothesis, for example, rapists tend to be young men from lower socioeconomic classes, who supposedly have limited access to mates. (Thornhill and Palmer offer no evidence for this supposed correlation between class status and access to mates.) But poorer men are disproportionately represented among *all* violent criminals, including those committing murder, armed robbery, and assault. Why does this observation confirm the direct-selection hypothesis instead of the simpler view that deprived, angry males commit violent acts that could gain them reputation, sex, or money?

Similarly, women between the ages of 18 and 30 are over-represented as rape victims compared to older women, a trend predicted by the notion that rapists prefer fertile victims. But what is the relative vulnerability of women of different ages to being raped? Could they differ in their availability to men who would molest them, or in their relative tendency to report rape? Or could the mostly young rapists merely be finding victims within their easily accessed peer group?

Why, exactly, is rape "a horrendous experience for the victim?" Thornhill and Palmer have an answer: the loss of her ability to choose her mate or the possibility that the rape will alienate her existing mate. But this answer is not only offensive, it is also incoherent. Why not argue that *any* violation of the body is traumatic, with rape being the most extreme intrusion? Surely victims of *homosexual* rape do not walk away mentally unscathed. The reader may find it amusing, and not all that hard, to devise plausible alternatives for the other half-dozen observations that Thornhill and Palmer offer as proof of the direct-selection theory.

Thornhill and Palmer also cite earlier psychological studies that seem to support the direct-selection theory, but a trip to the library shows that the authors misrepresent at least some of this literature. Lacking the time to look up every citation, I decided to check three claims about rape taken from Thornhill's own earlier publications. I was shocked to find that none of these claims are supported by the cited articles.

According to Thornhill and Palmer, the literature shows that female rape victims of reproductive age suffer more trauma than do older and younger victims (this is an essential element of their argument, since they see rape trauma as a direct adaptation); that older and younger victims suffer less rape-inflicted violence than do reproductive-age women (the latter fight harder to protect their eggs, and males fight harder to fertilize them); and that, compared to either pre- or postreproductive victims, raped females of reproductive age experience a higher proportion of penile-vaginal intercourse (rapists can recognize fertile females). These three claims derive from a study of 790 rape victims examined at Philadelphia General Hospital in 1973 and 1974. The study was published by McCahill, Meyer, and Fischman (1979), and its data further analyzed in three papers by Thornhill and Nancy Thornhill, the latter an anthropologist and his former wife (Thornhill and Thornhill 1990a, b, 1991).

In the three publications by Thornhill and Thornhill, the data show that while younger women (under twelve years) do indeed experience less trauma, violence, and vaginal rape than do reproductive-age women between the ages of twelve and forty-four, *older women do not differ from reproductive-age females*. Thornhill and Palmer thus achieve their "supportive" results by statistical sleight of hand: they lump together younger and older women when comparing them to reproductive-age women, and the difference between these "reproductive" and nonreproductive" victims results entirely from the effect of the youngest age class. This improper combining of heterogeneous data allows the authors to state, misleadingly, that "the study showed that reproductive-age victims suffered significantly more psychological trauma than non-reproductive-age rape victims" (p. 90), and that "reproductive-age rape victims were more often subjected to violent attacks than victims in the other two categories" (p. 91).

These three "predictions," then, are supported by the one comparison (younger versus reproductive) but not by the other (older versus reproductive). The general claim for rape and trauma as adaptations is achieved only by fiddling with the data. This is not the way that scientists normally behave. Moreover, even the differences between the youngest class and the two older classes may be caused by phenomena other than natural selection. Lack of vaginal intercourse in younger victims, some of them babes in arms, may be due to mechanical problems. And in the trauma study, the reactions of young girls (from two months to eleven years old) were often measured in a bizarre way—by consulting third parties. As noted in Thornhill and Thornhill (1990a, p. 161): "the child's caretaker sometimes helped the child respond to interview questions, or with very young victims, the caretaker gave the responses to the questions based on his/her perception of the effect of the sexual assault on the child." Does anyone really believe that a third party can accurately judge the degree to which a young child suffers increased "insecurities concerning sexual attractiveness" or "fear of unknown men"? (These were two criteria used to measure trauma.) Is it possible that caretakers may consciously or unconsciously try to minimize the trauma suffered by young girls? Or that young girls—or women of any age—will show full trauma only after a period of time? (All victims were interviewed within *five days* of the rape.)

There are other problems with these cited studies, including the failure to apply standard statistical corrections that, when used, weaken the "supportive" results; but we need not go further. The studies discredit themselves. I emphasize again that these are the only bits of supporting "evidence" that I checked. Did I happen, by chance, to find the only three inaccurate citations in the book?[3]

Thornhill and Palmer can be very nasty about those who differ with their analysis, mainly sociologists and feminists. "[A]ccording to the assumptions of the social science explanation of rape," they write, "the problem of rape could be solved simply by teaching women that rape is a wonderful experience" (p. 152). Also, "because the evolutionary approach threatens the theories and approaches that have traditionally been used to study human behavior, it poses a serious threat to the status of those who have achieved success in their fields using non-evolutionary approaches" (p. 115). It appears that Thornhill and Palmer alone care about truth, and everyone else cares about status.

In fact, Thornhill and Palmer are accusing others of what are really their own failings: "Not only is the bulk of the social science literature of rape clearly indifferent to scientific standards; many of the studies exhibit overt hostility toward scientific approaches, and specifically toward biological approaches. The message of these studies is clearly political rather than scientific" (p. 148). It is Thornhill and Palmer who are guilty of indifference to scientific standards. They buttress strong claims with weak reasoning, weak data, and finagled statistics. Their book lacks the measured tone and the openness to alternative theories that characterize truly scientific work. (Compare their sledgehammer approach with the moderate tone of *On the Origin of Species*.) It is perfectly clear to any fair-minded reader of *A Natural History of Rape* that its objective is not to test whether rape is an adaptation, but to prove it. Their evolutionary-psychological explanation of rape is not their conclusion, but their premise.

6

By claiming that rape is a natural biological act, Thornhill and Palmer immediately lay themselves open to the accusation of making excuses for rapists. They repeatedly distance themselves from this accusation (who wouldn't?), properly claiming that to equate "natural" with "allowable" or "good" is a common error known as "the naturalistic fallacy." They add that evolved biological impulses should not be used in court as a defense of rapists, even though their own work has made such a defense possible.

But they do declare that social policies to eliminate rape will not work unless they take into account the crime's evolutionary origin. Their "evolutionarily informed" suggestions are either obvious and derivable from nonevolutionary views of rape (punish rapists more harshly, teach young men not to rape, urge women to avoid secluded spots), fatuous (build male and female summer camps farther apart, use chaperones early in a relationship), or invidious (counsel rape victims by telling them that their trauma is adaptive).

Thornhill and Palmer justify Darwinian anti-rape courses for men by noting (p. 154) that "individuals who really understood the evolutionary bases of their actions might be better able to avoid behaving in an 'adaptive' fashion that is damaging to others." Does anyone imagine that young men will be less inclined to rape when they hear that it is in their genes? Or that rape victims will be consoled by understanding the supposed evolutionary roots of their trauma and depression?

There is a curious two-valued logic in the idea that those who understand the evolutionary basis of a crime will be less likely to commit it. Such a belief implies that we can, by force of will, overcome our genetic legacy. As Thornhill and Palmer observe:

To the extent that knowledge about the causes of things becomes a part of the environment and increases our ability to change things, men who are made aware of the evolutionary reasons for their suspicions about their wives' or girlfriends' claims of rape should be in a better position to change their reactions to such claims. (p. 159)

But Thornhill and Palmer also believe that rapists are not stopped by knowing that their crime is both immoral and criminal—knowledge that is also "part of the environment." Why should knowing that rape is an adaptation be any different?

Thornhill and Palmer also claim that women in scanty dress are more likely to be raped, and should keep this risk in mind when picking their clothes (p. 181):

Young women should also be informed that female choice, over the course of the evolution of human sexuality, has produced men who will be quickly aroused by signals of a female's willingness to grant sexual access. . . . And it should be made clear that, although sexy clothing and promises of sexual access may be means of attracting desired males (Cashdan 1993), they may also attract undesired ones.

Of all the book's claims, this one has caused the most furor among women, feminist or otherwise. But the reader will search in vain for any evidence that showing more skin provokes more rape. The source of Thornhill and Palmer's advice on this point is a complete mystery.

This brings us to the largest question broached by this book. Can knowledge about evolution play a useful role in reforming society? I strongly doubt it. The best approach to stopping crime, for example, is likely to be the pragmatic one: do what works best, regardless of the crime's evolutionary underpinnings. Must we study the evolutionary basis of murder to deal effectively with it? Should we think about the evolution of greed when making antitrust laws?

A useful parallel may be drawn from medicine. Can understanding the evolutionary origin of a disease facilitate its cure? We know both the genetic and evolutionary roots of only one malady: sickle-cell anemia. The gene that causes this disease also helps to fight malaria, and thus sickle-cell anemia is common in residents of mosquito-infested areas of Africa (and in their black American relatives). But this knowledge is of absolutely no comfort to those suffering from the disease, and it has been of no use to physicians trying to cure it.[4]

While denouncing feminists and sociologists for their misguided and scientifically uninformed attempts to deal with rape, Thornhill and Palmer overlook the major improvements that these groups have made in legal and cultural attitudes toward rape. The dropping of the legal requirement for eyewitness corroboration of rape; the restriction on courtroom presentation of a victim's prior sexual history; the founding of rape crisis centers; the establishment of more compassionate attitudes toward victims by police, hospital staff, psychiatric counselors, and juries: All of these constructive policy changes were brought into being by (to use Thornhill and Palmer's phrase) "individuals uninformed by evolutionary theory."

Thornhill and Palmer's attempts to gain control of rape counseling, laws, and punishments, despite the weakness of their science, reveal their larger goal: the engulfment of social science and social policy by the great whale of evolutionary psychology. This attempted takeover is not new. It was first suggested in 1978 in E. O. Wilson's *On Human Nature*. More recently, in *Consilience*, Wilson extended the program to nearly every area of human thought, including aesthetics and ethics. We are witnessing a new campaign for the Darwinization of Everything. Thornhill and Palmer's theory of rape is just the most recent attempt at annexing all human experience to evolutionary psychology.

After all, if one can give a credible evolutionary explanation for the difficult problem of rape, then no human behavior is immune to such analysis, and the cause is significantly advanced. The apocalyptic tone pervading Thornhill and Palmer's book reveals the party to which they belong: "The biophobia that has led to the rejection of Darwinian analyses of human behavior is an intellectual disaster" (p. 122). And "in addressing the question of rape, the choice between the politically constructed answers of social science and the evidentiary answers of evolutionary biology is essentially a choice between ideology and knowledge" (Thornhill and Palmer 2000b, p. 36).

Let us be clear. It is not "biophobia" to reject the reduction of all human feelings and actions to evolution. Quite the contrary. It is biophilia; or at least a proper respect for science. The "choice between ideology and knowledge" is a real choice; but it is Thornhill, Palmer, and the doctrinaire evolutionary psychologists who choose ideology over knowledge. Unfortunately, they enjoy the advantage that people like scientific explanations for their behavior and the certainty that such explanations provide. Attributing our traumas and misdeeds to our savannah-dwelling ancestors lessens the moral pressure on our lives. And so the disciplinary hubris of evolutionary psychology and the longing for certainty of ordinary men and women have combined to create a scientific cargo cult, with everyone waiting in vain for evolutionary psychology to deliver the goods that it doesn't have.

Amid this debacle—for *A Natural History of Rape* is truly an embarrassment to the field—I am consoled by the parallels between evolutionary psychology and Freudianism. Freud's views lost credibility when people realized that they were not based on science, but were actually an ideological edifice, a myth about human life, that was utterly resistant to scientific refutation. By judicious manipulation, every possible observation of human behavior could be (and was) fitted into the Freudian framework. Evolutionary psychologists are now building a similar edifice. They, too, deal in dogmas rather than the propositions of science. Evolutionary psychology will have its day in the sun, but versions of the faith such as Thornhill and Palmer's will disappear when people realize that they are useless and unscientific.

Acknowledgments

This essay is a revision of a piece originally published in the *New Republic* (April 3, 2000). I thank Andrew Berry, Susan Brownmiller, and Anne Magurran for discussion and critique of the manuscript, and Leon Wieseltier for his perceptive editing of the original essay.

Notes

1. All unattributed quotes in the rest of this chapter are taken from *A Natural History of Rape*.

2. Jennifer Pozner discusses the media's sensationalistic and nonscientific treatment of the controversy in her (2000) article, "In rape debate, controversy trumps credibility."

3. At least one author of the original study by McCahill, Meyer, and Fischman (1979) has repudiated Thornhill and Palmer's conclusions. Linda Williams (formerly Linda Meyer) was interviewed by the *Chicago Tribune* about *A Natural History of Rape* ("A researcher blasts rape theory," by Jeremy Manier, Mar. 12, 2000, p. 4):

Moreover, the original survey was not intended to accurately record trauma levels among children, said Linda Williams, a sociologist who helped direct the study. "We did not have a clue that so many of the rape victims were going to be children and old ladies," said Williams, now a researcher at Wellesley College in Massachusetts. "This was 1973, remember. We still thought rape victims were almost all women of child-bearing age."

Likewise, Pozner (2000, p. 9) notes:

This alarm at Thornhill's misrepresentation of statistics is shared by Anthony Goldsmith, director of the Joseph Peters Institute (formerly the Center for Rape Concern), the group that conducted the 1973–74 research on rape victims. Describing Thornhill's claims about victims' varying rates of trauma as a "bad analysis of the data," Goldsmith told *Extra!*, "The research doesn't support what they claim, and that's bad science. It's not nice when our data is misused. I don't like it . . . particularly when it's used to support a theory that hinders the way we work with offenders."

4. Evolutionary biology may be useful in medicine by helping us understand the evolution of disease-causing organisms, as in cases of antibiotic resistance in bacteria. It is unlikely, however, that understanding the evolutionary basis of human genetic diseases will lead to new treatments.

References

Cashdan, E. (1993). Attracting mates: Effects of parental investment on mate attraction strategies. *Ethology and Sociobiology* 14: 1–24.

Manier, Jeremy (2000). A researcher blasts rape theory. *Chicago Tribune*, March 12, p. 4.

McCahill, T. W., L. C. Meyer, and A. M. Fischman (1979). *The Aftermath of Rape*. Lexington, Mass.: Heath.

Pozner, Jennifer (2000). In rape debate, controversy trumps credibility. *Extra!* 13: 8–10.

Thornhill, R. and C. T. Palmer (2000a). *A Natural History of Rape: Biological Bases of Sexual Coercion*. Cambridge, Mass.: MIT Press.

Thornhill, R. and C. T. Palmer. (2000b). Why men rape. *The Sciences* Jan./Feb.: 30–36.

Thornhill, R. and N. W. Thornhill. (1983). Human rape: An evolutionary analysis. *Ethology and Sociobiology* 4: 137–173.

Thornhill, N. W. and R. Thornhill (1990a). An evolutionary analysis of psychological pain following rape: I. The effects of victim's age and marital status. *Ethology and Sociobiology* 11: 155–176.

Thornhill, N. W. and R. Thornhill (1990b). An evolutionary analysis of psychological pain following rape: III. Effects of force and violence. *Aggressive Behavior* 16: 297–320.

Thornhill, N. W. and R. Thornhill (1991). An evolutionary analysis of psychological pain following human (*Homo sapiens*) rape: IV. The effect of the nature of the sexual assault. *Journal of Comparative Psychology* 105: 243–252.

al distress over rape than single women or menopausal women
192–193). The logic behind predictions (1) and (2) is that for
special adaptation you need to show it has reproductive con-
in this case by demonstrating that it is done primarily to
o could bear children as a result, and who were not so seri-
d by the forced impregnation that they died, miscarried, or
o defective offspring. Predictions (3) through (5) are based on
former wife Nancy Thornhill. Her thinking was that women's
distress should be greater the more rape had an impact on re-
interests. The link of these hypotheses to the special adapta-
is never explained, and they appear tangential.

h most of the documentation provided by Thornhill and Palmer
sects and birds, they also use standard social science data. They
eductions with secondary analysis of a data set originally pre-
McCahill, Meyer, and Fischman in the pioneering work *The Af-
Rape* (1979). The source of the data was rape survivors seeking
a Philadelphia emergency room. The authors fail to address po-
cerns with these data such as validity: How well were the con-
essed given data collection predated formulation of the theory?
urement of the constructs reliable and valid? Nor is generaliz-
rape survivors examined. It is certainly questionable given that
rcent of rape victims sought emergency room care according to
al survey conducted for the U.S. Department of Justice (Tjaden
nnes 1998).

esentation concludes with suggestions for rape prevention activ-
rnhill and Palmer confidently predict that any prevention effort
unless based on an understanding that rape evolved as a form of
roductive behavior. Their recommendations include: (1) educat-
that all men are potential rapists who must learn to inhibit their
mpulses; (2) sensitizing women to the biological proclivities of men
e role that women's apparel plays in triggering rape; (3) suggesting
nen should exert more control over the circumstances of dating,
g only in public places; and (4) providing a Darwinian perspec-
omen undergoing counseling to help them understand why they
essed about being raped.

8

Evolutionary Models of Why Men Rape: Acknowledging the Complexities

Mary P. Koss

Randy Thornhill and Craig Palmer's book *A Natural History of Rape: Biological Bases of Sexual Coercion* (2000a) sets up a stark contrast between evolutionary theory and "feminist theory" that performed perfectly its intended role as a media hook (for a summary of the book see Thornhill and Palmer 2000b). The authors have appeared on CNN, *Dateline,* and other television programs, as well as on National Public Radio, disseminating their position. Victim advocates, National Organization of Women officers, experts on evolutionary biology, and Susan Brownmiller herself rebutted. This media phenomenon was a sad incident for rape prevention advocates, evolutionary biology, and science itself. The framing of the issues by Thornhill and Palmer increased resistance to evolutionary analysis, ill represented the process of science, and encouraged harmful prevention suggestions. This commentary examines in more depth than permitted in the public media selected hypotheses, supporting evidence, and recommendations for rape prevention. The complexity of causal analysis of rape is highlighted, including the consensus of expert panels on violence against women that no theory emphasizing a single cause is adequate to explain why men rape, no matter what its ideology.

The Evolutionary Thesis

Not only do Thornhill and Palmer have some evolutionary ideas to advance, they want to do so on a battlefield. The authors frame their presentation as a battle of evolution versus the social sciences, likening those who reject a reproductive explanation for rape to right-wing fundamentalists. As Thornhill and Palmer see it, evolutionary biology is armed with a knowledge-based approach to the issues whereas social science mounts only an ideologically driven advance. They repeatedly put on the armor of science. The battle cries echoed repeatedly include: Science is value free. Science is the only road to the truth. Science has the answers. Science will win. Most of these sentiments are naive from the perspective of the social construction of science—no theory or measurement is free from shaping by the human mind. Paradigms guiding designs of studies are human creations and are well known for their resistance to change even in the face of compelling empirical data. And, as soon as statements about the meaning of results are made, numbers become subject to interpretation. As Moore and Travis note, "Biologically based science has the nice quality of disguising politics" (2000, p. 25). By cloaking themselves in science talk ("bio-proof"), Thornhill and Palmer aim to camouflage their unstated ideological agenda, deflect attention from the obvious flaws in their logic and supporting evidence, and inflate the importance of their own work. They succeed only in diminishing the stature of science and fueling anti-intellectualism by the public.

Now that we have examined the framing of the issues, let's inspect the evolutionary arguments themselves. Thornhill and Palmer's primary aim is to challenge the idea that rape is an expression of power, which they correctly identify as the prevailing view in the advocate community. The book actually presents two alternative hypotheses of human rape. The first is the idea that rape is a special adaptive strategy that human males have developed because it helps them to sire more offspring. The second is that rape is a by-product of male sexual desire and preference for higher numbers of sexual partners. The latter alternative is totally undeveloped and the entire text is designed to describe, support, and consider the implications of rape as a special adaptation. In so doing, Thornhill and Palmer commit the same error for which their work has already been taken to task by colleagues (e.g., Figueredo 1992). The peer review process is the best system yet devised to ensure that science moves forward and that bad ideas are separated from good ideas. Given the mantle of science the authors have gathered around them, it is surprising to see so little attention devoted to acknowledging and responding to peer criticism of which they have long been aware. Elaborating the by-product model would have been more palatable to the general public because its links with reproduction are more indirect and would have provided a basis for integration of feminist

---

thought about rape. But in the media w scholars fall prey to its lures. In the field this all before.

Grasping the gist of rape as a reproducti view of the principles of Darwinian natur succinctly summarize (1999, p. 44), "Th selection are not inherently sexist and si iduals vary; some variations are more fav variation is heritable; differential reproduc fering gene frequencies may result" (p. 44) views rape as one of three strategies that males find mates, gain sexual access, and genes. These strategies are possessing physi erful warrior, and when all else fails, rapin that men resort to rape when they cannot looks, wealth, or status. To the extent that by rape, any genes associated with raping a

A cornerstone of Thornhill and Palmer's tr ferential parental investment (Trivers 1972). animals differ in their parental effort. Male monogamous species, which leads to greate males and chosiness by females (Thornhill & Since the male's *minimum* investment in chi the egg, the parental investment theory state genes will be represented in future generati number of females. If they cannot obtain ma rape is better than leaving no offspring from

To support their model, Thornhill and Pa strategy, listing the predictions that logically purported supportive evidence. Some of the m hill and Palmer make about rape as a special a rape victims will be women of childbearing age not seriously injure their victims (p. 76); (3) ra more violence will suffer less emotional distre penetration will be more distressing than othe (5) married women and women of childbear-in

The Evidence

Disputing the "Facts"

Had each of the deductions been the subject of a peer-reviewed empirical paper, they would have been examined in the context of related findings from existing literature. Thornhill and Palmer make virtually no reference to other empirical findings on sexual assault that contradict their thesis. The bulk of available data makes fiction of the facts, thus eliminating all the data that the authors purport are supportive of their theory except their observations of insect and bird behavior.

Many Rape Victims Are Children, Not Women of Reproductive Age

Contrary to the assertion that rapists favor reproductive age women, The *Rape in America* national survey (Kilpatrick, Edmunds, and Seymour 1992) reported that exactly $1/3$ of victims were under 11 years old when first raped, and a total of $2/3$ were younger than 17. The National Violence Against Women survey reported that 22 percent of rape victims were under age 12 when first sexually assaulted, and 32 percent were between 12 and 17 years old. Even without taking into account data on rapes of post-menopausal women, men, and boys, these figures establish that a sizable number of rapes lack reproductive consequences.

Women of Childbearing Age Do Not Experience the Most Distress

The literature on the impact of sexual trauma fails to support a link of childbearing potential to distress. Instead, child sexual abuse is consistently associated with the most severe, broad, and long-lasting effects, including lifelong elevated risks of physical problems, emotional distress, and more unsafe health behaviors like smoking, excessive drinking, and lack of physical activity (see Saunders et al. 1999; Walker et al. 1999a; Walker et al. 1999b; for a review see Messman and Long 1996). In terms of greatest fear, the elderly suffer from rape the most (Muram, Miller, and Cutler 1992; Warr 1985).

Distress Does Not Vary Inversely with Rapist's Violence

The idea that less violence causes more distress is not only counterintuitive, it is at odds with the bulk of trauma literature. Recent nationwide studies established that the major predictors of posttraumatic stress disorder were objective severity of the violence inflicted, the subjective fear of death or serious injury, and whether penetration of the body occurred (Epstein, Saunders, and Kilpatrick 1997). Also important were how much a woman blamed herself for what happened, and how threatening to her worldview she saw the rape (Frazier 1990; Frazier and Schauben 1994; Norris and Kaniasty 1991; Koss, Figueredo, and Prince, in press). Most people intuitively understand these findings because they support the obvious: The harder you are hit, the more it hurts.

All Unwanted Penetration is Traumatic in Women of All Ages

Is vaginal rape, because of its potential for impregnation, more traumatic than other forms of penetration? This hypothesis is faulty on its face because it overlooks the invention of modern methods of birth control including postconception interventions that restore to women control over reproduction and render moot any selective advantage for rape. Even if this issue had the importance attributed to it by Thornhill and Palmer, there are several methodological obstacles that raise questions as to whether they or anyone else could establish that vaginal penetration is most distressing. Among the barriers to establishing a clear cut relationship are: (1) the meaning of different forms of penetration is culturally conditioned, precluding universal statements about how they would be viewed by the survivor; (2) many rapes may involve multiple forms of penetration thereby resisting categorization; and (3) the amount of injury caused by rape is highly significant and would need to be measured and controlled for before the relationship of distress and form of penetration could be disentangled. Current literature establishes that all unwanted penetration is traumatic. It may not really matter if a Chevy truck or a Ford truck hits you; in either case you are seriously harmed.

Although Rapists Rarely Kill, Life Threat Is High

Thornhill and Palmer conclude that rapists rarely harm their victims. This statement is somewhat true about half the picture. According to the *Rape in America* study, 28 percent of rapes involve some degree of physical injury. However, as we saw earlier, postassault impact is predicted not just by objective severity but also by subjective severity. Half of all women feared that they would be seriously harmed or killed during their rape.

Prevention Recommendations are Naive and Harmful

Although good scientific practice dictates not generalizing beyond the capability of the data, Thornhill and Palmer move from consideration of insects and lower animals to making recommendations for preventing human rape and treating rape survivors. They address prevention at the individual level of causation. Ignored is the need for prevention initiatives at broader societal levels. Even from their biological perspective, several societal-level strategies would be helpful, such as revamping the legal system to better deter rape by enforcing penalties for men who fail to restrain, or advocating legislation that would continue to guarantee women access to the means to control the outcomes of forced sexual contact. Bioprevention based on the flawed assumptions listed below will not solve the rape problem.

Men as Potential Rapists

One of the critical problems faced by those who design rape prevention education is backlash that results in male attendees leaving even more resentful and angry at women than they were prior to the program (Lonsway 1996). Thornhill and Palmer suggest that prevention programs for young men teach them about their biological propensities to rape and warn of the need to inhibit these impulses. In short, men should be taught that they are all potential rapists. Years of experience in rape prevention have taught me that this approach is not productive. Men vociferously challenge any presenter who fails to distinguish between rapists and regular guys who want emotional relationships with women who will eventually end up raising kids they love and invest in. Nor is the recommendation grounded in established fact. The jury is still out on men's potential to rape, even among evolutionary psychologists. When pushed, many who assert that all men are potential rapists limit their assertion to the moment of birth. From there on, the potential is shaped by social and environmental influences that render most men incapable of raping. This is similar to saying that all humans are potential killers at birth. Men differ greatly in the extent to which they are aroused by sexual aggression and in their self-reported likelihood they would force sex on a woman. Few men say they would rape even if guaranteed not to be caught or punished, and even with a softer wording about forcing a woman to have sex only a minority indicate any likelihood of sexual coercion (Malamuth and Dean 1991).

Thornhill and Palmer's suggestion that time in rape prevention should be spent explaining Darwinian theory is laughable from the practical perspective. Even when rape seminars are marketed as "How To Be a Better Lover" workshops, attendance by men is low and limited to the already converted. And, such material takes time away from more critical prevention targets, such as teaching how to get consent from a woman so that their advances are reciprocated and educating them about what acts constitute rape. For example, men need to know that having sex with a drunken woman, something commonly seen as a stroke of good luck, is actually rape under the law. And they need to know that adding a drug to her drink elevates the crime to an aggravated level with the harsh sentences typical of the country's war on drugs. Thornhill and Palmer's suggestion to focus on harsh penalties also isn't honest about actual judicial outcomes for date rape (Koss 2000; Koss, in press).

Women Should Dress to Avoid Rape . . . How?

How would you advise women to dress to avoid rape? There have been rapists who were acquitted because the victims dressed "provocatively" in a turtleneck sweater and a mid-calf skirt (Bublick 1999). Where would it end? The mindset behind this advice is not far from that of countries where women are required by law to dress in shapeless head-to-toe black bags with a mask and two slits for the eyes so as not to provoke sexual attack.

As Thornhill and Palmer see it, the capacity for women to avoid rape has been selected for because those female ancestors who reproduced most successfully were very distressed about rape, learned how to identify the circumstances that resulted in rape, and avoided them. The implication is that many women today know how to avoid rape but prevention programs are needed for those poor souls who don't. We are not told how these highly vulnerable women would be identified.

The entire premise is based on an empirically unfounded assumption that women can protect themselves from rape. In fact, there has been no success in separating those women who have and haven't been raped on the basis of routine activities, personalities, or beliefs. Although there have been isolated reports that women who drink in bars have a high rape rate (Parks and Miller 1997), longitudinal study has demonstrated that alcohol use is triggered by past victimization and does not predict future victimization (Kilpatrick et al. 1997). Furthermore, sexual assault is an exception to the rule in criminology that routine activities have some power to predict vulnerability to crime (Mustaine and Tewsbury 1998). To the extent that rape can be predicted, history of sexual abuse in childhood is the most prominent factor. But even sexual abuse fails the test of practical significance. Chance would allow 15 percent of rape victims to be predicted correctly, whereas child abuse increases the figure only to 19 percent (Abbey et al. 1996; Himelein 1995; Koss and Dinero 1989). Thus, it has not been for lack of study that no powerful correlates of vulnerability are known.

It is also hard to see how formulating an acquaintanceship would be a protection against rape. Fully 86 percent of rape victims knew the man who raped them, and 20 percent of ever married women have been raped by a spouse (Bergen 1996; Browne 1993; Tjaden and Thoennes 1998). Furthermore, socializing in public places isn't going to eliminate rape. Among women raped by nonstrangers, the U.S. Department of Justice (Bureau of Justice Statistics (1997) reported that 32 percent of rapes occurred in the street or in a restaurant or bar, commercial building, parking lot, school, park, or playground (these figures are virtually identical to those for women raped by strangers). Giving up going out at night won't help either—30 percent of rapes happened in the daytime. The most scientifically appropriate reading of the data is that rape is predictable only on the grounds of being female and the best protection would be avoiding all men including family members.

Advice on women's dress and conduct should be rejected not only because it is unscientific, but also because of its tacit assumption that women have a responsibility to act "reasonably" and live their lives in fear of rape. This thinking is absolutely unacceptable in a democratic society. Because rape is a gendered crime, such recommendations harm equality by infringing more on women's liberties than men's. "Women citizens have a legal entitlement to act on a day-to-day basis on the premise that others will not intentionally rape them" (Bublick 1999, p. 1443). The U.S. Constitution guarantees freedom of movement, a right to travel, a right of locomotion, and a right to associate with others. In other words, women have the right to use public transportation, travel geographically, socialize with whom they choose, and express themselves through their dress in anyway they find comfortable that doesn't violate public decency laws. If as a society we are to have a citizen duty to take reasonable steps to avoid crime, the steps should be the same for sex crimes as other crimes, and by extension, the same for men as for women.

Problems with Bioprevention

From a public policy perspective, conceptualizing rape largely as a biological issue reframes it as "A problem to be punished but still expected in certain unavoidable numbers of occurrences, rather than as social problem with the possibility of social remediation" (Moore and Travis 1999, p. 47). The work becomes misguided "When the biology of sexual reproduction is taken as a general template or justification for a wide range of stereotypic gender role behaviors, often producing prescriptions for behavior that limit individual opportunity and choice" (Moore and Travis 1999, p. 50). Biologically based public policy recommendations in the area of rape are downright scary. Jones (1999) has analyzed a number of possible policy outcomes, which include: (1) performing chemical castration as the penalty for rape; (2) varying punishments for rape by the age of the victim with lesser penalties for older women as they are purportedly less traumatized; (3) having male judges refrain from making judgments on rape owing to inherent sex differences that render them incapable of making assessments of female psychology; (4) repealing of the Violence Against Women Act of 1994 on the grounds that gender animus as a motivation for rape is inconsistent with biological models; (5) legalizing prostitution to make "voluntary" sex partners available to men; and (6) using evolutionary material on relative harm by form of penetration, amount of violence, and age of victim to set damages in civil trials.

Conceptualizing rape as a sex act alone ignores that it is a serious crime where the penis is used as a weapon. Clearly a man is not engaging in a sex act when he screams "You know you like this Bitch" while penetrating a woman and forcefully restraining her. The force behind the criminal act of rape is a mixture of sexual motives and motives to control/dominate/ punish that vary in degree from case to case. My example would be low in sexual motives. Some date rapes might provide scenarios for rapes in which sexual motives appear more prominently. The important semantic distinction is that rape is not a sex act, it is a crime that can be impelled by sexual motives. Acknowledging this mixture of motives is not new. In a 1991 review, Barbaree and Marshall concluded that rape is best defined as an integration of both components and that learning how sex and aggressive elements interact will advance the field.

Dismissing One-Factor Theories

As a one-factor, one-level theory, the model of rape as a special adaptation implicates a single set of causes that reside within individuals. Rape long ago proved itself too complex to yield to such simplistic thinking. And, although cloaked in biology, individual-level evolutionary analysis is also out of step with modern biology's focus on more complex issues, such as evolution of a successful adaptation between a species and its environment and survival of the group and the species (Hyde and Oliver 2000). It is widely accepted that sexual assault is influenced by causes at multiple levels that range from the broader society through institutions such as the media and religion, the family, peer group, intimate relationships, and ultimately by features interior to each individual.

Researchers have demonstrated the links of sexual aggression to heredity, physiology, neurophysiology, social learning, gender schemas, sexual scripts, personality traits, attitudes regarding rape, power and sex motives, and alcohol as causes of rape interior to the individual. At the dyadic level, studies have examined contextual features of relationships such as communication styles, the type and stages of relationships, and features that may render women more vulnerable to sexual predation. Institutional influences that have been linked to rape include family, school, athletic teams, religion, and media promotion of sex role stereotypes that teach or reinforce female and male role imbalances, favor impersonal sex, downplay the seriousness of violence against women, and fail to present successful alternatives to male aggression (see Crowell and Burgess 1996 for a review).

Evolutionary influences have been acknowledged as part of a comprehensive model of rape by panels of experts such as the National Academy of Science Panel on Violence Against Women (Crowell and Burgess 1996) and the American Psychological Association Taskforce on Male Violence Against Women (Koss et al. 1994). Those who wish to learn how evolutionary concepts can be integrated in a model that also addresses environmental and social causation are referred to the work of Neil Malamuth and colleagues (Malamuth, 1998; Malamuth et al. 1995; also see Heise

1998). Alone, biological explanations will not solve social problems because people cannot change their evolutionary history. However, a conceptualization of biological influences not as hardwiring but as potential pathways that are shaped by the environment can lead to research with practical implications. Viewing men as inherently rapacious is hopeless. On the other hand, knowing how harsh environments, lack of secure attachments, or social learning favor the development of promiscuous male sexuality sets a prevention agenda.

Conclusions

Evolutionary psychologists must be pulling their hair out over Thornhill and Palmer's book. Having recently changed the name of their field from sociobiology, they must hope this is a perfect time to show the public the new face of evolutionary psychology: Instead, they find the spotlight grabbed by a work that is offensive, scientifically flawed, misguided, reckless, and unreflective of the field's contributions to knowledge. It will be much harder now in many quarters to advocate for the explanatory role of evolutionary factors in violence against women. This is unfortunate because scholars on sexual assault, like most scientifically oriented people, place themselves somewhere in the evolutionary camp regarding the origins of human behavior.

Acknowledgments

The author may be contacted at 1632 E. Lester St., Tucson, AZ 85719. (520)626.9511 (V). (520)626.9515 (F), and electronic mail: mpk@ u.arizona.edu.

Deepest appreciation is expressed to Aurelio José Figueredo and Patricia Rozée for their comments on earlier drafts and sharing their expertise in the development of this essay.

References

Abbey, A., L. Thomson-Ross, D. McDuffie, and P. McAuslan (1996). Alcohol and dating risk factors for sexual assault among college women. *Psychology of Women Quarterly* 20: 147–169.

Barbaree, H. E. and W. L. Marshall (1991). The role of male sexual arousal in rape: Six models. *Journal of Consulting and Clinical Psychology* 59: 621–630.

Bergen, R. K. (1996). *Wife Rape: Understanding the Response of Survivors and Service Providers.* Newbury Park, Calif.: Sage Publications.

Browne, A. (1993). Violence against women by male partners: Prevalence, outcomes, and policy implications. *American Psychologist* 48: 1077–1087.

Boudreaux, E., D. G. Kilpatrick, H. S. Resnick, C. L. Best, and B. E. Saunders (1998). Criminal victimization, posttraumatic stress disorder, and co-morbid psychopathology among a community sample of women. *Journal of Traumatic Stress* 11: 665–678.

Bublick, E. M. (1999). Citizen no duty rules: Rape victims and comparative fault. *Columbia Law Review* 99: 1413–1490.

Bureau of Justice Statistics (1997). Criminal victimization in the United States, 1994. NCJ-162126. Washington, D.C.: U.S. Government Printing Office.

Crowell, N. A., and A. W. Burgess, eds. (1996). *Understanding Violence against Women.* Panel on Research on Violence Against Women, National Research Council. Washington, D.C.: National Academy Press.

Epstein, J. N., B. E. Saunders, and D. G. Kilpatrick (1997). Predicting PTSD in women with a history of childhood rape. *Journal of Traumatic Stress* 10: 573–588.

Figueredo, A. J. (1992). Does rape equal sex plus violence? *Behavioral and Brain Sciences* 15: 384–385.

Frazier, P. (1990). Victim attributions and postrape trauma. *Journal of Personality and Social Psychology* 59: 298–304.

Frazier, P. and L. Schauben (1994). Causal attributions and recovery from rape and other stressful life events. *Journal of Social and Clinical Psychology* 14: 1–14.

Heise, L. L. (1998). Violence against women: An integrated, ecological framework. *Violence against Women* 4: 262–290.

Heise, L., M. Ellsberg, and M. Gottemoeller (1999). Ending violence against women. *Population Reports, Issues in World Health* 27 (series 50, no. 11), December, 1–44.

Himelein, M. J. (1995). Risk factors for sexual victimization in dating: A longitudinal study of college women. *Psychology of Women Quarterly* 19: 31–48.

Hyde, J. S. and M. B. Oliver (2000). Gender differences in sexuality: Results from meta-analysis. In J. G. White and C. B. Travis, eds., *Sexuality, Society, and Feminism*, pp. 57–77. Washington, D.C.: American Psychological Press.

Jones, O. D. (1999). Sex, culture, and the biology of rape: Toward explanation and prevention. *California Law Review* 87: 827–909.

Kilpatrick, D. G., C. N. Edmunds, and A. Seymour (1992). *Rape in America: A Report to the Nation.* Arlington, Va.: National Victim Center.

Kilpatrick, D. G., R. Acierno, H. S. Resnick, B. E. Saunders, and C. L. Best (1997). A 2-year longitudinal study of the relationships between violent assault and substance use in women. *Journal of Consulting and Clinical Psychology* 65: 834–847.

Koss, M. P. (2000). Shame, blame, and community: Justice responses to violence against women. *American Psychologist* 55: 1332–1343.

Koss, M. P. (in press). Restorative justice for sexual violence: Repairing victims, building community, and holding offenders accountable. In R. Prentky and A. Burgess, eds., *Understanding and Managing Sexual Coercion.* New York: New York Academy of Sciences.

Koss, M. P. and T. E. Dinero (1989). Discriminate analysis of risk factors for sexual victimization among a national sample of college women. *Journal of Consulting and Clinical Psychology* 57: 242–250.

Koss, M. P., A. J. Figueredo, and R. J. Prince (2002). Cognitive mediation of rape's mental, physical, and social health impact: Tests of four models in cross-sectional data. *Journal of Consulting and Clinical Psychology* 70.

Koss, M. P., L. A. Goodman, A. Browne, L. F. Fitzgerald, G. P. Keita, and N. F. Russo (1994). *No Safe Haven: Male Violence against Women at Home, at Work, and in the Community.* Washington, D.C.: American Psychological Press.

Lonsway, K. A. (1996). Preventing acquaintance rape through education: What do we know? *Psychology of Women Quarterly* 20: 229–265.

Malamuth, N. M. (1998). An evolutionary-based model integrating research on the characteristics of sexually coercive men. In R. C. Geen and E. Donnerstein, eds., *Human Aggression: Theories, Research, and Implications for Social Policy,* pp. 229–245. San Diego, Calif.: Academic Press.

Malamuth, N. M. and K. Dean (1991). Attraction to sexual aggression. In A. Parrot and L. Bechofer, eds., *Acquaintance Rape: The Hidden Crime,* pp. 229–248. New York: Wiley.

Malamuth, N. M., D. Linz, C. L. Heavey, G. Barnes, and M. Acker (1995). Using the confluence model of sexual aggression to predict men's conflict with women: A 10-year follow-up study. *Journal of Personality and Social Psychology* 69: 353–369.

McCahill, T. W., L. C. Meyer, and A. M. Fischman. (1979). *The Aftermath of Rape.* Lexington, Mass.: D.C. Heath.

Messman, T. L. and P. J. Long (1996). Child sexual abuse and its relationship to revictimization in adult women: A review. *Clinical Psychology Review* 16(5): 307–420.

Moore, D. S. and C. B. Travis (2000). Biological models and sexual politics. In J. G. White and C. B. Travis, eds., *Sexuality, Society, and Feminism,* pp. 35–56. Washington, D.C.: American Psychological Press.

Muram, D., K. Miller, and A. Cutler (1992). Sexual assault of the elderly victim. *Journal of Interpersonal Violence* 7: 70–77.

Mustaine, E. E. and R. Tewksbury (1998). Victimization risks at leisure: A gender-specific analysis. *Violence and Victims* 13: 231–24x.

Norris, F. H. and K. Kaniasty (1991). The psychological experience of crime: A test of the mediating role of beliefs in explaining the distress of victims. *Journal of Social and Clinical Psychology,* 239–261.

Parks, K. A. and B. A. Miller (1997). Bar victimization of women. *Psychology of Women Quarterly* 21: 509–525.

Saunders, B. E., D. G. Kilpatrick, R. F. Hanson, H. S. Resnick, and M. E. Walker (1999). Prevalence, case characteristics, and long-term psychological correlates of child rape among women: A national survey. *Child Maltreatment: Journal of the American Professional Society on the Abuse of Children* 4: 187–200.

Thornhill, R. and C. T. Palmer (2000a). *A Natural History of Rape: Biological Bases of Sexual Coercion.* Cambridge, Mass.: MIT Press.

Thornhill, R. and C. T. Palmer (2000b). Why men rape: Prevention efforts will founder until they are based on the understanding that rape evolved as a form of male reproductive behavior. *The Sciences* (January/February): 30–36.

Trivers, R. L. (1972). Parental investment and sexual selection. In B. Campbell, ed., *Sexual Selection and the Decent of Man, 1871–1971,* pp. 136–179. Chicago: Aldine.

Tjaden, P. and N. Thoennes (1998). Prevalence, incidence, and consequences of violence against women: Findings from the National Violence Against Women Survey. National Institute of Justice Centers for Disease Control and Prevention Research in Brief, November, 1–16.

Walker, E. A., A. Gelfand, W. Katon, M. P. Koss, M. VonKorff, D. Bernstein, and J. Russo (1999). Adult health status of women HMO members with histories of childhood abuse and neglect. *American Journal of Medicine* 107: 332–339.

Walker, E. A., J. Unutzer, C. Rutter, A. Gelfand, K. Saunders, M. VonKorff, M. P. Koss, and W. Katon (1999). Costs of health care use by women HMO members with a history of childhood abuse and neglect. *Archives of General Psychiatry* 56: 609–613.

Warr, M. (1985). Fear of rape among urban women. *Social Problems* 32: 239–250.

9

Theory and Data on Rape and Evolution

Cheryl Brown Travis

The general thesis of Randy Thornhill and Craig Palmer in *A Natural History of Rape: Biological Bases of Sexual Coercion* is that there is an adaptive genetic basis for rape that evolved through natural selection. They do not in any way condone rape; in fact, they spend some time to denounce it and to acknowledge its psychologically painful consequences. Their argument is that unless we acknowledge the evolutionary and genetic basis for rape, we cannot hope to contain it. They acknowledge that cultural factors are relevant for the control of rape. However, the suggestions they offer to limit rape are simplistic and suspiciously reminiscent of patriarchal "protection" of women. While they accept that culture has a role in the causes of rape, they believe that the best way to understand culture and rape is through evolutionary theory.

A Natural History of Rape is especially objectionable because it distorts evolutionary theory as a basis for rape and by doing so disguises issues of social power and privilege that might provide a more comprehensive and useful approach to containing rape. The book represents one of many publications that play into the cultural desire to be reassured of fundamental and categorical differences between women and men. As such, it is part of a larger social construction of gender politics. It sells and is "news" because the thesis of the book plays a confirmatory role in cultural models about fundamental, and "natural," sex differences.

Thornhill and Palmer offer two possibilities for the evolutionary basis of rape. They do not advance one hypothesis conclusively over the other and indicate that they are in some disagreement among themselves regarding which is the more compelling hypothesis. One option is that rape is a by-product of another adaptation. The other option they offer is that rape is an adaptive reproductive strategy evolved directly through natural selection pressures and consequences specific to rape.

Rape as a By-product

Thornhill and Palmer's best guess for the by-product option is that men are just naturally highly sexed. The sexy by-product hypothesis argues that having a high and relatively indiscriminant sex drive is advantageous, to males, because the more sex males have the more successful they will be in reproducing and raising their overall fitness. They argue that "Sexual stimulation is a proximate cause of raping and is *the common denominator across rapes of all kinds.* Men's sexual motivation is an ultimate product of selection pressures in human evolutionary history" (*Albuquerque Times,* July 7, 2000, emphasis added). As support for the by-product hypothesis, Thornhill and Palmer note the highly sexed nature of males. Rape is a by-product of this hyper sexuality. They point out that males are more easily aroused, more often aroused, more desirous of sexual variety, less discriminating about sexual partners, have a reduced ability to abstain from sexual activity, and have a greater willingness to engage in casual sex. This leads to more sex acts. The more sex men have, the more offspring they will have, and the more offspring, the more fitness they attain. According to this model, females do not benefit in the same degree from lots of sex with lots of partners and therefore are reluctant to participate. This difference of interest is seen to be fundamental and in part underlies the battle of the sexes where reproductive strategy is concerned. The general argument is based on parental investment theory (Trivers 1972).

Differing levels of parental investment are often cited as a fundamental basis for conflict between the sexes. The bottom line is that optimal mating strategies for males are not equivalent to those of females. Richard Dawkins summarized the situation: "The female sex is exploited, and the fundamental evolutionary basis for the exploitation is the fact that eggs are larger than sperms" (1976, p. 158). Thornhill and Palmer rely heavily on the tenets of parental investment theory in their depiction of rape as part of an exploitative male-female dynamic.

An assumption of this model is that males have little to lose and, equally important, *little to gain* by being selective or choosy. According to the theory, one female is as good as another, so there was no natural selective pressure on males to be choosy or to spend much time assessing females as potential mates. That is, all females have about the same reproductive potential. Therefore, males have little to lose in acting indiscriminately, even rashly. Carey Yeager and I have critiqued this model more fully elsewhere (Travis and Yeager 1991).

The fact is that primate females do vary considerably in their reproductive efficacy and it would be to any male's advantage to pay attention to these individual differences among females. Among nonhuman primates, compared to low-ranking females, high-ranking females are more consistent in producing offspring that actually survive year to year. This may be the result of an increased number of anovulatory cycles in low ranking females (Chapais 1983). There can be as much as a sixfold difference in the reproductive success of individual females (Casebolt, Henrickson, and Hird 1985). The reproductive success of certain females may also be passed along to their offspring in the form of social rank. This kind of variation among females is biologically important to a male, because it is likely that he will have to establish a breeding territory or will have to take risks in contests with competitor males. In a random, opportunistic approach to mating, the male may be forgoing opportunities to mate with the most fecund females. All of this involves time, energy, and forgone opportunity and constitutes costs or investments that must be weighed against any potential gains. Mating and reproductive strategies that reduce overall investment costs or that offer a higher return on investments are likely to prevail.

The oversexed by-product proposition for rape further suggests that it was relatively easy for males to abandon one female and *find another.* Maynard Smith (1977) points out that desertion works as an adaptive strategy only so long as certain conditions are met. First, males face the nontrivial task of finding another fertile female and doing so without in the process being eaten, injured, or otherwise depleted. Remember that among early humans, most fertile females would be affiliated with a more or less stable family group constellation, and for most of the time these females would be pregnant or nonfertile owing to lactation. Thus, the overall effort required to secure another female might be considerable and in any case have a relatively low probability of success. Recent evidence also suggests that sperm may not be as energetically cheap as previously thought and that there are some biological limits on success through multiple mating. Among feral sheep, dominant rams may reach a point where they lose out to subordinate rams because they suffer sperm depletion over the period of the rut (Preston et al. 2001).

Conceptual Bias in the By-product Option

Along with observations about rape, Thornhill and Palmer make use of a biological view of sexuality. In their framework, sexuality is a universal biological process derived from evolution and rooted in anatomy. It is an energy system located inside the individual. Critiques of this general understanding of sexuality and of conventional sex research are available elsewhere by Mary Boyle (1994) and Leonore Tiefer (1995, 2000). Alternative frameworks (White, Bondurant, and Travis 2000) view human sexuality as interactive and emergent, something that is created in the moment, and something that is understood and experienced as a function of social constructions.

In addition to problems in their basic conceptualization of sexuality, there are a host of confounding variables ignored or dismissed by Thornhill and Palmer. For example, there are a number of confounds that undermine their idea that rape has evolved largely as a side effect of hyper sexuality in males. This line of reasoning includes an implicit proposition that men are less able than are women to abstain from sexual activity, that is, men are not fully able to control their sexual behavior.

However, it is not the case that men are unable to control their sexual behavior. Most men are perfectly able to contain their sexual inclinations (if any) when it is to their advantage to do so. This is especially true when there is high risk, such as a high probability of being caught or when being caught (even if infrequently) involves a very high cost. Male self-control, like female self-control, is largely dependent, not on evolution, but on context and social structural conditions of power. If we observe that males are less likely to restrain their sexual impulses, it is most readily explained by the probabilities associated with potential risks and gains in the immediate context.

Evidentiary requirements have also been bypassed in the rape-evolution account. Even if all the assertions about hyper-sexed males were accurate, one would have to question whether other explanations might not account for the same observations. As long as different theories forecast or account for the same behavior, the mere existence of the behavior cannot be taken as confirmation of any one theory over the others. One such piece of supporting evidence is that men report being more comfortable with the idea of casual sex with a stranger. Thornhill and Palmer offer this as proof of the hyper sexuality of men and implicitly locate this reported inclination in the natural, universal biological realm of evolution. However, the mere existence among men of greater comfort with casual sex is not significant support for the rape as by-product idea, because social structural considerations provide a viable alternative account for the same behavior. Research findings of greater male inclinations toward casual sex may reflect a variety of social, rather than biological, conditions. For example, society is more tolerant of such behavior among males and in fact encourages it. It is part of our cultural idea of masculinity. In addition, males may report more likelihood of engaging in casual sex, because they assume they can physically protect themselves if necessary. Further, what males report about hypothetical events may have more to say about their willingness to endorse traditional gender role ideology than it says about their actual behavior. Moreover, casual sex is not rape. That men may be more willing than women to engage in casual sexual encounters does not mean they are likely to engage in rape.

Rape as a By-product of Desire

The most fundamental error made by Thornhill and Palmer is to characterize rape as largely an act of desire. The proposition that sexual motivation is the common denominator of all rape was debunked by feminists decades ago. Some of the relevant arguments and data were elaborated in the 1975 foundational work of Susan Brownmiller (*Against Our Will*). Aggression, intimidation, and violence are the major dynamics of rape. Sexual arousal may or may not be salient, and in any case may be a by-product of aggression and violence rather than a precursor. Neil Malamuth (who is not adverse to evolutionary approaches) and his colleagues have found that sexualized violence against women is in fact linked to violence and aggression in general (Malamuth 1983; Malamuth, Haber, and Feshback 1980). This research found that exposure to media images of aggressive sex, not simply erotic sexuality, increases the likelihood of aggressiveness in laboratory experiments and increases in the self-reported likelihood of sexualized violence. The violent nature of sexual assault is further evidenced by the fact that many victims report that they thought they might be murdered or maimed. Lingering fears and anxiety following rape are clearly based on a sense of physical vulnerability and a lack of safety that are prompted by the violence inherent in such assaults. Even if serious physical wounds are not inflicted, the potential of brutality is a form of violence and is a kind of personalized terrorism.

In any case, it's not entirely clear that Thornhill and Palmer wish to fully endorse the hypothesis of sexual pleasure as the single most important motivation for rape. Regardless of the proximate factors underlying rape, the evolutionary principles for natural selection must at some point be activated, that is, the principle of increased fitness. The alternative hypothesis they offer is that rape is an adaptive reproductive strategy evolved through direct natural selection and is retained in the gene pool because males who rape have increased biological fitness.

Rape as Reproduction

The second proposition Thornhill and Palmer make is that rape could be a product of direct natural selection acting directly on rape as a reproductive strategy. A key requirement for the natural selection of any attribute or behavior is that it must result in a net reproductive benefit to those individuals that express the attribute. Rapists must beget offspring fairly consistently through their acts of rape. Additionally, if rape is a specific adaptation that adds to inclusive fitness, individuals who rape must differ genetically from those who do not rape and there must be differential reproductive success for individuals with a genetic propensity to rape. Both of these are necessary requirements for support of the hypothesis. Thornhill and Palmer provide no evidence on these points.

Who Are the Rapists?

So who are these genetic rapists? Thornhill and Palmer give a general description of rapists as those who do not otherwise have access to normal reproductive options. This is the "limited access" feature of rapists. There are two kinds of individuals that might fit this "limited access" condition, young individuals of junior standing and societal misfits who are simply lacking in social skill or merit. Further, for rape to be an evolutionarily based adaptation, rapists should differ genetically from the nonrapists *in the same category*, that is, the category of youths or of misfits. Some youths have rape genes and some do not. Some misfits have rape genes and some do not. Supposedly those youths that express their rape genes in rape behavior have greater lifetime inclusive fitness than those youths that do not have the rape gene(s). Ditto for the misfits.

Marginal misfits might be ostracized or disregarded owing to their poverty, poor social skills, and so on, or perhaps they are a kind of scurrilous criminal element. They would rape because they would have only limited access to other channels of courtship and mating (Frankie and Johnny and Bonnie and Clyde notwithstanding). The implication of the rape as reproduction argument is that members of these marginalized groups differ genetically from members of mainstream society, who supposedly don't need to resort to rape. Arguments about the genetic basis for social class and criminal behavior have been advanced in the past to justify political and social inequities. This is called social Darwinism. However, lack of education, poverty, and so on are not genetic conditions, but rather matters of sociology, economics, and politics. In contrast to this "limited access" view, there is plenty of evidence to indicate that ordinary men, including men of high standing and power, engage in rape.

The other set of rapist candidates includes young males in junior standing who have limited access. The idea would be that it is to the advantage of junior males to sneak copulations and thus to extend their breeding years. It is important to note that sneaky copulations are not the same thing as rape. In fact, it's not entirely clear who is doing the sneaking. Field studies of primates indicate that females often are the ones to initiate sexual interplay (Hrdy 1977; Smuts 1985). Among humans, young males who regularly relied on violence and forcible rape (or who engaged in *any* behavior that consistently disrupted the social network of the group) probably would achieve only limited integration into the community. Disruptive youth would be more often shunned or expelled than they would be embraced by the larger group, and two or three years as a promiscuous young rogue could hardly compensate for decades as a fully integrated adult. Short-term benefits would be exchanged for long-term adult opportunities.

Pregnancy Rates

If rape is a reproductive strategy it must result in pregnancies. This requires the consistent and successful operation of some basic mechanics. These include penile-vaginal penetration and the ejaculation of viable sperm in sufficient number to offer a better than average likelihood of insemination and conception. Thornhill and Palmer suggest that if rape were a specific adaptation (with differential reproductive success), there should be more sperm produced in ejaculates associated with rape (p. 74). They infer that appropriate data are not available to test this hypothesis. However, relevant data do exist. Data indicate that rapists often do not have erections, fail to penetrate the vagina, or do not ejaculate. Medical studies report that these problems occur in 30 to 40 percent of cases (Bownes and O'Gorman 1991, Hook, Elliot, and Harbison 1992). During medical examination, traces of sperm may be found in only 50 percent of rape cases (Ferris and Sandercock 1998). Case reports note that rapists often have one or more of sexual dysfunctions and that these dysfunctions may precipitate additional violence, degradation, and brutalization of the victim (Groth and Burgess 1977).

Furthermore, Thornhill and Palmer propose the evolution of rape as reproduction with little or no attention to the co-evolution of female reproductive strategies. It is as if females did not evolve at all. Drea and Wallen, in this volume, discuss the active female role in the shaping of sex and reproduction. Thornhill and Palmer seem to ignore the fact that in a sexually reproducing species it is difficult for one sex to evolve any strategy that seriously impairs or limits the well being or fitness of the other sex.

For rape to be a successful reproductive strategy, a rape pregnancy must occur and be successfully carried to term. This means that the female must be ovulating (at most a 4–5 day window in a monthly cycle), the egg must be fertilized, the fertilized blastocyte must implant in the uterus, and so on. Spontaneous abortion or the use of natural abortifacients would have constituted another barrier to reproductive goals of the rapist. The estimate by Thornhill and Palmer is that pregnancy occurs in approximately 2 percent of rapes. Despite these barriers, Thornhill and Palmer argue that reproduction is, or has been, a significant outcome of rape. Remember, in addition, that genetic fitness is advanced not only by having immediate offspring, but by having offspring who themselves reproduce.

Thornhill and Palmer argue that a reproductive function can be inferred because rapists choose to rape young women of reproductive age. It is more likely the case that rapists rape those who are most often in situations where rape is possible. Thus, the age distribution may reflect opportunity rather than choice. Rapists also choose to rape adult women who are not fertile and choose young girls as well as boys and men as their targets. A third of all cases of rape perpetrated by a family member involve children under age 12 (FBI 1998). A national study of the Bureau of Justice Statistics found that one third of all emergency department (ED) cases of violence involving patients under age 12 were admitted for completed or suspected rape or sexual assault (Rand and Strom 1997). There are plenty of other instances where rape occurs when reproductive interests would not be served, for example gang rapes and rapes of men. Rapes during social upheaval and war often involve the brutal maiming or killing of victims. Rape is practiced in wars of ethnic cleansing, and one would hardly think that racial purists are motivated to rape as a reproduction strategy.

The Cost/Benefit Ratio

One must ask after all what general costs and risks are incurred in the effort to get this supposed 2 percent reproductive return. It seems unlikely that a dedicated strategy of rape as reproduction or even rape as a by-product of hyper sexuality would have produced a positive cost benefit ratio. We're talking about risks, contingencies, and benefits as they would have existed a long time ago, sometimes referred to as the environment of evolutionary adaptedness. One might pick roughly 100,000 years ago at the beginning of the last major ice age, which imposed significant selection pressures. Alternatively, one might settle on a more recent period dating back only 14,000 years ago when the last ice age began to thaw out. For any of these time periods, it's pretty clear that finding and subduing an unwilling victim involves a number of risks. Humans lived most successfully in groups, at least somewhat sociable and collaborative. Individuals who committed egregious violations of community interests would surely have been harassed, shunned, or driven out. Remember this is a time before there were formal court systems or prisons. Violators might be killed outright, or expelled, where being expelled might well have amounted to a death sentence. If instead the rapist treks to the locale of another band in order to reproduce through rape, he risks the travails of any wilderness journey. He must get there and back without becoming a prey item himself. In addition, he may be hunted and killed by members of the other band.

Surviving Offspring

For rape to be a successful reproductive strategy, rape not only must result in pregnancies, but the offspring must survive to produce offspring. The offspring that are products of rape must fare well. They must be nourished and protected to the same degree and intensity as other offspring. They must additionally be integrated and welcomed into the social group with the same opportunities and acceptance of other offspring. They must be viewed as good partners in all the basic aspects of community life, including and most importantly as potential mates. Since rapists abandon any offspring produced through rape, how might these conditions be met? One of two conditions must prevail. One option is that surrogate fathers might readily be found to provide for a child what the rapist does not. Alternatively, the conditions for thriving offspring could be met if one assumes that the contributions of a father are more or less irrelevant.

The first set of conditions requires the support and investment of male caretakers other than the biological father. The probability seems slim that such providers could be readily recruited, and that fatherly contributions would be forthcoming. Sons or brothers might have an interest in providing these contributions, but since they would have lower genetic relatedness they would also have less vested interest than a biological father. Alternatively, replacement of fatherly contributions could be obtained if surrogates could be easily and consistently deceived about paternity. Such deception may be successfully practiced on occasion, but it appears to have limited potential. Thornhill and Palmer themselves point out that evolution has operated to guard against male investment in offspring fathered by other males. Thus, it seems problematic that offspring of rapists consistently would receive the needed nurturing, protection, and social integration.

Perhaps after all, these fatherly investments are not necessary or particularly beneficial. The reproductive advantage of rape might be retained if a second set of conditions held sway, namely that offspring reared without fatherly contributions fared as well as those reared with such contributions.

This second set of conditions could be met if one assumes that the contributions of a father are more or less irrelevant. Perhaps women and their children were the basic social unit and survived well without the input of men. However, there is general agreement among scholars that males probably did contribute significantly to the provisioning, protection, and socialization of young. An important aspect of male caretaking may actually be as a mediator of intrusions by other group members that might separate the mother and infant (Altmann 1980). This is not trivial, because among nonhuman primates, junior or low-status females often have their infants confiscated for episodes of rough and tumble play or general kidnapping by more senior and dominant females. The result of such harassment and interference can easily result in the death of the infant. An invested partner would reduce these risks.

Comparative fieldwork in primates indicates that for many species males play significant roles in caretaking. The incidence of male parental care among a wide range of species suggests the importance of such care. Male-infant affiliation is reported to be normative and striking in its intimacy (Smuts 1985). In times of emergency, nonhuman primate males may even adopt infants. Such behavior has been reported among nonhuman primates and probably characterized humans too. Wade Mackey in this volume provides an extensive discussion of these issues.

The significance of human fathers and fathering has long been endorsed by research from a number of disciplines. Cultural anthropology studies have included detailed descriptions of daily life that document the central role played by fathers. For example, among the Kalahari hunter-gatherers men spend substantial hours within the social milieu of the group, with immediate family, children, and friends (Lee and DeVore 1976). Among contemporary nonindustrialized societies, fathering and father roles are held to be very important. In these societies, the cultural concept of father may appear in a relatively elaborate form. A number of tribal groups of the Amazonian basin have constructed complex definitions of biological father. They believe that the sperm of many men contribute to the layered development of a child. For example, when asked to identify their fathers, members of the Ache of eastern Paraguay almost always list more than one father (Hill and Hurtado 1996). Data from similar groups indicate that children with only one acknowledged father are significantly less likely to survive to adolescence than those able to identify a secondary father as well.

Alternative Models

Two of the requirements for advancing a scientific causal model are that it account for a notable percentage of the variance in the observed outcome and that alternative explanations for the same outcome can be discounted. The proposal that rape is an evolutionary reproductive success story fails on both counts. Thornhill and Palmer note that rape is observed in virtually all cultures, and since rape is so common it therefore must be biologically based. This proposition in its most simple form is flawed because evolutionary theory does not specify that all common behaviors are genetically coded. Almost all people in China eat rice, but it is not necessary to suppose there is a specific evolutionary adaptation for rice-eating.

The rape-evolution account is also flawed because Thornhill and Palmer fail to note that there is a good deal of cultural variation in the incidence of rape, as Peggy Reeves Sanday in this volume and elsewhere has ably demonstrated. A cultural approach considers the processes and conditions that elicit and sustain rape behaviors, including belief systems, expectations, and sexual scripts. Sanday argues that rape is culturally, not naturally, selected and can be predicted in the context of this broader cultural configuration.

Considerations of relative power, privilege, and the status of women allow one to understand rape as a social and cultural phenomenon. This framework suggests different rudimentary causes and interventions to reduce rape. Larry Barron and Murray Strauss (1989) have offered a comprehensive model for rape based on analysis of rates of rape for individual U.S. states. They found that the rate of rape varies in predictable ways from state to state. Their model examined regional culture, social organization and disorganization, and gender equality as a function of economic, political, and legal status in each state. Among other things, their study found that having high rank on one measure of equality does not ensure similarly high status on other indicators of equality. A quantitative path analysis regressing rates of rape in each of the fifty states against carefully quantified variables documented that direct and indirect indicators of gender inequality were significantly associated with increased rates of rape. Alice Eagly and Wendy Wood in this volume take a cross-cultural perspective to demonstrate that it is the status of women in various cultures that influences rape and other forms of abuse. Jackie White in this volume and elsewhere has formulated a comprehensive model of sexualized violence. In her model, rape is conceptualized as a function of five interacting factors, including sociocultural and social networks as well as dyadic, situational, and intrapersonal factors.

References

Altmann, J. (1980). *Baboon Mothers and Infants*. Cambridge: Harvard University.

Barron, Larry, and Murray A. Straus (1989). *Four Theories of Rape in American Society*. New Haven, Conn.: Yale University Press.

Bownes, I. T., and E. C. O'Gorman (1991). Assailants' sexual dysfunction during rape reported by their victims. *Medical Science Law* 31 (4): 322–328.

Boyle, M. (1994). Gender, science, and sexual dysfunction. In T. R. Sarbin and J. I. Kitsuse, eds., *Constructing the Social,* pp. 101–118. Thousand Oaks, Calif.: Sage.

Casebolt, D. B., R. V. Henrickson, and D. W. Hird (1985). Factors associated with birth rate and live birth rate in multi-male breeding groups of rhesus monkeys. *American Journal of Primatology* 8: 289–297.

Chapais, B. (1983). Matriline membership and male rhesus reaching high ranks in natal troops. In R. A. Hinde, ed., *Primate Social Relationships: An Integrated Approach,* pp. 171–175. Sunderland, Mass.: Sinauer.

Cohen, Jacob (1994). The earth is round. *American Psychologist* 49 (12): 997–1003.

Dawkins, Richard (1976). *The Selfish Gene*. New York: Oxford Univ. Press.

Eagly, Alice, and Valerie J. Steffen (1986). Gender and aggressive behavior: A meta-analytic review of the social psychological literature. *Psychological Bulletin* 100: 309–330.

FBI (1998). *Uniform Crime Report*. http://www.FBI.gov.

Ferris, L. E. and J. Sandercock (1998). The sensitivity of forensic tests for rape. *Medicine and Law* 17 (3): 333–350.

Gould, S. J. and R. Lewontin (1970). The spandrels of San Marco and the Panglossian paradigm: A critique of the adaptationist programme. *Proceedings of the Royal Society of London* 205: 581–598.

Gould, S. J. (1981). *The Mismeasure of Man*. New York: W. W. Norton.

Groen, George, Arthur P. Wunderlich, Manfred Spitzer, Reinhard Tomczak, and Matthias W. Riepe (2000). Brain activation during human navigation: Gender-different neural networks as substrate of performance. *Nature Neuroscience* 3 (4): 404–408.

Groth, A. N. and A. W. Burgess (1977). Sexual dysfunction during rape. *New England Journal of Medicine* 297 (14): 764–766.

Gur, Ruben C., Bruce I. Turetsky, Mie Matsui, Michelle Yan, Warren Bilker, Paul Hughett, and Raquel E. Gur (1999) *Journal of Neuroscience* 19 (10): 4065–4072.

Hamilton, W. D. (1964). The genetical evolution of social behavior, I, II. *Journal of Theoretical Biology* 7: 1–52.

Hill, K. and A. M. Hurtado (1996). *Ache Life History: The Ecology and Demography of a Foraging People*. New York: Aldine de Gruyter.

Hook, S. M., D. A. Elliot, and S. A. Harbison (1992). Penetration and ejaculation: forensic aspects of rape. *New Zealand Medical Journal* 105 (929): 87–89.

Hrdy, S. B. (1977). *The Langurs of Abu.* Cambridge, Mass.: Harvard Univ. Press.

Hyde, Janet. (1984). How large are gender differences in aggression? A developmental meta-analysis. *Developmental Psychology* 20: 722–736.

Lee, R. B. and I. DeVore, eds. (1976). *Kalahari Hunter-gatherers.* Cambridge, Mass.: Harvard University Press.

Malamuth, Neil M. (1983). Factors associated with rape as predictors of laboratory aggression against women. *Journal of Personality and Social Psychology* 45 (2): 432–442.

Malamuth, N. M., S. Haber, S. Feshbach. (1980). Testing hypotheses regarding rape: Exposure to sexual violence, sex differences, and the "normality" of rapists. *Journal of Research in Personality.* 14 (1): 121–137.

Maynard Smith, J. (1977). Parental investment: A prospective analysis. *Animal Behaviour* 25: 1–9.

Maynard Smith, J. and G. R. Price (1973). The logic of animal conflict. *Nature* 246: 15–18.

Miller, Dale T., Brian L. Taylor, and Michelle L. Buck (1991). Gender gaps: Who needs to be explained? *Journal of Personality and Social Psychology* 61: 5–12.

Preston, B. T., I. R. Stevenson, J. M. Pemberton, and K. Dominant Wilson (2001). Rams lose out by sperm depletion. *Nature* 409: 681–682.

Rand, M. R. and K. Strom (1997). Violence-related injuries treated in hospital emergency departments. *Bureau of Justice Statistics: Special Report.* August 1997, NCJ-156921.

Smuts, B. B. (1985). *Sex and Friendship in Baboons.* New York: Aldine.

Tiefer, L. (1995). *Sex Is Not a Natural Act and Other Essays.* Boulder, Colo.: Westview.

Tiefer, L. (2000). The social construction and social effects of sex research: The sexological model of sexuality. In C. B. Travis and J. W. White, eds., *Sexuality, Society, and Feminism,* pp. 79–108. Washington, D.C.: American Psychological Association.

Travis, C. B. and C. P. Yeager (1991). Sexual selection, parental investment, and sexism. *Journal of Social Issues* 47 (3): 117–129.

Trivers, R. L. (1972). Parental investment and sexual selection. In B. Campbell, ed., *Sexual Selection and the Descent of Man 1871–1971,* pp. 136–179. Chicago: Aldine Publishing.

White, J. W., B. Bondurant, and C. B. Travis (2000). Social constructions of sexuality: Unpacking hidden meanings. In C. B. Travis and J. W. White, eds., *Sexuality, Society, and Feminism,* pp. 11–34. Washington, D.C.: American Psychological Association.

10

An Unnatural History of Rape

Michael Kimmel

We must not treat the unknown as known and too readily accept it; and he who wishes to avoid this error [as all should do] will devote both time and attention to the weighing of evidence.

—Cicero, *De Officiis*

The ability of ideology to blind people to the utter implausibility of their positions is perhaps the greatest threat to accumulating the knowledge necessary to solve social problems.

—Randy Thornhill and Craig Palmer, A Natural History of Rape (p. 152)

I was tempted to ignore *A Natural History of Rape* and its modest moment of cultural excitement entirely as just another silly and unwarranted extension of evolutionary psychology's preposterously reductionist sociobiology written by two vainglorious and self-promoting researchers who have never done any research with actual human beings but feel perfectly comfortable making all sorts of cross-cultural generalizations about them anyway.[1] These claims were so ridiculous, the authors so narcissistically self-aggrandizing in their public pronouncements—why, I asked myself, should I give it, or them, any more press? Who would believe this nonsense anyway?

It was while watching my 22-month-old son playing with our neighbor's daughter the other day that I was convinced to respond in some way to the view Thornhill and Palmer have of my little boy, and their view of his future—a future of unbridled sexual predation, of the evolutionary justification for using any means necessary—fraud or force, drugs or alcohol—to sexually conquer an unwilling female (or male, but Thornhill and Palmer think other males would be more compliant). And the life of our little neighbor is even more bleak: She will have to be constantly on her guard

because boys will be boys—which is to say that boys will be violent little rapacious predatory beasts. She will have to modify her behavior, watch what
she wears, where she walks, and at what time, because there's certainly no
way we're going to be able to protect her from those little male monsters.

I see a different reality, and I want a different future for my children than
that which Thornhill and Palmer lay out for them. Fortunately, in the real
world, in which I happen to live, Thornhill and Palmer's prognosis is
merely political resignation with a pseudo-scientific façade. My son will
live in a different world, because he already does, because the real world
he and I live in bears little resemblance to the world Thornhill and Palmer
describe, and because works like Thornhill and Palmer's, however politically resigned they are, offer no real vision and no real hope.

And no real science either. I will argue that this "natural history" contains dreadfully poor understanding of nature, of history, and of "natural
history." The book tells us less about "the biological bases of sexual coercion" than the ideological fantasies of those who justify sexual coercion.
It's bad science, bad history, and bad politics—or, more accurately, it's bad
politics masquerading as science.

On top of that, it's also appallingly badly written. Let me put it this
way: compared to *A Natural History of Rape,* your typical NSF research
report reads like Virginia Woolf. Bad science, bad writing, and bad politics—makes you wonder not only how such a work was vetted through a
reputable university press, but also how it has received so much attention.
I believe that as unconvincing an argument as it is, it is one that has a certain currency in the current political climate. "Bad" does not mean "useless"; indeed, this is a work that is enormously useful to some groups.

Bad Science

Evolutionary psychology is a social science, which is to say it is an oxy-
moron. It cannot conform to the canons of a science like physics, in which
falsifiability is its chief goal and replication its chief method. It does not
account for variations in its universalizing pronouncements, nor does it
offer the most parsimonious explanations. It is speculative theory, often
provocative and interesting, but no more than that. It is like—gasp!—my
own discipline of sociology. And, like sociology, there are some practitioners who will do virtually anything to be taken seriously as "science,"

despite the fact that individual human beings happily confound all predictions based on aggregate models of behavior.

Typically, to stake its claim for legitimacy, pseudo-science cloaks itself in vociferous denunciations of all other pseudo-sciences. In this case, Thornhill and Palmer set up straw man arguments, attribute them to a social science utterly in the thrall of feminist rape hysteria, and then claim to demolish them with pseudo-scientific assertions based on selective evidence. No wonder one medical reviewer noted the irony "that a book purporting such devotion to science should have so little in it" and evolutionary biologist Jerry Coyne calls the work "utterly lacking in sound scientific grounding," "an embarrassment to the field," and "useless and unscientific" (Hung 2000; Coyne 2000, pp. 28, 34).

The "argument" of the book is actually a tautology. Rape, they claim, is "a natural, biological phenomenon that is a product of human evolutionary heritage" (2000a, p. 30). Well, of course it is. As is *any* behavior or trait found among human primates. If it exists in nature, it's natural. Some "natural" beverages contain artificial—"social"—additives that give them their color, their texture, their taste, their "meaning" or "significance." This is equally true of rape. Telling us that it is natural tells us nothing about it except that it is found in nature. Years ago, in our quest for scientific legitimacy we social scientists jettisoned "functionalist" explanations of social phenomena—if they exist they must be there for a reason (manifest), even if the reason is not entirely clear to us (latent). It's amusing to see evolutionary psychology, in its quest for credibility, dusting off the structural functionalism of Talcott Parsons.

Proof of this argument is based first on Robert Trivers's reductionist evolutionary theory, which suggests that males and females have different reproductive strategies based on the size and number of their reproductive cells. From sperm and egg we get motivation, intention, perhaps even cognition. Male reproductive success comes from impregnating as many females as possible; females' success comes from enticing a male to provide and protect the vulnerable and dependent offspring. Thus males have a natural predisposition toward promiscuity, sex without love, and parental indifference; females have a natural propensity for monogamy, love as a precondition of sex, and parental involvement.

This arrangement gives women a lot of power. Since males are more eager for sex than females, this gives females the power to choose which males are going to be successful. Thornhill and Palmer offer rape as the evolutionary mating strategy of losers, males who cannot otherwise get a date. "But getting chosen is not the only way to gain sexual access to females," they write. "In rape, the male circumvents the females' choice" (p. 53).

Trivers's arguments have been effectively refuted by primatologist Sarah Blaffer Hrdy, who has used the same empirical observations to construct an equally plausible case for females' natural propensity toward promiscuity (to seduce many males into believing the offspring is theirs and thus ensure survival by increasing food and protection from those males) and males' natural propensity toward monogamy (to avoid being run ragged providing for offspring that may—or may not—be their own).

Some Bad Assumptions

Thornhill and Palmer's use of Trivers's speculations makes two assumptions about rape and sex. First, they assume that rape is only about sex. "Rapists are sexually motivated," they write (p. 134). Second, they assume that sex is only about reproduction. Neither of these is supported by the evidence.

To be sure, as Thornhill and Palmer note, rape *can be* about sex. Surely, three decades of feminist advocacy and social science research on date and acquaintance rape indicates that some rapes are a product of a combination of sexual desire, contempt for women's bodily integrity, and a feeling of sexual entitlement. (Ironically, Thornhill and Palmer's thesis works better for date and acquaintance rape than it does for stranger rape, which is their model. After all, at least some modicum of desire is potentially present.) There are few, if any, feminists or social scientists who would, today, argue that rape is *never* about sex.

But if rape can sometimes also be partly about sex, it is not *only* about sex. Gang rape, prison rape, military rape of entire subject populations, rape prior to murder, rape *after* murder—these don't necessarily admit to rape-as-alternate-strategy-to-express-sexual-desire. Rape may also be about sexual repulsion, about rage and fear, about domination. Rape of women may be a homosocial event, by which one group of men expresses its domination over another group of men. Rape is a multidimensional phenomenon, offering a large amount of variation. Thornhill and Palmer's view of rape is monochromatic and embraces only a small fraction of its remarkable variety.

Men use their penises for many motivations, and they aren't all necessarily reproductive. Sex can be about play, about pleasure, about cementing bonds between females and males, or between males or between females. It may—or it may not—have anything to do with reproduction. (I would bet that neither Thornhill nor Palmer has more than three children each, and that both have made love more than three times. I hope that their partners would tell a story of two men who know sex is not only about reproduction.) The clitoris, for example, seems to have evolved strictly because of its capacity for pleasure. Since it evolved, then, it means that women's pleasure has something to do with reproductive success in humans.

Selective Generalization

Thornhill and Palmer's use of evidence is so selective that it may well constitute scholarly fraud. Thornhill, himself, has actually done research only on scorpion flies, who are not exactly our closest genetic neighbors. "In some animal species," they write, "rape is commonplace" (2000a, p. 33). How do they know this? By what logic do they label any mating behavior "rape"? Is this possibly a case of anthropomorphizing mating behavior that might instead be female preference for vigorous males? By legal canon, "rape" requires more than aggressive sexual contact—it involves the absence of consent and the threat or actual use of force. If we don't think that children or pets are legally capable of consent, why would we think scorpion flies are? What Thornhill and Palmer call "rape" is *their* term, but not by any means the only one that could adequately describe these species' sexual behavior.

And in many species there's nothing that even looks remotely like what they (mis)label rape. Actually, my two favorite sentences in the book (so cluttered with references that it becomes a seventeen-line paragraph) are these:

In the ten years that followed Brownmiller's claim, studies of rape in non-human species grew too numerous to be ignored. Evolutionary explanations of rape were put forth in regard to insects, birds, fishes, reptiles and amphibians, marine mammals, and non-human primates. (p. 144)

And the absence of rape behaviors has been equally found for varieties of each of those species as well. Oops.

And it may turn out that the cases in which rape does not take place—cases that Thornhill and Palmer are utterly unable to explain—are more instructive than those in which it does. Rape is virtually absent among primates in which females are seen as equally sexual as males—and equal to them in other ways as well. Primatologist Meredith Small reminds us that among some monkeys and apes, the female approaches the male, pushing her genitals in his face, slapping him, initiating sexual advances and clearly enjoying sexual games. Jane Goodall and Barbara Smuts showed that adult female chimpanzees mate successively with virtually every male in the group, while adult males are the ones who are sexually choosy. Or at least try to be. Female baboons too; Barbara Smuts comments that she has "seen them literally hop from one guy to the next. They'll mate with ten different males in the space of an hour" (cited in Angier 1999, p. 381). And Frans de Waal shows how among bonobos there's lots of female-female gento-genital rubbing, lots of masturbation, and lots of egalitarian sex, initiated largely by the females. Oh yeah, and there's no rape.

Unable to account for variation among animal species, Thornhill and Palmer are equally unable to account for human variation—the fact that in some cultures rape is quite rare and in others quite common. Indeed, they ignore any evidence of variation. In an article in the *Sciences* summarizing their book, they cite approvingly Donald Symons's ridiculous pronouncement that, as they write, "people everywhere understand sex as 'something females have that males want'" (2000b, p. 33). Symons's understanding of sex as a commodity is a particularly silly example of the assumptions of advanced consumer society being read back onto cultures for which sex might be any number of other things. But while Symons simply asserts that *sex* is this gendered commodity, Thornhill and Palmer add the words "people everywhere," rendering the merely ridiculous sublimely so.

In several cultures, we have evidence that sex is not a commodity, that women and men "have" equal amounts of it, and that it's not the basis of some putative feminine "power." We have evidence of the absence of rape, and evidence of the presence of female promiscuity designed to promote the likelihood of an offspring's survival. Among the Ache foragers in eastern Paraguay, each of the 66 children of the 17 women interviewed by two anthropologists was attributed to an average of 2.1 proginating men. In fact the Ache differentiate among three different categories of father: (1) the man to whom a woman is married when the child is born; (2) the man or men she had extramarital sex with just before or during her pregnancy; (3) the man whom the woman believes is that actual father (Angier 1999: 382–383).

Bari women in Venezuela also engage in significant amounts of extramarital sex during pregnancy. When the child is born, the woman tells the midwife who her lovers were, and the midwife then goes to each man and says "Congratulations. You have a child." The men are then expected to help care and provide for the child—much to the benefit of the child. These children have a much higher likelihood of survival than the offspring of rape, where the men would invest little or nothing.

That leads to another problem of evidence and assumption. Thornhill and Palmer claim that "selection favored males who mated frequently," and that "rape increased reproductive success" (2000a, pp. 32, 34). But why should this be true? Might it not also be the case that being hardwired to be good lovers and devoted fathers enabled us to be reproductively successful? One might argue that selection favored males who mated *well,* since successful mating is more than spreading of seed. After all, human males are the only primates for whom skillful lovemaking, enhancing *women's* pleasure, is normative, at least in many societies. (Don't go talking about "her pleasure" to gorillas and especially not those pesky little scorpion flies!)

Being an involved father assured reproductive success far better than rape. After all, babies are so precious, so fragile that they need extraordinary—and extraordinarily long!—care and devotion. Infants conceived during rape would have a far lower chance of survival, which is probably one reason we invented love. Infants conceived in rape might well have been subject to infanticide—which has been, historically, the most common form of birth control before the modern era. "The children of guys who raped-and-ran must have been a scrawny lot and doomed to end up on some leopard's lunch menu," as Barbara Ehrenreich (herself a Ph.D. in biology) writes (2000, p. 88). It is quite unlikely that very many rape-conceived babies would have survived. Rape's persistence and its enormous variation have other origins than the hypothesis that our great-great-great-granddaddies to the 14th power did it.

Other evidence for their theory is explained equally well—perhaps better—by alternate hypotheses, which both weaken their theory and reveal their political agenda. For example, they argue that women in their peak childbearing years are far more likely to be raped, and that this is an evolutionary holdover. "Women in their teens and their early twenties are highly overrepresented among rape victims around the world" (p. 139; see also p. 72).

But is this not better explained by the simple fact that younger women, ages 16 to 24, are the least likely to be married and the most likely to be out on dates with men with whom they are not in permanent relationships? That is to say, they are women who are most likely to be raped because of "opportunity"—social exposure and marital status—not age and fecundity, which probably have little or nothing to do with it. (This is, of course, not to say that married women are not raped. They are. Rape by intimates—lovers, partners, husbands, boyfriends, and yes, fathers, uncles, brothers, and step-fathers—is by far the most common form of rape, and one that Thornhill and Palmer's thesis is utterly unable to comprehend, because they suggest that rape is a function of thwarted sexual desire and limited sexual access.)

Simple demographics offer a far more parsimonious and convincing explanation of ages of vulnerability to rape. But let's look at this demographic argument a little more closely. By their logic, the likelihood of rape should correlate with the ratio of females to males in a society. In a society in which females outnumber males, the possibility of reproductive success would be significantly higher for males; that is, the guy would likely find a female who would be willing to have sex with him. In such societies, by their logic, women's power would be lower, because they would have to make compromises with their "natural" propensity for selectivity. Some men whom they might have rejected were their circumstances different will simply have to do. In such societies rape rates would be lower.

In societies in which males outnumber females, by contrast, Thornhill and Palmer's thesis would predict significantly higher rape rates because males would have less likelihood of reproductive success simply by being nice guys. Male dominance hierarchies would be more in evidence, and males would compete for the right to mate. Women's scarcity would increase their power, because they could be choosier about with whom they would mate. Rape rates would be high, then, because those males left out of the reproductive mix might use rape as an alternative mating strategy.

Actually, societies in which females outnumber males are likely to be warrior societies, in which women's relative power is *lower* and rape rates higher. Rape is a crime of entitlement not evolution, of opportunity not imperatives, of permission not passion.

Bad History

Thornhill and Palmer's bad science is complemented by equally bad history. It's hard to explain the persistence of rape in modern society, except as some unnecessary evolutionary residue like the appendix or tonsils. But they compound this by arguing against all their own evidence that rape is more prevalent today than ever before.

Rape rates in modern society are so high because "in such societies women rarely are chaperoned and often encounter social circumstances that make them vulnerable to rape" (p. 194). More: "The common practice of unsupervised dating in cars and private homes, which is often accompanied by the consumption of alcohol, has placed young women in environments that are conducive to rape to an extent that is probably unparalleled in history" (2000a, p. 36).

I would hypothesize precisely the opposite, that rape rates are lower today than ever before. Rape was *far* more likely in medieval Europe, for example. It's just that we called it something else. Ever hear of "right of first night"? (That's coerced sex without consent, that is, rape.) In many societies, rape was a common and legitimate punishment for all sorts of perceived crimes against men. And it is *by far* safer to be a woman alone walking on the street at night today in a modern society than it has ever been. (This is decidedly *not* to say it is safe—just safer.)

I believe that rape rates are lower today because women have more power, including the power to redefine behavior that was once seen as normative sexual "etiquette" as date rape. In my high school locker room, I was counseled by older athletes that "it doesn't count unless you put it in." I was advised to "keep going, even if she says no, even if she screams, even if she pushes you away. Don't stop until she hits you," was the felicitous way they put it. (Incidentally, when I mentioned this to my students a few weeks ago, one of the men said, sardonically, "You stopped too soon, man. It's 'don't stop until she *hurts* you.'")

If we were honest about it, then, men of my generation (I'm 50) would have to confess that virtually all of us are "failed attempted date rapists." What we called "dating" is now against the law. (Yes, of course, some were successful. But my point is that the norms have changed, and that such behavior is increasingly problematized, thus making dating safer for women than ever.)

Comparatively, rape rates vary enormously among cultures. And the best variable that determines those rape rates is women's status. Those countries in which women's wages come closer to matching men's (so the men won't feel they are owed something after spending money on their date) have rape rates lower than ours. Those countries in which women hold more political offices, in which women equal men in the professions, in which there is adequate sex education—all have lower rape rates than we do.

Bad Politics

Lowering rape rates is a political discussion, a discussion about the effectiveness of specific policy proposals. And here Thornhill and Palmer's bad history leads inevitably to bad politics. They make two policy recommendations that they believe will reduce the scourge of rape. The first is transparently silly because it blames the victim. Women must be informed about men's biological predisposition to rape because it *does* matter how they dress and which parties they choose to go to. The best our authors can offer is that women should be warned about how predatory men are. After that, well, they're on their own. (It's a good idea to give them that warning when they get their driver's licenses, since they will need their cars to escape men's violent predations. But, of course, Thornhill and Palmer actually want to use driver's licenses to warn *men* of their own base proclivities.)

The press release that accompanied my copy of the book notes that the authors recommend that "young women consider the biological causes of rape when making decisions about dress, appearance, and social activities." "But where is the evidence that women in mini-skirts are more likely to be raped than women in dirndls?" asks Barbara Ehrenreich (2000, p. 88). "Women were raped by the thousands in Bosnia for example, and few if any of them were wearing bikinis or bustiers." Many rapes—in war, in prison—have nothing to do with ensuring reproductive success and everything to do with domination and humiliation of other men. Rape may be far more of a homosocial act than a heterosexual one.

The second policy recommendation—about males—reveals Thornhill and Palmer's real political agenda—and it is not a pretty picture. You see, Thornhill and Palmer hate men.

Rarely, if ever, have I read a book that is so resolutely and relentlessly anti-male. *A Natural History of Rape* is the best example I can find of male-bashing masquerading as academic pseudo-science. In their eyes, all men are violent, rapacious predators, seeking to spew their sperm far and wide, at whatever creature happens in their testosterone-crazed evolutionary path. Oh, sure, they try and sugarcoat it:

human males in all societies so far examined in the ethnographic record possess genes that can lead, by way of ontogeny, to raping behavior when the necessary environmental factors are present, and . . . the necessary environmental factors are sometimes present in all societies studied to date. (p. 142)

So all men have the genetic "motivation" to rape and all they need is a social permission.

Wait a minute? Isn't that what they claim the feminists they are trying to discredit argued also? Is that not the justification for zero-tolerance for rape? Isn't that the justification for sensible arguments, like those of Peggy Reeves Sanday, to reduce risk of rape by increasing women's status?

As a policy recommendation, Thornhill and Palmer propose that we institute "an evolutionarily informed education program for young men that focuses on increasing their ability to restrain their sexual behavior."

"Restrain"? Is it that bad? How about "express"—their equally evolution-based biological drive to experience pleasure, mutuality, and fun? Might we not be "hard wired" for that as well? Education for restraint is perhaps the second most politically bankrupt policy initiative around, and utterly ineffective. (The first is demanding that women "just say no.") If Thornhill and Palmer were right—and of course they are not—then the only sensible solution would be to lock all males up and release them for sporadic, reproductive mating after being chosen by females.

Thornhill and Palmer offer a far more "misandrous" account of rape than anything offered by their nemeses, radical feminists. In the process, they do an enormous disservice to thinking about rape, and, ironically, they end up reproducing the very canards about men that they project onto feminist women. Feminists, by contrast, believe that men are capable of doing better, of stopping rape and expressing an equally evolutionarily ordained imperative toward pleasure, mutuality, and equality.

Conclusion

Bad science, bad history, and bad politics add up to a pretty dreadful book. What's missing, ultimately, from Thornhill and Palmer's facile reductionism is the distinctly human capacity for change, for choice. What's missing is human agency.

To them, men are driven by evolutionary imperatives to rape, pillage, destroy to make sure our seed gets planted. If women are not compliant, we men are hard wired to take what we want anyway. They have the power of choice, but when we're not chosen—well, we get testy. "They made us do it because we can't get them any other way. And we simply *must* have them."

I've heard this before. From rapists! That's who will really find Thornhill and Palmer's arguments comforting. I can imagine that Thornhill's phone has been ringing off the hook with attorneys defending men accused of rape, asking him to be an expert witness for the defense. "You see, your honor, as I wrote, 'rape has evolutionary—and thus genetic—origins.'"

"Aha!" Comments the defense lawyer. "So he was driven by his biological imperative to reproduce? How could he be held accountable for some behavior that he was compelled to do by his body? He simply had to have her!"

Feminists believe we can do better than this politically; social scientists believe that we can do better than this book scientifically.

Nowhere is this better expressed than on a "splash guard" that a colleague devised for Rape Awareness Week at his university. (For those who don't know, a splash guard is the plastic grate that is placed in men's public urinals that prevents splatter.) He had thousands made up with a simple and hopeful slogan. It says simply: "You hold the power to stop rape in your hand."

References

Angier, Natalie (1999). *Woman: An Intimate Geography.* New York: Houghton Mifflin.

Brownmiller, Susan (1975). *Against Our Will: Men, Women, and Rape.* New York: Simon and Schuster.

———. (2000). Rape on the brain. *Feminista!* March 8.

Coyne, Jerry (2000). "Of Vice and Men," *New Republic*, April 3.

De Waal, Frans B. M. (2000). "Survival of the Rapist," *New York Times Book Review*, April 2.

Ehrenreich, Barbara. (2000). "How 'Natural" is Rape?" *Time*, January 31.

Hung, Mindy. (2000). Review of *A Natural History of Rape*, in *Medscape*, September 14. <http://www.womenshealth.medscape.com>

Thornhill, Randy and Craig T. Palmer. (2000a). *A Natural History of Rape: Biological Bases of Sexual Coercion*. Cambridge, Mass.: The MIT Press.

———. (2000b). Why men rape. *The Sciences*, January.

11

Violence against Science: Rape and Evolution

Elisabeth A. Lloyd

It is clear where the opposition is coming from—it's coming from ideology. . . .
Most of the ideology is coming from certain feminist groups. It's not feminism,
per se, that's against us. It is certain groups of feminists that are against the application of science for dealing with this problem. That is a socially very irresponsible
position.
—Randy Thornhill, quoted in Dano (2000)

Throughout *A Natural History of Rape,* co-authors Randy Thornhill and
Craig Palmer resort to what is known among philosophers of science as
"The Galileo Defense," which amounts to the following claim: "I am telling the Truth and doing excellent science, but because of ideology and
ignorance, I am being persecuted."[1] The authors have repeated and elaborated on this defense during the sizable media flurry accompanying the
book's publication in February 2000.[2]

Now, history has accepted this defense from Galileo. But in order for it
to work for Thornhill and Palmer, of course, they must be telling the Truth
and doing excellent science. In this essay I shall argue that the Galileo defense is impotent in the hands of Thornhill and Palmer because of glaring
flaws in their science.

1 Their Claims

Thornhill and Palmer present two alternative evolutionary explanations
for the existence of human rape. They claim that rape behavior must either
have evolved through a process of natural selection, that is, rape behavior
must be a specific adaptation, or it must be the by-product of some underlying traits that are themselves adaptations.

Their main arguments for these theses all rest on a hypothesis about the evolution of sex differences: that because women bear the brunt of the effort in reproduction—through pregnancy, nursing, and infant care— they have evolved to be very selective about their mates.

Men, on the other hand, by virtue of the possibility of being able to reproduce with the minimal investment of mere ejaculation, have evolved to seek out as many mates as possible, and to copulate with no intention of co-parenting or providing. This has led to such traits of male sexuality as the desire for casual sex, the seeking out of a wide variety of mates, and a stronger disregard for the particular features of a given mate. Hence, female and male "reproductive strategies" differ: Women choose mates carefully, whereas men seek multiple mates.[3]

Here is how each of Thornhill and Palmer's two theses about rape rely on this picture of evolved male sexuality. They call their first hypothesis— that men have evolved, through natural selection, a specific tendency to- ward rape behavior—the "rape-specific" hypothesis. On this view, men who had trouble attaining sexual access to females—especially because of low status or evidence of inferior genetic make-up—must have resorted to rape in order to satisfy their sexual urges to mate with a larger number of women. This trait, a disposition to rape behavior, helped get these males' genes into the human gene pool by increasing mate number and thereby increasing the frequency of "rape genes" in the population through the process of natural selection. In other words, the reproductive problems facing our human ancestors were very specific, and therefore the mecha- nism, that is, the tendency to rape itself, that "solved" these problems is also specific. Therefore, the rape-specific adaptation hypothesis is favored.

Evolution by natural selection occurs when individuals of one type of genetic makeup (genotype) reproduce more successfully than individuals of other types of genetic makeup, resulting in a change within the whole population of the proportions of each type. For natural selection to work in favor of a particular genotype, the genotype must be associated with a trait that is inheritable, that is, transmitted from one generation to another through the genes, and that increases the organism's reproductive success. In this case, the rapists would succeed reproductively while men who were otherwise genetically equivalent but who were not rapists would have failed at reproducing. The long-term effect of this pattern of reproductive success on human demographics would thus have been the increasing fre- quency of the rapist type within the human population.

When a trait evolves (or is "chosen") through natural selection, it is called an evolutionary *adaptation*. Thus, the *primary* hypothesis defended in Thornhill and Palmer's book is that rape is an evolutionary adaptation, that is, it evolved because rape behavior itself was reproductively superior to nonraping behavior.

Under Thornhill and Palmer's second hypothesis, which they call the "by-product" view, evolved psychological traits such as the male desire for a wide variety of mates led accidentally to the existence of rape, but rape itself was not directly selected. On this view, the act of rape is an incidental by-product of other male sexual adaptations, "especially those that function to produce the sexual desire of males for multiple partners without commitment" (2000b, p. 60). The phenomenon of evolutionary by-products is frequent in human evolution. Manual dexterity was directly selected because it was reproductively advantageous to our ancestors for making tools, and so on, and is therefore an adaptation. Our use of manual dexterity in playing the piano is a by-product of the selection on manual dexterity. It is not an evolutionary adaptation itself. Note that selection leading to evolutionary adaptation is involved in this scenario, but the trait of playing the piano is distinct from the evolutionary adaptation itself; it is an epiphenomenon.

Thornhill and Palmer consider two hypotheses about the evolution of human rape—the hypothesis that rape is a specifically selected adaptation, and the hypothesis that rape is an evolutionary by-product of selection on other traits. Although they do not find any evidence they consider decisive in favor of either hypothesis, nevertheless, most of the evidence they advance is explicitly intended to support the adaptive view. Thus, in what follows, I shall evaluate primarily their claims about this adaptive view.

To buttress the rape-specific hypothesis, Thornhill and Palmer propose a number of subsidiary psychological adaptations that would have increased men's chance of reproductive success when attempting to rape. Proposed mechanisms include men having: (1) a special psychological adaptation that enables them to evaluate females' vulnerability to rape (2000b, p. 66); (2) a special psychological adaptation to prefer to rape women at peak fertility (2000b, p. 71); (3) a psychological adaptation to be sexually aroused by gaining physical control over an unwilling sexual partner (2000b, p. 75); (4) a psychological adaptation to rape wives and girlfriends if they believe their women are cheating on them (2000b, pp. 77–78); and finally, (5) a psychological adaptation for male paranoia about women's claims of being raped (2000b, p. 158).

But under either evolutionary scenario, women are also hypothesized to have evolved rape-related adaptations—specifically, an adaptation for psychological anguish on being raped. The supposition is that rape victims suffer an overall loss in reproductive success. Psychological anguish is thus hypothesized to have been an adaptation to help women guard against such reproductive loss. The psychological adaptation focuses the victim's attention on the causes of the loss and helps her avoid repetition of those causes (2000b, p. 85). The basic evolutionary assumptions here are that rape reduces a woman's reproductive success by circumventing her mate choice, that it reduces her mate's reproductive success by lowering his certainty of paternity, and that it reduces the fitness of the relatives of the victim and her mate (2000b, p. 85). In addition, reproductive losses could be expected from getting raped, insofar as the act causes physical injury, the loss of a victim's ability to use copulation as a means of obtaining material benefits from men, the interference with a victim's mate's protection of her, or a reduction in the quality or quantity of parental care given by her mate (2000b, p. 86).

According to Thornhill and Palmer, the adaptation of psychological anguish manifests itself differently in different circumstances of rape. Women of peak reproductive age are hypothesized to experience more psychological pain than females of either pre- or postreproductive age (2000b, pp.89–90). This is because the reproductive costs to these young women of getting raped are higher.

In addition, Thornhill and Palmer predict that reproductive-age victims will experience more violent attacks than the pre- or postreproductive-age rape victims (2000b, pp. 91–92). The basis of this prediction lies in the hypothesis that reproductive-age women are more likely to fight back "because of the greater evolutionary historical cost to their reproductive success of being raped" (2000b, pp. 91–92), and that rapists would be more highly sexually motivated to complete the rape in reproductive-age victims because of these victims' greater sexual attractiveness relative to victims in the other two categories (2000b, p. 92).

Other hypothesized adaptations among females include: (1) the tendency to experience decreased psychological pain as the violence of the attack increases—this is because physical injury helps to prove to her mate that the sex really was forced and not consensual (2000b, p. 92); (2) "the absence of orgasm during rape" (2000b, p. 99); and (3) the tendency to avoid risky situations, especially during the fertile phase of her cycle (2000b, p. 100).

Thornhill and Palmer then use the supposed existence of female psychological rape adaptations to bolster their claims for specific male psychological rape-adaptations and to counter two alternatives to their theory. One would expect to find rape behavior to be ubiquitous in human societies, if it is genuinely adaptive for men; women's "apparent adaptation to deal with rape . . . implies that rape has been common enough in human evolutionary history to select for counter-adaptations in women" (2000b, p. 57). This, they claim, refutes the alternative explanation that rape results from a low-frequency mutation, where a rape mutation would occur in the population, but would not be selected either for or against. Such an explanation would imply that rape is not an evolutionary adaptation (2000b, p. 57). They also use the hypothesized female adaptations against rape to argue that rape is not a recently derived cultural anomaly generated by new circumstances in the human environment (2000b, p. 58). In other words, they use the supposed female adaptations against rape to rule out two possible alternatives to their two favored hypotheses.

In sum, the authors focus their attention on what they present as the only two plausible candidates for the evolutionary explanation of rape: Either it is an adaptation itself, or it is a by-product of other aspects of evolved male sexuality. There is much more to be said regarding the evidence that they offer for this panoply of male and female rape-related psychological adaptations, some of which I shall cover in section 3, below. But first, we must investigate the soundness of the entire evolutionary framework within which the authors work.

2   The Theory

Let us examine Thornhill and Palmer's use of evolutionary biology. They begin by claiming that "selection is the most important cause of evolution" (2000b, p. 8). What is evident from this bit of theoretical positioning is that Thornhill and Palmer are in the business of looking for explanations of traits in relation to the selective causes that produced them, thus downplaying the other four accepted forces of evolution (drift, mutation, recombination, and gene flow among groups in subdivided populations; see Lloyd, 1988/1994). Evolutionary biologists standardly refer to strategies like Thornhill and Palmer's as "adaptationism," since such approaches seek to explain all interesting traits in terms of selective forces alone. In fact, Thornhill and Palmer explicitly equate an "ultimate or evolutionary analysis" with adaptationism. They claim that the challenge for such an analysis is "to determine the nature of the selective pressure that is responsible for the trait. That selective pressure will be apparent in the functional design of the adaptation" (2000b, p. 9). In other words, they want to infer information about the selection pressure from the "design" of a trait, and to assume that the only relevant evolutionary force shaping the trait was natural selection.

Identification of the trait under evolution is an essential part of an adaptation explanation. When explaining the evolution of rape, Thornhill and Palmer emphasize that rape is a reproductive act brought into play when other means of reproduction are thwarted. It is, fundamentally, from their evolutionary point of view, sexual intercourse with fertile female partners. But is this a plausible description of rape? A very wide variety of acts are considered by Thornhill and Palmer to fall under the rubric of "rape" that they are trying to explain in evolutionary terms, including the rape of babies, men, postmenopausal women, and so on, which turn out to make up the majority of rapes, and which are clearly not intercourse with fertile females (Kilpatrick, Edmunds, and Seymour 1992; Coyne 2000).[4] How does this compare with evolutionary accounts of a clear single trait such as bipedalism? There seems to be a striking disunity among the various acts that are classed as rape. Why should we expect that one evolutionary explanation be appropriate for all of these diverse behaviors? Thornhill and Palmer proceed on the assumption that all rapes are fundamentally the same. If this assumption is wrong, then there are serious problems with Thornhill and Palmer's evolutionary account of what may well be disparate phenomena.

Given that there are alternative hypotheses that see, for example, male on male rape as predominantly a dominance behavior, Thornhill and Palmer cannot simply assume that all rape is a single type of behavior, that is, one involving incentives to reproduce. Thornhill and Palmer could respond that the majority of rapes, that is, all the other, nonreproductive cases of rape, are simply generalized misfirings of the fundamental adaptation, which is one of having intercourse with fertile women. Thus, they could claim, because they explained the "fundamental" behavior of rape, the misfirings are evolutionarily uninteresting. But this strategy is defensible only in the absence of other alternative explanations for the occurrences of the nonreproductive rapes, that is, in the absence of explanations based on dominance or aggression. Thus, Thornhill and Palmer use an undefended and contentious assumption about the unity of rape behaviors to launch their evolutionary adaptive explanation. On the face of it, this is a bad start to their evolutionary project.

The traits in any adaptation account must also be inheritable. Because Thornhill and Palmer hypothesize a species-wide trait—of universal condition-dependent raping behavior—asking for information regarding whether rapists' children are more likely to rape than nonrapists' children may seem to be irrelevant. After all, a universal trait has no variation in the population: everyone has it, and all offspring are expected to have it. Nevertheless, evidence regarding whether rapists' children are more likely to rape *is* relevant to our consideration of Thornhill and Palmer's hypothesis. This is because the most promising *alternate* theories of rape, for example, those involving psychopathology of various sorts, are expected to have a genetic component, and thus to be reflected in the degree of resemblance between parent and offspring. Hence, information about the heritability of rape is an important—and missing—part of the evidence needed to evaluated Thornhill and Palmer's claims.

One also needs to show that the trait *is* an adaptation. There are a number of ways to do this. One is to look at existing genotypic and phenotypic[5] variations in the current population of the trait: Given that few men rape, there would seem to be ample evidence of phenotypic variation from which to work. From this variation, the scientist can then compare the differences in reproductive success between those exhibiting the trait and those not. If a positive reproductive advantage for those exhibiting the trait is found, then the evolutionist starts to look for the possible adaptive scenarios under which the trait could have evolved.

The problem with applying the above method to Thornhill and Palmer's case is that they claim the trait of potential raping behavior is universal. Because they are positing a conditional reproductive strategy, which includes rape, as the adaptation, any variation in rates of rape among individuals or societies can be explained away: Different societies construct different costs and benefits to raping, and therefore there are varying frequencies of rape. The form of the hypothesis itself may seem to make it untestable, because differences in costs and benefits can always be hypothesized. But the hypothesis of a conditional strategy is not untestable, it is merely difficult to test: Different costs and benefits must be *shown* to exist in the societies with corresponding variations in rape rates. However, Thornhill and Palmer have not attempted to offer any evidence of the required type. Hence their hypothesis is, in fact, untested.

Another important research avenue exists for establishing that a trait is an adaptation. Evolutionary biologists often compare the species in question (in this case, human beings) with their closest relatives to see if the trait is manifested elsewhere in the lineage. This approach is not foolproof, but it does provide important information regarding when the trait might have evolved and under what circumstances. If the trait is found to be an adaptation in closely related species, then it can be viewed with more confidence as an adaptation in human beings.

Finally, especially if the trait is not exhibited with any frequency in closely related species, the scientist must examine the past evolutionary circumstances of human beings very carefully for evidence that there was, indeed, a plausible set of circumstances under which the trait could have evolved. This would involve examination of past social structures, population sizes, migration rates, and material culture. However, despite their own warning that the trait of rape behavior is not necessarily adaptive to *current* conditions, nearly all of the evidence they offer concerns precisely contemporary circumstances of rape (2000b, pp. 71–73, 88–89). This could be relevant evidence if they showed the relative reproductive success of rapists and nonrapists, but they do not. Instead, they *begin* by assuming that the trait is an adaptation, and reason backward from there. I have reviewed above the customary standards for adaptation explanations in evolutionary biology. Not all of these evidentiary standards may be met, in which case the conclusion that a trait is an adaptation is correspondingly weakened.

Even if we accept that rape is a coherent evolutionary trait, that it is related to increasing reproductive success, and that it is inherited, the fact remains that Thornhill and Palmer have given no historical evidence of the process of selection that supposedly led to rape as an adaptation (e.g., from archaeology or current anthropology).

One puzzle is that Thornhill and Palmer claim that one can rule out drift and mutation as forces in explanations of evolutionary history when a trait "shows evidence of functional design" (2000b, p. 10). But they make no mention of Sewall Wright's (1931) results to the contrary in population genetics, which clearly demonstrate the possibility of mutation and drift playing a major role in producing adaptations, in his Shifting Balance theory.

Thornhill and Palmer seem to misunderstand the role of mutation per se in evolution, by claiming that "mutation, as an evolutionary cause for traits, may apply only to those traits that are only slightly above zero frequency in the population" (2000b, p. 10). In fact, this is true only for strongly deleterious traits.[6]

One especially startling aspect of Thornhill and Palmer's version of evolutionary theory is their claim that "the study of the profound implications of evolutionary theory—particularly the ability of selection to form adaptations—has, until recently, been relatively unexplored" (2000b, p. 106). Reconciling this claim with the actual history of evolutionary biology is, to say the least, a challenge (see Clausen, 1951; Darwin 1859 /1964; Dobzhansky 1937; Grant 1963; Lack 1954; Lewontin 1997; Mayr 1942; Sheppard 1958; Simpson 1953; Stebbins 1950; Weismann 1904; Wright 1931). This is just part of the so-called evolutionary psychologists' valorization of themselves as starting a "new" movement in evolutionary biology.

These oversights are not trivial; Thornhill and Palmer's fringe version of the actual theory of evolution damages their credibility—especially in light of their repeated claims that they are experts in evolutionary theory.

Is it possible, though, that their unusual view of the actual workings of evolutionary theory has no real consequences for their overall line of reasoning? No, for they rely on these misunderstandings to eliminate alternative hypotheses regarding the evolution of rape. For example, they list four evolutionary causes of trait change or trait maintenance in evolutionary lines—selection, drift, gene flow, and mutation—and in the end, discard all but selection as a possible evolutionary cause of rape behavior (2000b, pp. 56–59). The most bizarre aspect of the little set of arguments that they use is that, despite their later acknowledgment that population geneticists are the experts in determining the balances and possibilities of those four causes (2000b, p. 106), they cite *no* population geneticists in their arguments that selection alone explains the existence of rape. Instead, they fabricate their own conclusions about the likelihood of each cause, and then present their foregone conclusion: that only selection could have caused the propensity to rape.

But let us return to Thornhill and Palmer's main fallacious conclusion, that "the diversity of life has two major components: adaptations and the effects of adaptations" (2000b, p. 11). Regarding "effects of adaptations," they give the useful example of the trait of the red color of human blood: This trait is a by-product or epiphenomenon of the chemistry of oxygen and hemoglobin in the blood, plus the existence of human color vision. By-products or epiphenomena are not directly selected for their advantages to reproductive success, unlike real adaptations.

Thornhill and Palmer make a contentious claim about these epiphenomena, namely, that they are *always* by-products of adaptations for other things. This does not follow, and it is not the mainstream evolutionary view. For example, many traits categorized as evolutionary by-products are understood as phyletic remnants, that is, leftovers from the evolutionary ancestors of the species in question. But this entails neither that they ever were nor that they were not under selection pressure. Take the human trait of having five fingers on each hand. This trait traces to the near beginnings of the vertebrate lineage. Some vertebrates, for example, horses, have endured selection pressure to change the number of phalanges, from five down to one for each limb. Other vertebrates underwent selection for grasping branches, reducing the number to four, and yet most vertebrates retain the five-digit limb. Does the fact that human beings customarily have five digits signify that there was selection for five and only five digits in human ancestry? The generally accepted evolutionary answer is "no" (Gould 1977). *Deviations* from the basic vertebrate body plan of five digits are understood as having undergone mutation and selection for those mutations, while the default property of having five digits is not seen as having been directly selected in this case. This phenomenon is called "phyletic inertia," wherein a trait remains the same unless it is actively selected to change. This is true even in the deep evolutionary past, at the beginnings of the vertebrate line, where having five rather than four digits was perhaps an incidental side effect of selection on other aspects of the vertebrate skeleton, or may well have been the only variant that, for other reasons, survived to found the lineage of vertebrates.

Thornhill and Palmer hold an extreme evolutionary view of the role of phyletic inertia in evolutionary explanations. They claim that phyletic inertia—or the difficulty of changing body plans and the resultant continuation of a trait in a lineage—*is not an evolutionary explanation of anything,* because it does not involve an evolutionary "cause" of the maintenance of a trait in a lineage of species. This is because the phylogenetic cause of a trait in a given species does not identify the "ultimate cause of the continuance" (2000b, p. 55). They use a clever choice of example to bolster this view: the trait of the crossing over of the digestive and respiratory tracts in (land) vertebrates. Here, they claim, the trait is maintained in all relevant species through constant selection. Such a set-up, awkward and dangerous though it is, was necessary to maintain the digestive and respiratory functions through the history of vertebrates. And (land) vertebrates not conforming to the basic body plan would be nonviable and would be selected against. Therefore, they conclude, "all evolutionary constraints and phylogenetic legacies ultimately involve selection in some way" (2000b, p. 56). But think: Does this argument apply equally well to having five digits, a trait that just as likely was fixed in the phylogenetic past as an incidental correlate to a basically successful body plan? Of course not.

Thus it is incorrect, according to modern evolutionary theory, to say that *every trait* is either an adaptation or an effect of an adaptation in the sense that Thornhill and Palmer use this dichotomy. And this mistake profoundly weakens Thornhill and Palmer's basic position, for they use this false dichotomy to set up a false choice: Either rape is a *specific adaptation,* directly selected for in virtue of its superior reproductive success, or it is a *by-product of other adaptations,* an incidental side effect of special-purpose adaptations to circumstances other than rape. These two options are not, in fact, exhaustive.

Having set up their supposedly exhaustive choice between a direct-adaptation and a by-product, they proceed to argue that *very specific* psychological adaptations should be selected for in evolution. This discussion reveals their adherence to the scientifically undefended thesis—in fact, one contradicted by neurophysiological evidence (Buller and Hardcastle, in press)—that the brain is constructed of a high number of very special-purpose physiological mechanisms. This view is a familiar hobby-horse of a group of authors calling themselves "evolutionary psychologists" (Thornhill and Palmer 2000b, pp. 15–20; cf. Lloyd 1999).

While on the topic, I should point out the exceedingly high density of references to this small group of authors in this book, who themselves engage in heavy cross-citation, and the fact that these authors are considered a fringe group by most evolutionary theorists. This group repeatedly demonstrates its narrow understanding of evolutionary theory and its misinterpretations of some elements of modern evolutionary biology; they rarely cite more mainstream evolutionary theory or genetics, either contemporary or historical (see Lloyd and Feldman 2002).

At any rate, Thornhill and Palmer toe the party line among evolutionary psychologists in their claim that we should expect human psychological adaptations to be special-purpose rather than general-purpose. This supposedly buttresses the rape-specific adaptation hypothesis in the following way: The reproductive problems facing our human ancestors were very specific; therefore the mechanism, that is, the tendency to rape itself, that "solved" these problems is also likely to be specific and not a by-product of a more general adaptation. Therefore, the rape-specific adaptation is favored.

There is another literature on the relations between human culture/psychology and genetics in evolutionary biology, oddly absent from Thornhill and Palmer's book. Thornhill and Palmer ignore the careful, quantitative and theoretical work that has been done on the co-evolution of genes and culture (Boyd and Richerson 1985; Cavalli-Sforza and Feldman 1978; 1981; Durham 1991; Laland, Odling-Smee, and Feldman 1996, 2000; Lewontin 1982). These authors concentrate on the mutual effects that genes and culture have had and can have on human evolution. Unlike Thornhill and Palmer, they do not see cultural and biological explanations as on the same *level* of explanation, nor do they attempt to reduce one to the other.[7] Although Thornhill and Palmer do appeal to one of these authors' works (once), conclusions in this section of their book aim toward showing that cultural research has no legitimate explanatory role outside of direct evolutionary considerations. They quote Margo Wilson approvingly, when she writes, "Darwinian selection is the only known source of the functional complexity of living things, and biologists have no reason to suspect that there are any others" (Wilson, Daly, and Scheib 1997, p. 433; quoted in Thornhill and Palmer 2000b, p. 122). Contrary to this claim, the biologists working on gene-culture co-evolution see culture as an important contributor to the evolved complexity of human beings. Nevertheless, Thornhill and Palmer maintain, "the realization that culture is behavior places it clearly within the realm of biology, and hence within the explanatory realm of natural selection" (2000b, p. 25). But contra Thornhill and Palmer, the above authors have shown that different explanatory levels are legitimate in evolutionary theory.

3 The Evidence

Let us now consider some of the specific evidence and arguments Thornhill and Palmer offer to support their various claims about evolutionary adaptations, keeping in mind the usual evolutionary standards of evidence discussed previously. Overall, as Jerry Coyne and Andrew Berry pointed out in their review in *Nature,* there are serious weaknesses and misrepresentations in Thornhill and Palmer's presentation of their evidence (see Coyne, this volume).

Let us consider a few other examples of Thornhill and Palmer's handling of evidence and reasoning. Take their claim that rape is all and only about sexual reproduction—the club they use to batter the view of feminists who hold that rape is about both sex and domination or control of women. Thornhill and Palmer admit, in passing, that some holders of the by-product view see rape as resulting from a combination of male sexual desire and the "drive to possess and control" (2000b, p. 61; they cite Ellis 1989, 1991; and Malamuth 1996). But they dismiss this very plausible evolutionary view by claiming that ordinarily there is no drive to possess and control victims "for prolonged periods of time" (2000b, p. 62). But, of course, the period of time is irrelevant to whether that desire is a contributing proximate cause to rape.

We should also scrutinize Thornhill and Palmer's claim that the ability to detect vulnerability in potential victims is a special psychological adaptation in men to facilitate rape (2000b, p. 66). While we are telling evolutionary stories, isn't it more likely that the ability to detect vulnerability evolved as a broadly valuable social and parenting capacity? For example, the ability to detect vulnerability would have been very advantageous in the evolutionary past when men were protecting their families. This obvious alternative is not considered by Thornhill and Palmer.

And what happened to the patently obvious hypothesis that raping behavior is due to psychopathology? In one of the two studies of developmental factors affecting rape that Thornhill and Palmer do discuss in the book, psychopathology played a leading explanatory role. This study of adolescent male sexual criminals by Figueredo et al. (2000) found that these rapists were characterized by backgrounds of repeated frustration, failed romantic and sexual relationships, as well as lower psychosocial functioning, learning disabilities, and psychological disorders (2000b, p. 67). But Thornhill and Palmer want to treat psychopathic men as a distinct group from rapists, claiming (with no evidence) that psychopaths make up a distinct genetic form, and that normal men don't have the same adaptations.[8] In fact, they suggest that "psychopathic and normal men possess two *distinct* psychological adaptations with regard to rape—both of which could be condition dependent" (2000b, p. 82; emphasis added). Here we have a clear candidate for special pleading. Interestingly, this resembles a similar problem that Thornhill and Palmer have with the fact that high-status men, who are otherwise able to secure sexual partners, rape, thus challenging their theory that only "losers" rape. In that case, they propose that "their raping must result from adaptations other than that suggested by the [low-status] hypothesis" (2000b, p. 68). Thus, we have two more specific psychological adaptations proposed in order to deal with anomalies from the main rape adaptation theory, under which the genetic underpinnings of rape were supposedly fixed among human beings. We can see an evasive tactic emerging: If ever an anomaly threatens Thornhill and Palmer's project, they simply propose more psychological adaptations.

There is yet another type of data that is patently relevant to Thornhill and Palmer's hypotheses that is not considered: comparisons between human beings and our closest relatives, the chimpanzee and the bonobo. Thornhill and Palmer seem to have an internal conflict about whether to use comparative evidence, even though it is standard in contemporary evolutionary analyses. In one place, they argue for the importance of comparative analysis, "which is a fundamental tool in biology for understanding causation" (2000b, p. 120). They follow this approach when they appeal to the claim that rape occurs in many nonhuman species. But when it comes to our closest relatives, the standards change: They claim that it is erroneous to think that the behavior of nonhuman primates is necessarily salient to human adaptations (2000b, p. 56). What is motivating this sudden switch? Perhaps this: The rate of rape among chimpanzees is very low, and the majority of these are brother-sister rapes; moreover, rape has never been observed at all in bonobos (Wrangham, personal communication, 2000; see also Goodall 1986).[9] These are our two closest living relatives. This information is clearly damaging to their case. It places extra burdens on them to produce a uniquely human account of the evolution of rape, one that does not rely on common traits about sex differences in sexuality that we share with our nearest relatives. Instead, Thornhill and Palmer rely heavily on comparative evidence from scorpion flies (2000b, pp. 63–64). I leave the reader to judge whether comparisons with scorpion flies are more relevant than comparisons with nonhuman primates.

Moreover, the chimps and bonobos show that their by-product view is also inadequate. If rape resulted simply from the design of male sexuality for multiple partners, then we should expect our closest relatives to exhibit the same rape-as-by-product behavior, given that they have similarly evolved male sexualities. But we find the incidence of rape is either low or nonexistent. Hence, it seems that the structure of male sexuality is, itself, insufficient to support a by-product analysis of rape. Other authors suggest that aggression and dominance are also involved, which, in the case of human beings, might make a dangerous cocktail of causes that leads to rape as an evolutionary by-product. Nevertheless, Thornhill and Palmer reject these alternate views.

Finally, perhaps the crucial assumption of their entire book is that rape was indeed, at some time in evolution, a reproductively successful strategy—but they leave this assumption almost completely unsupported. In fact, the current rape statistics provide a potential challenge to their conclusions. According to a study they cite themselves, the success rate that reported rapists currently have at inseminating their victims is only about 2 percent. This 2 percent must be compared within the context of the overall lifetime reproductive success of those using the rape strategy, those not, and mixed cases. Even though Thornhill and Palmer do not compare these various strategies, it is still possible that a 2 percent rate of insemination is strong enough to provide a selective pressure, even with high abortion rates. However, what such a scenario requires is that raping provided, at some time in history, a higher frequency of fertilization than nonraping for these individuals. But they have not shown this.

Worse for Thornhill and Palmer, 50 percent of pregnant rape victims in a U.S. study terminated their pregnancy through therapeutic abortions, and another 12 percent resulted in spontaneous abortion (2000b, p. 100). Thornhill and Palmer are not deterred by these contemporary results. They dismiss objections to their views by stating that such contemporary evidence is not relevant to whether rape was an adaptation in our evolutionary past.[10] They are certainly correct about this. However, the problem is that Thornhill and Palmer make no effort to describe the relevant environmental (including cultural) circumstances in our evolutionary past in any detail, either in support of or against the rape hypotheses they consider. What we would normally demand is some evidence regarding, for example: the percentage of women who either abort or kill their rape-begotten infants,[11] the likelihood that any given woman of reproductive age either is nursing (with its concomitant reduction in fertility) or is already pregnant at any given moment; or what percentage of rapists were caught and punished, which could be calibrated to the ancestral group size and culture, and the likelihood of being caught. But Thornhill and Palmer make no effort to provide this crucial evidence, which is badly needed in order to evaluate their hypotheses.

4   The Enemy

Thornhill and Palmer begin their chapter entitled "Law and Punishment" with a caricature of social scientists, who supposedly believe in "cultural determinism." They claim: "Cultural determinism is consistent with free will and with the ability of humans to change their behavior *easily* by adopting new social constructs" (2000b, p. 153; emphasis added). Needless to say, the "ease" of adopting new social constructs is an imaginative piece of misinterpretation by Thornhill and Palmer; social scientists tend to view social and cultural forces as entrenched and as acting over the lifetime of the individual's development, and thus as very *difficult* to change. Hence, when Thornhill and Palmer point out that the "ease" of change "is in conflict with everything that is known about the interaction of genetic and environmental factors in the development of all behavioral abilities" (2000b, p. 153), they are in agreement, not opposition, with their supposed targets.

They continue by stating that our real need is to understand "how human-mediated alterations in the developmental environment can produce desirable behavioral changes" (2000b, p. 153), thus stating the obvious, and outlining the standard goal of many socialization, criminalistic, and psychological studies. Thornhill and Palmer see their stated goals as conflicting with the social sciences only because they see evolutionary theory as "crucial, since it predicts that the developmental events of interest will occur in response to specific cues that, in our history as a species, were most reliably correlated with reduced consensual sex with females" (2000b, p. 154). But these specific cues are part of what the social scientists in question study.

Moreover, instead of including fair critical examination of various alternative hypotheses for the development of rape in men, Thornhill and Palmer attack a caricature of what they call the "feminist psychosocial" position. They spend a full 60 pages of this slim 200-page book attacking feminist views on rape, which they inexplicably equate with "the social science theory." The feminist view supposedly says that sex has absolutely nothing to do with rape (the "not sex" view), and that rape is instead exclusively about the power and control over women, about misogyny, and about the exercise of patriarchal values. Their ultimate target for this view is Susan Brownmiller, who successfully inspired changes in the political and legal atmosphere surrounding treatment of rapists and victims with her 1975 book, *Against Our Will.* In Thornhill and Palmer's précis of their book, published in the *Sciences,* they wrote:

In 1975 the feminist writer Susan Brownmiller asserted that rape is motivated not by lust but by the urge to control and dominate. In the twenty-five years since, Brownmiller's view has become mainstream. All men feel sexual desire, the theory goes, but not all men rape. Rape is viewed as an unnatural behavior that has nothing to do with sex, and one that has no corollary in the animal world. (2000a, p. 30)

But Brownmiller never professed the primary mistake attributed to her, namely, that rape does not involve sex. In fact, Brownmiller refers to rape as a sexual act throughout the whole 1975 book. For example, she calls rape "a 'taking' of sex through the use of threat or force" (1975, p. 377). Elsewhere she recounts instances in which rape is a *sexual* reward for the male slave, and a *sexual* privilege for the masters (1975, pp. 157–158). In other words, she clearly and repeatedly categorizes rape as sex.

More recently, in an appearance on the National Public Radio show "Talk of the Nation" with Thornhill, Brownmiller insisted:

I never said that rape was not involved with sex. Obviously, it uses the sex organs. What the women's movement did say, starting in the 1970s, was that rape was not *sexy*, you see. The men, up to that point, had romanticized rape and always presented scenarios of beautiful but just slightly unwilling, but really teasing victims. And the act was construed as sort of a Robin Hood act of machismo. When women started to speak up about their own experiences of rape, the first thing they said was, "No, there's nothing sexy about this. This was pure power humiliation, degradation." And that's where the feminist theory came from, out of listening to the experiences of women. (Appearing on Penkava 2000; emphasis added)

Thornhill expressed surprise during this radio show at Brownmiller's statement that sex was involved in rape.[12] But this response was disingenuous at best, because Brownmiller had previously attempted to correct Thornhill's specific misrepresentation of the feminist view as the "not sex" view of rape. She and Barbara Mehrhof (1992) were commentators on a 1992 target article in *Brain and Behavioral Sciences* written by Thornhill and his former wife, Nancy Thornhill. In the commentary, Brownmiller and Mehrhof state, "the central insight of the feminist theory of rape identifies the act as a crime of violence. . . . The sexual motivation, orgasmic release, is a secondary component" (1992, p. 382).

So then why does Thornhill now publicly feign surprise at Brownmiller's resistance to the former's characterization of her view as the "not sex" view? Perhaps because in their book, Thornhill and Palmer attribute to Brownmiller a series of strawperson "arguments" that depend on her maintaining the "not sex" view. They then attempt to debunk these arguments. Let us take a closer look at what they say Brownmiller says, and compare it to what Brownmiller actually said.

Take Thornhill and Palmer's "Argument 9," supposedly put forward by Brownmiller: "It is not a crime of lust but of violence and power . . . rape victims are not only the 'lovely young blondes' of newspaper headlines—rapists strike children, the aged, the homely—all women" (2000b, p. 138).[13] In elaborating their rebuttal to this claim, Thornhill and Palmer focus on the ages of rape victims, and argue as follows:

The statement that "any female may become a victim of rape" (Brownmiller 1975, p. 348) does not imply that the "rapist chooses his victim with a striking disregard for conventional 'sex appeal'" (ibid., p. 338). Contrary to Brownmiller, although any female *might* become a victim of rape, some women are far more likely to become victims of rape than others. Indeed, one of the most consistent findings of studies on rape, and one not likely to be due entirely to reporting bias, is that women in their teens and their early twenties are highly overrepresented among rape victims around the world. (Thornhill and Palmer, 2000b, pp. 138–139; their emphasis)

Now let us look at what Brownmiller actually said. On the very same page as the second sentence they quote, Brownmiller continues:

Statistical probability does matter. Just as there is a calculable "typical" rapist, there is also, to a lesser degree of certainty, a "typical" victim. While any woman is a natural target for a would-be rapist, the chances are that a rape victim will be of the same class and race as her attacker, at least between 70 and 90% of the time. More often than not, she will also be the same age as her attacker, or slightly younger. Overall, the danger to women is greatest between the ages of 10 and 29. Teenage girls, simply by being teenage girls, run the greatest risk of any age group. (Brownmiller 1975, p. 348)

In other words, Brownmiller *explicitly denies* that all women are equally likely to become rape victims, and in fact emphasizes the same results as Thornhill and Palmer, in direct contradiction to their charge.

In all, four of the nine "feminist" arguments they attempt to debunk are attributed to Brownmiller, so it is very significant that the textual evidence and the verbal reports of that author deny the basic premise of these arguments, namely, that sex is not involved in rape. There are further difficulties, though. Feminist "Argument 1" consists of a quote taken from *opponents* to a feminist understanding of rape (2000b, p. 133). Ordinarily, honest scientists consider versions of arguments from their proponents and not their proponents' enemies. This is not the only time, however, that Thornhill and Palmer use the tactic of representing their enemies' views unfairly. For example, they also use the work of antifeminist Dwight C. Murphy (1992), who presents a popular press version of Brownmiller's view of rape that misrepresents Brownmiller's position as a "not sex" view (Thornhill and Palmer 2000b, p. 125). In sum, Thornhill and Palmer must be considered unreliable on the issue of what feminists have said and how it relates to their own views.

Now consider the following argument: All matter is subject to the laws of quantum mechanics. Therefore, population geneticists cannot have a legitimate explanation of the behavior of genes, because they are failing to appeal to the *fundamental causes* of matter's behavior.[14] This amounts to a denial of the legitimacy of an independent level of explanation for any "nonfundamental" theory.

Implausibly, Thornhill and Palmer use the same form of argument in this book, wherein higher, independent levels of explanation above the ordinary biological level are rejected as not being fundamental enough. This argument is unacceptable regarding population genetics, and it is unacceptable concerning the social science levels of explanation that Thornhill and Palmer want to delegitimate.

One of the most confused and confusing aspects of Thornhill and Palmer's arguments is the claim that "every aspect of every living thing is, by definition, biological" (2000b, p. 20). Their argument runs as follows. All behavior is biological because it evolved. Therefore all explanations of that behavior must be biological, since there is no psychological, sociological, or cultural explanation that is not fundamentally biology. Therefore, all research into behavior must involve and be guided by evolutionary biology. As they put it, culture is "still biological and subject to the only general biological theory—evolution by selection" (2000b, p. 24). (Never mind the false equation of evolutionary theory itself with evolution by selection.)

Shockingly, this line of argument is supposed to show that social scientists such as psychologists and sociologists cannot do their research— investigating and identifying the range of environmental factors influencing behavior—without doing evolutionary biology simultaneously.[15] Of course, it implies nothing of the kind: The search for environmental factors affecting phenotypes can proceed in the complete absence of a specific evolutionary hypothesis. Furthermore, having an evolutionary hypothesis about a trait does not by any means isolate the relevant learning factors that go into producing that trait. Both of these points are denied vehemently by Thornhill and Palmer (2000b, pp. 84, 153, 156).

Note how the apparently trivial claim that "everything is biological" is now doing real work here. They want to claim that if someone is not using the evolutionary level of explanation for a human phenomenon, then they are not doing any explaining at all. But even according to their own view, research into the *relevant causes* of different developmental outcomes in human beings is a necessary part of the explaining that they want to do. If some of the relevant causes are cultural, then cultural research into such causes is totally legitimate, and in fact necessary. Or do they want to rule out cultural causes as possible influences on human development? It seems that they do not, for they say, "Yes, some differences in behavior between individuals could be due entirely to cultural influences that have affected their behavior" (2000b, pp. 24–25). But this does not mean, they say, that "an individual's culturally influenced behavior is due entirely to environmental causes and hence is not biological" (2000b, p. 25). But they've just admitted that, in the case at hand, the differences between one individual and another can be entirely cultural, and not *explicable* at the level of biology.

And there's the rub. They want to deny that cultural explanations can really *explain* anything—that the cultural level of investigation is a legitimately explanatory one. On what basis? On the basis that "an individual's cultural behavior is still a product of gene-environment interactions. And the individual can learn nothing without underlying adaptation for learning" (2000b, p. 25). Well, this is no doubt true, but we can agree to these last statements and yet believe that a purely cultural investigation of individual differences in development is both necessary and explanatory. Nevertheless, Thornhill and Palmer insist that "The cultural behavior of individuals is *never* independent of the human evolutionary history of selection for individual reproductive success" (2000b, p. 29). What they mean by "independent" here is *explanatory* independence, as becomes painfully obvious in their fierce attack on the possibility of the social sciences telling us anything useful about human rape. But they have not successfully argued for *explanatory* dependence of the social on the biological; at best, they have argued the reverse, with their own admission of the explanatory power of cultural explanation of difference.

5   Legal and Social Consequences

Thornhill and Palmer repeatedly promise that moving to the evolutionary level of explanation will make everything better: therapeutic treatment of rape victims; reduction in the incidence of rape; improvements in how rape is treated in the courts; and understanding of the developmental, social, and cultural "conditional" factors producing rapists from male babies (2000b, pp. 82, 84, 97, 114, 153, 154, 156, 158, 187). Despite this repetition, they offer no evidence whatsoever for any of these claims; all we get are promises. But they do offer a few concrete remarks, well-supported or not, concerning the legal treatment of rapists. They also suggest ways to improve rape-prevention training.

As Thornhill and Palmer acknowledge, people have a strong tendency to react to their theories by indulging in what is known as the "naturalistic fallacy": equating claims of what is "natural" with claims of what is good or morally defensible. Since the authors do not condone rape, they attempt to deter this reaction repeatedly. But their eagerness to publish a poorly supported and inflammatory theory—one that predictably evokes the naturalistic fallacy[16]—seems irresponsible. Accusing people of a "lack of scholarship" just is not good enough (2000b, p. 122).

Their response to the naturalist fallacy is as follows: "Contrary to the common view that an evolutionary explanation for human behavior removes individuals' responsibility for their actions, individuals who really understood the evolutionary bases of their actions might be better able to avoid behaving in an 'adaptive' fashion that is damaging to others" (2000b, p. 154). Specifically how is this knowledge supposed to help change the rapist's behavior? Do they have evidence that such knowledge would be connected with a lower incidence of rape? Is this even plausible? They propose a rape-prevention education program for teenage boys—one that could perhaps be required before they get their driver's licenses—which involves explaining the evolutionary basis of their sexual desires, and which encourages them to control their sexual impulses (2000b, p. 179). (And these are the authors who criticized the sociologists for allegedly believing that behavior can easily be changed!) After such an education, they suggest, "refusal to refrain from damaging behavior in the face of scientific understanding could be seen as a ground for holding irresponsible individuals *more* culpable, not less so" (2000b, p. 154; their emphasis).

This suggestion raises a host of questions. For instance: Since they emphasize that evolutionary theory is very complicated and difficult, how are they planning to teach it in this minicourse?[17] Also, since they know that most people's reaction to their view *is* to commit the naturalistic fallacy, why assume that the instructees (or their instructors) would be any different, and would not also conclude that rape is natural and therefore inevitable or acceptable? They do emphasize that teaching that the naturalistic fallacy *is* a fallacy will be part of their suggested course (2000b, pp. 179–180), but can we assume that it will be understood?

One very striking thing about Thornhill and Palmer's discussion of rape prevention and punishment is how many of their ideas are borrowed *directly* from the feminist accounts they deride. For instance, they note that "rape has traditionally been defined and punished not from the victim's perspective but from a male perspective, and particularly from the perspective of the victim's mate" (2000b, pp. 154–155; see Brownmiller 1975, pp. 14, 18–30, 376–377). They also note that rules and laws generally serve the interests of the powerful—for example, men as opposed to women (2000b, p. 162; see Brownmiller 1975, p. 17). Furthermore, statutory rape laws should be understood in the context that, in most societies, "daughters have been viewed as their father's property" (2000b, p. 162;

see Brownmiller 1975, pp. 17–18, 376). As far as rape prevention goes, their suggestions are nearly all features that have been central to the feminist revolution in rape counseling: advising caution about being alone in isolated places; advocating self-defense training; urging women to exert greater control over circumstances "in which they consent to be alone with men" (2000b, p. 186). They differ from feminist advice in their recommendation that women wear more concealing clothing (even though they offer no evidence of a correlation between the amount of skin shown and rape). But Thornhill and Palmer claim that all this follows only from the evolutionary perspective, and that only the evolutionary perspective can help direct research toward treatment that will alleviate the pain and suffering caused by rape (2000b, pp. 187–188).

As far as legal punishment goes, Thornhill and Palmer do not propose a specific program; they simply claim that any such program of punishment should be informed by what is known about evolution. They do discuss one possible punishment in detail, though—*chemical castration.* They defend chemical castration on the basis of evolution, claiming that since rape is about reproductive sex, chemical castration might be an effective preventative (2000b, pp. 165–166).[18] They fail to address the problem, however, that such an approach has a chance of reducing the conviction rate of rapists, since juries may be more reluctant to interfere with the suspect's "manhood" than they are to sending him to prison for a few years.

In sum, Thornhill and Palmer encourage their readers to see rape as *purely* a sexual act, proximally motivated by an out-of-control male libido. The public needs to decide if this reduced view of rape as sex alone really represents the truth about rape. On the bases of the weaknesses in their evolutionary biology alone, I think the answer is clear. When the data-fudging and gross misrepresentation of other explanatory approaches are added to the mix, I take it to be the responsibility of educated people to resist Thornhill and Palmer's conclusions about rape.

Notes

1. Thornhill and Palmer write: "Why have researchers attempting to discover the evolutionary causes of rape been denied positions at universities? Why have organizers of scholarly conferences attempted to keep papers on evolutionary analysis of rape from being presented? Why have editors of scholarly journals refused to publish papers treating rape in a Darwinian perspective?" (2000b, p. 105). And

later: "The choice between the social science explanation's answers and the evolutionarily informed answers provided in this book is essentially a choice between ideology and knowledge" (2000b, p. 189).

2. "In the future, I anticipate, hopefully not the too distant future, that we'll turn this thing around in a sense that people will look back with horror at the kinds of attitudes that Brownmiller is expressing today and, to a degree, Dr. Coyne. And the horror will be in the fact that people did not understand that, in the Dark Ages, the validity and importance of science for correcting our social problems. But specifically in response to the kind of data that we have in there, it's all scientific approach . . ." (Randy Thornhill, appearing on "Talk of the Nation." Penkava 2000; see also Goode 2000; Spohn 2000; Sandlin 2000).

3. This is a standard view among many biologists working in human and animal evolution.

4. According to a 1998 U.S. study, about 302,1000 women and 92,700 men are raped each year nationwide ("Men can't help it," 2000).

5. The phenotype of an organism is the particular collection and arrangement of all its manifest physical and behavioral traits.

6. Thornhill and Palmer (2000b) make use of their mistaken view about mutation on p. 57, in the context of dismissing the hypothesis that rape could have arisen as a mutation balanced by selection.

7. Different "levels of explanation" appeal to different entities and laws, at distinct levels of the organization of life. *See* notes 15–16 and accompanying text.

8. Geoffrey Miller, an evolutionary psychologist at University College, London, also challenges Thornhill and Palmer's neglect of the psychopathology explanation: "Psychopaths are discussed on only one page, though they account for a substantial proportion of all rapists, and the majority of multiple rapists. . . . [R]esearch shows that there are heritable genetic differences in many traits that may predict the tendency to use sexual coercion, such as disagreeableness, psychoticism, low intelligence and alcoholism" (2000).

9. Despite Thornhill and Palmer's approving citations of Wrangham and Dale Peterson (1996), Wrangham notes there that feminists are right in seeing rape as involved with power relations, not just as a conceptive strategy (personal communication, 2000).

10. This, in spite of their heavy usage of such contemporary evidence in other contexts.

11. Sarah Blaffer Hrdy (1999) argues for the prevalence of abortion and infanticide in human evolutionary history.

12. Thornhill to Brownmiller: "And that you're saying now that rape is sex and so forth is kind of amazing" (Penkava 2000).

13. Thornhill and Palmer chose this quote from the back cover of Brownmiller's book.

14. This example is due to Michael Dickson, History and Philosophy of Science Department, Indiana University.

15. In criticizing social scientists, Thornhill and Palmer actually claim that evolved cognition itself may interfere with evolutionary investigation into cultural phenomena: "Evolved psychological intuitions about behavioral causation can mislead individuals into believing that they know as much as *experts* do about proximate human motivation" (2000b, p. 114; emphasis added). The experts on social behavior here seem to be the evolutionists, rather than the social scientists.

16. A survey of the available published reviews, editorials and letters to the editor involving this book shows that most readers, in fact, commit precisely this fallacy.

17. Thornhill himself argued in a radio appearance, "you know, evolutionary biology is complex. Science is complex. In fact, many have pointed out that the facts and theory of evolution are the most complex set of ideas we have out there . . ." (appearing on Penkava 2000).

18. According to Dani Robbins Zulich, Director of the Women's Coalition at Case Western Reserve University, experiments in treating rapists with surgical and chemical castration have not proven effective (Sandstrom 2000, p. 111).

References

Blaffer Hrdy, Sarah (1999). *Mother Nature: Maternal Instincts and How They Shape the Human Species*. New York: Ballantine Books.

Brownmiller, S. (1975). *Against Our Will: Men, Women, and Rape*. New York: Simon and Schuster.

Brownmiller, S. and B. Mehrhof (1992). A feminist response to rape as an adaptation in men. *Behavioral and Brain Sciences* 15 (2): 381–382.

Boyd, R. and R. J. Richerson (1985). *Culture and the Evolutionary Process*. Chicago, IL: University of Chicago Press.

Buller, D. and V. G. Hardcastle (2001). Evolutionary psychology, meet the developing brain: Combating promiscuous modularity. *Brain and Mind* 1(3):307–325.

Cavalli-Sforza, L. L. and M. W. Feldman (1978). Darwinian selection and "altruism." *Theoretical Population Genetics* 14: 180–218.

Cavalli-Sforza, L. L., and M. W. Feldman (1981). *Cultural Transmission and Evolution*. Princeton, N.J.: Princeton University Press.

Clausen, Jens (1951). *Stages in the Evolution of Plant Species*. Ithaca, N.Y.: Cornell University Press.

Coyne, J. A. (2000). Of vice and men [review of the book *A Natural History of Rape*]. *The New Republic,* April 3.

Dano, Mike (2000). Media blitz surrounding controversial theory works for U. New Mexico prof. *University of New Mexico Daily Lobo*, February 4, p. 1.

Darwin, C. (1859/1964). *On the Origin of Species* (reprinted). Cambridge, Mass.: Harvard University Press.

Dobzhansky, T. (1937). *Genetics and the Origin of Species*. New York: Columbia University Press.

Durham, W. H. (1991). *Coevolution: Genes, Culture, and Human Diversity.* Palo Alto, Calif.: Stanford University Press.

Ellis, L. (1989). *Theories of Rape: Inquiries into the Causes of Sexual Aggression.* New York: Hemisphere Press.

Ellis, L. (1991). The drive to possess and control as a motivation for sexual behavior: Applications to the study of rape. *Social Science Information* 30: 633–675.

Figueredo, A. J., B. D. Sales, J. V. Becker, K. Russell, and M. Kaplan (2000). A Brunswikian evolutionary-developmental model of adolescent sex offending. *Behavioral Sciences and the Law* 18 (2–3): 309–329.

Goodall, Jane (1986). *The Chimpanzees of Gombe.* Cambridge, Mass.: Harvard University Press.

Goode, Erica (2000). Human nature: Born or made? *New York Times,* March 14, p. F1.

Gould, S. J. (1977). *Ontogeny and Phylogeny.* Cambridge, Mass.: Harvard University Press.

Grant, V. (1963). *The Origin of Adaptations.* New York: Columbia University Press.

Kilpatrick, D., C. Edmunds, and A. Seymour (1992). *Rape in America: A Report to the Nation.* Arlington, Virginia: National Victim Center.

Lack, D. (1954). *The Natural Regulation of Animal Numbers.* Oxford: Oxford University Press.

Laland, K. N., F. J. Odling-Smee, and M. W. Feldman (1996). The evolutionary consequences of niche construction: A theoretical investigation using two-locus theory. *Journal of Evolutionary Biology* 9: 293–316.

Laland, K. N., F. J. Odling-Smee, and M. W. Feldman (2000). Niche construction, biological evolution, and cultural change. *Behavioral and Brain Sciences* 23: 31–175.

Lewontin, R. C. (1982). Organism and environment. In H. C. Plotkin, ed., *Learning, Development, and Culture,* pp. 151–170. New York: John Wiley and Sons.

Lewontin, R. C. (1997). Dobzhansky's *Genetics and the Origin of Species:* Is it still relevant? *Genetics* 147: 351–355.

Lloyd, Elisabeth A. (1988/1994). *The Structure and Confirmation of Evolutionary Theory.* Princeton, N.J.: Princeton University Press.

Lloyd, Elisabeth A. (1999). Evolutionary psychology: The burdens of proof. *Biology and Philosophy* 14: 211–233.

Lloyd, Elisabeth A. (2001). Science gone astray: Evolution and rape. *Michigan Law Review* 99: 1536–1559.

Lloyd, E. A. and M. W. Feldman (2002). Evolutionary psychology: A view from evolutionary biology. *Psychological Inquiry.*

Malamuth, N. (1996). The confluence model of sexual aggression: Feminist and evolutionary perspectives. In D. Buss and N. Malamuth, eds., *Sex, Power, Conflict,* pp. 269–295. New York: Oxford University Press.

Mayr, E. (1942). *Systematics and the Origin of Species.* New York: Columbia University Press.

Men can't help it, the. (2000). *Guardian,* January 25, p. 4.

Miller, Geoffrey (2000). Review of the book *A Natural History of Rape. Evening Standard,* March 6.

Murphy, Dwight C. (1992). Feminism and rape. *Journal of Social, Political, and Economic Studies* 17 (1): 13–27.

Penkava, Melinda (Host). (2000). *Talk of the Nation.* January 26 broadcast. Washington, D.C.: National Public Radio.

Sandlin, Scott (2000). Rape a biological act, UNM professor writes. *Albuquerque Journal,* January 22, p. A1.

Sandstrom, Karen (2000). Study of rape hits ideological nerve; linking cause to evolution ignites backlash. *Plain Dealer,* February 27, p. 11I.

Sheppard, P. M. (1958). *Natural Selection and Heredity.* New York: Harper and Row.

Simpson, G. G. (1953). *The Major Features of Evolution.* New York: Columbia University Press.

Spohn, Lawrence (2000). Their argument provokes thought—and ire. *Grand Rapids Press* (Scripps Howard News Service), January 14, p. A2.

Stebbins, G. L. (1950). *Variation and Evolution in Plants.* New York: Columbia University Press.

Thornhill, R. and C. T. Palmer (2000a). Why men rape. *Sciences,* January/February, pp. 30–36.

Thornhill, R. and C. T. Palmer (2000b). *A Natural History of Rape: Biological Bases of Sexual Coercion.* Cambridge, Mass.: MIT Press.

Thornhill, R. and N. W. Thornhill (1992). The evolutionary psychology of men's coercive sexuality. *Behavioral and Brain Sciences* 15 (2): 363–421.

Weismann, A. (1904). *The Evolution Theory* (2nd ed., 2 vols.; J. A. Thomson and M. R. Thomson, trans.). London: Edward Arnold.

Wilson, M., M. Daly, and J. Scheib (1997). Femicide: An evolutionary psychological perspective. In P. Gowaty, ed., *Feminism and Evolutionary Biology,* pp. 431–465. New York: Chapman and Hall.

Wrangham, R. and D. Peterson (1996). *Demonic Males: Apes and the Origins of Human Violence.* Boston: Houghton Mifflin.

Wright, S. (1931). Evolution in Mendelian populations. *Genetics* 1 (6): 97–159.

Integrative and Cultural Models of Gender and Rape

12

The Origins of Sex Differences in Human Behavior: Evolved Dispositions versus Social Roles

Alice H. Eagly and Wendy Wood

As more research psychologists have become willing to acknowledge that some aspects of social behavior, personality, and abilities differ between women and men (e.g., Eagly 1995; Halpern 1997), their attention has begun to focus on the causes of these differences. Debates about causes center, at least in part, on determining what can be considered the basic or ultimate causes of sex differences. Theories of sex differences that address causes at this level are termed in this article *origin theories* (Archer 1996). In such theories, causation flows from a basic cause to sex-differentiated behavior, and biological, psychological, and social processes mediate the relation between the basic cause and behavior. In this article, we consider two types of origin theories: One of these implicates evolved psychological dispositions, and the other implicates social structure. Evolutionary psychology, as illustrated in the work of Buss (1995a), Kenrick and Keefe (1992), and Tooby and Cosmides (1992), thus represents the first type of origin theory, and social psychological theories that emphasize social structure represent the second type of origin theory (e.g., Eagly 1987; Eagly, Wood, and Diekman, 2000; Lorenzi-Cioldi 1998; Ridgeway 1991; West and Zimmerman 1987; Wiley 1995).

In the origin theory proposed by evolutionary psychologists, the critical causal arrow points from evolutionary adaptations to psychological sex differences. Because women and men possess sex-specific evolved mechanisms, they differ psychologically and tend to occupy different social roles. In contrast, in the social structural origin theory, the critical causal arrow points from social structure to psychological sex differences. Because men and women tend to occupy different social roles, they become psychologically different in ways that adjust them to these roles.

One important feature is shared by these two origin theories: Both offer a functional analysis of behavior that emphasizes adjustment to environmental conditions. However, the two schools of thought differ radically in their analysis of the nature and timing of the adjustments that are most important to sex-differentiated behavior. Evolutionary psychologists believe that females and males faced different pressures in primeval environments and that the sexes' differing reproductive status was the key feature of ancestral life that framed sex-typed adaptive problems. The resolutions of these problems produced sex-specific evolved mechanisms that humans carry with them as a species and that are held to be the root cause of sex-differentiated behavior. Although evolutionary psychologists readily acknowledge the abstract principle that environmental conditions can influence the development and expression of evolved dispositions, they have given limited attention to variation of sex differences in response to individual, situational, and cultural conditions (e.g., Archer 1996; Buss 1995b; Buss and Kenrick 1998). For example, Buss (1998) emphasized "universal or near-universal sex differences" (p. 421) in preferences for long-term mates.

Social structuralists maintain that the situations faced by women and men are quite variable across societies and historical periods as social organization changes in response to technological, ecological, and other transformations. From a social structural perspective, a society's division of labor between the sexes is the engine of sex-differentiated behavior, because it summarizes the social constraints under which men and women carry out their lives. Sex differences are viewed as accommodations to the differing restrictions and opportunities that a society maintains for its men and women, and sex-differentiated behavior is held to be contingent on a range of individual, situational, and cultural conditions (see Deaux and LaFrance 1998). Despite this emphasis on the social environment, social structuralists typically acknowledge the importance of some genetically mediated sex differences. Physical differences between the sexes, particularly men's greater size and strength and women's childbearing and lactation, are very important because they interact with shared cultural beliefs, social organization, and the demands of the economy to influence the role assignments that constitute the sexual division of labor within a society and produce psychological sex differences (Eagly 1987; Wood and Eagly in press).

These thumbnail sketches of these two origin theories should make it clear that this debate about the origins of sex differences cannot be reduced to a simple nature-versus-nurture dichotomy. Both evolutionary psychology and social structural theory are interactionist in the sense that they take both biological and environmental factors into account, but they treat these factors quite differently. Evolutionary psychology views sex-specific evolved dispositions as psychological tendencies that were built in through genetically mediated adaptation to primeval conditions; the theory treats contemporary environmental factors as cues that interact with adaptations to yield sex-typed responses. Social structural theory views sex-differentiated tendencies as built in through accommodation to the contemporaneous sexual division of labor; in this approach, physical differences between the sexes serve as one influence on role assignment.

Another caution is that these theories do not merely reflect different levels of analysis. In some attempts to reconcile the two perspectives, writers have proposed that social structural theories identify proximal, contemporaneous causes for the behavior of women and men, whereas evolutionary analyses invoke more distal causes that arose early in human history (e.g., Borkenau 1992; Jackson 1992; Schaller 1997). Although the timing of the human adjustment to environmental conditions that is deemed critical is indeed different in the two theories, they propose causes that are similar in their position on the proximal versus distal continuum of causality. Both theories thus identify psychological causes (i.e., evolved dispositions, role expectations) that operate in the present and that exert their impact through more proximal processes (e.g., emotions, perceptions). The social structural perspective is thus in stark contrast to evolutionary psychology models that attribute sex differences in contemporary society to sex-typed evolved mechanisms. The causes of sex differences in evolutionary psychology involve these mechanisms, which are intended to replace the social psychological mechanisms featured in theories that give a key role to social structure.

It also would be inappropriate to conclude that the social structural approach is incompatible with the general perspective of evolutionary theorizing. Social structural analyses suggest an evolved organism, but one in which evolutionary pressures yielded a variety of dispositions, such as the capacity for group living and for culture. These analyses do not imply that people's minds are blank slates, because humans possess facilities, such as for language, that develop in certain ways, given appropriate environments. Moreover, our critique of theorizing in evolutionary psychology is not meant to apply to evolutionary principles in general. Evolutionary reasoning pertaining to humans is diverse (Smith, 2000) and provides the basis, not only of evolutionary psychology, but also of models of the relation between biology and culture (Janicki and Krebs 1998) and human behavioral ecology approaches that emphasize behavioral variability in response to socioecological conditions (Cronk 1991). The implications of these other evolutionary theories for psychological processes have yet to be fully developed and are not discussed in this article.

To illustrate the contrasting approaches of evolutionary psychology and social structural theory, we first present and discuss each theory. Then we examine their predictions concerning the criteria men and women use in selecting mates. This domain of behavior has been central to evolutionary theorizing about human sex differences (e.g., Buss and Schmitt 1993; Kenrick and Keefe 1992), and the cross-cultural findings available in this area provide an opportunity to examine empirically some of the predictions of evolutionary and social structural analyses.

Evolutionary Psychology as an Origin Theory of Sex Differences

From the perspective of evolutionary psychology, human sex differences reflect adaptations to the pressures of the differing physical and social environments that impinged on females and males during primeval times (Buss 1995a; Tooby and Cosmides 1992). Evolutionary psychologists thus label the environment that produced a species' evolved tendencies as its environment of evolutionary adaptedness (EEA; Cosmides, Tooby, and Barkow 1992; Symons 1979, 1992; Tooby and Cosmides 1990b). They loosely identify the Pleistocene era as the human EEA and generally assume that it was populated by hunter-gatherer groups. To the extent that males and females faced different adaptive problems as they evolved, the two sexes developed different strategies to ensure their survival and to maximize their reproductive success. The resolutions to these problems produced evolved psychological mechanisms that are specific to each problem domain and that differ between women and men.

Although humans' evolved mechanisms developed in response to the types of problems consistently encountered by their ancestors and thus are presumed to be universal attributes of humans, environmental input affects how these mechanisms develop in individuals and how they are expressed in behavior (e.g., Buss and Kenrick 1998). Because culture influences developmental experiences and patterns current situational input, culture is in principle important to the expression of adaptive mechanisms (Tooby and Cosmides 1992). However, evolutionary psychologists have devoted relatively little attention to the interaction between such broader attributes of the social and cultural environment and the evolved mechanisms that may underlie sex differences. The contextual factors that have interested them generally relate directly to these hypothesized mechanisms. For example, Buss and Schmitt (1993) maintained that the characteristics that people seek in mates depend, not only on their sex, but also on whether they are engaging in short-term or long-term mating. Because of a relative neglect of broader social context, evolutionary psychologists have generated little understanding of how variation in sex-differentiated behavior arises from developmental factors and features of social structure and culture (for an exception, see Draper and Harpending 1982).

The aspect of evolutionary theory that has been applied most extensively to sex differences is the theory of sexual selection initially proposed by Darwin (1871) and further developed by Trivers (1972). In the evolutionary psychologists' rendition of these views, sex-typed features of human behavior evolved through male competition and female choice of mates. Because women constituted the sex that devoted greater effort to parental investment, they were a limited reproductive resource for men, who were the less investing sex. Women were restricted in the number of children they could propagate during their life span because of their investment through gestating, bearing, and nursing their children; men did not have these restrictions. Men therefore competed for access to women, and women chose their mates from among the available men. As the more investing sex, women were selected for their wisdom in choosing mates who could provide resources to support their parenting efforts. Women's preferences for such men, in turn, produced sexual selection pressures on men to satisfy these criteria.

Proponents of sexual selection theory argue that sex differences in parental investment favored different strategies for reproductive success for men and women and consequently established different adaptive mechanisms governing mating behavior (Buss 1996; Kenrick, Trost, and Sheets 1996).

It was to men's advantage in terms of fitness outcomes to "devote a larger proportion of their total mating effort to short-term mating than do women" (Buss and Schmitt 1993, p. 205)—that is, to be relatively promiscuous. Women, in contrast, benefited from devoting a smaller proportion of their effort to short-term mating and a larger proportion to long-term mating. Also, because of women's concealed fertilization, men were unable to determine easily which children could proffer the fitness gains that follow from genetic relatedness. Men ostensibly adapted to this problem of paternity uncertainty by exerting sexual control over women and developing sexual jealousy and a motive to control women's sexuality (Daly and Wilson 1998).

According to evolutionary psychologists (e.g., Buss 1995b; Buss and Kenrick 1998), sex differences in numerous psychological dispositions arose from differing fitness-related goals of women and men that followed from their contrasting sexual strategies. Because men competed with other men for sexual access to women, men's evolved dispositions favor violence, competition, and risk taking. Women in turn developed a proclivity to nurture and a preference for long-term mates who could support a family. As a result, men strived to acquire more resources than other men in order to attract women, and women developed preferences for successful, ambitious men who could provide resources.

Critical to some of evolutionary psychologists' claims about sex differences is the assumption that ancestral humans living in the EEA had a hunter-gatherer socioeconomic system (e.g., Buss 1995b; Cosmides et al. 1992; DeKay and Buss 1992). The idea of a division of labor in which men hunted while women gathered suggests sex-differentiated pressures linked to survival and reproduction. Such an ancestral division of labor might have favored men who were psychologically specialized for hunting and women who were specialized for gathering. For example, cognitive abilities could have been affected, with men acquiring the superior spatial skills that followed from ancestral hunting, and women acquiring the superior spatial location memory that followed from ancestral gathering (e.g., Geary 1995; Silverman and Phillips 1998).

Various mediating processes are implied in evolutionary psychology models of behavioral sex differences. The first and most important involves some means of retaining effective adaptations in human design and perpetuating them over time. Thus, sex-differentiated psychological mechanisms and developmental programs, like other adaptations, are "genetic, hereditary, or inherited in the sense that . . . their structured design has its characteristic form because of the information in our DNA" (Tooby and Cosmides 1990a, p. 37; see also Buss, Haselton, Shackelford, Bleske and Wakefield 1998; Crawford 1998). Some evolutionary accounts also emphasize that genetic factors trigger biochemical processes that mediate psychological sex differences, especially by means of sex differences in hormone production (e.g., Daly and Wilson 1983; Geary 1995, 1996). In addition, sex-typed evolved mechanisms are translated into behavioral sex differences by various cognitive and affective processes. Establishing these links requires theoretical understanding and empirical documentation of the range of processes by which the genetic factors implicated in innate dispositions might affect human behavior (e.g., Collear and Hines 1995).

Buss and Kenrick (1998) described evolutionary psychology's approach to understanding sex differences as a "metatheory" and summarized it as follows: "Men and women differ in domains where they faced different adaptive problems over human evolutionary history" (p. 994). These theorists thus derive sex differences from heritable adaptations built into the human species. Because these differences are assumed to follow from evolutionary adaptations, they are predicted to occur as central tendencies of male versus female behavior. Human behavior would thus be characterized by a deep structure of sex-differentiated dispositions, producing similar, albeit not identical, behavioral sex differences in all human societies.

Critique of the Evolutionary Origin Theory

A number of questions can be raised about evolutionary psychology's account of the origins of sex differences. One consideration is that evolutionary analyses have generally identified adaptations by relying on "informal arguments as to whether a presumed function is served with sufficient precision, economy, efficiency, etc. to rule out pure chance as an adequate explanation" (Williams 1966, p. 10). Explanations that reflect this approach consist of an analysis of the functional relations served by a particular psychological mechanism, along with the construction of a convincing story about how the adaptation might have made an efficient contribution to genetic survival or to some other goal contributing to reproduction in the EEA. These explanations serve as hypotheses that require additional validation and thus can be useful for initiating scientific research.

In developing these analyses of the possible functions of behaviors, evolutionary scientists face special challenges in distinguishing adaptations from other possible products of evolution—for example, features that were random or that had utility for one function but were subsequently coopted to fulfill a new function (see Buss et al. 1998; Gould 1991; Williams 1966). Moreover, the products of evolution must be distinguished from the products of cultural change. Behaviors that provide effective solutions to problems of reproduction and survival can arise from inventive trial-and-error among individuals who are genetically indistinguishable from other members of their living groups; such beneficial behaviors are then imitated and transmitted culturally.

An understanding of humans' primeval environment might help validate evolutionary hypotheses because adaptations evolved as solutions to past environmental challenges. Various bodies of science have some relevance, including observational studies of other primates, the fossil record, and ethnographic studies. However, models of human nature constructed from the behavior of nonhuman primates do not yield a uniform picture that reflects key features of sex differences in modern human societies (see Fedigan 1986; Strier 1994; Travis and Yeager 1991). Similarly ambiguous concerning sex differences are the models of early human social conditions that paleontologists and paleoanthropologists have developed from fossil evidence. Anthropologists continue to debate fundamental points—for example, whether hunting of dangerous prey might have emerged during the period that is usually identified as the human EEA (e.g., Potts 1984; Rose and Marshall 1996). As a consequence, assumptions that certain traits were adaptive and consequently are under genetic control cannot be firmly supported from analyzing attributes of the EEA. Moreover, early human societies likely took a wide variety of forms during the period when the species was evolving toward its modern anatomical form (Foley 1996). Variability in social organization is consistent with observations of more contemporary hunter-gatherer societies, which show great diversity in their social organization (Kelly 1995). For example, studies of power relations between the sexes across diverse cultures show variability in the extent to which men control women's sexuality (Whyte 1978), although evolutionary psychologists have assumed that this control is a defining feature of male-female relations. Therefore, because the EEA likely encompassed a variety of conditions, tracing humans' evolution requires understanding of the timing, social organization, and ecological circumstances of multiple periods of adaptation (Foley 1996). The ambiguity and complexity of the relevant scientific findings leave room for evolutionary psychologists to inadvertently transport relatively modern social conditions to humans' remote past by inappropriately assuming that the distinctive characteristics of contemporary relations between the sexes were also typical of the EEA.

Given the difficulty of knowing the functions of behaviors and the attributes of the EEA, other types of scientific evidence become especially important to validating the claims of evolutionary psychologists. The most convincing evidence that a behavioral pattern reflects an adaptation would be that individuals who possessed the adaptation enjoyed a higher rate of survival and reproduction than individuals who did not possess it. However, such evidence is difficult, if not impossible, to produce. Because humans' evolved mechanisms emerged in relation to past selection pressures, present reproductive advantage does not necessarily reflect past advantage, and evolutionary psychologists have warned against relying on measures of current reproductive success to validate hypothesized adaptations (Buss 1995a; Tooby and Cosmides 1992). In the absence of evidence pertaining to reproductive success, scientists might document the genetic inheritance of postulated mechanisms and the processes by which genetic factors result in sex differences in behavior. However, for the psychological dispositions considered in this article, such evidence has not been produced. Instead, the scientific case for these sex-differentiated evolved dispositions rests on tests of evolutionary psychologists' predictions concerning the behavior of men and women in contemporary societies (e.g., Buss and Schmitt 1993; Kenrick and Keefe 1992). We evaluate some of these predictions in this article.

Social Structural Theory as an Origin Theory of Sex Differences

A respected tradition in the social sciences locates the origins of sex differences, not in evolved psychological dispositions that are built into the human psyche, but in the contrasting social positions of women and men.

In contemporary American society, as in many world societies, women have less power and status than men and control fewer resources. This feature of social structure is often labeled gender hierarchy, or in feminist writing it may be called patriarchy. In addition, as the division of labor is realized in the United States and many other nations, women perform more domestic work than men and spend fewer hours in paid employment (Shelton 1992). Although most women in the United States are employed in the paid workforce, they have lower wages than men, are concentrated in different occupations, and are thinly represented at the highest levels of organizational hierarchies (Jacobs 1989; Reskin and Padavic 1994; Tomaskovic-Devey 1995). From a social structural perspective, the underlying cause of sex-differentiated behavior is this concentration of men and women in differing roles.

The determinants of the distribution of men and women into social roles are many and include the biological endowment of women and men. The sex-differentiated physical attributes that influence role occupancy include men's greater size and strength, which gives them priority in jobs demanding certain types of strenuous activity, especially activities involving upper body strength. These physical attributes of men are less important in societies in which few occupational roles require these attributes, such as postindustrial societies. Also important in relation to role distributions are women's childbearing and in many societies their activity of suckling infants for long periods of time; these obligations give them priority in roles involving the care of very young children and cause conflict with roles requiring extended absence from home and uninterrupted activity. These reproductive activities of women are less important in societies with low birthrates, less reliance on lactation for feeding infants, and greater reliance on nonmaternal care of young children.

In general, physical sex differences, in interaction with social and ecological conditions, influence the roles held by men and women because certain activities are more efficiently accomplished by one sex. The benefits of this greater efficiency can be realized when women and men are allied in cooperative relationships and establish a division of labor. The particular character of the activities that each sex performs then determines its placement in the social structure (see Wood and Eagly in press). As historians and anthropologists have argued (e.g., Ehrenberg 1989; Harris 1993; Lerner 1986; Sanday 1981), men typically specialized in activities (e.g., warfare, herding) that yielded greater status, wealth, and power, especially as societies became more complex. Thus, when sex differences in status emerged, they tended to favor men.

The differing distributions of men and women into social roles form the basis for a social structural metatheory of sex differences, just as evolutionary theory provides a metatheory. The major portion of this social structural theory follows from the typical features of the roles of men and women. Thus, the first metatheoretical principle derives from the greater power and status that tends to be associated with male-dominated roles and can be succinctly stated as follows: Men's accommodation to roles with greater power and status produces more dominant behavior, and women's accommodation to roles with lesser power and status produces more subordinate behavior (Ridgeway and Diekema 1992). Dominant behavior is controlling, assertive, relatively directive and autocratic, and may involve sexual control. Subordinate behavior is more compliant to social influence, less overtly aggressive, more cooperative and conciliatory, and may involve a lack of sexual autonomy.

The second metatheoretical principle follows from the differing balance of activities associated with the typical roles of each sex. Women and men seek to accommodate sex-typical roles by acquiring the specific skills and resources linked to successful role performance and by adapting their social behavior to role requirements. A variety of sex-specific skills and beliefs arise from the typical family and economic roles of men and women, which in many societies can be described as resource provider and homemaker. Women and men seek to accommodate to these roles by acquiring role-related skills, for example, women learning domestic skills such as cooking and men learning skills that are marketable in the paid economy. The psychological attributes and social behaviors associated with these roles have been characterized in terms of the distinction between communal and agentic characteristics (Bakan 1966; Eagly 1987). Thus, women's accommodation to the domestic role and to female-dominated occupations favors a pattern of interpersonally facilitative and friendly behaviors that can be termed communal. In particular, the assignment of the majority of child rearing to women encourages nurturant behaviors that facilitate care for children and other individuals. The importance of close relationships to women's nurturing role favors the acquisition of superior interpersonal skills and the ability to communicate nonverbally. In contrast, men's accommodation to the employment role, especially to male-dominated occupations, favors a pattern of assertive and independent behaviors that can be termed agentic (Eagly and Steffen 1984). This argument is not to deny that paid occupations show wide variation in the extent to which they favor more masculine or feminine qualities. In support of the idea that sex-differentiated behaviors are shaped by paid occupations are demonstrations that to the extent that occupations are male dominated, they are thought to require agentic personal qualities. In contrast, to the extent that occupations are female dominated, they are thought to require communal personal qualities (Cejka and Eagly 1999; Glick 1991).

In social structural theories, differential role occupancy affects behavior through a variety of mediating processes. In social role theory (Eagly 1987; Eagly et al 2001) an important mediating process is the formation of gender roles by which people of each sex are expected to have characteristics that equip them for the tasks that they typically carry out. These expectations encompass the preferred or desirable attributes of men and women as well as their typical attributes. Gender roles are emergents from the productive work of the sexes; the characteristics that are required to perform sex-typical tasks become stereotypic of women or men. To the extent that women more than men occupy roles that demand communal behaviors, domestic behaviors, or subordinate behaviors for successful role performance, such tendencies become stereotypic of women and are incorporated into a female gender role. To the extent that men more than women occupy roles that demand agentic behaviors, resource acquisition behaviors, or dominant behaviors for successful role performance, such tendencies become stereotypic of men and are incorporated into a male gender role. Gender roles facilitate the activities typically carried out by people of each sex. For example, the expectation that women be other-oriented and compassionate facilitates their nurturing activities within the family as well as their work in many female-dominated occupations (e.g., teacher, nurse, social worker).

People communicate gender-stereotypic expectations in social interaction and can directly induce the targets of these expectations to engage in behavior that confirms them (e.g., Skrypnek and Snyder 1982; Wood and Karten 1986). Such effects of gender roles are congruent with theory and research on the behavioral confirmation of stereotypes and other expectancies (see Olson, Roese, and Zanna 1996). Gender-stereotypic expectations can also affect behavior by becoming internalized as part of individuals' self-concepts and personalities (Feingold 1994). Under such circumstances, gender roles affect behavior through self-regulatory processes (Wood, Christensen, Hebl, and Rothgerber 1997). The individual psychology that underlies these processes is assumed to be the maximization of utilities. People perceive these utilities from the rewards and costs that emerge in social interaction, which takes place within the constraints of organizational and societal arrangements.

Gender roles coexist with specific roles based on factors such as family relationships and occupation. These specific social roles contribute directly to sex-differentiated behavior when women and men are differently distributed into them—for example, women into the homemaker role and men into the provider role. In contrast, when men and women occupy the same specific social role, sex differences would tend to erode because specific roles are constraining (e.g., Eagly and Johnson 1990). However, gender roles ordinarily continue to have some impact on behavior, even in the presence of specific roles (see Gutek and Morasch 1983; Moscowitz, Suh, and Desaulniers 1994; Ridgeway 1997). Moreover, experimental evidence (e.g., Hembroff 1982) suggests that people combine or average the expectations associated with specific roles and more diffuse roles such as gender roles in a manner that weights each set of expectations according to its relevance to the task at hand.

The social structural perspective provides a broad theoretical outline within which many social scientific theories of sex-differentiated behavior can be placed. These theories focus on different aspects of the processes by which societies produce sex-differentiated behavior, and many theories have spawned detailed predictions and a substantial body of empirical research (see Beall and Sternberg 1993; Canary and Dindia 1998; England and Browne 1992). For example, developmental psychologists have studied socialization in the family, school, and peer group. Social psychologists have examined the impact of gendered self-schemas, men's greater status, sex-differentiated expectations about behavior, and gendered patterns of social interaction. Sociologists have implicated organizational factors such as discriminatory employment practices, societal factors such as

men's greater ownership of capital, and cultural factors such as the ideologies that legitimize gender inequality. Social scientists have thus provided an array of interrelated theories, each of which illuminates certain
aspects of the processes by which sex-differentiated behavior is produced.

In summary, in social structural accounts, women and men are differently distributed into social roles, and these differing role assignments can
be broadly described in terms of a sexual division of labor and a gender
hierarchy. This division of labor and the patriarchal hierarchy that sometimes accompanies it provide the engine of sex-differentiated behavior because they trigger social and psychological processes by which men and
women seek somewhat different experiences to maximize their outcomes
within the constraints that societies establish for people of their sex. Sex
differences in behavior thus reflect contemporaneous social conditions.

Response to Critiques of the Social Structural Origin Theory

A number of criticisms have been leveled against the social structural theory of sex differences and more specifically against social role theory (see
Archer 1996; Buss 1996). At least some evolutionary psychologists have
expressed skepticism that culture and social structure could have any independent causal role in relation to behavior. Instead, culture and social
structure are seen as reflecting the underlying logic of evolved dispositions,
and consequently they do not constitute the causal force underlying behavioral sex differences (Buss 1995a; Tooby and Cosmides 1992). However, from our perspective, culture and social structure can influence
behavior. Culture consists of knowledge, beliefs, and evaluations shared
among members of a society and reflects, not only the biological endowment of humans, but also the constraints of their social and physical
environments. Social structure reflects culture and consists of "persisting
and bounded patterns of behavior and interaction among people or positions" (House 1995, p. 390). Gender roles and other social roles are
simultaneously aspects of culture, because they represent shared knowledge, and of social structure, because they represent bounded patterns of
interaction.

Another criticism is that in social structural theories, individuals are
treated as mere passive receptacles of the roles they are assigned (Buss
1996). Although social scientists often do refer to *role assignment,* this
term does not imply that people are typically assigned to roles arbitrarily,

as if they were passive actors in the social system. On the contrary, social and organizational psychologists have demonstrated that the assumption of roles in a complex and dynamic process (e.g., Kerckhoff 1995; Pfeffer 1998). In deciding whether to attempt to assume particular roles at all, individuals take their own attributes, skills, and personal preferences into account, although in some cultural contexts some roles are imposed on people regardless of their own preferences (e.g., the practice of early betrothal of girls). In general, social systems are arranged to shape people's self-concepts, skills, beliefs, and values so that the majority of people actively seek out experiences that help them to become appropriate occupants of existing social roles by meeting the expectations of these roles.

Evolutionary psychologists also claim that sociocultural theorists view gender roles as "essentially arbitrary" (Buss 1996, p. 19) or as arising by "historical accident" (Archer 1996, p. 915). On the contrary, as we have explained, the content of gender roles is not arbitrary but is embedded in social structure and culture. Roles must thus facilitate the endeavors of a society, if its members are to prosper and survive. Therefore, different types of role systems become effective under differing circumstances. For example, in industrial economies, many roles are organized by a market pricing system that takes into account factors such as ownership of property and contribution to production (see Fiske 1992). The analytical frameworks for understanding how systems of social roles change over time have been developed by scholars in other disciplines (e.g., Diamond 1997; Toynbee 1934–1961). Yet, understanding the principles by which women and men distribute themselves into a society's roles is part of the agenda of social psychologists as well as other social scientists.

A related criticism is that from a social structural perspective, "differences between cultures are random with respect to evolutionary hypotheses and therefore that, for example, sex differences should occur as frequently in one direction as the other" (Tooby and Cosmides 1989, p. 37). However, our theoretical perspective is not consistent with random variation in sex differences across societies. Instead, societal variation in the roles of men and women depends on multiple factors, including men's greater size and physical strength, women's reproductive activities, and the activities required by a society's economy and social organization, which in turn reflect technological developments and the current ecology. Because these factors are not randomly distributed, certain types of social arrangements are more common than others, and sex differences appropriate to the common arrangements should be more frequent than reversals of these differences.

The social structural approach has also been criticized for treating the minds of women and men as identical except by virtue of the constraints that follow from externally assigned roles (Buss 1996). We acknowledge that the social structural perspective does imply that differences in the minds of women and men arise primarily from experience and socialization, which reflect the physical attributes of women and men and the characteristics of the social and physical environment. This assumption that humans' psychological attributes are minimally constrained by genetically encoded sex differences is consistent with the diversity of behaviors and skills exhibited by men and women across societies and within societies. Yet, our perspective is fully compatible with the idea that people possess evolved facilities, such as for language, that develop in predictable ways in appropriate environments.

Sex Differences in Mate Selection Criteria Predicted from Evolutionary Psychology and Social Structural Theory

One reasonable area for comparing the predictive power of the evolutionary and the social structural origin theories of sex differences is human mating behavior, especially the criteria that people use for selecting mates. Evolutionary predictions have been articulated especially clearly for mating activities, and these behaviors can also be used to test a social structural perspective. Furthermore, empirical findings concerning mate selection preferences have been well-established for many years in the literature on the sociology of the family (e.g., Coombs and Kenkel 1966). Powers's (1971) summary of 30 years of research concluded that at least in the United States, women generally prefer mates with good earning potential, whereas men prefer mates who are physically attractive and possess good domestic skills. Furthermore, women typically prefer a mate who is older then them, whereas men prefer a mate who is younger. Feingold's (1990, 1991, 1992a) meta-analyses of studies drawn from various research paradigms established that the sex differences in valuing potential mates' earning potential and physical attractiveness are robust, despite sex similarity on most criteria for selecting mates. Subsequent research based on a national probability sample of single adults provided further confirmation of the sex differences in age preferences as well as in valuing earning potential and physical attractiveness (Sprecher, Sullivan, and Hatfield 1994).

Evolutionary psychologists have adopted mate preferences as signature findings of their analysis. Women's valuing of mates' resources and men's valuing of mates' youth and physical attractiveness are thought to arise from the different parental investment of the sexes that was outlined in Trivers's (1972) sexual selection theory. It is commonly argued that women, as the more investing sex, seek mates with attributes that can support their parenting efforts. However, human mate selection does not follow a strict version of Trivers's males-compete-and-females-choose model, because among humans, selection is a product of the behavior of both sexes, a process Darwin (1871) called "dual selection." In Buss's (1989a) account, male choice derives from women's time-limited reproductive capacity and the tendency for men to seek mates with attributes that suggest such capacity. In Kenrick and Keefe's (1992) account, men and women are both selective about potential mates and both invest heavily in offspring but with different kinds of resources. In particular, "males invest relatively more indirect resources (food, money, protection, and security), and females invest relatively more direct physiological resources (contributing their own bodily nutrients to the fetus and nursing child)" (Kenrick and Keefe 1992, p. 78). As a result, women prefer mates who can provide indirect resources, and men prefer healthy mates with reproductive potential.[1]

In contrast, from a social structural perspective, the psychology of mate selection reflects people's effort to maximize their utilities with respect to mating choices in an environment in which these utilities are constrained by societal gender roles as well by as the more specific expectations associated with marital roles. Consistent with these ideas, Becker's (1976) economic analysis of mating decisions characterized marriage as occurring between utility-maximizing men and women who can reach an equilibrium with a variety of types of exchanges, including, for example, an exchange between men's wages and women's household production and other attributes such as education and beauty. This cost-benefit analysis of mating appears even on occasion in the writings of evolutionary scientists.

For example, Tattersall (1998) maintained that behavioral regularities, such as sex differences in mate selection criteria, are as likely to be due to rational economic decisions as to inherited predispositions, and Hrdy (1997) wrote that "a woman's preferences for a wealthy man can be explained by the simple reality that . . . males monopolize ownership of productive resources" (p. 29).

The outcomes that are perceived to follow from mating decisions depend on marital and family arrangements. To the extent that women and men occupy marital and family roles that entail different responsibilities and obligations, they should select mates according to criteria that reflect these divergent responsibilities and obligations. Consider, for example, the family system based on a male provider and a female domestic worker. This system became especially pronounced in industrial economies and is still prevalent in many world societies. To the extent that societies have this division of labor, women maximize their outcomes by seeking a mate who is likely to be successful in the economic, wage-earning role. In turn, men maximize their outcomes by seeking a mate who is likely to be successful in the domestic role.

The sex differences in the preferred age of mates also can be understood as part of the general tendency of men and women to seek partners likely to provide a good fit to their society's sexual division of labor and marital roles. Specifically, the marital system based on a male breadwinner and a female homemaker favors the age gap in marriage. Marriageable women who are younger than their potential mates tend to have lesser wages, social status, and education and knowledge than women who are the same age as potential mates. With the combination of a younger, less experienced woman and an older, more experienced man, it would be easier to establish the power differential favoring men that is normative for marital roles defined by a male breadwinner and a female domestic worker (Lips 1991; Steil 1997). Moreover, compared with somewhat older women, young women lack independent resources and therefore are more likely to perceive that their utilities are maximized in the domestic worker role. In complementary fashion, older men are more likely to have acquired the economic resources that make them good candidates for the provider role. The older man and younger woman thus fit more easily than same-age partners into the culturally expected pattern of breadwinner and homemaker.

Cross-Cultural Evidence for Sex Differences in Mate Preferences

Evolutionary psychologists' predictions that women select for resources and older age and men for attractiveness and younger age have been examined cross-culturally. Buss's (1989a; Buss et al. 1990) impressive study in 37 cultures of the characteristics that people desire in mates suggested that consistent with evolutionary psychology, these sex differences in mate preferences emerged cross-culturally. Similarly, Kenrick and Keefe (1992) examined the preferred ages of mates in five countries and across various time periods in the twentieth century and concluded that all provided evidence of sex differences in these preferences. Specifically, for dating and marriage, women preferred older men and men preferred younger women, although men's preferences were moderated by their age, with teenage boys preferring girls of similar age.[2]

On the basis of these investigations, evolutionary accounts have emphasized the cross-cultural commonality in women's preference for resources and older age and men's preference for attractiveness and younger age. According to Buss (1989a) and Tooby and Cosmides (1989), uniformity across diverse cultures and social circumstances suggests powerful sex-differentiated evolved mechanisms that reflect an innate, universal human nature. Kenrick and Keefe (1992) also argued that "invariance across cultures is evidence that supports a species-specific, rather than a culture-specific, explanation" (p. 76).

Despite evidence for cross-cultural commonality in sex differences in mate selection criteria, these investigations also yielded evidence for cultural variation. For example, Kenrick and Keefe (1992) found that the preference for younger wives was evident among Philippine men of all ages, but only among older men (i.e., age 30 or over) in the United States. However, the simple existence of uniformity or variability does not provide a definitive test of either the evolutionary or the social structural origin theory. Although evolutionary psychologists emphasize uniformity and social structural theorists emphasize variability, both perspectives have some power to explain both of these cross-cultural patterns. To account for uniformity, social structuralists can point to similarities in the sexual division of labor in the studied societies and can argue that these similarities produce these relatively invariant sex differences. As Buss (1989a) noted, his 37 cultures, which were drawn from 33 nations, were biased toward urbanized cash-economy cultures, with 54 percent from

Europe and North America. Furthermore, respondents selected from each society tended to be young, comparatively well-educated, and of relatively high socioeconomic status. To the extent that these societies similarly defined the roles of women and men and that the respondents were similarly placed in these societies' social structures, commonality in the sex differences that follow from social structure should characterize these societies.

To account for cross-cultural variability, both evolutionary and social structural origin theories recognize that developmental processes and social factors that are unique to each society direct behavior in ways that can yield variability in sex differences across cultures. Beyond this insight that some evidence of cross-cultural variability would not surprise theorists in either camp, the particular pattern of cross-cultural variation provides an informative test of the mechanisms underlying sex differences. Specifically, the social structural argument that a society's sexual division of labor and associated gender hierarchy are responsible for sex differences in social behavior yields predictions concerning cross-cultural variability in mate preferences.

In the nations included in Buss et al.'s (1990) cross-cultural sample, whose economies ranged from agrarian to postindustrial, some cultures were still strongly marked by this division of labor between the provider and domestic worker, whereas other cultures had departed from it. In advanced economies like the United States, women have entered the paid labor force and spend a smaller proportion of their time in domestic labor (Haas 1995; Shelton 1992). Although the tendency for men to increase their hours of domestic work is much more modest, the lives of men and women become more similar with greater gender equality. Therefore, people of both sexes should lessen their emphasis on choosing mates whose value is defined by their fit to the division between domestic work and wage labor. Even in postindustrial economies such as the United States, however, the sex-typed division of labor remains in modified form, with men devoting longer hours than women to wage labor and women devoting longer hours to domestic work (e.g., Ferree 1991; Presser 1994; Shelton 1992). Therefore, the social structural prediction is that the sex differences in mate selection criteria that follow from the male-female division of labor should be substantially weakened in societies characterized by greater gender equality, albeit they should still be present to the extent that complete equality has not been achieved.[3]

Reanalysis of Buss et al.'s (1990) 37 Cultures Data

To evaluate whether the division of labor within a society could explain the mate preferences of men and women, we reanalyzed Buss et al.'s (1990) 37 cultures data. Our efforts focused on men's tendencies to select wives for domestic skill and younger age and women's tendencies to select husbands for earning capacity and older age. To test the hypothesis that a higher level of gender equality lessens these sex differences, we represented societies' gender equality in terms of archival data available from the United Nations (United Nations Development Programme 1995).

Buss et al. (1990) derived the data on criteria for selecting mates from questionnaire measures of preferences for a wide range of characteristics that might be desired in a mate: (a) One instrument obtained rankings of a set of 13 characteristics according to "their desirability in someone you might marry" (p. 11); (b) the other instrument obtained ratings on a 4-point scale of each of 18 characteristics on "how important or desirable it would be in choosing a mate" (p. 11). Buss et al. represented each culture by the male and female respondents' mean ranking of each of the 13 mate selection criteria and by their mean rating of each of the 18 criteria. A separate question inquired about preferences for a spouse's age. The data that we reanalyzed consisted of mean preferences for each culture.

Our reanalysis confirmed Buss et al.'s (1990) conclusion that women placed more value than men on a mate's wage-earning ability. Furthermore, consistent with the greater domestic responsibility of women than men in most cultures, men valued *good cook and housekeeper* more than women did, a sex difference that has received little attention from evolutionary psychologists. When the sex differences in the mean preference ratings were averaged across the cultures, this difference was of comparable magnitude to those obtained on the attributes most strongly emphasized by evolutionary psychologists. Specifically, in both the rating and ranking data, the criteria of *good earning capacity, good housekeeper and cook,* and *physically attractive* produced the largest sex differences. The appropriateness of focusing on the criteria pertaining to earning ability and domestic skill within Buss et al.'s data was also supported by the good agreement across the ranking and rating data sets for sex differences in the valuation of the qualities of financial prospect, $r(33) = .76$, $p < .001$, and domestic skill, $r(33) = .68$, $p < .001$, whereas the agreement in the valuation of physical attractiveness was poorer, $r(33) = .34$, $p < .05$. In addition, as Buss et al. reported, the sex difference in the preferred age of mates was fully intact in the 37 cultures data.[4]

Additional evidence for the social structural predictions emerged when we evaluated the pattern of sex differences in preferences across societies. Consistent with the division of labor principle, a substantial relation emerged between the sex difference in valuing a spouse's domestic skills and the sex difference in valuing a spouse's capacity to provide a good income. Specifically, on the basis of the ranking measure, the sex differences in the good earning capacity criterion and the good housekeeper criterion were correlated across the cultures, $r(33) = .67$, $p < .001$. On the basis of the rating measure, the sex differences in the financial prospect criterion and the housekeeper-cook criterion were also correlated, $r(35) = .38$, $p < .05$. These positive correlations indicate that to the extent that women more than men reported seeking a mate who is a good breadwinner, men more than women reported seeking a mate who is a good homemaker. In addition, the sex difference in the preferred age of one's spouse bore a positive relation to the sex difference in preference for a good earner, $r(33) = .34$, $p < .05$ for the ranking data, and $r(35) = .32$, $p < .06$ for the rating data. Similarly, the sex difference in preferred age bore a positive relation to the sex difference in preference for a good housekeeper and cook, $r(33) = .58$, $p < .001$ for the ranking data, and $r(35) = .60$, $p < .001$ for the rating data. These relationships show that to the extent that the sex-difference in the preferred age of spouses was large, women more than men preferred mates who were good providers and men more than women preferred mates who were good domestic workers. The division of labor provides the logic of all of these relationships: Women who serve in the domestic role are the complement of men who serve as breadwinners, and the combination of older husbands and younger wives facilitates this form of marriage.

Analysis of gender equality   To test our hypothesis that sex differences in mate preferences erode to the extent that women and men are similarly placed in the social structure, we sought cross-national indicators of gender equality. Among the many such indicators compiled by United Nations researchers, the most direct indicator of gender equality is the aggregate Gender Empowerment Measure, which represents the extent to which women participate equally with men in economic, political, and decision-making roles (United Nations Development Programme 1995). This index increases as (a) women's percentage share of administrative and managerial jobs and professional and technical jobs increases, (b) women's percentage share of parliamentary seats rises, and (c) women's proportional share of earned income approaches parity with men's.

The Gender-Related Development Index is another useful indicator of societal-level gender equality provided by United Nations researchers. It increases with a society's basic capabilities to provide health (i.e., greater life expectancy), educational attainment and literacy, and wealth, but imposes a penalty for gender inequality in these capabilities (United Nations Development Programme, 1995). Whereas this measure reflects equality in basic access to health care, education and knowledge, and income, the Gender Empowerment Measure is a purer indicator of equal participation in economic and political life.

In the set of 37 cultures, the Gender Empowerment Measure and the Gender-Related Development Index were correlated, $r(33) = .74$, $p < .001$, and both of these indexes were moderately correlated with general indexes of human development and economic development. One limitation of the indexes of gender equality is that they are based on data from the early 1990s. Because Buss et al.'s (1990) data were collected in the mid-1980s, these indexes are from a slightly later time period, but the relative positions of the cultures should remain approximately the same.[5]

To examine the relation between societal gender equality and mate preferences, we calculated the correlations of these indexes with the sex differences in valuing a mate as a breadwinner and as a domestic worker—the two criteria most relevant to the traditional division of labor. These correlations for the ranking and the rating data, which appear in Table 12.1, are generally supportive of the social structural predictions. As the Gender Empowerment Measure increased in value, the tendency decreased for women to place greater emphasis than men on a potential spouse's earning capacity, although the correlation with the rated criterion was relatively weak. Also, as the Gender Empowerment Measure increased, the tendency decreased for men to place greater emphasis than women on a potential spouse's domestic skills. As expected in terms of the Gender-Related Development Index's less direct representation of the similarity of the roles of women and men, its correlations with these sex differences were somewhat weaker.

Table 12.1
Correlations of mean rankings and ratings of mate selection criteria with United Nations Indexes of Gender Equality for Buss et al.'s (1990) 37 cultures sample.

Mate selection criterion	Rater	Ranked Criteria		Rated criteria	
		Gender Empowerment Measure (n = 33)	Gender-Related Development Index (n = 34)	Gender Empowerment Measure (n = 35)	Gender-Related Development Index (n = 36)
Good earning capacity (financial prospect)	Sex difference	-.43*	-.33†	-.29†	-.23
	Women	-.29	-.18	-.49**	-.42**
	Men	.24	.27	-.40*	-.36*
Good housekeeper (and cook)	Sex difference	-.62***	-.54**	-.61***	-.54**
	Women	.04	-.01	.11	-.07
	Men	-.46**	-.42*	-.60***	-.61***
Physically attractive (good looks)	Sex difference	.13	-.12	.20	.18
	Women	.14	.34†	-.45**	-.25
	Men	.20	.28	-.33†	-.14

†p < .10. *p < .05. **p < .01. ***p < .001.

Note: The criteria were described slightly differently in the ranking and the rating tasks: The ranking term is given first, with the rating term following in parentheses. Higher values on the gender equality indexes indicate greater equality. For the preferences of women or men, higher values of the mean rankings and ratings of mate selection criteria indicate greater desirability in a mate; therefore, a positive correlation indicates an increase in the desirability of a criterion as gender equality increased, and a negative correlation indicates a decrease. Sex differences in these preferences were calculated as female minus male means for good earning capacity and male minus female means for good housekeeper and physically attractive. A positive correlation thus indicates an increase in the sex difference as gender equality increased, and a negative correlation indicates a decrease in the sex difference.

The preference data for each sex reported in table 12.1 provide insight into these sex-difference findings. For good housekeeper and cook, the correlations for both the rating data and the ranking data indicated that as gender equality increased, men decreased their interest in choosing mates for their skill as domestic workers, and women showed no change in this preference. In contrast, for good earning capacity, as gender equality increased, women decreased their emphasis on mates' earning potential in the rating data (although nonsignificantly in the ranking data). However, men's preferences for good earning capacity are more difficult to interpret because their relations to gender equality were inconsistent across the ranking and rating measures. Inconsistencies between the two measures may reflect that rankings are judgments of the relative importance of the criteria in relation to the others in the list, whereas ratings are judgments of the absolute importance of the different criteria.

As shown in table 12.2, examination of preferences for a spouse's age showed that as gender equality increased, women expressed less preference for older men, men expressed less preference for younger women, and consequently the sex difference in the preferred age of mates became

Table 12.2
Correlations of mean preferred age difference between self and spouse with United Nations Indexes of Gender Equality for Buss et al.'s (1990) 37 cultures sample.

Rater	Gender Empowerment Measure ($n = 35$)	Gender-Related Development Index ($n = 36$)
Sex difference	−.73*	−.70*
Women	−.64*	−.57*
Men	.70*	.70*

*$p < .001$.
Note. Higher values on the gender equality indexes indicate greater equality. Positive ages indicate preference for an older spouse, and negative ages indicate preference for a younger spouse. Therefore, for the preferences of women, a negative correlation indicates a decrease in the tendency to prefer an older spouse as gender equality increased, whereas for the preferences of men, a positive correlation indicates a decrease in the tendency to prefer a younger spouse. Because the sex difference in preferred age was calculated as female minus male mean preferred spouse age in relation to self, a negative correlation indicates a decrease in the sex difference in preferred age as gender equality increased.

smaller. These relations suggest that sex differences in age preferences reflect a sex-differentiated division of labor.[6]

Interpretation of the magnitudes of the correlations reported in tables 12.1 and 12.2 should take several considerations into account. One feature limiting the strength of these relationships is the assessment of the mate selection preferences with one-item questionnaire measures. Also, the indexes of gender equality imperfectly represented the critical conceptual variable, the extremity of the division of labor between male providers and female homemakers. In addition, the sampling of respondents was not uniformly implemented across the 37 cultures, nor would these samples have corresponded to those that contributed to the indexes of gender equality. Finally, there may be a time lag between the social and economic changes reflected in these indexes and shifts in the individual preferences that constitute the 37 cultures data. For these several reasons, it is plausible to conclude that the correlations we report underestimate the true magnitude of the predicted relationships.

Preference for physical attractiveness   As also shown in table 12.1, correlations between the sex difference in valuing potential mates' physical attractiveness and the United Nations indexes of gender equality were low and nonsignificant. These findings are not surprising, because this mate selection criterion does not mirror the division between wage labor and domestic labor in the manner that earning potential, domestic skill, and age do. Nevertheless, under some circumstances, physical attractiveness may be part of what people exchange for partners' earning capacity and other attributes.

Assuming that attractiveness is sometimes exchanged for other gains, the social structural perspective offers possibilities for understanding its value. Research on the physical attractiveness stereotype has shown that attractiveness in both sexes conveys several kinds of meaning—especially social competence, including social skills, sociability, and popularity (Eagly, Ashmore, Makhijani, and Longo 1991; Feingold 1992b). Therefore, men's greater valuing of attractiveness might follow from the greater importance of this competence in women's family and occupational roles, including women's paid occupations in postindustrial societies (Cejka and Eagly 1999; Lippa 1998), and the consequent inclusion of this competence in the female gender role. If women's roles demand greater interpersonal competence in societies with greater and lesser gender equality, the tendency for men to place greater value on mates' attractiveness would not covary with indexes that assess equality.

Another possibility is that the value of attractiveness stems from its perceived association with the ability to provide sexual pleasure. This idea receives support from research showing that attractiveness conveys information about sexual warmth (Feingold 1992b). If so, men might seek sexiness in a mate in all societies, in addition to attributes such as domestic skill, whose importance varies with the society's level of gender equality. Given that the female gender role often includes sexual restraint and lack of sexual autonomy, women may place less emphasis on sexiness in mates than men do.

It is less certain that physical attractiveness conveys information about women's fertility, as should be the case if men's preference for attractiveness in mates developed because attractiveness was a cue to fertility (Buss 1989a; Jones 1995; Singh 1993). It seems reasonable that perceptions of attractiveness and potential fertility would covary even in contemporary data, but these relations have proven to be inconsistent (e.g., Cunningham 1986; Tassinary and Hansen 1998). Moreover, Singh's (1993) research on judgments of female figures that varied in weight and waist-to-hip ratio suggested three somewhat independent groupings of attributes: health, attractiveness, and sexiness; capacity and desire for children; and youth.

Although little is known about the relation between women's attractiveness and their actual fecundity, Kalick, Zebrowitz, Langlois, and Johnson (1998) found that facial attractiveness in early adulthood was unrelated to number of children produced or to health across the life span. Although the few participants in their sample who did not marry were less attractive than those who did marry, once the nonmarried were excluded, physical attractiveness was unrelated to the number of children produced by male or female participants. Kalick et al. (1998) concluded that "any relation between attractiveness and fecundity was due to mate-selection chances rather than biological fertility" (p. 10). Of course, as we noted in our critique of evolutionary psychology in this article, proponents of the theory do not predict that hypothesized evolved dispositions, such as men's preference for physically attractive partners, would necessarily be related to current reproductive success. Evolutionary psychologists argue instead that actual fertility in modern societies may bear little relation to the factors indicative of reproductive success in the EEA.

In summary, several aspects of the findings from Buss et al.'s (1990) 37 cultures study are compatible with the social structural origin theory of sex differences. The idea that the extremity of the division between male providers and female homemakers is a major determinant of the criteria that people seek in mates fits with the observed covariation between men placing more emphasis than women on younger age and domestic skill and women placing more emphasis than men on older age and earning potential. The lessening of these sex differences with increasing gender equality, as represented by the United Nations indexes, is consistent with our claim that these sex differences are by-products of a social and family structure in which the man acts as a provider and the woman acts as a homemaker. More ambiguous are the sex differences in valuing mates' physical attractiveness. Without evidence that men's greater valuing of attractiveness follows from one or more specific mechanisms, the simple absence of a relation between gender equality and sex differences in valuing attractiveness in our reanalysis does not advance the claims of evolutionary psychology or the social structural theory. Convincing evidence for either interpretation has yet to be generated. However, with respect to the other sex differences emphasized by evolutionary psychologists, their cross-cultural patterning suggests that they arise from a particular economic and social system.

Within-Society Effects of Social Position

As evidence that presumably counters the social structural interpretation of sex differences in mate selection criteria, evolutionary psychologists (e.g., Buss and Schmitt 1993) have sometimes cited studies that examined the relation within a given culture between individuals' mate preferences and their economic resources (e.g., Buss 1989b; Kenrick and Keefe 1992; Townsend 1989). In one of the most extensive of these studies, Wiederman and Allgeier (1992) assessed mate preferences and anticipated income of undergraduate students from a midwestern university and of a convenience sample of Ohio residents. Mate preference ratings from both samples yielded the typical sex differences in ratings of good looks and good financial prospect. The central finding was that women's anticipated income and their valuing of mates as a good financial prospect were positively related in the college sample, $r(635) = .17$, $p < .001$, and unrelated in the community sample, $r(165) = .04$, *ns*. That women who expected to earn higher incomes still valued financial resources in their mates was taken as evidence in favor of the evolutionary theory of mate preferences.

On the basis of such data, any conclusions about the validity of the evolutionary or the social structural origin theory are unwarranted because such studies confound women's income with their socioeconomic status. Women who themselves have higher incomes would tend to come from higher socioeconomic groups and would anticipate selecting mates from their own stratum of society. In the United States, both sexes' homogamous mating on the basis of education, occupation, and economic resources is a well-established phenomenon (e.g., Kalmijn 1991, 1994; Mare 1991). Therefore, women's socioeconomic status typically should be positively related to expectations concerning mates' financial prospects.

An additional consideration is that, because societal gender roles coexist with specific roles, achieving a high-paying job does not completely neutralize the impact of broader gender role expectations. Therefore, consistent with these broader norms, even women with higher-than-average income commonly regard themselves as secondary wage earners in their marriages (Ferree 1991) and often prefer to leave the labor force entirely or to become employed part-time while raising a family (Herzog, Bachman, and Johnston 1983; Tittle 1981). Despite earning a substantial income, most women likely anticipate being fully or partially dependent on their husband's income during a portion of their life span. Consequently, within-society analyses of mate preferences that seek to draw conclusions about the effects of women's own economic resources must control for the influences of expectations based on social class and education as well as actual and anticipated marital roles.

Conclusion

Considered at the level of a general metatheory of sex differences, social structural theories provide alternative explanations of the great majority of the general predictions about sex-differentiated social behavior that have been featured in evolutionary psychology. Because the central tendencies of sex differences (see Eagly 1995; Halpern 1997; Hyde 1996) are

readily encompassed by both of these perspectives, neither the evolutionary metatheory nor the social structural metatheory is convincingly substantiated by a mere noting of the differences established in the research
literature. It is far too easy to make up sensible stories about how these differences might be products of sex-differentiated evolved tendencies or the
differing placement of women and men in the social structure. This overlap in general main-effect predictions calls for more refined testing of the
two theoretical perspectives, and each perspective is associated with numerous more detailed predictions and empirical tests.

Certainly there are many possibilities for distinguishing between the
two approaches with appropriate research designs (see Jackson 1992).
Evolutionary psychologists have been especially resourceful in obtaining
cross-cultural data intended to support their claims of invariance across
cultures in sex-differentiated behavior. To be maximally informative about
social structural factors, cross-cultural research should be systematically
designed to represent cultures with differing forms of social organization
and levels of gender equality. In addition, a variety of other research methods, including experiments and field studies, can yield tests of predictions
that emerge from evolutionary and social structural perspectives.

Although this article contrasts social structural explanations of sex differences with those based on evolutionary psychology, social structural
analyses may be generally compatible with some evolutionary perspectives, as we noted in the introductory section of this article. Our argument
that sex differences in behavior emerge primarily from physical sex differences in conjunction with influences of the economy, social structure,
ecology, and cultural beliefs is potentially reconcilable with theories of
coevolution by genetic and cultural processes (Janicki and Krebs 1998).
Our position is also sympathetic to the interest that some evolutionary
biologists and behavioral ecologists have shown in the maintenance of
behavioral patterns from generation to generation through nongenetic,
cultural processes (e.g., Sork 1997). However, despite our acknowledge-
ment of the importance of some evolved genetic influences on the behavior of women and men, an implicit assumption of our approach is that
social change emerges, not from individuals' tendencies to maximize their
inclusive fitness, but instead from their efforts to maximize their personal
benefits and minimize their personal costs in their social and ecological
settings.

One test of the evolutionary psychology and social structural origin theories of sex differences lies in the future—that is, in the emerging postindustrial societies in which the division between men's wage labor and women's domestic labor is breaking down. Notable is the increase in women's paid employment, education, and access to many formerly male-dominated occupations. Accompanying these changes is a marked attitudinal shift toward greater endorsement of equal opportunity for women in the workplace and role-sharing in the home (e.g., Simon and Landis 1989; Spence and Hahn 1997; Twenge 1997). Nonetheless, occupational sex segregation is still prevalent with women concentrated in occupations that are thought to require feminine qualities and with men in occupations thought to require masculine qualities (Cekja and Eagly 1999; Glick 1991). Given that occupational distributions currently take this form and that the homemaker-provider division of labor remains weakly in place, social structuralists would not predict that sex differences in behavior should have already disappeared. Instead, to the extent that the traditional sexual division between wage labor and domestic labor disappears and women and men become similarly distributed into paid occupations, men and women should converge in their psychological attributes.

Acknowledgments

This article was completed while Alice H. Eagly was a Visiting Scholar at the Murray Research Center of Radcliffe College and was supported by a Sabbatical Award from the James McKeen Cattell Fund. The research received support from Grants SBR-9729449 and SBR-9514537 from the National Science Foundation.

Thanks are extended to David Buss for making available for reanalysis data from his 37 cultures study (Buss, 1989b; Buss et al., 1990) and to Michael Bailey, April Bleske, Judith S. Bridges, Galen Bodenhausen, David Buss, Stephen M. Colaretti, Lee Cronk, Amanda Diekman, Steven W. Gangestad, Patricia Adair Gowaty, Judith Hall, Martie Haselton, Sarah Hrdy, Douglas T. Kenrick, Mary Kite, Richard Lippa, Dan McAdams, Anne McGuire, Felicia Pratto, Radmila Prislin, Dean Pruitt, Eshkol Rafaeli, Neal Roese, Alice Schlegel, and Jeffry Simpson for comments on a draft of the article. Also, Crystal Toures and Heather Franzese provided assistance in locating and entering relevant data.

Notes

1. Darwin (1871) expressed skepticism about the applicability of the processes of sexual selection to modern human societies. He argued that sexual selection was more powerful among early humans, who were guided by instinctive passions, than among contemporary members of society, who show greater foresight and reason in mating behavior. In fact, Darwin maintained that "civilized men are largely attracted by the mental charms of women, by their wealth, and especially by their social position" (Darwin 1871, p. 178).

2. Although Kenrick and Keefe (1992) showed that teenage boys prefer girls of similar age, this tendency is most likely a product of the lower age limits that exist for culturally and maturationally appropriate marital partners (Broude 1992).

3. Prior efforts to test social structural hypotheses within Buss et al.'s (1990) 37 cultures data produced mixed or nonsignificant findings (Buss 1989a; Glenn 1989).

4. We did not also focus on the criterion of *ambition and industriousness* because it produced a substantially smaller sex difference in the 37 cultures data than the criteria of *good earning capacity, good housekeeper and cook,* and *physically attractive.* From the social structural perspective, industriousness is important for performance of domestic work as well as wage labor, and therefore both men and women should seek this quality in mates under the traditional division of labor between homemakers and providers.

5. Another compromise consisted of representing differing subsamples from the same broader culture (e.g., mainland United States and Hawaiian United States) with the same values of the United Nations indexes. For the Gender Empowerment Measure and the Gender-Related Development Index, data for all represented nations were published in 1995, with the exception of data for two nations published in 1996 and one in 1997 (United Nations Development Programme 1995, 1996, 1997). For two cultures, ranking data for mate selection preferences were not available.

6. The United Nations indexes of economic development and fertility showed relationships to mate preferences that were similar to those displayed in tables 12.1 and 12.2. The magnitude of these relationships was in general nonsignificantly smaller than those involving the Gender Empowerment Measure. These relationships were expected, given that this measure increased with economic development (real gross domestic product per capita), $r(33) = .71$, $p < .001$, and decreased with fertility, $r(33) = -.61$, $p < .001$.

References

Archer, J. (1996). Sex differences in social behavior: Are the social role and evolutionary explanations compatible? *American Psychologist, 51,* 909–917.

Bakan, D. (1966). *The Duality of Human Existence: An Essay on Psychology and Religion.* Chicago: Rand McNally.

Beall, A. E. and R. J. Sternberg (eds.). (1993). *The Psychology of Gender.* New York: Guilford Press.

Becker, G. S. (1976). *The Economic Approach to Human Behavior.* Chicago: University of Chicago Press.

Borkenau, P. (1992). Age preferences: The crucial studies have yet to be done. *Behavioral and Brain Sciences* 15: 93–94.

Broude, G. J. (1992). The May–September algorithm meets the 20th century actuarial table. *Behavioral and Brain Sciences* 15: 94–95.

Buss, D. M. (1989a). Sex differences in human mate preferences: Evolutionary hypotheses tested in 37 cultures. *Behavioral and Brain Sciences* 12: 1–14.

Buss, D. M. (1989b). Toward an evolutionary psychology of human mating. *Behavioral and Brain Sciences* 12: 39–49.

Buss, D. M. (1995a). Evolutionary psychology: A new paradigm for psychological science. *Psychological Inquiry* 6: 1–30.

Buss, D. M. (1995b). Psychological sex differences: Origins through sexual selection. *American Psychologist* 50: 164–168.

Buss, D. M. (1996). The evolutionary psychology of human social strategies. In E. T. Higgins and A. W. Kruglanski, eds., *Social Psychology: Handbook of Basic Principles,* pp. 3–38. New York: Guilford Press.

Buss, D. M. (1998). The psychology of human mate selection: Exploring the complexity of the strategic repertoire. In C. Crawford and D. L. Krebs, eds., *Handbook of Evolutionary Psychology: Ideas, Issues, and Applications,* pp. 405–429. Mahwah, NJ: Erlbaum.

Buss, D. M. et al. (1990). International preferences in selecting mates: A study of 37 cultures. *Journal of Cross-Cultural Psychology* 21: 5–47.

Buss, D. M., M. G. Haselton, T. K. Shackelford, A. L. Bleske, and J. C. Wakefield (1998). Adaptations, exaptations, and spandrels. *American Psychologist* 53: 533–548.

Buss, D. M. and D. T. Kenrick. (1998). Evolutionary social psychology. In D. T. Gilbert, S. T. Fiske, and G. Lindzey, eds., *The Handbook of Social Psychology,* 4th ed., vol. 2, pp. 982–1026. Boston: McGraw-Hill.

Buss, D. M. and D. P. Schmitt. (1993). Sexual strategies theory: An evolutionary perspective on human mating. *Psychological Review* 100: 204–232.

Canary, D. J. and K. Dindia (eds.). (1998). *Sex Differences and Similarities in Communication: Critical Essays and Empirical Investigations of Sex and Gender in Interaction.* Mahwah, NJ: Erlbaum.

Cejka, M. A. and A. H. Eagly. (1999). Gender-stereotypic images of occupations correspond to the sex segregation of employment. *Personality and Social Psychology Bulletin* 25: 413–423.

Collear, M. L. and M. Hines. (1995). Human behavioral sex differences: A role for gonadal hormones during early development? *Psychological Bulletin* 118: 55–107.

Coombs, R. H. and W. F. Kenkel. (1966). Sex differences in dating aspiration and satisfaction with computer-selected partners. *Journal of Marriage and the Family* 28: 62–66.

Cosmides, L., J. Tooby, and J. H. Barkow. (1992). Introduction: Evolutionary psychology and conceptual integration. In J. H. Barkow, L. Cosmides, and J. Tooby, eds., *The Adapted Mind: Evolutionary Psychology and the Generation of Culture*, pp. 3–15. New York: Oxford University Press.

Crawford, C. (1998). The theory of evolution in the study of human behavior: An introduction and overview. In C. Crawford and D. L. Krebs, eds., *Handbook of Evolutionary Psychology: Ideas, Issues, and Applications*, pp. 3–41. Mahwah, NJ: Erlbaum.

Cronk, L. (1991). Human behavioral ecology. *Annual Review of Anthropology* 20: 25–53.

Cunningham, M. R. (1986). Measuring the physical in physical attractiveness: Quasi-experiments on the sociobiology of female facial beauty. *Journal of Personality and Social Psychology* 50: 925–935.

Daly, M. and M. Wilson. (1983). *Sex, Evolution, and Behavior* (2nd ed.). Boston: Grant Press.

Daly, M. and M. Wilson. (1998). The evolutionary social psychology of family violence. In C. Crawford and D. L. Krebs, eds., *Handbook of Evolutionary Psychology: Ideas, Issues, and Applications*, pp. 431–456. Mahwah, NJ: Erlbaum.

Darwin, C. (1871). *The Descent of Man and Selection in Relation to Sex*. London: Murray.

Deaux, K. and M. LaFrance. (1998). Gender. In D. T. Gilbert, S. T. Fiske, and G. Lindzey, eds., *The Handbook of Social Psychology*, 4th ed., vol. 1, pp. 788–827. Boston: McGraw-Hill.

DeKay, W. T. and D. M. Buss. (1992). Human nature, individual differences, and the importance of context: Perspectives from evolutionary psychology. *Current Directions in Psychological Science* 1: 184–189.

Diamond, J. (1997). *Guns, Germs, and Steel: The Fates of Human Societies*. New York: Norton.

Draper, P. and H. Harpending. (1982). Father absence and reproductive strategy: An evolutionary perspective. *Journal of Anthropological Research* 38: 255–273.

Eagly, A. H. (1987). *Sex Differences in Social Behavior: A Social-role Interpretation*. Hillsdale, NJ: Erlbaum.

Eagly, A. H. (1995). The science and politics of comparing women and men. *American Psychologist* 50: 145–158.

Eagly, A. H., R. D. Ashmore, M. G. Makhijani, and L. C. Longo. (1991). What is beautiful is good, but . . . : A meta-analytic review of research on the physical attractiveness stereotype. *Psychological Bulletin* 110: 109–128.

Eagly, A. H. and B. T. Johnson. (1990). Gender and leadership style: A meta-analysis. *Psychological Bulletin* 108: 233–256.

Eagly, A. H. and V. J. Steffen. (1984). Gender stereotypes stem from the distribution of women and men into social roles. *Journal of Personality and Social Psychology* 46: 735–754.

Eagly, A. H., W. Wood, and A. Diekman. (2000). Social role theory of sex differences and similarities: A current appraisal. In T. Eckes and H. M. Trautner, eds., *The Developmental Social Psychology of Gender*, pp. 123–174. Mahwah, NJ: Erlbaum.

Ehrenberg, M. (1989). *Women in Prehistory*. London: British Museum Publications.

England, P. and I. Browne. (1992). Internalization and constraint in women's subordination. In B. Agger, ed., *Current Perspectives in Social Theory*, vol. 12, pp. 97–123. Greenwich, CT: JAI Press.

Fedigan, L. M. (1986). The changing role of women in models of human evolution. *Annual Review of Anthropology* 15: 25–66.

Feingold, A. (1990). Gender differences in effects of physical attractiveness on romantic attraction: A comparison across five research paradigms. *Journal of Personality and Social Psychology* 59: 981–993.

Feingold, A. (1991). Sex differences in the effects of similarity and physical attractiveness on opposite-sex attraction. *Basic and Applied Social Psychology* 12: 357–367.

Feingold, A. (1992a). Gender differences in mate selection preferences: A test of the parental investment model. *Psychological Bulletin* 112: 125–139.

Feingold, A. (1992b). Good-looking people are not what we think. *Psychological Bulletin* 111: 304–341.

Feingold, A. (1994). Gender differences in personality: A meta-analysis. *Psychological Bulletin* 116: 429–456.

Ferree, M. M. (1991). The gender division of labor in two-earner marriages: Dimensions of variability and change. *Journal of Family Issues* 12: 158–180.

Fiske, A. P. (1992). The four elementary forms of sociality: Framework for a unified theory of social relations. *Psychological Review* 99: 689–723.

Foley, R. (1996). The adaptive legacy of human evolution: A search for the environment of evolutionary adaptedness. *Evolutionary Anthropology* 4: 194–203.

Geary, D. C. (1995). Sexual selection and sex differences in spatial cognition. *Learning and Individual Differences* 7: 289–301.

Geary, D. C. (1996). Sexual selection and sex differences in mathematical abilities. *Behavioral and Brain Sciences* 19: 229–284.

Glenn, N. D. (1989). Intersocietal variation in the mate preferences of males and females. *Behavioral and Brain Sciences* 12: 21–23.

Glick, P. (1991). Trait-based and sex-based discrimination in occupational prestige, occupational salary, and hiring. *Sex Roles* 25: 351–378.

Gould, S. J. (1991). Exaptation: A crucial tool for an evolutionary psychology. *Journal of Social Issues* 47: 43–65.

Gutek, B. A. and B. Morasch. (1983). Sex-ratios, sex-role spillover, and sexual harassment of women at work. *Journal of Social Issues* 38 (4): 55–74.

Haas, L. L. (1995). Household division of labor in industrial societies. In B. B. Ingoldsby and S. Smith, eds., *Families in Multicultural Perspective: Perspectives on Marriage and the Family,* pp. 268–296. New York: Guilford Press.

Halpern, D. F. (1997). Sex differences in intelligence: Implications for education. *American Psychologist* 52: 1091–1102.

Harris, M. (1993). The evolution of human gender hierarchies: A trial formulation. In B. D. Miller, ed., *Sex and Gender Hierarchies,* pp. 57–79. New York: Cambridge University Press.

Hembroff, L. A. (1982). Resolving status inconsistency: An expectation states theory and test. *Social Forces* 61: 183–205.

Herzog, A. R., J. G. Bachman, and L. D. Johnston. (1983). Paid work, child care, and housework: A national survey of high school seniors' preferences for sharing responsibilities between husband and wife. *Sex Roles* 9: 109–135.

House, J. S. (1995). Social structure, relationships, and the individual. In K. S. Cook, G. A. Fine, and J. S. House, eds., *Sociological Perspectives on Social Psychology,* pp. 387–395. Boston: Allyn & Bacon.

Hrdy, S. B. (1997). Raising Darwin's consciousness: Female sexuality and the prehominid origins of patriarchy. *Human Nature* 8: 1–49.

Hyde, J. S. (1996). Where are the gender differences? Where are the gender similarities? In D. M. Buss and N. M. Malamuth, eds., *Sex, Power, Conflict: Evolutionary and Feminist Perspectives,* pp. 107–118. New York: Oxford University Press.

Jackson, L. A. (1992). *Physical Appearance and Gender: Sociobiological and Sociocultural Perspectives.* Albany: State University of New York Press.

Jacobs, J. A. (1989). *Revolving Doors: Sex Segregation and Women's Careers.* Stanford, CA: Stanford University Press.

Janicki, M. G. and D. L. Krebs. (1998). Evolutionary approaches to culture. In C. Crawford and D. L. Krebs, eds., *Handbook of Evolutionary Psychology: Ideas, Issues, and Applications,* pp. 163–207. Mahwah, NJ: Erlbaum.

Jones, D. (1995). Sexual selection, physical attractiveness, and facial neoteny: Cross-cultural evidence and implications. *Current Anthropology* 36: 723–748.

Kalick, S. M., L. A. Zebrowitz, J. H. Langlois, and R. M. Johnson. (1998). Does human facial attractiveness honestly advertise health? Longitudinal data on an evolutionary question. *Psychological Science* 9: 8–13.

Kalmijn, M. (1991). Status homogamy in the United States. *American Journal of Sociology* 97: 496–523.

Kalmijn, M. (1994). Assortative mating by culture and economic occupational status. *American Journal of Sociology* 100: 422–452.

Kelly, R. L. (1995). *The Foraging Spectrum: Diversity in Hunter-Gatherer Lifeways.* Washington, D.C.: Smithsonian Institution Press.

Kenrick, D. T. and R. C. Keefe. (1992). Age preferences in mates reflect sex differences in human reproductive strategies. *Behavioral and Brain Sciences* 15: 75–91.

Kenrick, D. T., M. R. Trost, and V. L. Sheets. (1996). Power, harassment, and trophy mates: The feminist advantages of an evolutionary perspective. In D. M. Buss and N. M. Malamuth, eds., *Sex, Power, and Conflict: Evolutionary and Feminist Perspectives*, pp. 29–53. New York: Oxford University Press.

Kerckhoff, A. C. (1995). Social stratification and mobility processes: Interaction between individuals and social structures. In K. S. Cook, G. A. Fine, and J. S. House, eds., *Sociological Perspectives on Social Psychology*, pp. 476–496. Boston: Allyn and Bacon.

Lerner, G. (1986). *The Creation of Patriarchy*. New York: Oxford University Press.

Lippa, R. (1998). Gender-related individual differences and the structure of vocational interests: The importance of the "people-things" dimension. *Journal of Personality and Social Psychology* 74: 996–1009.

Lips, H. M. (1991). *Women, Men, and Power*. Mountain View, CA: Mayfield.

Lorenzi-Cioldi, F. (1998). Group status and perceptions of homogeneity: In W. Stroebe and M. Hewstone, eds., *European Review of Social Psychology*, vol. 9, pp. 31–75. Chichester, England: Wiley.

Mare, R. D. (1991). Five decades of educational assortative mating. *American Sociological Review* 56: 15–32.

Moscowitz, D. W., E. J. Suh, and J. Desaulniers. (1994). Situational influences on gender differences in agency and communion. *Journal of Personality and Social Psychology* 66: 753–761.

Olson, J. M., N. J. Roese, and M. P. Zanna. (1996). Expectancies. In E. T. Higgins and A. W. Kruglanski, eds., *Social Psychology: Handbook of Basic Principles*, pp. 211–238. New York: Guilford.

Pfeffer, J. (1998). Understanding organizations: Concepts and controversies. In D. T. Gilbert, S. T. Fiske, and G. Lindzey, eds., *The Handbook of Social Psychology*, 4th ed., vol. 2, pp. 733–777. Boston: McGraw-Hill.

Potts, R. (1984). Home bases and early hominids. *American Scientist* 72: 338–347.

Powers, E. A. (1971). Thirty years of research on ideal mate characteristics: What do we know? *International Journal of Sociology of the Family* 1: 207–215.

Presser, H. B. (1994). Employment schedules among dual-earner spouses and the division of household labor by gender. *American Sociological Review* 59: 348–364.

Reskin, B. F. and I. Padavic. (1994). *Women and Men at Work*. Thousand Oaks, CA: Pine Forge Press.

Ridgeway, C. L. (1991). The social construction of status value: Gender and other nominal characteristics. *Social Forces* 70: 367–386.

Ridgeway, C. L. (1997). Interaction and the conservation of gender inequality: Considering employment. *American Sociological Review* 62: 218–235.

Ridgeway, C. L. and D. Diekeman. (1992). Are gender differences status differences? In C. L. Ridgeway, ed., *Gender, Interaction, and Inequality*, pp. 157–180. New York: Springer-Verlag.

Rose, L. and F. Marshall (1996). Meat eating, hominid sociality, and home bases revisited. *Current Anthropology* 37: 307–338.

Sanday, P. R. (1981). *Female Power and Male Dominance: On the Origins of Sexual Inequality.* New York: Cambridge University Press.

Schaller, M. (1997). Beyond "competing," beyond "compatible." *American Psychologist* 52: 1379–1380.

Shelton, B. A. (1992). *Women, Men, and Time: Gender Differences in Paid Work, Housework, and Leisure.* New York: Greenwood Press.

Silverman, I. and K. Phillips. (1998). The evolutionary psychology of spatial sex differences. In C. Crawford and D. L. Krebs, eds., *Handbook of Evolutionary Psychology: Ideas, Issues, and Applications,* pp. 595–612. Mahwah, NJ: Erlbaum.

Simon, R. J. and J. M. Landis. (1989). The polls—A report: Women's and men's attitudes about a woman's place and role. *Public Opinion Quarterly* 53: 265–276.

Singh, D. (1993). Adaptive significance of female physical attractiveness: Role of waist-to-hip ratio. *Journal of Personality and Social Psychology* 65: 293–307.

Skrypnek, B. J. and M. Snyder. (1982). On the self-perpetuating nature of stereotypes about women and men. *Journal of Experimental Social Psychology* 18: 277–291.

Smith, E. A. (2000). Three styles in the evolutionary study of human behavior. In L. Cronk, W. Irons, and N. Chagnon, eds., *Adaptation and Human Behavior: An Anthropological Perspective,* pp. 27–46. Hawthorne, NY: Aldine de Gruyter.

Sork, V. L. (1997). Quantitative genetics, feminism, and evolutionary theories of gender differences. In P. A. Gowaty, ed., *Feminism and Evolutionary Biology: Boundaries, Intersections, and Frontiers,* pp. 86–115. New York: Chapman and Hall.

Spence, J. T. and E. D. Hahn. (1997). The Attitudes Toward Women Scale and attitude change in college students. *Psychology of Women Quarterly* 21: 17–34.

Sprecher, S., Q. Sullivan, and E. Hatfield. (1994). Mate selection preferences: Gender differences examined in a national sample. *Journal of Personality and Social Psychology* 66: 1074–1080.

Steil, J. M. (1997). *Marital Equality: Its Relationship to the Well-being of Husbands and Wives.* Thousand Oaks, CA: Sage.

Strier, K. B. (1994). Myth of the typical primate. *Yearbook of Physical Anthropology* 37: 233–271.

Symons, D. (1979). *The Evolution of Human Sexuality.* New York: Oxford University Press.

Symons, D. (1992). On the use and misuse of Darwinism in the study of human behavior. In J. H. Barkow, L. Cosmides, and J. Tooby, eds., *The Adapted Mind: Evolutionary Psychology and the Generation of Culture,* pp. 137–159. New York: Oxford University Press.

Tassinary, L. G. and K. A. Hansen. (1998). A critical test of the waist-to-hip-ratio hypothesis of female physical attractiveness. *Psychological Science* 9: 150–155.

Tattersall, I. (1998). *Becoming Human: Evolution and Human Uniqueness.* New York: Harcourt Brace.

Tittle, C. K. (1981). *Careers and Family: Sex Roles and Adolescent Life Plans.* Beverly Hills, CA: Sage.

Tomaskovic-Devey, D. (1995). Sex composition and gendered earnings inequality: A comparison of job and occupational models. In J. A. Jacobs, ed., *Gender Inequality at Work,* pp. 23–56. Thousand Oaks, CA: Sage.

Tooby, J. and L. Cosmides. (1989). The innate versus the manifest: How universal does universal have to be? *Behavioral and Brain Sciences* 12: 36–37.

Tooby, J. and L. Cosmides. (1990a). On the universality of human nature and the uniqueness of the individual: The role of genetics and adaptation. *Journal of Personality* 58: 17–67.

Tooby, J. and L. Cosmides. (1990b). The past explains the present: Emotional adaptations and the structure of ancestral environments. *Ethology and Sociobiology* 11: 375–424.

Tooby, J. and L. Cosmides. (1992). The psychological foundations of culture. In J. H. Barkow, L. Cosmides, and J. Tooby, eds., *The Adapted Mind: Evolutionary Psychology and the Generation of Culture,* pp. 19–136. New York: Oxford University Press.

Townsend, J. M. (1989). Mate selection criteria: A pilot study. *Ethology and Sociobiology* 10: 241–253.

Toynbee, A. J. (1934–1961). *A Study of History,* vols. 1–12. New York: Oxford University Press.

Travis, C. B. and C. P. Yeager. (1991). Sexual selection, parental investment, and sexism. *Journal of Social Issues* 47 (3): 117–129.

Trivers, R. (1972). Parental investment and sexual selection. In B. Campbell, ed., *Sexual Selection and the Descent of Man: 1871–1971,* pp. 136–179. Chicago: Aldine.

Twenge, J. M. (1997). Attitudes toward women, 1970–1995: A meta-analysis. *Psychology of Women Quarterly* 21: 35–51.

United Nations Development Programme. (1995). *Human Development Report 1995.* New York: Oxford University Press.

United Nations Development Programme. (1996). *Human Development Report 1996.* New York: Oxford University Press.

United Nations Development Programme. (1997). *Human Development Report 1997.* New York: Oxford University Press.

West, C. and D. H. Zimmerman. (1987). Doing gender. *Gender and Society* 1: 125–151.

Whyte, M. K. (1978). *The Status of Women in Preindustrial Societies.* Princeton, NJ: Princeton University Press.

Wiederman, M. W. and E. R. Allgeier. (1992). Gender differences in mate selection criteria: Sociobiological or socioeconomic explanation? *Ethology and Sociobiology* 13: 115–124.

Wiley, M. G. (1995). Sex category and gender in social psychology. In K. S. Cook, G. A. Fine, and J. S. House, eds., *Sociological Perspectives on Social Psychology,* pp. 362–386. Boston: Allyn and Bacon.

Williams, G. C. (1966). *Adaptation and Natural Selection: A Critique of Some Current Evolutionary Thought.* Princeton, NJ: Princeton University Press.

Wood, W., P. N. Christensen, M. R. Hebl, and H. Rothgerber. (1997). Conformity to sex-typed norms, affect, and the self-concept. *Journal of Personality and Social Psychology* 73: 523–535.

Wood, W. and A. H. Eagly. (In press). A cross-cultural analysis of the behavior of women and men: Implications for the origins of sex differences. *Psychological Bulletin.*

Wood, W. and S. J. Karten. (1986). Sex differences in interaction style as a product of perceived sex differences in competence. *Journal of Personality and Social Psychology* 50: 341–347.

13

The Evolutionary Value of the Man (to) Child Affiliative Bond: Closer to Obligate Than to Facultative

Wade C. Mackey

Rule #1: All politics are local.
—Rep. Tip O'Neill

Rule #2: All long-term politics are reproductive strategies.
Rule #3: All effective long-term politics camouflage Rule #2.
—Ipsoc Macquire

The Thornhill and Palmer Thesis

Thornhill and Palmer (2000) proffer the intriguing idea that human "rape" represents a specialized neuro-hormonal—motivational—module that is an evolutionarily successful adaptation. The adaptation could take the form of either a specialized module or a generalized increase in men's sex drive or sexual assertiveness or overall aggression. For example, it might have proven advantageous for men to maintain an increased interest in sexuality across the woman's menstrual cycle. If Thornhill and Palmer are correct, and, if, as is traditional, the burden of scientific proof falls on the shoulders of those stating the thesis, then Thornhill and Palmer need to demonstrate the following:

When compared to the much more typical pattern of social fathers who conceive and nurture their own children to effective adulthood, the bio-cultural behavior of "rape" is, at least, competitive in terms of generating grandchildren who generate grandchildren.

Thornhill and Palmer fail to offer any evidence—at all—that would indicate that children conceived via "rape" survive, mate, and procreate in greater or equal competence when compared to children conceived via ongoing social fathers.

The evidence presented by Thornhill and Palmer consists of the following:

During Rwanda's recent civil war, as many as 35 percent of 304 rape victims surveyed may have become pregnant, and a high percentage of the rape conceptions resulted in offspring despite the fact that most of the women claimed not to want the pregnancies. (p. 99)

"Estimates of rates of pregnancy resulting from rape in peacetime settings vary from 1 percent to 33 percent" (p. 99). Quoting from Holmes et al. (1996) they write: "the rape-related pregnancy rate was 5 percent per rape, or 6 percent per victim" (p. 100). Because many of the pregnancies after the rape were the result of impregnation by a consensual mate, Thornhill and Palmer note that "[T]he figure reported by Holmes et al. probably should be corrected to about 2 percent" (p. 100).

The Thornhill and Palmer evidence for a "rape" as a specialized motivational module is restricted to an estimated 2 percent pregnancy rate per rape. The fates of the pregnancies are totally unknown. The necessary data for a substantiation of their thesis, namely grandchildren who have grandchildren, are not presented, nor do Thornhill and Palmer acknowledge the singular necessity of such data for the support of their hypothesis.

Accordingly, their thesis becomes an intriguing idea or speculation. To wit: "Children of rape are as competitive in achieving effective adulthood as are children with on-going social fathers." Thornhill and Palmer do not provide evidence to advance this thesis, perhaps better labeled a hypothesis, beyond the domain of the speculative.

The rest of this chapter argues that such equality of competitiveness is unlikely.

Because counterindicative data are no more available than are indicative data, no Popperian falsification is available. What is available is the clear value of the ongoing social father to the well-being of the developing child and that this value is very, very old. And it may be reiterated that "rape" is a phenomenon that effectively precludes the biological father from being the ongoing social father.

First, the argument is presented that there does exist, in fact, a man (to) child affiliative bond that is independent of the man-woman bond and of the woman (to) child bond.

Second, the very recent social experiment, in parts of the industrialized world, of abrading or excluding the father from the mother-child dyad is analyzed in terms of the consequences for the commonweal across generations.

Social Fathering as a Human Trait

Fathering Is Neither a Thin Veneer Nor a Social Invention: The Cross-cultural Theme of Marriage

Although there are a myriad of exotic and arcane variations on rituals of marriage across the world's community of cultures, an invariant is the sheer existence of marriage. Leach (1955) has distilled a list of commonalities that are universally aligned with "marriage." Three of the commonalities are germane here. Namely, marriage serves:

1. to give the husband a monopoly in the wife's sexuality ("husbands" in the case of polyandry);
2. to give the wife a monopoly in the husband's sexuality ("wives" in the case of polygyny); and
3. to establish the legal father of a woman's children.

Point (3) is of special interest. A key component to marriage is the universal imprimatur or designation of legitimacy. Virtually all cultures have the notion that children should be legitimized through marriage: A man—the husband—has special responsibility for the nurturance and protection of his children (Hartley 1975; Malinowski 1927; Stephens 1963; Van den Berghe 1979). That is, the man—the husband—becomes a social father. Because the presence of a social father is mandated, his presence is a constant in the structure of virtually all societies. Accordingly, the function of the social father is difficult to analyze as long as it remains a constant. Variation of cause is essential to evaluate variation of effect.

Framed a little differently, in the hurly-burly assemblage of very diverse cultures with large differences in economic bases and cosmologies, a constant that thematically emerges is the "social father" (Hewlett 1992; Mackey 1985, 1986, 1996, 2001). Because it is difficult to explain a "constant/consistent" with a variable, a second constant/consistency would loom as a more attractive explicator. The most likely candidate to explain the catholicity of the "social father" is the human genetic mosaic: That is, fathering is a human trait. Phrased in a more prosaic manner: Men are built to like their kids.

The man (to) child affiliative bond The question can then be legitimately asked: "Why would such a male (to) child affiliative bond arise and be competitive in our evolutionary trajectory or history?" The pongids (chimpanzees, bonobos, and gorillas)—our closest genetic relatives—are not predictive of such a bond. Pongid males and the males of other terrestrial primates generally tolerate the young of the troop (at least his young), but leave nurturing to the mothers (Goodall 1986; McGinnis 1979; McGrew, Marchant, and Nishida 1996; Smuts et al. 1986; Smuts and Guberick 1992; Taub 1984). Yet, across cultural boundaries, human males—men—are clearly fond of their own children, nurture them, play with them, and are quite willing to provision and protect them (Hewlett 1992; HRAF #22–#26 1949; Lamb 1987; Mackey 1976, 1985, 1996).

Men systematically provisioning their children   A cross-cultural universal is that men will gather resources—food is an excellent example—from outside the perimeter of their camp/village and then return to the camp/village and share that resource with particular children (their children) as well as with the men's wives. The pattern is highly predictable (Hewlett 1992; HRAF #22–#26 1949; Lamb 1987; Mackey 1985, 1986, 1996) and occurs across societal structures and across ecologies (Murdock 1957, 1967) such as the Yanomamo (Chagnon 1977), China (Chance 1984), Tibet (Ekvall 1968), the Tiwi of Australia (Hart and Pilling 1960), the Dani of New Guinea (Heider 1979), Eskimos (Chance 1966), Japan (Norbeck 1976), the Yuqui of Amazonia (Stearman 1989), Australian aborigines (Tonkinson 1978), and the Dobe !Kung in southern Africa (Lee 1984). The provisioning is not totally exclusive. Systematic food sharing has been ritualized in many, if not all, societies. Rarely can a hunter claim a large kill for only his own family (Coon 1971; Lee 1982; Tonkinson 1978; Chance 1966). But, within these contexts, a man provides singular attention in terms of provisioning and protection to the legitimate children that he has fathered and to his wife or wives (see HRAF 1949, #22–26, and see Malinowski 1927 and Hendrix 1996 for theoretical discussions).

When resources are not forthcoming from a prospective groom, brides are difficult to acquire (Cashdan 1993) and wives are difficult to keep (Betzig 1989). When the pattern does break down across the overall society, for example, the Ik (Turnbull 1972), the breakdown signals an overall societal disintegration and is a focused topic of the ethnographer's analysis.

Adult males' active and systematic food sharing is not a primate trait. That is, men, but not other adult male primates, (i) procure food from outside of the group's perimeter, and (ii) they then return to the group for the sharing with females and their young. The adult male primates may allow a shared feeding from the same source, or may relinquish food to a "begging" female, for example, as in the chimpanzee (Boesch 1994; Boesch and Boesch 1989; de Waal 1997, 1998; de Waal and Lanting 1997; Goodall 1986; Nishida and Hosaka 1996; Stanford 1996; Teleki 1973; cf. Parish 1996); however, the adult males do not leave the perimeter of the troop, obtain food, and then return to the troop to give the food to adult females, who might then give it to their young.

Although not a primate characteristic, food sharing by adult males does occur in many—if not most—bird species, especially if the species tends toward monogamy (Kleiman 1977), and in the canids: wolves (Mech 1966; Mowat 1963; Murie 1944), coyotes (Dobie 1949; McMahan 1976; Ryden 1974; Young and Jackson 1951), jackals (Lawick and Lawick-Goodall 1971; Moehlman 1980), hunting dogs (Kuhme 1965), and foxes (Alderton 1994). See King (1980), Mackey (1976, 1996), Schaller and Lowther (1969), and Thompson (1978) for discussions (cf. Lovejoy 1981). The canid analogue is of most interest to the argument being presented here. For example, the adult male wolf will catch prey, return to the den and give the food via regurgitation to the mother wolf and the pups for their consumption (Mech 1970). Of further interest, these canids—parallel with humans—also tend toward monogamy and toward minimal sexual dimorphism (Kleiman 1977). As detailed below, this minimal sexual dimorphism of *Homo* presents a problem for the Thornhill and Palmer thesis. An argument can be made that convergent evolution has occurred between adult male canids and adult male Homo (see Mackey 1976, 1996 for expanded discussion). A key difference between the canids (e.g., hunting dogs or wolves) and humans is that breeding within the canid pack is often restricted to one (alpha) pair; whereas any and all men who "marry" are expected to have offspring.

The problem of reduced sexual dimorphism   Paternal provisioning is aligned with reduced sexual dimorphism (Kleiman 1977). Accordingly, the model presented here and the pressures for reduced sexual dimorphism exerted on men who uniquely provisioned their wives and their (own) children are mutually supportive concepts (cf. Foley and Lee 1989). In terms of sexual dimorphism, there are three items Thornhill and Palmer need to address. First, *Homo*'s predecessor *Australopithecus* did exhibit a large degree of sexual dimorphism by size (Hall 1985; Plavcan and van Schaik 1997). Second, *Homo,* compared to *Australopithecus,* gradually increased in size (Aiello 1994; Fleagle 1988; Hall 1985). Third, *Homo* became exclusively terrestrial. From these three givens a not unreasonable inferred assumption would be that *Homo* would follow the basic trend of maintaining or increasing sexual dimorphism. However, sexual dimorphism decreased (Aiello 1994; Arsuaga et al. 1997; *Economist* 1984; Lewin 1987; Lockwood et al. 1996; McHenry 1991; see Martin, Willner, and Dettling 1994 for a discussion).

In terms of height, the sexual dimorphism of contemporary humans is 107 (s.d. 1.5; $n = 93$ [societies], that is, women are 94 percent the height of men) (Alexander et al 1979). The human canine is virtually (sexually) isomorphic, and piloerection is not a functional human trait. In terms of weight, the sexual dimorphism of (U.S.) humans is 130.0. Since the linear correlation between the weight of primate males and the sexual dimorphism of their species is significant ($r_p = .569$; $p < .01$; two-tailed; $n = 47$) (Hall 1985), then the sexual dimorphism of human males could be predicted from their weight. When the "sexual dimorphism ratio" is predicted from the average man's weight, the predicted value is a sex ratio for male-to-female of 187.4. This predicted value overestimates the actual value of 130.0 by 1.55 standard deviations. (Using a similar method for data from Plavcan and van Schaik 1997 resulted in a similar finding. The correlation [r_p of .389 was significant] [$p < .01$; 2-tailed; $n = 86$]. The predicted sexual dimorphism ratio was 155 or 1.15 standard deviations larger than the actual male-to-female ratio.)

"Rape" is a behavior involving physical aggression. Large size is advantageous in physical confrontations. If "rape" were a specific and adaptive evolutionary strategy, then Thornhill and Palmer need to explain why human sexual dimorphism decreased when a "rape" strategy would predict the reverse.

Synopsis   It is argued here that those males, whether late *Australopithecines* or early *Homo*, who did have a rudimentary affiliative bond toward (their) children—"liked" them—would have a clear reproductive advantage over those men who did not "like" (their/any) children. If sexual exclusivity were becoming a norm, then the children of the wife also tended to be the children of the husband. (See Fisher 1983 for a discussion of the "sex contract.") His nurturing of her children was also the nurturing of his children, that is, his genes, his inclusive fitness. Framed a little differently, the father's emotion of affection for his children would be the drivewheel to allow paternal certainty to be a fruitful and effective strategy. Just as a husband's jealousy may reduce his wife's straying, his nurturing of his own (very altricial) children would increase the man's chances of having his own grandchildren. A measure of intuition infers that it is much more palatable for someone to nurture other people and to give them treasure if those people were liked by the dispenser. Any other combination of a giver-receiver relationship seems a nonviable competitor. In times of scarcity, especially during an intense winter, systematic provisioning by a man to his young would certainly enhance the survivability quotient of those children. Children who survive are more likely to have grandchildren than those children who do not. Children who did survive became our ancestors. Children who did not survive did not.

Female Reproductive Calculus and the Paternalistic Man

From what was probably a fairly simple choice for her female ancestors, a qualitatively different strategy would have unfolded for those females who were in the transition period between mothering-only and co-parenting. For eons, her ancestors merely had to notice which male out-tussled his competitors. Such a winner would sire the females' children.

Her descendants would have had a much more complex evaluation to make. She, in competition, with other females, had to shift from what the male's physical dominance had achieved in the past—he had won the tussle—to what a man would do in the future—would he be able and be willing to share valuable resources with her (and her children).

Of the two traits, "able" and "willing," "willing" would be much, much harder to evaluate. She now had to evaluate the male's psychology, his personality. Although the words "trust," "honest," "reliable" were undoubtedly not part of the woman's worldview, the concepts, *de facto,* had to have been. An incompetent read by her of the male would have left her hungry and pregnant and the mother of incompetent offspring. A competent read by her of the male would have left her sated and pregnant and the mother of competent offspring. Thus, across millennia, as the women were slowly biasing toward finding the qualities of "affiliation," "reliability," and "sharing" to be attractive in mating partners, they were simultaneously sculpting male descendants who were "affectionate," "reliable," and "sharing" toward the males' own children. Such traits in a mate lent enhanced survivability to the woman and her (and his) children. The men who possessed such traits would have increased their proportion of the next generation's gene-pool, as did the women who found such men attractive.

Social context of fathering   It is not known, nor will it ever be known, when the biological "pair-bonding" slid into the cultural "marriage." However, whenever "marriage," as a cultural institution, was devised as an overlay to pair-bonding, it was a success. "Marriage" became a universal. The individual woman's choice of a mating partner, a.k.a. husband, was now in the context of familial politics (Stephens 1963; Van den Berghe 1979). Some societies were content to let women maintain high levels of discretion. But other societies had input from elders. The input would vary from suggestion to veto to complete control, for example, preferential cross-cousin marriage, arranged marriages. The dowry and brideprice were invented. "Political" and alliance formation were inserted into the mix. Again the "input" occurs independent of ecology or subsistence technique, as in the Yanomamo (Chagnon 1977), China (Chance 1984), Tibet (Ekvall 1968), the Tiwi of Australia (Hart and Pilling 1960), the Dani of New Guinea (Heider 1979), Eskimos (Chance 1966), Japan (Norbeck 1976), the Yuqui of Amazonia (Stearman 1989), Australian aborigines (Tonkinson 1978) and the Dobe !Kung of southern Africa (Lee 1984).

Suitors who were handsome, virile, energetic, reliable, and trustworthy would generally receive approval from the debutante as well as her family. However, men who either portended to become or had become ineffectual providers, that is, ineffectual fathers, threatened not only the/their wife and their children, but also the extended family, and, to the extent that such men were becoming more numerous, the entire commonweal. As the irresponsibility of an effectual father becomes more and more self-evident, the burdens of caring for the woman and her/his children are either ignored by her/his kin or the kin must shift their resources to keep the woman and her children viable. Any systematic ignoring of her by her/his kin threatens the woman and her children's very existence. Any shift in resources weakens the corporate or extended family. The more ineffectual fathers there are in the extended family, the more the extended family's resources are diluted.

Similarly, the more families that are faced with sustaining women-child(ren) dyads that have an ineffectual husband/father, the weaker is the overall society. In a very competitive world, weakened societies do not enjoy prolonged longevity.

The preceding argument is not merely hypothetical. Given the social experiment begun in the 1960s and the widespread availability of the "pill" and other effective contraceptive techniques, it can be tested, that is, falsified. The "social experiment" is the systematic separation of the child from his or her social father. The main locus of the separations is Western Europe and its extensions. The two mechanisms are out-of-wedlock births (father preclusion) and divorce (father abrasion). We focus on out-of-wedlock births in this exercise. The equation of an absent father with an ineffectual father seems fairly intuitive. The basic question being addressed is: "Does the systematic separation of children from their social and biological fathers have negative consequences for the commonweal?"

Potential Costs to the Commonweal of Absent/Ineffectual Fathers

This section offers the notion that the early or total preclusion of a social father from the mother-child dyad is aligned with dysfunctional consequences for the child, both in childhood and in the child's later adulthood. These dysfunctional consequences can be exemplified (I) in rates of violent crime (for sons), (II) in sexually transmitted diseases (for daughters), (III) in vulnerability to child abuse, plus (IV) in the differential access to resources. Given that any children conceived by a "rape" would be systematically deprived of an ongoing social and biological father, the dysfunctions described below would be concentrated in this category of children.

1   Sons and Violent Behavior

There is a tendency for children from fatherless homes to be overrepresented in categories of unwanted behavior, and this tendency has been known for decades (Adams, Milner, and Schrepf 1984; Anderson 1968; Bereczkei and Csanaky 1996; Blau and Blau 1982; Chilton and Markle 1972; Coney and Mackey 1998; Monahan 1972; Mosher 1969; Robins and Hill 1966; Stevenson and Black 1988). See Mischel (1961a,b) and

Mackey (1985, 1996) for theoretical orientations on the suggested linkage. See Wilson and Herrnstein (1985), Draper and Harpending (1982), Blankenhorn (1995), and Popenoe (1996) for reviews of the literature.

Cross-cultural data   Three surveys of violent crime are presented. The first survey is restricted to Nordic nations. The next two are more universal and span the globe.

For these cross-cultural comparisons, the unit of analysis was "nation." It may be noted that nations represent coarse units of analysis, thereby elevating the opportunity for false-negatives to occur. However, if a signal were to be found in all the potential noise, then the signal may represent an alignment of some potency. And, as presented below, patterns were found.

Nordic out-of-wedlock births and levels of assault   Percentages of out-of-wedlock births and rates of assault per 100,000 population 15 years or older (14 years for Norway) were available from Denmark, Finland, Norway, and Sweden for the interval 1959 to 1990 (Nordic Statistical Secretariat 1960–1992). The correlation between percentage of out-of-wedlock births and levels of assault were significant for all four nations (Denmark, $[r_p = .970; p < .001; n = 23]$, Finland $[r_p = .851; p < .001; n = 20]$; Norway $[r_p = .973; p < .001; n = 23]$, and Sweden $[r_p = .945; p < .001; n = 22]$; because not all nations had indices for all years, the "ns" vary). All four countries were ethnically homogeneous and relatively wealthy. Accordingly, neither ethnic antagonisms nor absolute levels of poverty would seem a likely variable in affecting the results.

If an interval of 19 years is used to separate the levels of out-of-wedlock births and rates of assault, the correlations are still significant (the correlations $[r_p]$ range from .889 to .949; $p < 13$). Of course, after 19 years the sons are no longer infants and are quite capable of energetic behaviors.

Global sample 1: Murder and illegitimacy across cultures   Cross-cultural analyses are hampered by the problems of meaningful and comparable units of analysis. (See Ford 1961 and Levinson and Malone 1980 for a discussion of cultural units.) Analyses on rates of crime are often problematic because of the lack of consonance among countries in the definitions and reporting of various crimes. However, one crime—murder—does seem to be universally accepted as a crime with reasonably concordant definitions (Archer and Gartner 1984; Daly and Wilson 1988). One may muse on the high validity of the level of death as a dependent variable. Accordingly, rates of murder were correlated with illegitimacy rates in each nation (Smith-Morris 1990; United Nations 1985–1992).

There were usable data from the U.N. sources for 44 countries in which murder rates and illegitimacy rates were both reported to the satisfaction of the United Nations. The relationship was positive and significant (r_p = .443; p < .01; 2-tailed; df = 42).[1] Across cultures, as murder rates went up, so did the proportion of single-parent births. Nearly 20 percent ($.443^2$ = .196 = 19.6 percent) of the differences in murder rates could be attributed to differences in rates of illegitimacy.

Global sample 2   In a wider sample of 60 nations (40 of these had data useful for this inquiry) (INTERPOL 1990), rates of serious assault and out-of-wedlock births were found to be related. As the percentage of all live births that were out-of-wedlock increased, so did the rates of serious assault (r_p = .436; p < .05; 2-tailed; n = 38).

These data refer to father separation due to out-of-wedlock births (father-preclusion). Although "divorce" also tends to separate the father from his child (father-abrasion), the data described above are not easily generalizable from father-preclusion to father-abrasion. "Divorce" and "out-of-wedlock births" are diagnostically separable phenomena.

2   Daughters and Promiscuity

Out-of-wedlock births and multiple partners   As presented earlier, it is— at base—women (as a class), compared to men (as a class), who tend to control sexual interactions. (See Symons 1979 for a discussion.) A woman could be more discerning in her selection of sexual partners or less discerning. Accordingly, the inclusion and patterning of multiple sexual partnerships, in the context of fatherlessness, were examined.

In the United States, as elsewhere, sexual activity is a secreted activity. Accordingly, compiling data via naturalistic observation would be difficult, highly illegal, and unwelcomed by all. Thus, a proxy for multiple sexual partners becomes necessary. It has been noted by several authors (e.g., Aral, Mosher, and Cates 1991; Brunham and Plummer 1990; Hunter et al.

1994; Laumann et al. 1997; Moore and Cates 1990; Weström and Mårdh 1990) that having multiple sexual partners is the best marker for acquiring a sexually transmitted disease: an STD. The Division for STD Prevention of the Centers for Disease Control compiles data by state (plus D.C.), which enabled rates of gonorrhea and congenital syphilis to be used as markers for multiple sexual partners.

Note that, if an individual contracts an STD, the infection does not necessitate that the individual has had multiple sexual partners. However, if someone is infected with an STD, then it is highly likely that the individual either has had multiple partners or has chosen a mating partner who has had multiple partners.

STDs and threat to the commonweal   STDs are not benign occurrences. Current problems related to human fertility that stem from contemporary STDs involve a myriad of pathogenic agents. These organisms include bacteria, viruses, ectoparasites, fungi, and protozoa. The pathologies caused by these organisms include, but are not limited to, infertility, chronic pelvic pain, copulatory pain, and ectopic pregnancy due to gonorrhea and chlamydia; anal, cervical, penile and vulvar carcinoma due to human papilloma virus; acquired immunodeficiency due to HIV; hepatitis and hepatic cancer due to hepatitis B virus; and life-threatening fetal, neonatal, and infant infections (i.e., syphilis, HIV herpes simplex virus, hepatitis B virus) (Aiken 1992; Allen et al. 1992; Brunham, Holmes, and Embree 1990; Holmes et al. 1990; McDermott, Steketee, and Wirima 1996; McDermott et al. 1993; Schulz, Cates, and O'Mara 1987; Villa 1997; zur Hausen 1996).

These contemporary STDs present a wide range of consequences that can lower a woman's fertility and neonatal viability. Important to this chapter is that STDs would lower a community's ability to replace itself in proportion to the prevalence of the STDs within that community as in, for example, the Sub-Saharan Africa's epidemic of acquired immunodeficiency syndrome AIDS. For example, if syphilis is contracted by a woman, the chances for miscarriage, infant death, still-births, and prematurity are all increased (Newell et al. 1993; Schulz et al. 1990; Waugh 1990). Furthermore, if the mother is infected, then the chances are also substantial that the fetus will contract syphilis from the mother, which would decrease the child's life chances: life chances that would include a reproductive history. In addition, the proportions are not small. Untreated syphilis during pregnancy is passed to virtually 100 percent of the infants: 50 percent resulting in prematurity or perinatal death (Schulz et al. 1990). In a 1917 (pre-antibiotic) study of 1000 syphilitic pregnancies, 8 percent ended in still-births, 23 percent infant deaths, and 21 percent of the infants had contracted syphilis. The corresponding numbers for the controls ($n =$ 826) were 2 percent, 11 percent, and 0 percent respectively (Schulz et al. 1990). Examples of *sequelae* following congenital syphilis to the neonate include deafness, dental defects, bony lesions, eye lesions, and nervous system lesions including mental retardation, obstructive hydrocephalus, and seizure disorders. None of these conditions would seem to enhance an individual's reproductive history or an individual's desirability as a mate.

AIDS, of course, is a fatal disease and is also associated with higher infant and children mortality (Taha et al. 1995). See Haldane (1949), Barkow (1989), Graves and Duvall (1995), Hamilton and Zuk (1982), and Ridley (1993) for complementary discussions and examples from non-humans. Cf. Sheldon (1993).

The current leading cause of infertility is pelvic inflammatory disease (PID) as caused by STDs (e.g., chlamydia, gonorrhea) (Aral, Mosher, and Cates 1991; Weström and Mårdh 1990; Harrison and Alexander 1990; Peterson, Galaid, and Cates 1990; Gutman and Wilfert 1990; Wolner-Haussen, Kiviat and Holmes 1990; Moore and Cates 1990; Weström 1987, 1991; Moore and Spadoni 1984). Basically, these STDs can infect (salpingitis) and scar the fallopian tubes and thereby impair uterine conception. Consequently, such afflicted women can have impaired fertility or have a tubal (ectopic) pregnancy. Note that ectopic pregnancies represent the leading cause of maternal deaths during the first trimester in the United States (Herbertson and Storey 1991; *JAMA* 1995; Joesoef et al. 1991). Prior to effective and sterile surgical procedures, for example, in 1880, the prognosis for an ectopic pregnancy was death (72 percent to 90 percent death, 28 percent to 10 percent survival). The current prognosis is greater than 99 percent survival and less than 1 percent death (Lurie 1992). A recent study in Sweden (Weström et al. 1992) indicated that occluded fallopian tubes significantly decreased the chances for a successful attempt at becoming pregnant and, if pregnancy did occur, also (significantly) increased the chances of an ectopic pregnancy by at least a factor of five.

Moore and Cates (1990) estimate that after a single episode of PID, infertility resulted in 6 percent of the mild cases, 13 percent of the moderate cases and 30 percent of the severe cases. (Note that these figures arose even when effective treatment was available.)

Each successive bout of PID acts to double the chances of infertility (Weström and Mårdh 1990). An analogous sequence occurs with successive pregnancies in a woman who has contracted syphilis.

It should be reiterated that these statistics arise in a time and a society with readily available medical information, medical technology, and inexpensive antibiotics. In the pre-antibiotic era, after being infected with gonorrhea, up to 70 percent of the women had tubal obstruction (Moore and Cates 1990). Holtz (1930) estimated that 1.3 percent of the PIDs were lethal. Mosher and Aral (1985) calculated that PID accounted for a third to a half of recent increases in infertility.

Similar *sequelae* result from infections of herpes simplex virus. For example, a herpes simplex virus infection in an infant can spread to multiple organs including the central nervous system, the lung, the liver, adrenals, the eyes, the mouth, and the skin. When the virus affects multiple organs, there is a 60 percent mortality rate at one year. Of the survivors, 44 percent are left with permanent neurologic impairment (Stagno and Whitley 1990). Again, these statistics are from a time and a place that uses modern medical techniques.

Although these pathologies, inter alia, are not necessarily lethal to the nubile woman, the symptoms of these pathologies would tend to decrease the afflicted individual's level of competitiveness in attracting desirable mates. To the extent that these infections affect skin texture, body odors, genital secretions, general activity level, and romantic tendencies (see Buss 1989, 1994; Buss and Schmitt 1993; and Cashdan 1993 for examples), the chances for a successful impregnation are similarly decreased. And, again, if someone does not have children, then that someone will not have grandchildren. (See Mackey and Immerman in press for examples of how quickly an epidemic of STDs can virtually eradicate a community.)

Method The rates of gonorrhea and congenital syphilis were analyzed, across the 50 states plus D.C., for the three consecutive years of 1991, 1992, and 1993 (Division of STD Prevention 1996, 1999). The percentage of all births that were out-of-wedlock was compiled across (available)

Table 13.1
Correlations (i) between the percentage of births that are out-of-wedlock and rates of STDs (from the same time interval) and (ii) between percentage of births that are out-of-wedlock (from a prior time interval) and rates of STDs (from a subsequent time interval).

Year of out-of-wedlock births	Year of STD rates	STD	N	r_p
1991	1991	Gonorrhea	51	.835*
1992	1992	Gonorrhea	51	.786*
1993	1993	Gonorrhea	51	.791*
Mean			51	.804*
1991	1991	Congenital syphilis	51	.751*
1992	1992	Congenital syphilis	51	.722*
1993	1993	Congenital syphilis	51	.784*
Mean			51	.752*
1971	1991	Gonorrhea	39	.940*
1972	1992	Gonorrhea	39	.932*
1973	1993	Gonorrhea	39	.927*
Mean			39	.933*
1971	1991	Congenital syphilis	39	.858*
1972	1992	Congenital syphilis	39	.822*
1973	1993	Congenital syphilis	39	.858*
Mean			39	.846*

* $p < .001$

states plus D.C. for two intervals of three years each (U.S. Bureau of the Census 1970–1996). The first interval of three years was the same interval as the data on STDs: 1991 to 1993. The second interval of three years was from a generation before the analyzed interval of the data on STDs. Twenty years is used to index a generation. (Note that approximately one-third of the cases of gonorrhea in females occurred in females 20 years of age or less, and approximately 90 percent of the cases of primary and secondary syphilis occur in women younger than 40 years of age; Division of STD Prevention 1990, 1996.) Hence, the second interval was from 1971 to 1973.

Results: Out-of-wedlock births and (i) gonorrhea and (ii) congenital syphilis (1991–1993) For all three years, 1991 to 1993, the percentage of all births that were out-of-wedlock births were significantly and positively related to rates of gonorrhea, as well as to rates of congenital syphilis. See table 13.1. As would be expected, the mean correlation for the three-year interval was also significant and positive for gonorrhea ($r_p = .804, p < .001$, df = 49) and for congenital syphilis ($r_p = .752, p < .001$, df = 49).

Results: Out-of-wedlock births and (i) gonorrhea and (ii) congenital syphilis (1971–1973) to (1991–1993)   For all three years, the percentage of all births that were out-of-wedlock births from the prior interval (1971–1973) was significantly and positively correlated (i) to the rates of gonorrhea as well as (ii) to the rates of congenital syphilis in the subsequent interval (1991–1993). The mean correlation was also significant and positive for gonorrhea ($r_p = .933$; $p < .001$; df = 37) and for congenital syphilis ($r_p = .846$; $p < .001$; df = 37). In fact, the mean correlation between the prior interval (1971–1973) and the subsequent interval (1991–1993) of (r_p) .933 was higher ($t = 5.803$; $p < .001$; df = 36) than the mean correlation between the out-of-wedlock births and gonorrhea from the same interval (1991–1993): (r_p) = .804. In a similar manner, the correlation ($r_p = .846$) between out-of-wedlock births and congenital syphilis from the prior interval (1971–1973) was higher ($t = 3.701$; $p < .001$; df = 36) than the relationship between out-of-wedlock births and congenital syphilis from the same time interval (1991–1993): $r_p = .752$. See table 13.1. Again, "divorce" and "out-of-wedlock births" should not be conflated. The interpretations here are restricted to "out-of-wedlock births."

3   Choice of Partner and Child Abuse

Although rarely phrased in such a way, a resident father is a reliable health insurance policy for his children. As soon as any other domestic arrangement occurs, that is, as soon as any other man other than the biological and social father becomes proximate to children who are not his own, the children are at increased risk to physical abuse (Daly and Wilson 1982, 1985, 1987; Gil 1970; Hegar, Zuravin, and Orme 1994; Lenington 1981; Levine, Freeman, and Compaan 1994; Mann 1996; Widom 1992; see Kasim, Shafie, and Cheah 1994 for an example outside of the U.S.; cf. Hausfater and Hrdy 1984). If the child is a girl, then the increase in physical abuse risk is complemented with an increased risk to sexual abuse (Gordon and Creighton 1988; Mynatt and Allgeier 1990; Russell 1986;

Tyler 1986). The *sequelae* of sexual abuse on prepubescent girls will be examined separately in the next section.

Hence, if a mother (i) chooses not to co-reside with the biological and
social father of her children, and (ii) chooses a lifestyle other than unre-
lenting chastity, then her choices elevate the chances that her children will
be physically or sexually abused. In the short-term, dead, maimed, and
traumatized children are probably not the best route to family cohesion
and effectiveness and certainly not to Darwinian success. The long-term
sequelae of physical abuse on either boys or girls is an unknown entity
(aside from death, which has a predictable future).

On the other hand, the long-term *sequelae* of sexual abuse on girls is
known and is extremely expensive to the violated-girl-grown-to-adult-
hood and to whatever social group in which she would find herself. See
Browne and Finkelhor (1986), Finkelhor (1979), Finkelhor and Dziuba-
Leatherman (1994), and Garnefski and Arends (1998) for reviews of the
literature.

Sequelae to sexual abuse of the girl   That the (adult) woman suffers deficits as a consequence of being raped has been well documented. Such
deficits include post-traumatic stress syndrome, or rape trauma syndrome
(Burgess and Holmstrom 1979; Clum, Calhoun, and Kimerling 2000;
Feeny, Zoellner, and Foa 2000; Nishith, Mechanic, and Resick 2000).
Here, the *sequelae* of unwanted sexual behavior coerced on the prepubescent girl is the focus. Note that the psychopathologies aligned with incestuous relationships are closely paralleled with those psychopathologies
aligned with instances of childhood sexual abuse that were not incestuous.
Hence, the frame of reference for this section is "sexual abuse": both incestuous and nonincestuous. It should be noted that methodological problems are clearly evident in generating a database. Problems in definitions,
validity, control groups, and sampling are nontrivial. See Green (1993)
for a review of the difficulties in teasing out sexual abuse from other variables (e.g., socioeconomic status) as a contributing variable to a psychopathology, rather than as merely a correlative. Nevertheless, a number of
analyses from diverse perspectives do tend to converge and to point in
the direction that sexual abuse, itself, has a direct effect on elevating the
chances of the woman developing a psychopathology, even years after the

episodes had terminated. From the model presented in this chapter, it is the violation of the female's "choice" that is hypothesized to be the prepotent dynamic.

Candidates of psychopathologies that are generated or intensified by sexual abuse of prepubescents include (1) depression (see Sloman and Price 1987 and de Catanzaro 1987 for a theoretical discussion), (2) anxieties or negative self-image, (3) revictimization, (4) sexual dysfunctions/poor relationships with men, and (5) poor parenting. Note that 40 percent of the victims in Courtois's (1979) sample had never married.

The factors that seem to intensify the psychopathology include (a) the level of invasiveness (more invasive, more trauma); (b) level of force (more force, more trauma); (c) sex of perpetrator (men are aligned with more trauma than are women). The father-daughter or stepfather-daughter incestuous relationship involving penetration seems to be aligned with the most debilitating combination (Kluft 1990a; Russell 1986; Herman 1981; Courtois 1979, 1988; Groth 1978).

Although the qualities that determine attractiveness in the selection of spouses do vary across cultures, *sequelae* from childhood sexual abuse would seem to diminish attractiveness in the woman regardless of cultural expectations. For example, women who were victimized as children were found to have higher rates of "fear" or "anxiety-related difficulties" during sexual contact (Meiselman 1978) and higher levels of "pain" during sexual intercourse with lower levels of "orgasms" experienced (Maltz and Holman 1987). (Psycho)somatic difficulties in adult women that are linked with childhood sexual violations include headaches, stomach pain, asthma, bladder infections, and chronic pelvic pain (Cunningham, Pearce, and Pearce 1988; Morrison 1989; Springs and Friedrich 1992). Women who had been sexually abused as children have increased tendencies for substance abuse (Briere and Runtz 1988), as well as increased levels of promiscuous behavior, unintended pregnancies, and sexually transmitted diseases (Wyatt et al. 1993). These women are also more likely to be fearful of men (Briere and Runtz 1990). Accordingly, these traits would not seem to auger well for a successful marital history, and, indeed, these women are more likely to remain single, and—if married—more likely to divorce or to separate (Briere and Runtz 1990). There is a certain intuition that a depressed, anxious woman with poor personal habits and poor interpersonal and romantic skills would seem to have a lowered prospect for becoming a bride and for remaining a wife under virtually any circumstance.

Note that these psychosocial conditions or reactions are somewhat out of proportion to the physical event. If sexual intercourse, in and of itself, were capable to creating psychological dysfunction, then prostitution and honeymoons would be clearly the hotbeds of psychopathologies, and such appears not to be the case. However, essentially the same act of sexual intercourse that occurs in both "rape" and "(step)father-daughter incest" can leave severe emotional scars far in excess of what the physical act itself would warrant. The violation of a very old mating-strategy template—the woman's choice—on which hominid evolution depended for viability may help explain the genesis of the trauma. And, again, the presence of a biological and social father minimizes the chances of the girl being abused.

The more the community maximizes the presence of the biological and social father with the developing daughter, the greater the reproductive health of the community as the daughters mature to adulthood. Conversely, as the presence of biological and social fathers is minimized within a community, the more risk that occurs to the reproductive health of the community.

4　Choice of Mating Partner and Access to Resources

If a woman mates with a man, and both the man and the woman are virtually oblivious to the level of resources that the man might bring to the union, then such randomness ought to result in a number of mother-child dyads with low levels of available resources. The feminization of poverty (within the United States) is much more than a cliché. It is demographic fact. Families headed by an unwed mother are easily the families that have the least earned income available to them. Accordingly, as was mentioned earlier, either other family members dilute their own resources to aid and abet the otherwise isolated woman-child dyad, or they choose to ignore them and allow the deficits attributed to reduced resources to occur. The greater the prevalence of father absence within a community, the more that the community is weakened and threatened with being supplanted or displaced. This dynamic, found in contemporary societies, is expected to have a very long history.

Summary

Obviously the above statistics do not constitute a Newtonian proof. Nonetheless, the statistics are consonant with the notion that the early preclusion of a social and biological father from the mother-child dyad is aligned with dysfunctional events for the child, both in childhood and in the child's later adulthood. Current data in contemporary societies point out deficits that occur when the social father is not consistent and ongoing in the lives of (especially) very young children. The separation of the child from his or her father is aligned with (i) increased tendencies of violent crime, specifically murder, on the part of sons grown to adulthood; (ii) reduced levels of reproductive health (as indexed by higher levels of STDs) on the part of daughters grown to adulthood; (iii) an increased exposure to child abuse, including psychopathologies on the part of sexually abused girls grown to adulthood; and (iv) increased levels of poverty.

While each person who illustrates such dysfunctions will represent an individual tragedy, the commonweal or community is also weakened to the extent that the tragedies are pervasive and systematic. In any between-group competition, those communities with less internal mayhem, better reproductive health, physically and mentally healthier children (who would grow into adulthood), better coping skills, and better access to resources have an inherent advantage over those communities with excessive internal violence, problematic reproductive health, abused children, lessened coping skills, and lower access to resources.

An ongoing social and biological father increases not just his own children's well-being, but also the well-being of his group, his community, which, in turn, promises an enhanced opportunity for the community's longevity across generations. The absence of such fathers augurs just the reverse.

Note

1. The two rates—for illegitimacy (6.7) and for murder (38.7)—were also available for the Philippines. However, the Philippines' murder rate of 38.7 was over 8.5 standard deviations (s.d. = 4.09) over the sample mean of 3.62. Accordingly, the Philippines was enough of an outlier to be excluded from the sample. If rankings were used to generate the correlation coefficient (r_s) and if the Philippines is included in the sample, then the relationship between illegitimacy and murder rates

is significant ($r_s = .889$; $p < .01$; 2-tailed; $n = 45$). If the Philippines is not included in the sample, the correlation, based on ranks, is still significant ($r_s = .896$; $p < .01$; 2-tailed; $n = 44$).

References

Adams, P. L., J. R. Milner, and N. A. Schrepf (1984). *Fatherless Children.* New York: John Wiley and Sons.

Aiello, L. C. (1994). Variable but singular. *Nature* 368: 399–400.

Aiken, C. G. (1992). The causes of perinatal mortality in Bulawayo, Zimbabwe. *Central African Journal of Medicine* 38: 263–281.

Alderton, D. (1994). *Foxes, Wolves, and Wild Dogs of the World.* New York: Facts on File.

Alexander, P. C. (1993). The differential effects of abuse characteristics and attachment in the prediction of long-term effects of sexual abuse. *Journal of Interpersonal Violence* 93: 346.

Alexander, R. D., J. L. Hoogland, R. D. Howard, K. M. Noonan, and P. W. Sherman (1979). Sexual dimorphisms and breeding systems in pinnipeds, ungulates, primates, and humans. In N. A. Chagnon and W. Irons, eds., *Evolutionary Biology and Human Social Behavior,* pp. 402–435. North Scituate, Mass.: Duxbury Press.

Allen, S. et al. (1992). Human immunodeficiency virus infection in urban Rwanda. *JAMA* 266: 1657–1663.

Anderson, R. E. (1968). Where's dad? *Archives of General Psychiatry* 18: 641–649.

Aral, S. O., W. D. Mosher, and W. Cates, Jr. (1991). Self-reported pelvic inflammatory disease in the United States. *JAMA* 266: 2570–2573.

Archer, D. and R. Gartner (1984). Homicide in 110 nations. In L. I. Shelly, ed., *Readings in Comparative Criminology,* pp. 78–100. Carbondale, Ill.: Southern Illinois University Press.

Arsuaga, J. L. et al. (1997). Size variation in Middle Pleistocene humans. *Science* 277: 1086–1089.

Bagley, C. and R. Ramsay (1985). Disrupted childhood and vulnerability to sexual assault: Long-term sequels with implications for counseling. Paper presented at the Conference on Counseling the Sexual Abuse Survivor. Winnipeg, Canada.

Barkow, J. (1989). *Darwin, Sex, and Status.* Toronto: University of Toronto Press.

Bartol, C. R. (1995). *Criminal Behavior: A Psychosocial Approach,* 4th ed. Englewood Cliffs, N.J.: Prentice Hall.

Bereczkei, T. and A. Csanaky (1996). Evolutionary pathway of child development. *Human Nature* 7: 257–280.

Betzig, L. L. (1989). Causes of conjugal dissolution. *Current Anthropology* 30: 654–676.

Blankenhorn, D. (1995). *Fatherless America.* New York: Basic.

Blau, J. R. and P. M. Blau (1982). The cost of inequality. *American Sociological Review* 47: 114–129.

Boesch, C. (1994). Cooperative hunting in wild chimpanzees. *Animal Behaviour* 48: 653–667.

Boesch, C. and H. Boesch (1989). Hunting behavior of wild chimpanzees in the Tai National Park. *American Journal of Physical Anthropology* 78: 547–573.

Briere, J. (1984). The effects of childhood sexual abuse on later psychological functioning: Defining a post-sexual-abuse syndrome. Paper presented at the Third National Conference on Sexual Victimization of children. Washington, D.C.

Briere, J. and M. Runtz (1985). Symptomatology associated with prior sexual abuse in a non-clinical sample. Paper presented at the annual meeting of the American Psychological Association, Los Angeles, Calif.

Briere, J. and M. Runtz (1988). Post-sexual abuse trauma. In G. E. Wyatt, and G. J. Powell, eds., *Lasting Effects of Child Sexual Abuse*, pp. 85–100. Newbury Park, Calif.: Sage.

Briere, J. and M. Runtz (1990). Differential adult symptomatology associated with three types of child abuse histories. *Child Abuse and Neglect* 14: 357–364.

Browne, A. and D. Finkelhor (1986). Impact of child sexual abuse: A review of the research. *Psychological Bulletin* 99: 75–86.

Brunham, R. C., K. K. Holmes, and J. E. Embree (1990). Sexually transmitted diseases in pregnancy. In K. K. Holmes, P. Mårdh, P. F. Sparling, and P. J. Wiesner, eds., *Sexually Transmitted Diseases*, pp. 771–802. New York: McGraw-Hill.

Brunham, R. C. and F. A. Plummer (1990). A general model of sexually transmitted disease epidemiology and its implications for control. *Medical Clinics of North America* 74: 1339–1352.

Burgess, A. W. and L. L. Holmstrom (1979). Adaptive strategies and recovery from rape. *American Journal of Psychiatry* 136: 1278–1282.

Buss, D. (1989). Sex differences in human mate preferences. *Behavioral and Brain Sciences* 12: 1–49.

Buss, D. (1994). *The Evolution of Desire.* New York: Basic.

Buss, D. M. and D. P. Schmitt (1993). Sexual strategies theory. *Psychological Review* 100: 204–232.

Cashdan, E. (1993). Attracting mates. *Ethology and Sociobiology* 14: 1–24.

Chagnon, N. (1977). *Yanomamo.* New York: Holt, Rinehart and Winston.

Chance, R. A. (1966). *The Eskimo of North Alaska.* New York: Holt, Rinehart and Winston.

Chance, N. (1984). *China's Urban Villages.* New York: Holt, Rinehart and Winston.

Chilton, R. J. and G. E. Markle (1972). Family disruption, delinquent conduct, and the effects of subclassification. *American Sociological Review* 37: 93–99.

Clum, G. A., K. S. Calhoun, and R. Kimerling (2000). Associations among symptoms of depression and posttraumatic stress disorder and self-reported health in sexually assaulted women. *Journal of Nervous and Mental Diseases* 188: 671–678.

Coney, N. S. and W. C. Mackey (1998). Social fatherhood as a prophylactic against violent behavior: An empirical analysis of the kinder, gentler side of Freud's Oedipus Complex. *Mankind Quarterly* 38 (4): 381–412.

Coon, C. S. (1971). *The Hunting Peoples.* Harmondsworth: Penguin.

Courtois, C. (1979). The incest experience and its aftermath. *Victimology: An International Journal* 4: 337–347.

Courtois, C. (1988). *Healing the Incest Wound.* New York: Springer-Verlag.

Cunningham, J., T. Pearce, and P. Pearce (1988). Childhood sexual abuse and medical complaints in adult women. *Journal of Interpersonal Violence* 3: 131–144.

Daly, M. and M. I. Wilson (1982). Homicide and kinship. *American Anthropologist* 84: 372–378.

Daly, M. and M. I. Wilson (1985). Child abuse and other risks of not living with both parents. *Ethology and Sociobiology* 6: 197–210.

Daly, M. and M. I. Wilson (1987). Evolutionary psychology and family violence. In C. Crawford, M. Smith, and D. Krebs, eds., *Sociobiology and Psychology: Ideas, Issues, and Applications,* pp. 293–310. Hillsdale, N.J.: Lawrence Erlbaum.

Daly, M. and M. I. Wilson (1988). *Homicide.* New York: Aldine De Gruyter.

de Catanzaro, D. (1987). Evolutionary pressures and limitations to self-preservation. In C. Crawford, M. Smith, and D. Krebs, eds., *Sociobiology and Psychology: Ideas, Issues, and Applications,* pp. 311–333. Hillsdale, N.J.: Lawrence Erlbaum.

de Waal, F. B. M. (1997). The chimpanzee's service economy. *Evolution and Human Behavior* 18: 375–396.

de Waal, F. B. M. (1998). *Chimpanzee Politics,* revised ed. Baltimore: Johns Hopkins University Press.

de Waal, F. and F. Lanting (1997). *Bonobo.* Berkeley: University of California Press.

DeYoung, M. (1982). *The Sexual Victimization of Children.* Jefferson, N.C.: McFarland.

Division of STD/HIV Prevention (1990). *Division of STD/HIV Prevention Annual Report 1990.* U.S. Dept. of Health and Human Services, Public Health Service. Atlanta, Georgia: Centers for Disease Control.

Division of STD Prevention (1996). *Sexually Transmitted Disease Surveillance 1995.* Atlanta, Georgia: Centers for Disease Control.

Division of STD Prevention (1999). *Sexually Transmitted Disease Surveillance 1998.* Department of Health and Human Services. Atlanta, Georgia: Centers for Disease Control.

Dobie, J. F. (1949). *The Voice of the Coyote.* Boston: Little, Brown.

Draper, P. and H. Harpending (1982). Father absence and reproductive strategy: An evolutionary perspective. *Journal of Anthropological Research* 38: 255–272.

Dudley, J. R. (1991). Increasing our understanding of divorced fathers who have infrequent contact with their children. *Family Relations* 40: 279–285.

Economist (1984). Big hairy ape-men. *Economist* 331: 85–86.

Ekvall, R. B. (1968). *Fields on the Hoof.* New York: Holt, Rinehart, and Winston.

Feeny, N. C., L. A. Zoellner, and E. B. Foa (2000). Anger, dissociation, and post-traumatic stress disorder among female assault victims. *Journal of Traumatic Stress* 13: 89–100.

Finkelhor, D. (1979). *Sexually Victimized Children.* New York: Free Press.

Finkelhor, D. and J. Dziuba-Leatherman (1994). Victimization of children. *American Psychology* 49: 173–183.

Fisher, H. (1983). *The Sex Contract.* New York: Quill.

Fleagle, J. G. (1988). *Primate Adaptation and Evolution.* New York: Academic.

Foley, R. A. and P. C. Lee (1989). Finite social space, evolutionary pathways, and reconstructing hominid behavior. *Science* 243: 901–905.

Ford, C. S. (1961). *Readings in Cross-cultural Methodology.* New Haven, Conn.: HRAF Press.

Fromuth, M. E. (1983). *The Long-Term Psychological Impact of Childhood Sexual Abuse.* Unpublished doctoral dissertation, Auburn University, Auburn, AL.

Garnefski, N.and E. Arends (1998). Sexual abuse and adolescent maladjustment. *Journal of Adolescence* 21: 99–107.

Gil, D. G. (1970). *Violence against Children.* Cambridge, Mass.: Harvard University Press.

Goodall, J. (1986). *The Chimpanzees at Gombe.* Cambridge, Mass.: Belknap.

Goodwin, J., T. McCarthy, and P. Divasto (1981). Prior incest in mothers of abused children. *Child Abuse and Neglect* 5: 87–96.

Gordon, M. and S. J. Creighton (1988). Natal and non-natal fathers as sexual abusers in the United Kingdom. *Journal of Marriage and the Family* 50: 99–105.

Graves, B. M. and D. Duvall (1995). Effects of sexually transmitted diseases on heritable variation in sexually selected systems. *Animal Behavior* 50: 1129–1131.

Green, A. H. (1993). Child sexual abuse: Immediate and long-term effects and intervention. *Journal of the American Academy of Child and Adolescent Psychiatry* 32(5): 890–902.

Groth, N. A. (1978). Guidelines for assessment and management of the offender. In A. Burgess, N. Groth, S. Holmstrom, and S. Sgroi, eds., *Sexual Assault of Children and Adolescents,* pp. 25–42. Lexington, Mass.: Lexington Books.

Guggisberg, C. A. W. (1963). *Simba.* Philadelphia: Chilton.

Gutman, L. T. and C. M. Wilfert (1990). Gonococcal diseases in infants and children. In K. K. Holmes et al., eds., *Sexually Transmitted Diseases,* pp. 803–810. New York: McGraw-Hill.

Haldane, J. B. S. (1949). Disease and evolution. In *Symposium sui fattori ecologi e genetici della specilazione negli animali, Supplemento a la Ricerca Scientifica Anno 19th,* pp. 68–75.

Hall, R. (ed.) (1985). *Sexual Dimorphism in Homo Sapiens.* New York: Praeger.

Hamilton, W. and M. Zuk (1982). Heritable true fitness and bright birds. *Science* 218: 384–387.

Harrison, H. R. and E. R. Alexander (1990). Chlamydial infections in infants and children. In K. K. Holmes, P. Mårdh, P. F. Sparling, and P. J. Wiesner, eds., *Sexually Transmitted Diseases,* pp. 811–820. New York: McGraw-Hill.

Hart, C. W. M. and A. R. Pilling (1960). *The Tiwi of North Australia.* New York: Holt, Rinehart and Winston.

Hartley, S. F. (1975). *Illegitimacy.* Berkeley: University of California Press.

Hausfater, G. and S. B. Hrdy (1984). *Infanticide.* Chicago: Aldine.

Hegar, R. L., S. J. Zuravin, and J. G. Orme (1994). Factors predicting severity of physical child abuse injury: A review of the literature. *Journal of Interpersonal Violence* 9: (2): 170–183.

Heider, K. (1979). *Grand Valley Dani.* New York: Holt, Rinehart and Winston.

Hendrix, L. (1996). *Illegitimacy and Social Structures.* Westport, Conn.: Bergin and Garvey.

Herbertson, R. M., and N. D. Storey (1991). Ectopic pregnancy. *Crit. Care Clin.* 7: 899–915.

Herman, J. L. (1981). *Father-Daughter Incest.* Cambridge, Mass.: Harvard University Press.

Hewlett, B. S. (ed.) (1992). *Father-child Relations.* New York: Aldine de Gruyter.

Holmes, K. K., P. Mårdh, P. F. Sparling, and P. J. Wiesner (eds.) (1990). *Sexually Transmitted Diseases,* 2nd ed. New York: McGraw-Hill.

Holmes, M., H. Resnick, D. Kilpatrick, and C. Best (1996). Rape-related pregnancy: Estimates and descriptive characteristics from a national sample of women. *American Journal of Obstetrics and Gynecology* 175: 320–325.

Holmes, W. C. and G. B. Slap (1998). Sexual abuse of boys. *JAMA* 280: 1855–1862.

Holtz, F. (1930). [As reported in] Acute pelvic inflammatory disease (PID) by L. Weström and P. Mårdh. In K. K. Holmes, P. Mårdh, P. F. Sparling, and P. J. Wiesner, eds., *Sexually Transmitted Diseases,* 2nd ed., pp. 593–613. New York: McGraw-Hill.

HRAF (1949). *Human Relations Area Files.* New Haven, Conn.: HRAF.

Hunter, D. J., N. M. Baker, K. G. M. Japheth, P. M. Tukeik, and S. Mbugua (1994). Sexual behavior, sexually transmitted diseases, male circumcision and risk of HIV infection among women in Nairobi, Kenya. *AIDS* 8: 93–99.

INTERPOL (1990). *International Crime Statistics, 1989–1990.* Lyons, France: Interpol General Secretariat.

JAMA. (1995). Ectopic pregnancy—United States, 1990–1992. *JAMA* 273: 532.

Joesoef, M. R. et al. (1991). Recurrence of ectopic pregnancy. *American Journal of Obstetrics and Gynecology* 165: 46–50.

Kasim, M. S., M. S. Shafie, and I. Cheah (1994). Social factors in relation to physical abuse in Kuala Lumpur, Malaysia. *Child Abuse and Neglect* 18: 401–407.

King, G. E. (1980). Alternative uses of primates and carnivores in the reconstruction of early hominid behavior. *Ethology and Sociobiology* 1: 99–110.

Kleiman, D. G. (1977). Monogamy in mammals. *Quarterly Review of Biology* 52: 39–69.

Kluft, R. P. (1990a). *Incest-Related Syndromes of Adult Psychopathology.* Washington, D.C.: American Psychiatric Press.

Kluft, R. P. (1990b). Incest and subsequent revictimization: The case of therapist-patient sexual exploitation, with a description of the sitting duck syndrome. In R. P. Kluft, ed., *Incest-Related Syndromes of Adult Psychopathology,* pp. 25–51. Washington, D.C.: American Psychiatric Press.

Kruuk, H. (1972). *The Spotted Hyena.* Chicago: University of Chicago Press.

Kuhme, W. (1965). Communal food distribution of and division of labour in African hunting dogs. *Nature* 205: 443–444.

Lamb, M. E. (1987). *The Father's Role.* Hillsdale, N.J.: Erlbaum.

Langmade, C. J. (1983). The impact of pre- and post-pubertal onset of incest experiences in adult women as measured by sex anxiety, sex guilt, sexual satisfaction, and sexual behavior. *Dissertation Abstracts International* 44: 917B (University Microfilms, #3592).

Laumann, E. O., C. M. Masi, and E. W. Zuckerman (1997). Circumcision in the U.S. *JAMA* 277: 1051–1057.

Lawick, H. van and J. van Lawick-Goodall (1971). *Innocent Killers.* Boston: Houghton Mifflin.

Leach, E. R. (1955). Polyandry, inheritance, and the definition of marriage. *Man* 55: 182–186.

Lee, R. B. (1982). Eating Christmas in the Kalahari. In J. P. Spradley and D. W. McCurdy, eds., *Conformity and Conflict,* pp. 14–21. Boston: Little Brown.

Lee, R. B. (1984). *The Dobe !Kung.* New York: Holt, Rinehart and Winston.

Lenington, S. (1981). Child abuse. *Ethology and Sociobiology* 2: 17–29.

Levine, M., J. Freeman, and C. Compaan (1994). Maltreatment-related fatalities. *Law and Policy* 16: 454–465.

Levinson, D. and M. J. Malone (1980). *Toward Explaining Human Culture.* New Haven, Conn.: HRAF.

Lewin, R. (1987). The earliest "humans" were more like apes. *Science* 236: 1061–1063.

Lockwood, C. A., B. G. Richmond, W. L. Jungers, and W. H. Kimbel (1996). Randomization procedures and sexual dimorphism in Australopithecus. *Journal of Human Evolution* 31: 537–548.

Lovejoy, C. O. (1981). The origin of man. *Science* 211: 341–359.

Lurie, S. (1992). The history of the diagnosis and treatment of ectopic pregnancy. *European Journal of Obstetrics, Gynecology, and Reproductive Biology* 43: 1–7.

Mackey, W. C. (1976). The adult male-child bond. *Journal of Anthropological Research* 32: 58–73.

Mackey, W. C. (1985). *Fathering Behaviors.* New York: Plenum.

Mackey, W. C. (1986). A facet of the man-child bond. *Ethology and Sociobiology* 7: 117–135.

Mackey, W. C. (1996). *The American Father.* New York: Plenum.

Mackey, W. C. (2001). Support for the existence of an independent man-(to)-child affiliative bond: Fatherhood as a bio-cultural invention. *Psychology of Men and Masculinity* 2: 51–66.

Mackey, W. C. and R. S. Immerman (in press). Restriction of sexual activity as a partial function of disease avoidance: A cultural response to sexually transmitted diseases. *Cross-Cultural Research* 35.

Malinowski, B. (1927). *The Father in Primitive Society.* New York: Norton.

Maltz, W. and B. Holman (1987). *Incest and Sexuality: A Guide to Understanding and Healing.* Lexington, Mass.: Lexington Books.

Mann, C. R. (1996). *When Women Kill.* Albany, N.Y.: SUNY Press.

Martin, R. D., L. A. Willner, and A. Dettling (1994). The evolution of sexual size dimorphism in primates. In R. V. Short and E. Balaban, eds., *The Differences between the Sexes,* pp. 159–197. Cambridge: Cambridge University Press.

McDermott, J., R. Steketee, and J. Wirimia (1996). Perinatal mortality in rural Malawi. *Bulletin of the World Health Organization* 74: 165–171.

McDermott, J., R. Steketee, S. Larsen, and J. Wirima (1993). Syphilis associated perinatal and infant mortality in rural Malawi. *Bulletin of the World Health Organization* 71: 773–780.

McGinnis, P. R. (1979). Sexual behavior in free-living chimpanzees. In D. A. Hamburg and E. R. McCown, eds., *The Great Apes,* pp. 429–438. Menlo Park: Benjamin.

McGrew, W. C., L. F. Marchant, and T. Nishida (1996). *Great Ape Societies.* Cambridge: Cambridge University Press.

McHenry, H. M. (1991). Femoral lengths and stature in Plio-Pleistocene hominids. *American Journal of Physical Anthropology* 85: 149–158.

McMahan, P. (1976). The victorious coyote. *Natural History* 84: 42–51.

Mech, L. D. (1966). *The Wolves of Isle Royale Washington.* Washington, D.C.: U.S. Government Printing Press.

Mech, L. D. (1970). *The Wolf.* Garden City, N.Y.: Natural History.

Meiselman, K. C. (1978). *Incest: A Psychological Study of Causes and Effects with Treatment Recommendations.* San Francisco: Jossey-Bass.

Miller, J., D. Moeller, A. Kaufman, P. Divasto, P. Fitzsimmons, D. Pather, and J. Christy (1978). Recidivism among sexual assault victims. *American Journal of Psychiatry* 135: 1103–1104.

Mischel, W. (1961a). Father-absence and delay of gratification. *Journal of Abnormal and Social Psychology* 52: 116–124.

Mischel, W. (1961b). Preference for delayed reinforcement and social responsibility. *Journal of Abnormal and Social Psychology* 62: 1–7.

Moehlman, P. D. (1980). Jackals of the Serengeti. *National Geographic* 153: 840–843.

Monahan, T. P. (1972). Family status and the delinquent child. *Social Forces* 35: 250–258.

Moore, D. E. and W. Cates, Jr. (1990). Sexually transmitted diseases and infertility. In K. K. Holmes et al., eds., *Sexually Transmitted Diseases,* pp. 19–29. New York: McGraw-Hill.

Moore, D. E. and L. R. Spadoni (1984). Infertility in women. In K. K. Holmes, P. Mårdh, P. F. Sparling, and P. J. Wiesner, eds., *Sexually Transmitted Diseases,* pp. 763–770. New York: McGraw-Hill.

Morrison, J. (1989). Childhood sexual histories of women with somatization disorder. *American Journal of Psychiatry* 146: 239–241.

Mosher, L. R. (1969). Father absence and antisocial behavior in Negro and White males. *Acta Paedopsychiatrica* 36: 186–202.

Mosher, W. D. and S. O. Aral (1985). Factors related to infertility in the United States 1965–1976. *Sexually Transmitted Diseases* 12: 117–125.

Mowat, F. (1963). *Never Cry Wolf.* Boston: Little, Brown.

Murdock, G. P. (1957). World ethnographic sample. *American Anthropologist* 59: 664–687.

Murdock, G. P. (1967). Ethnographic atlas. *Ethnology* 6: 109–236.

Murie, A. (1944). *The Wolves of Mount McKinley.* Washington, D.C.: U.S. Government Printing Office.

Mynatt, C. R. and E. R. Allgeier (1990). Risk factors, self-attributions, and adjustment problems among victims of sexual coercion. *Journal of Applied Social Psychology* 20: 130–153.

Newell, J. et al. (1993). A population-based study of syphilis and sexually transmitted disease syndromes in north-western Tanzania. 2. Risk factors and health seeking behavior. *Genitourinary Medicine* 69: 421–426.

Nishida, T. and K. Hosaka (1996). Coalition strategies among adult male chimpanzees of the Mahale Mountains, Tanzania. In W. C. McGrew, L. F. Marchant, and T. Nishida, eds., *Great Ape Societies,* pp. 114–134. Cambridge: Cambridge University Press.

Nishith, P., M. B. Mechanic, and P. A. Resick (2000). Prior interpersonal trauma: The contribution to current PTSD symptoms in female rape victims. *Journal of Abnormal Psychology* 109: 20–25.

Norbeck, E. (1976). *Changing Japan,* 2nd ed. New York: Holt, Rinehart, and Winston.

Nordic Statistical Secretariat (ed.) (1960–1992). *Yearbook of Nordic Statistics,* vols. 1–31. Copenhagen: Nordic Council.

Parish, A. R. (1996). Female relationships in bonobo (Pan paniscus). *Human Nature* 7: 61–96.

Parke, R. D. and A. A. Brott (1999). *Throwaway Dads.* New York: Houghton Mifflin.

Peters, J. F. (1979). Divorce in Canada: A demographic profile. In G. Kurian, ed., *Cross-cultural Perspective of Mate-selection and Marriage,* pp. 376–390. Westport, Conn.: Greenwood Press.

Peters, S. D. (1988). Child sexual abuse and later psychological problems. In G. E. Wyatt and G. J. Powell, eds., *Lasting Effects of Child Sexual Abuse,* pp. 101–118. Beverly Hills, Calif.: Sage.

Peterson, H. B., E. I. Galaid, and W. Cates, Jr. (1990). Pelvic inflammatory disease. *Medical Clinics of North America* 74: 1603–1615.

Plavcan, J. M. and C. P. van Schaik (1997). Interpreting hominid behavior on the basis of sexual dimorphism. *Journal of Human Evolution* 32: 345–374.

Popenoe, D. (1996). *Life without Fathers.* New York: Free Press.

Pribor, E. F. and S. H. Dinwiddie (1992). Psychiatric correlates of incest in childhood. *American Journal of Psychiatry* 149: 52–56.

Rasa, O. A. E. (1986). Parental care in carnivores. In W. Sluckin and M. Herbert, eds., *Parental Behavior,* pp. 117–151. Oxford: Basil Blackwell.

Ridley, M. (1993). *The Red Queen.* New York: Macmillan.

Robins, L. N. and S. Y. Hill (1966). Assessing the contributions of family structure, class, and peer groups to juvenile delinquency. *Journal of Criminal Law, Criminology, and Police Science* 57: 325–334.

Rudnai, J. A. (1973). *The Social Life of the Lion.* Wallingford, Penn.: Washington Square.

Russell, D. E. H. (1986). *The Secret Trauma: Incest in the Lives of Girls and Women.* New York: Basic Books.

Russell, D. E. H., R. A. Schurman, and K. Trocki (1988). The long-term effects of sexual abuse. In G. E. Wyatt and G. J. Powell, eds., *Lasting Effects of Child Sexual Abuse,* pp. 119–134. Beverly Hills, Calif.: Sage.

Ryden, H. (1974). The "lone" coyote likes family life. *National Geographic* 146: 279–294.

Schaller, G. B. (1972). *The Serengeti Lion.* Chicago: University of Chicago Press.

Schaller, G. B. and G. R. Lowther (1969). The relevance of carnivore behavior in the study of early hominids. *Southwestern Journal of Anthropology* 25: 307–336.

Schetky, D. H., R. Angel, and C. Morrison (1979). Parents who fail: A study of 51 cases of termination of parental rights. *Journal of the American Academy of Child Psychiatry* 18: 366–383.

Schulz, K. F., W. Cates, Jr., and P. R. O'Mara (1987). Pregnancy loss, infant death, and suffering. *Genitourinary Medicine* 63: 320–325.

Schulz, K. F., F. K. Murphy, P. Patamasucon, and A. Z. Meheus (1990). Congenital syphilis. In K. K. Holmes, P. Mårdh, P. F. Sparling, and P. J. Wiesner, eds., *Sexually Transmitted Diseases,* 2nd ed., pp. 821–842. New York: McGraw-Hill.

Sedney, M. A. and B. Brooks (1984). Factors associated with a history of childhood sexual experience in a nonclinical female population. *Journal of the American Academy of Child Psychiatry* 23: 215–218.

Sheldon, B. C. (1993). Sexually transmitted disease in birds. *Philosophical Transactions of the Royal Society of London—Series B: Biological Sciences 339:* 491–497.

Siegel, L. J. (1992). *Criminology,* 4th ed. New York: West Pub.

Sloman, L. and J. S. Price (1987). Losing behavior (yielding subroutine) and human depression: Proximate and selective mechanisms. *Ethology and Sociobiology* 8 (3S): 99–110.

Smith, C. and M. D. Krohn (1995). Delinquency and family life among male adolescents: The role of ethnicity. *Journal of Youth and Adolescence* 24: 69–93.

Smith-Morris, M. (ed.) (1990). *The Economist Book of Vital World Statistics.* New York: Times Books.

Smuts, B. B. et al. (eds.) (1986). *Primate Societies.* Chicago: University of Chicago Press.

Smuts, B. B. and D. J. Gubernick (1992). Male-infant relationships in nonhuman primates. In B. S. Hewlett, ed., *Father-child Relations,* pp. 1–30. New York: Aldine de Gruyter.

Springs, F. E. and W. M. Friedrich (1992). Health risk behaviors and medical sequelae of childhood sexual abuse. *Mayo Clinic Proceedings* 67: 527–532.

Stagno, S. and Whitley, R. J. (1990). Herpesvirus infection in the neonate and children. In K. K. Holmes, P-A Mårdh, P. F. Sparling, and P. J. Wiesner, eds., *Sexually Transmitted Diseases,* 2nd ed., pp. 863–888. New York: McGraw-Hill.

Stanford, C. B. (1996). The hunting ecology of wild chimpanzees. *American Anthropologist* 98 (1): 96–113.

Stearman, A. M. (1989). *Yuqui.* New York: Holt, Rinehart and Winston.

Stein, J. A., J. M. Golding, J. M. Siegel, M. A. Burnam, and S. B. Sorenson (1988). Long-term psychological sequelae of child sexual abuse. In G. E. Wyatt and G. J. Powell, eds., *Lasting Effects of Child Sexual Abuse,* pp. 135–161. Beverly Hills, Calif.: Sage.

Stephens, W. (1963). *The Family in Cross-cultural Perspective.* New York: Holt, Rinehart, and Winston.

Stevenson, M. R. and K. N. Black (1988). Paternal absence and sex-role development. *Child Development* 59: 793–814.

Stone, M. H. (1990). Incest in the borderline patient. In R. P. Kluft, ed., *Incest-related Syndromes of Adult Psychopathology,* pp. 183–204. Washington, D.C.: American Psychiatric Press.

Symons, D. (1979). *The Evolution of Human Sexuality.* New York: Oxford University Press.

Taha, T. E. et al. (1995). The effect of human immunodeficiency virus infection on birthweight, and infant and child mortality in urban Malawi. *International Journal of Epidemiology* 24: 1022–1029.

Taub, D. M. (1984). *Primate Paternalism.* New York: Nostrand Reinhold.

Teleki, G. (1973). The omnivorous chimpanzee. *Scientific American* 228: 33–42.

Thompson, P. R. (1978). The evolution of territoriality and society of top carnivores. *Social Science Information* 17: 949–992.

Thornhill, R. and C. Palmer (2000). *A Natural History of Rape: Biological Bases of Sexual Coercion.* Cambridge, Mass.: MIT Press.

Tonkinson, R. (1978). *The Mardudjdara Aborigines.* New York: Holt, Rinehart, and Winston.

Turnbull, C. (1972). *The Mountain People.* New York: Simon and Schuster.

Tyler, A. H. (1986). The abusing father. In M. E. Lamb, ed., *The Father's Role,* pp. 256–275. New York: Wiley.

United Nations (1985–1992). *Demographic Yearbook.* New York: United Nations.

U.S. Bureau of the Census (1970–1996). *Statistical Abstract of the United States: 1970–1996,* 98th–124th ed. Washington, D.C.: Government Printing Office.

U.S. Department of Justice (1995). *Uniform Crime Reports.* Washington, D.C.: U.S. Government printing office.

Van den Berghe, P. L. (1979). *Human Family Systems.* New York: Elsevier.

Vander May, B. J. (1988). The sexual victimization of male children. *Child Abuse and Neglect* 12: 61–72.

Villa, L. L. (1997). Human papillomaviruses and cervical cancer. *Advances in Cancer Research* 71: 321–341.

Watkins, B. and A. Bentovim (1992). The sexual abuse of male children and adolescents. *Journal of Child Psychology and Psychiatry* 13: 197–248.

Waugh, M. A. (1990). History of clinical developments in sexually transmitted diseases. In K. K. Holmes, P. Mårdh, P. J. Sparling, P. J. Wiesner, eds., *Sexually Transmitted Diseases,* pp. 3–18. New York: McGraw-Hill.

Weström, L. (1987). Pelvic inflammatory disease: Bacteriology and sequelae. *Contraception* 36: 111.

Weström, L. (1991). Pelvic inflammatory disease. *JAMA* 266: 2612.

Weström, L. and P. Mårdh (1990). Acute pelvic inflammatory disease (PID). In K. K. Holmes et al., eds., *Sexually Transmitted Diseases,* pp. 593–613. New York: McGraw-Hill.

Weström, L., J. Riduan, G. Reynolds, H. Alula, and S. E. Thompson (1992). Pelvic inflammatory disease and fertility. *Sexually Transmitted Diseases* 19: 185–192.

Widom, C. S. (1992). *The Cycle of Violence.* Washington, D.C.: Government Printing Office.

Wilson, J. Q. and R. Herrnstein (1985). *Crime and Human Nature.* New York: Simon and Schuster.

Winfield, I., L. K. George, M. Swartz, and D. G. Blazer (1990). Sexual assault and psychiatric disorders among a community sample of women. *American Journal of Psychiatry* 147: 334–341.

Wolner-Haussen, P., N. B. Kiviat, and K. K. Holmes (1990). Atypical pelvic inflammatory disease: subacute, chronic, or subclinical upper genital tract infection in women. In K. K. Holmes, P. Mårdh, P. F. Sparling, and P. J. Wiesner, eds., *Sexually Transmitted Diseases,* pp. 615–620. New York: McGraw-Hill.

Wyatt, G. E., M. Newcomb, M. Reederle, and C. Notgrass (1993). *Sexual Abuse and Consensual Sex: Women's Developmental Patterns and Outcomes.* Newbury Park, Calif.: Sage.

Young, S. P. and H. T. Jackson (1951). *The Clever Coyote.* Washington, D.C.: Wildlife Management Institute.

Zeitlin, S. B., R. J. McNally, and K. L. Cassiday (1993). Alexithymia in victims of sexual assault: An effect of repeated traumatization? *American Journal of Psychiatry* 150: 661–663.

zur Hausen, H. (1996). Papillomavirus infection: A major cause of human cancers. *Biochimica et Biophysica Acta* 1288: F55–F78.

14

Rape-Free versus Rape-Prone: How Culture Makes a Difference

Peggy Reeves Sanday

Imagine a society in which rape is rare and women are respected as active participants in the economic system and play a role with men in shaping the processes of the public domain. Unlike U.S. society there is no consumer culture commodifying sexual allure nor is there a masculine peer culture shaping gender and sexual norms. In this society, older men and women regulate and enforce these norms. The value placed on mutual respect in personal relations extends to sexual relations. Sexually aggressive or abusive men are shunned in what can amount to social death. This is not a small, remote society but the fourth largest ethnic group in one of the most populous nations in the world. I refer to the Minangkabau of West Sumatra, Indonesia where I conducted anthropological field work.

Before embarking on field work in West Sumatra, I carried out a cross-cultural study of the sociocultural context of rape in 95 band and tribal societies. The goal of this study was to account for variation in the reported incidence of rape in these societies in light of related social factors. I found that there was a significant correlation between rape and the overall position of women. For example, in the more rape-free societies gender relations were marked by respect for women as citizens, significant female power and authority, and the near absence of interpersonal aggression in social relations. In the more rape-prone societies, social relations were marked by interpersonal violence in conjunction with an ideology of male dominance enforced through the control and subordination of women. Faced with such data the only reasonable conclusion by empirically minded social scientists must be that culture plays a role in the expression of male sexual aggression. The nature of that role is the subject of this chapter.

In the following, after contrasting my approach as a cultural anthropologist with that of Thornhill and Palmer, I summarize the results of my early cross-cultural study, which was first published in 1981. I then move to a discussion of follow-up research in the United States and West Sumatra in the 1980s and '90s on the sociocultural contexts promoting or inhibiting violence against women. I suggest that the near-absence of rape in West Sumatra in contrast to the more rape-prone United States can be explained by the hegemony of human social values promoted by the adult peer culture in West Sumatra in which males and females play equivalent roles. Minangkabau values and worldview stand in sharp contrast to the asymmetrical sexual values of the male peer culture in the United States. I suggest that the difference is due to the central role that an ideology of male sexual dominance plays in U.S. sexual culture as opposed to the central role played by values attached to the mother-child bond, social equity, and politesse in the Minangkabau system of values. These differences can be attributed to cultural rather than natural selection.

Cultural versus Natural Selection

My approach of examining the sociocultural context in which violence against women is accepted or condemned together with my argument that cues for sexual behavior circulate as part of a pattern of cultural selection departs significantly from Thornhill and Palmer's "natural history" approach to the "biological bases of sexual coercion." Thornhill and Palmer present two basic arguments for why men rape, both of which refer to the Darwinian doctrine of natural selection. The first argument is that rape is an evolved adaptation "that was directly favored by selection because it increased male reproductive success by way of increasing mate number." The second argument is that rape "may be only a by-product of other psychological adaptations, especially those that function to produce the sexual desires of males for multiple partners without commitment" (2000, pp. 59–60).

In both of these arguments, rape is assumed to be a characteristic in human males that is directly (the first argument) or indirectly (the second) related to genetic traits that evolve by natural selection. Natural selection in the Darwinian sense is the doctrine that in the struggle for existence evolutionary progress is achieved by the inheritance of advantageous characteristics that prosper at the expense of less advantageous ones. According to Darwin, natural selection operates somewhat like an all-seeing force in nature that scrutinizes, "daily and hourly," "throughout the world, every variation, even the slightest; rejecting that which is bad, preserving and adding up all that is good; silently and insensibly working. . . ." (Quoted by Thornhill and Palmer 2000, p. 5.) Thornhill and Palmer quote this passage from Darwin in order to comment on what Darwin might have meant by the statement that natural selection scrutinizes variation to reject the "bad" and preserve the "good." Citing the biologist George Williams, Thornhill and Palmer claim that the "good" refers to traits "that promote an individual's [viz. the male's] reproductive interests" irrespective of what is "morally right or wrong" (ibid., pp. 5–6).

Reducing the causes of rape behavior to the individual male psyche or to genes bypasses the facts of social and cultural life. Human beings do not live in a world devoid of other human beings. Nor do they exist in a cultural and social vacuum. Cultural anthropologists argue that without culture patterns (i.e., "organized systems of significant symbols") human behavior would be shapeless and without direction, "a mere chaos of pointless acts and exploding emotions" (Geertz 1973, p. 46). The relevance of culture patterns applies as much to human needs with a strong physiological component, such as sexual desire, hunger, thirst, and the experience of pain, as it does to the more metaphysical aspects of the human spirit.

Just as the food quest is managed by humans within a sociocultural context, so is sexual behavior. The gratification of sexual desire is shaped by cultural definitions of the erotic and social norms expressed between partners who bond according to their understanding of the rights and duties attendant to what they give and receive sexually. This means that sexual behavior is channeled by social norms defining masculinity and femininity, ideas about appropriate sexual relations, cues for sexual arousal, and a variety of social messages about the consequences of sexual expression including punishments for breaking sexual taboos. Even the gang rapes described below are filtered by a sociocultural apparatus.

Rape Cross-Culturally

My interest in the symbolic and social context of human sexual behavior began in the 1970s with a study of the factors related to the sociocultural context of rape cross-culturally. My primary motivation for conducting this study was not in establishing the presence or absence of rape, as Thornhill and Palmer (2000, p. 141) imply in their criticism of my work, but in examining the sociocultural context of variation in the incidence of rape. In the opening paragraphs of the first article I published on this subject, my goals and rationale were clearly stated.

> The research described in the present paper departs from the familiar assumption that male nature is programmed for rape, and begins with another familiar, albeit less popular, assumption that human sexual behavior, though based in a biological need, "is rather a sociological and cultural force than a mere bodily relation of two individuals" (Malinowski, 1929, p. xxiii). With this assumption in mind, what follows is an examination of the socio-cultural context of sexual assault and an attempt to interpret its meaning. . . . Two general hypotheses guided the research: first, the incidence of rape varies cross-culturally; second, a high incidence of rape is embedded in a distinguishably different cultural configuration than a low incidence of rape. (Sanday 1981, p. 6)[1]

In this study, I used the standard cross-cultural sample of band and tribal societies prepared by Murdock and White (1969).[2] The same sample was used by Broude and Greene (1976) for a study of rape cross-culturally. Although we disagree on coding, our findings are similar in demonstrating that the incidence of rape is not constant cross-culturally, but varies from rare to commonplace when a number of societies are considered. Broude and Greene (1976) found that rape was reported as absent or rare in 59 percent of the 34 societies they included in their sample. I found that rape was reported as absent or rare in 47 percent of the 95 societies I included in my sample (see Sanday 1981, pp. 7–9 for a comparison of the two samples). In addition to the rape-free and rape-prone categories, I developed a third category for cases where rape is reported as present but frequency is not mentioned. These categories, along with the number of societies classified in each, are presented in table 14.1.[3]

The pattern of correlations between the rape variable illustrated in table 14.1 and the variables listed in table 14.2 reveal that rape is not randomly distributed cross-culturally but is associated with interpersonal violence, male social dominance, and the subordination of women. The importance of male violence in rape-prone societies is seen in the fact that raiding other groups for wives is significantly associated with the incidence of rape, as is the intensity of interpersonal violence and the presence of an ideology that encourages men to be tough and aggressive (see table 14.2). When warfare is reported as frequent or endemic (as opposed to absent or occasional),

Table 14.1
Cross-Cultural Incidence of Rape. From Sanday (1981:9)

	N	%
1. Rape Free. Rape is reported as rare or absent.	45	47%
2. Rape is reported as present, no report of frequency, or suggestion that rape is not atypical.	33	35%
3. Rape Prone. Rape is an accepted practice used to punish women, as part of a ceremony, or is clearly an act of moderate to high frequency carried out against own women or women of other societies.	17	18%
Total	95	100%

Table 14.2
Most Significant Correlates of Rape reported in Sanday (1981:23.)*

1. Raiding other groups for wives $<r = .29; \ p = .004>$
2. Degree of Interpersonal violence $<r = .47; \ p = .000>$
3. Ideology of male toughness $<r = .42; \ p = .000>$
4. No female participation in political decision making $<r = .33; \ p = .001>$
5. No respect for women as citizens $<r = .28; \ p = .005>$

* This list represents the most significant results. For a list of additional variables which were correlated with rape at lower probability levels see discussion in text.

rape is also more likely to be present (see Sanday 1981, p. 23 for the list of variables that were associated at lower probability rates with the rape variable).[4]

The other significant relationships reported in table 14.2 prompted me to suggest that in rape-prone environments, violence against women is an expression of a social ideology of male dominance (Sanday 1981, pp. 22–24). Female power and authority are lower in rape-prone societies. Women do not participate in public decision making in these societies, and males express contempt for women as decision makers. In these cases, rape is the playing out of a sociocultural script in which the expression of personhood for males is directed by, among other things, interpersonal violence and an ideology of male toughness. If we see the sexual act as the ultimate emotional expression of the self, then it comes as no surprise that male sexuality is phrased in physically aggressive terms when other expressions of the self are phrased in these terms.[5] Violence against women is the means men use to express the power they are taught belongs to them either by natural or by social right. For example, Murphy and Murphy (1974) describe how Mundurucu men of the tropical forest of South America are socialized for male dominance. According to them, in this society "men . . . use the penis to dominate their women" (1974, p. 197). Some may wish to infer from the above analysis that rape is a by-product of a culture of violence and an ideology of male social dominance, but I believe that the focus is better placed on examining the cultural and social mechanisms by which violence against women becomes part of a sociocultural script for masculine identity. I can't address this issue fully in this chapter, but some observations are in order (see Sanday 1996 for an overview of cultural selection for rape in the American sexual culture).

Cultural Selection at Work: Denigrating the "Feminist Social Science" Explanation for Rape

Illustrative of a troubling bias in the work of Thornhill and Palmer is their tendency to denigrate all research that finds a functional relationship between male social dominance and rape. Thornhill and Palmer label such research "the feminist social-science explanation of rape" (2000, p. 141). Their argument against the functional theory stems from their disagreement with assertions by "feminist social scientists" who claim that "sexual coercion is motivated by power, not lust" (Thornhill and Palmer 2000, p. 124). Since the linchpin of Thornhill and Palmer's evolutionary argument for rape, in both of its versions, is in the claim that rape behavior promotes an individual's reproductive interests—which means that the behavior must involve intercourse and insemination—it is not surprising that they disagree so vehemently with the suggestion that rape is about power and not lust.

I suggest that by seeing rape mainly as a product of human evolution, the evolutionary argument provides scientific support for the well-known popular belief in U.S. society that "boys will be boys" and "girls ask for it." Although Thornhill and Palmer neither condone rape nor see it as good socially or psychologically, their arguments are nonetheless part of the same cultural selection process that legitimizes a discourse that looks the other way when young males rape on the grounds that they are, after all, only human.

The Minangkabau have quite a different approach. They argue that whatever the natural basis of rape might be, culture exists to override these tendencies. This point will become more apparent in light of the Minangkabau assertion, discussed below, that social norms and cultural values are responsible for the near absence of rape in their society. While our norms and values treat rape as natural, the Minangkabau construct a social system that demonstrates zero tolerance for rape.

Thornhill and Palmer say that "[i]t is difficult to overestimate the power the 'not sex' theory of rape continues to have" (2000, p. 125). They quote a series of scholars, including me, who, they say, argue that "rape is caused by supposedly patriarchal cultures where males are taught to dominate, and hence rape, women" (ibid.). They chose the following quote from my book *Fraternity Gang Rape* (1990) as an example of the "not sex" theory of rape.

Sanday (1990, p. 10) states that during rape "the sexual act is not concerned with sexual gratification but with the deployment of the penis as a concrete symbol of masculine social power." (ibid.)

I never use the word "patriarchy" or "patriarchal culture," nor does my work rule out sexual gratification in the deployment of the penis as a symbol of masculine power. With respect to the issue of sexual gratification, my research suggests that this is a secondary motivation, present in some but not all males. For example, with respect to the incident of fraternity gang rape to which the above quote pertains, one of the young men involved confessed that "he could not get it up" when he faced the unconscious body of the young woman who was "trained" (gang raped) by a number of brothers in his fraternity.

From accounts of the incident and its aftermath by brothers and female party goers who were present that night, whatever sexual gratification any of the young men might have experienced was secondary to the celebration of fraternity bonding and group pride in the conquest of this young woman's body. In their house minutes for that week, the brothers referred to the incident as the "XYZ [a pseudonym for the fraternity] Express." They pinned these minutes on their bulletin board and boasted all over campus about the incident, calling it "interviewing for the little sister's program." Their boasting stopped only when they realized that they were not getting good press in the campus newspaper.

Another case of campus gang rape of which I also had personal knowledge confirms the conclusion that male social dominance is intimately involved in such incidents (see Sanday 1996 for a lengthy description of this case). On the witness stand in a Queens courtroom, the complainant and several eyewitnesses to this event painted a vivid picture of what happened in an off-campus house rented by members of the lacrosse team. It started when Angela (a pseudonym) passed out after being given vodka to drink (which may have included a drug).

When she woke, it seemed as if there were five or more boys in the room. There was a guy sitting on the chair in front of the sofa and another sitting on the bed [nearby]. These two were just watching. . . . They hit their penises against her face. Walter put his penis in her mouth. When she gagged on Walter's penis, she heard him say, "Do it, choke on it." She heard someone say, "She is dead. She is not doing anything for me. I have to get a hard-on."

They had propped her up to a sitting position, but her head wouldn't stay up. Walter held her cheeks to force her mouth open so his friends could put their penises in her mouth. She tried to get up several times. Once her nails scratched Walter. He slapped her hands. She passed out again. When she came to, she screamed. Walter ordered her to stop, telling her it was a residential neighborhood and she might alarm the neighbors. When Walter put his hand on her neck, she felt that she had to be careful not to upset him. She didn't know what he might do to her. Dazed, she fell back on the couch.

[Later when she woke again] there were people wearing masks. One of the masked figures really scared her. The eyes behind the mask were bulging out and she couldn't understand how these could be human eyes. There was another figure wearing a Lone Ranger mask, which covered half his face. (Sanday 1996: 14–15)

It was clear from the testimony at the trial and from my interviews with Angela that the boys who sexually abused her ranged from those who found sexual pleasure in the act of abuse to those who didn't take advantage of her when they discovered that she was half conscious. Angela remembered that one of the guys present left the room when another commented "Her pupils are dilated. She doesn't know what's going on." It seems that some of the guys present thought Angela had consented to group sex when they were invited to the house where the incident took place. Some left when they realized she was unconscious; others stayed and watched. Others orally sodomized her in what amounted to a masturbation party in front of their buddies.

The homoerotic nature of this and the other cases of gang rape that have been described to me suggests that, whatever else might be at stake, establishing a heterosexual identity in a heterosexist society is a key factor. All the evidence suggests that gang rape in the U.S. adolescent male peer culture is primarily about power, homoerotic attraction, and heterosexual identity. While lust is involved, the lust is related only indirectly to reproductive interests. Even if we can assume that having established one's position in the male heterosexual culture makes a young male more desirable as a potential mate, thus promoting his reproductive interests according to Thornhill and Palmer's scheme, cultural selection is still the mechanism by which such males are defined as desirable. As I will show below, a male in West Sumatra who participates in a gang rape would be banished from village society, perhaps killed. In the Minangkabau marriage system, young men who display the kind of "macho" personality that seems to be the goal of U.S. fraternity bonding rituals would find themselves at the absolute bottom of the wish list of prospective mates.

To pursue the cultural selection argument a little further, in *Fraternity Gang Rape,* I describe what one of the brothers involved in the case had to say about sexual identity, dominance, and control.

Tom (pseudonym) told me that "sexual identity problems in both men and women lead them to casual sex." According to Tom,

male social dominance and sexual identity are frequently based on sexual performance. . . . The male ego is built on sexual conquests because through sex men gain respect from other men. (Sanday 1990, p. 72)

Tom also admitted that women are the objects of force in sex. Sex is the way for men to dominate women, he said. He added that

[a] gang bang is an assertion of dominance because the woman is objectified and dominated socially in a gang bang. Historically women are more subject to sexual oppression and this is why psychologically it is more important for women to have a commitment in sexual activity. (1990, pp. 72–73)

The pawns in such sexual socialization rituals include vulnerable young men as well as young women. One of the unknown stories of rape is the role it plays as a reaction to male-on-younger-male abuse. A masculine peer culture in which status depends on dominance means that young men are divided into three basic categories: the dominators, the dominated, and the followers. The magnitude of the stakes in the game of male dominance played by adolescent males is suggested by the school shooting incidents in which those who are bullied turn the tables in the ultimate expression of dominance by murdering their assailants. The story is different for boys who are abused in hazing only in the sense that they are given the license to turn on vulnerable young women as a reward for enduring abuse in the initiation rite that glues them to the male social body.

This conclusion is prompted by the fact that models for masculinity and male sexual aggression in some fraternity rituals and those of athletic teams (such as mounting a "train" or donning masks when engaging in group sex, described above) are almost always accompanied by hazing abuses. The pledge who is abused as he enters the fraternity or the new athlete who is abused by his teammates looks forward to the rewards of being a valued member and anxiously follows the pack in whatever they do. Numerous hazing rituals described to me and reported by others are devised to coerce pledges into obedience and cement them to the brotherhood (see Sanday 1990; and Nuwer 1990, 1999). Another way of inducing male bonding in the fraternal or athletic setting is the use of pornography to bond under a common view of female sexuality and male prowess in "getting sex." Such behaviors, although not universal in all-male circles, circulate widely and constitute an American sexual ethos promoting coercive, adversarial male sexuality—a scenario that can easily lead to rape.

Getting back to the power and not lust argument, it is clear that not all young males respond similarly to the sight of an exposed, vulnerable woman. What the so-called feminist social science tries to do, at least as I practice it, is to understand the difference between those who find sexual pleasure in acts of sexual male bonding and those who are disgusted and leave or who stay and try to perform for their buddies. The only conclusion one can come to is that it is culture that makes the difference here. Men who want to be accepted by their buddies and thereby gain entrance into the culture of male dominance behave in ways that they don't necessarily feel drawn to. In the absence of peer support for sexual abuse and in the presence of more oversight by adults, who don't condone abusive behavior by conveying the message that "boys will be boys," I am sure that many young men would not engage in it.

The United States as a Rape-Prone Society

Socialization for male sexual dominance and control is suggested by numerous studies on U.S. college campuses. In a study of a large southeastern university, Boeringer (1996, pp. 137–39) reports that one-quarter of the males reported using drugs or alcohol to obtain sex, and 9 percent reported using or threatening force to obtain sex. Boeringer also found that

56 percent of the men he interviewed used verbally coercive tactics to obtain sex, such as threatening to end the relationship, falsely professing love, or lying to render their partners more sexually receptive. He suggests that such tactics present an "adversarial view of sexuality in which one should use deceit and guile to win favors from a woman" (p. 140).

Sexually aggressive men in U.S. studies, from convicted rapists to college males answering questions on social surveys, share a remarkably similar set of attitudes. Most believe that sexual aggression is normal, that sexual relationships involve game playing, that men should dominate women, that women are responsible for rape, and that relations between the sexes are adversarial and manipulative on both sides (Koss and Leonard 1984, pp. 221, 223). Reanalyzing Koss's data to pinpoint attitudes held by the self-admitted sexually aggressive men of her study (i.e., those who admitted to forcing a woman to have sex in Koss's 1985 questionnaire discussed below), I found that these men often expressed adversarial-like beliefs (Sanday 1996, pp. 196–197). For example, many stated that they believe that a woman's "no" means "yes" and that women say no to intercourse because they don't want to seem loose but really hope the man will force her. Compared with men who do not admit to forcing a woman, more of these men also think that being roughed up by a man is sexually stimulating to women and that women have an unconscious wish to be raped. Few of the women in Koss's sample (described next) hold such attitudes.

Such attitudes are consistent with the prevalence of rape in U.S. society. The first major study was conducted by Mary Koss in conjunction with *Ms.* magazine in 1985. This study surveyed 6,159 students on 32 college campuses. Koss found that 1 in 4 of the women surveyed indicated that they had experienced rape or attempted rape due to force, threat, or the use of drugs or alcohol. Since this study, many others confirm the same basic statistic. Studying populations in communities across the nation, researchers report rape prevalence figures of 24 percent in Minnesota; 24 percent in San Francisco; 28 percent among college-educated women in Los Angeles; 25 percent for African-American and 20 percent for white women in Los Angeles County; 23 percent in Charleston, South Carolina; and 14 percent in a national sample (see Sanday 1996, p. 254 for citations to these studies).

The repetition of similar results in so many samples speaks to the issue of validity. In survey research, "validity" refers to conformity of the survey questions with the event being measured. Usually, this is tested by comparing the replies from independent samples. Based on this criterion, Koss's data are valid when compared with similar data collected in independent studies. Koss's results are supported by another national study of sex in America, conducted in 1992 and published in 1994. With a staff of 220 interviewers, this study utilized a national sample of 3,432 individuals. They found that "22 percent of women were forced to do something sexually at some time." The authors say that while the forced sexual behavior reported by women in this study may not have involved rape, "it is of considerable interest to find that as many as one in five women do consider themselves to have been forced against their will to do something sexually" (Sanday 1996, pp. 254–255, citing the study published by Michael, Gagnon, and Laumann 1994, p. 335).

"Boys Will Be Boys"/"She Asked for It": Cultural Selection and the Discourse of Sexology

The discourse of male sexual and social dominance described so far circulates widely in the United States, appearing in the media, the legal profession, and receiving the stamp of scientific truth in disquisitions on the nature of human sexuality such as found not just in Thornhill and Palmer's evolutionary explanation for rape but in the scientific study of sex called sexology as well. The Darwinian doctrine of sexual selection was central to the theories produced by the first sexologists, Krafft-Ebing and Havelock Ellis in the late nineteenth century. In his magnum opus, *Psychopathia Sexualis,* first published in German in 1886, Krafft-Ebing argued that "gratification of the sexual instinct [is] the primary motive in man as well as in beast" (quoted by Sanday 1996, p. 125). Following Krafft-Ebing, Havelock Ellis conceived of human sexual behavior as a game of combat in the third volume of his *Studies in the Psychology of Sex,* published in Philadelphia between 1897 and 1910. Ellis claimed that the female conceals her sexual passion by playing the role of hunted animal and adopting a demeanor of modesty in order that the male may be more ardent and forceful. Ellis claims that as the hunt becomes more sexually charged, "an element of real violence, of undisguised cruelty" is introduced. Accepting the Darwinian theory of natural selection with its emphasis on competition and brute strength, Ellis claimed that a woman who resisted "the assaults of the male" aided natural selection "by putting to the test man's most important quality, force" (quoted by Sanday 1996, pp. 127–128).

Ellis lived at a time when women were beginning to assert a female sexual discourse in a manner that broke with the cult of "true womanhood," so popular among middle-class women earlier in the nineteenth century, which required women to be sexually demur and chaste. In their search for greater sexual freedom, women looked to the theories of Ellis, and, later, those of Freud for scientific confirmation of female sexual desire. Unfortunately for women, these early scientists of sex put women in a sexual double bind by granting women sexual desire at the same time they claimed that this desire should be passive and wholly responsive to male desire. Freud gave the male sexual dominance hypothesis a new twist by defining the sex instinct as a basic biological drive, which in its active form was masculine and in its passive form was feminine. He claimed that for a woman to reach femininity, she had to transform active into passive desire, by which he meant transforming sensations from the clitoris to the vagina.

Another side of this argument was that the new woman would be one who said no when she meant yes, not because of the desire to display Victorian female purity but in obedience to her alleged (by Freud and Ellis) desire to be dominated. Domination not only defined the masculine in men, being dominated defined the feminine in women. Both Ellis and Freud saw these attributes as basic to the biology of male and female. Freud went further to suggest, however, that under a demur demeanor the raging fires of desire still lurked in the female breast, giving her an overactive sexual imagination that sometimes led to false accusations of rape. Thus, whereas in the nineteenth century the woman who cried rape was "fallen," in the early twentieth she was a hysteric.

Such attitudes made it virtually impossible for a woman to make an accusation of rape stick in the courtroom, unless it was accompanied by evidence that she had resisted to the "utmost" to preserve her "honor." Freud's ideas regarding female sexuality influenced rape law through the most important and widely cited legal treatise on rape of the twentieth century penned by the noted jurist John Henry Wigmore. Using Freudian terminology, Wigmore cautioned the legal establishment to beware of the female hysteric and the pathological liar and advised that all rape complainants be examined by a psychiatrist for nefarious complexes of a Freudian nature (Sanday 1996, pp. 121–139).

Throughout the twentieth century, the sexual discourse reflected in the theories of the sexologists functioned in popular culture to maintain a community of males in opposition to and superior over females. Although the details of the discourse changed granting sexual freedom to women, its ability to maintain male bonding and male dominance remained unaffected. To preserve her reputation and to show that she is not an aggressive hussy, a woman had to say no so that a man could take pride in his seduction and assure himself that she is not "loose."

The sexual revolution of the 1960s began with the concept of sexual freedom and ended with women seeking parity in sexual relationships. Although the women of the '60s were having sex in greater numbers than before, they were not seen as equal sexual partners with the enforceable right to say no. Although the so-called sexual revolution freed women to have sex, it was, once again, on male terms. The late twentieth-century feminist movement was sparked by the soaring rape rates of the 1960s. Getting together in consciousness raising sessions, young women began to discover the degree to which sexual expression for them was marked by either "giving in" or being forced. Few of them could say that they were in egalitarian sexual relationships characterized by mutual consent.

The discovery of the ubiquity of acquaintance rape led to a significant lobbying effort in the early to mid-1970s, which resulted in rape law reform in most of the states. "Earnest," "sufficient," or "utmost" resistance was abolished as being necessary to indicate nonconsent in most states. The legal reform was an attempt to equalize rape trials so that fear of false accusers and examining a woman's reputation no longer played a decisive role.

The reform changed outmoded laws and practices that had remained on the books since the seventeenth and eighteenth centuries. For example, in many states the death penalty for rape persisted up to the 1960s, making convictions highly unlikely. Another hold-over from the seventeenth century, abolished in the 1970s, was the practice of reading to the jury the cautions of the seventeenth-century English judge Sir Matthew Hale. By giving semilegal status to the fear of the false accuser, Hale's instructions to the jury read in many American courts created a prodefense bias (see Sanday 1996, p. 58 for Hale's cautions).

The anti-rape movement that got started in the 1970s was the first real sexual revolution in the twentieth century, or any century for that matter, because it was based firmly on the notion of sexual parity. The basic proposition was that a no means no and that sexual consent was to be established through speech. Although articulated in the 1970s, these ideas began to trickle down to large numbers of women only in the 1990s. Today, the anti-rape movement on many college campuses teaches men and women the necessity of affirmative, verbal consent. The sexual equivalence assumed by this development for male and female choice in sexual behavior is joined with the call for sexual equality in all aspects of social life. Whether this new, revolutionary discourse will expand and circulate more widely in U.S. society remains to be seen (Sanday 1996, pp. 265–287). To the extent that it replaces the current discourse of male sexual dominance, we will see a reversal of one cultural selection process in favor of another, one that is more respectful of women's sexual and social rights.

The Case of the Minangkabau: Worldview or Natural Selection?

The Minangkabau present an interesting case of how social assumptions regarding human nature inhibits violence against women. The social philosophy of the Minangkabau of West Sumatra is reflected in an ethos and worldview that makes matrilineal inheritance and preserving the mother-child bond the foundational social form. The same ethos and worldview explains why the Minangkabau are virtually rape free. Having said this, I want to caution the reader not to jump to the conclusion that matrilineal descent alone inhibits male violence against women. Most relevant is not matrilineal descent per se but the philosophy that underpins the Minangkabau version of matriliny and the relationship of this philosophy to issues of male violence. This point underscores once again my major point: Behavior cannot be considered separately from the system of symbols, rituals, and worldview that operate as models of and for behavior crafted over time molding the cup of clay anthropologists call culture.

Numbering some eight million people, about half in the province of West Sumatra—the traditional homeland of their culture—and another half in other parts of Indonesia, the Minangkabau are the fourth largest ethnic group in the archipelago. In Indonesia, the Minangkabau are famous for their "matriarchal *adat*," which they proudly proclaim by referring to their society as a *matriarchaat,* using the Dutch term for matriarchy. By this label, however, they don't refer to female rule as we define matriarchy but to a host of maternal meanings giving women an unusually authoritative role when compared to women's role in other societies (see Sanday 2002).

By all measures, the Minangkabau can be called a modern society. They are well known in Indonesia for their literary flair, democratic leanings, and business acumen, making them among the most prosperous and better known of Indonesia's ethnic groups. Tradition and modernity live in visible coexistence in the cities of West Sumatra. Malls, universities, banks, and book stores share the same streets with traditional marketplaces in the capital city of Padang. The colorful cities of the highlands attract tourists from all over the world. Buses link most villages to the cities. In the villages, satellite dishes beam CNN, Asian MTV, Indonesian soap operas, and Japanese and Indian movies to TVs in homes and food stalls. For eighteen years, beginning in 1981 and ending in 1999, I went to West Sumatra nearly every year for summers and sabbaticals. The following summarizes my findings with respect to questions regarding the implications of the Minangkabau discourse on the appropriate relationship between culture and nature.

It is fitting to begin with the Minangkabau version of natural selection, because it is quite different from the Darwinian version presented by Thornhill and Palmer in their arguments for why men rape. The Minangkabau also believe in an all-seeing force in nature. However, they sacralize this force, seeing it as the will of the ancestors that works for the common good, which means that it is eminently moral. The will of the ancestors represents the accumulated traditions passed down through the generations. This body of customs is said to have been formed from choosing the good and rejecting the bad of nature for the benefit and reproductive success of each generation.

Choosing the good and rejecting the bad of nature is at the core of Minangkabau philosophy and can be tied to the social arrangements related to reproduction, including customs related to descent, residence, and marriage, all of which are designed to protect the mother-child bond. The dominant principle determining these customs is expressed in the following proverb.

Take the small knife used for carving
Make a staff from the lintabuang tree
The cover of pinang flowers becomes a winnow

A drop of water becomes the sea
A fist becomes a mountain
Growth in nature is our teacher.

This proverb means that people derive the rules of culture from observing the benign aspects of nature. The standard explanation of this proverb goes something like this. Nature provides us with the wherewithal for rudimentary implements for food and shelter (first three lines). Social well-being is found in natural growth and fertility (second three lines) according to the dictum that the unfurling, blooming, and expansion of growth in nature is our teacher. As plants grow from seedlings, trees from transplanted branches, the sea from a trickle of water, and mountains from a clump of earth, so do people. Like the seedlings of nature, people and emotions must be fed patiently so that they will flower and grow to their fullness and strength. Thus nurture is the natural law that humans should follow in devising social rules. This means that culture must focus on nurturing the weak and turn away from the desire to resort to brute strength. The importance placed on nurturing the vulnerable emphasizes cooperation and elevates the moral and social authority of women. The construction of social forms to nurture the vulnerable is evident in the Minangkabau explanation for matrilineal descent.

In an interview, a well-known Minangkabau leader rationalized matrilineal descent as being "in accordance with the flora and fauna of nature in which it can be seen that it is the mother who bears the next generation and it is the mother who suckles the young and raises the child." Elaborating, he said:

As we all know, Minangkabau *adat* [custom] comes from nature according to the proverb *Alam takambang jadi guru* [growth in nature is our teacher]. In nature all that is born into the world is born from the mother, not from the father. Fathers are only known by a confession from the mother. *Adat* knows that the mother is the closest to her children and is therefore more dominant than the father in establishing the character of the generations. Thus, we must protect women and their offspring because they are also weaker than men. Just as the weak becomes the strong in nature, we must make the weaker the stronger in human life. If the mother abandons or doesn't recognize her own child, adat exists to recognize the child's descent line and to ensure the child's worldly welfare.

Male and female leaders in many villages expressed similar ideas. For example, one man explained to me that the matrilineal system was originally devised so that children would always have a family, food, and ancestral land. Speaking rhetorically he asked, "If a child is born without a father, or we don't know who the father is, where can the child find *pusaka* [land and ancestral home] and food? Like growth in nature, we always know from whom the child descends: the mother."

Such ideas cannot be reduced to ignorance about the father's role in conception as was commonly claimed in nineteenth-century discussions on the subject of matriarchy. The Minangkabau understand the biological basis of paternity perfectly well, yet choose not to make protecting the blood ties between a father and his children a social issue. To do so would be antithetical to the conviction that the job of culture (adat) is to nurture and care for the young. While the mother-child bond can always be counted on to perform this task, the father-child link is not as reliable for the reasons spelled out in the comments noted above. These comments suggest that concerns about paternity deflect emphasis from a child's well-being to concerns about biological fatherhood that may raise extraneous social issues inimical to the child's welfare. This is not to say that Minangkabau fathers don't play an important role in the lives of their children. Indeed, they play a key role; but, the connection of father to child is not tied to the transmission of land and houses. It is more an emotional than a material bond. Social rights are conceived so as to protect the weak. As I was told many times:

Here we elevate the weak instead of the strong. Women *must* be given rights *because* they are weak. Young men *must* be sent away from the village to prove their manhood so that there will be no competition between them and their sisters.

Protecting the mother-child bond is also the goal of customs related to mate selection and postmarital residence. Males don't chose marriage partners and wives are not exchanged in Minangkabau society. This is one of the few societies described by anthropologists in which husbands are exchanged by women. Marriage partners are chosen by women for their daughters in conjunction with family members, usually the mother's brothers and sisters. Certain types of men are more desirable than others. The least desirable is a category of male who fits the image of what we would call "macho." No one wants their daughter to marry such a man, because he is perceived as unreliable and a poor prospect for contributing to the household economy. Mothers seek hardworking men who will contribute to the agricultural labor on the matrilineal land their daughters will inherit. Wealthy men are also in high demand, but few families can afford a wealthy husband for their daughters. As a general rule all husbands live in the households of their wives.

The Minangkabau never speak directly about sexual abuse, domestic violence, or rape. Nor do they speak directly about preferred behavior. Rather, they convey cultural expectations through proverbs. For example, there are many proverbs about the importance of peacefulness in human interaction and of maintaining good relations by resorting to consensus deliberation rather than using power for social ends. In the relationships of daily life people stress politesse and harmony in resolving disputes, by speaking of how "where two or three sit together, the words seek truth, round like the water that flows in the bamboo tube, seeking common agreement." The Minangkabau liken their customs and traditions "to growing flowers," saying that a marriage conducted according to the rule of custom is like the planting of a seed that "will grow bearing flowers and fruit."

Good and evil are conceived as two sides of the same lesson to be learned from nature and the will of the ancestors. If human beings break the rules of matrilineal descent, they can be destroyed by the curse of the ancestors, shunned, or sent away from the village. A man who beats his wife reflects the evil of nature, which is also punishable by the curse of the ancestors. Such a man is separated from the household of his wife and sent back to the household of his mother. A man who rapes is turned over to the Indonesian state authorities for prosecution. The only case of rape I knew of in the village where I lived occurred many years before my arrival. This was a gang rape of a mentally retarded girl by a group of young males in another village when they found her wandering alone through their village. While in progress the rape was stopped by senior males. The next day the leader of the rape committed suicide for fear of what he faced from the senior males of the girl's extended family. The remaining males were turned over to the authorities.

After hearing about this case, I listened to the sexual gossip of the women I knew, asking many questions about instances of sexual abuse. I also studied the village sexual discourse. Just as the male peer culture in the United States is characterized by a sexual discourse, usually abusive to women, there is a sexual discourse that circulates in Minangkabau villages. However, its nature is completely different. First, it is a female sexual discourse; second, it is a public discourse.

A female-defined sexual discourse is communicated in public spaces to male and female audiences by female bards in songs sung in all-night performances staged to entertain villagers in association with the celebration of marriage and birth. The singing, which begins around 9 P.M. and lasts until 4:30 A.M., includes at minimum two female singers and one male flute player brought to the village to entertain guests. The songs are about love, sex, loss, joy, and sorrow. Many are funny songs about women and men in various states of sexual desire. In all the performances I attended and recorded, the theme of male sexual coercion was never voiced, even though many sexual complaints were aired, including songs about male sexual performance and songs likening unsatisfied female desire to a dried, unwatered, unhoed rice field (see Sanday 2002 for the text of typical songs). The Minangkabau can be classified as one exception to the general statement made by Thornhill and Palmer (p. 160) that "people everywhere understand sex to be something that women have and men want." I am sure that there are many anthropologists who could provide additional exceptions.

It is clear that the Minangkabau have a concept of rape. Their understanding of rape is in part conditioned by the sexual abuse women experienced during the occupation by the Japanese at the end of World War II. It was during this time of general chaos that the gang rape mentioned above took place. Today, the Minangkabau categorize rape behavior as barbaric, the epitome of the uncivilized. Any form of violence against women is not tolerated in village life. Reproductive success for men in Minangkabau society is guaranteed to those who conform to the etiquette expected in personal relationships. Men who follow this etiquette are in more demand by mothers seeking husbands for their daughters than young men who engage in rough, unseemly behavior. The latter type of male finds it hard to find a wife and usually ends up migrating to other parts of Indonesia.

Minangkabau thought and practices with respect to interpersonal violence is a timeless reminder of an old anthropological axiom. Although human beings have the potential for aggression, it is culture (not biology) that redirects, dampens, or activates that potential. When I talked to the Minangkabau about the incidence of rape and wife abuse in the United States they were always astounded. Interpersonal violence and rape are impossible in our society, I was told, because custom not power determines the way people act. We need customs to temper behavior, I was informed. Otherwise people would be like wild animals in the jungle in which the strong would conquer the weak. This comment illustrates both an awareness of raw physical power and the idea that such power can be regulated.

With respect to the expression of individual reproductive interests in this society, it is obvious that reproduction is highly social in the sense that what counts is not so much sexual union as the context in which this union takes place. The Minangkabau understand that their society is structured to favor the vulnerable, namely women and children, through the practice of matrilineal descent. Ancestral land and houses are inherited in the female line so that women and children will never be homeless. Husbands go to live with their wives at marriage so that if there is a divorce mother and child will not be in want. Providing for the vulnerable is seen as a source of strength after the proverb "growth in nature is our teacher." Applied to sex, the Minangkabau social philosophy teaches that aggression weakens rather than strengthens the body's tie to nature and society. This explains why there is no discernible incidence of sexual abuse or domestic violence in the village of my field work. In other parts of West Sumatra I was able to document very few rapes either from police reports in the cities, personal observation, or interviews. The assailants in the few cases I identified were tried, convicted, and jailed. I conclude that this is a rape-free society not because rape is entirely absent but because it is infrequent.

Conclusion

The incidence of rape is far lower among men raised in stable peaceful environments be it a family context in a complex society like the United States or the intimate village communities of the Minangkabau people in the province of West Sumatra where one finds an ethos of mutual respect between the sexes. To say that at least some men rape in all societies and to use this fact to make generalizations about the natural history of rape and the biological bases for sexual coercion obfuscates the dramatic cultural differences between a rape-free society like the Minangkabau and a rape-prone society like the United States. Naturalizing and universalizing rape as an adaptation related to male reproductive success may bring about the very sexual culture one is trying to avoid by creating a lore that makes sexual aggression inevitable to masculinity. Looking to the male psyche for the rapelike structures of scorpion flies—as Thornhill and Palmer do in one of their arguments for why men rape—is profoundly belittling to men and boys, reducing them to biological material just as women are reduced to their bodily attributes in the pornographic scenarios of rape cultures.[6]

In contrast to the generalizations Thornhill and Palmer offer about the evolved nature of male rape, other students of evolution suggest that the primary selective pressure in human evolution was not for violent men but for those who were able to cooperate with women and other males in organized food gathering. This viewpoint suggests that what happened over time was cultural selection *against* violent males by means of the institution of socially determined forms of mate selection and reproductive practices. Some anthropologists believe that female selection of cooperative males as mates in a foraging environment where food acquisition and childrearing tasks had to be divided up was responsible for the evolution of humans (Tanner 1981).

Keeping women in a state of fear with the threat of rape may increase social bonding among young males for whatever reason (hunting or warfare) but it is unlikely to have contributed to the evolution of human society and culture. Fear splits the sexes into ranked camps and reduces the overall level of cooperation. By increasing levels of stress in females, fear may reduce fertility rates and a female's capability to bear children. It also reduces the ability of the sexes to coordinate food-gathering activities. It is hard to imagine how the combination of fearful, dependent females and aggressive, belligerent males could have helped us through the many evolutionary crises created by changing environmental circumstances and the widespread extinctions on the long road toward humanity. Indeed, one could easily argue that male aggression hastens extinction because of the culture of violence it encourages, where death rather than life excites men.

The Minangkabau provide living proof of how cooperation and complementary roles between the sexes work in a society that values the kinds of nurturing males that anthropologist Nancy Tanner (1981) describes in her book *On Becoming Human*. In light of the ever-increasing incidence of life-threatening sexually transmitted diseases, rape can no longer be viewed as contributing to reproductive success. Additionally, it has been clear since the discovery of HIV and other sexually transmitted diseases that giving boys free reign to pursue their "individual reproductive interests," such as seen in the "boys will be boys" discourse, must now be judged not only in moral but in criminal terms as well. Because males are largely in charge of deciding to use force, be it sexually or in warfare, it will be males who decide whether we continue down the path of violence against women. With its emphasis on the role of culture, the "feminist social-science explanation of rape," which Thornhill and Palmer denigrate as bad science, has a better chance than the so-called natural history of rape to light the way by demonstrating that because culture counts humans have it in their power to produce a more equitable sexual culture.

Notes

1. See Vance (1984) and Caplan (1987) for more recent anthropological statements on the variation of human sexual behavior cross-culturally.

2. This sample offers to scholars a representation of the world's known and well-described societies. The complete sample consists of 186 societies, each "pinpointed" to an identifiable subgroup of the society in question at a specific point in time. The time period for the sample societies ranges from 1750 B.C. (Babylonians) to the late 1960s. The societies included in the standard sample are distributed relatively equally among the six major ethnographic regions of the world: Sub-Saharan Africa, Circum-Mediterranean, East Eurasia, Insular Pacific, North America, South and Central America. Information on the incidence of rape was available in only 95 societies of the full sample. For more information on the sample employed for the cross-cultural incidence of rape and related variables, see Sanday (1981).

3. As part of their criticism of my "rape-free" category, Thornhill and Palmer (2000, p. 141) claim that I misclassify the Mbuti Pygmies of the Ituri forest in Africa. They point out that Turnbull's description of the Mbuti is ambiguous, making my "rape-free" categorization of the Mbuti suspicious. Thornhill and Palmer (ibid.) quote Turnbull on the subject of Mbuti rape: "I know of no cases of rape, though boys often talk about their intentions of forcing reluctant maidens to their will." Thornhill and Palmer could not know that I had a long talk with Turnbull regarding rape among the Mbuti, at which time he told me that rape was "infrequent" in Mbuti society. If a girl lay down with a boy, Turnbull reported to me, it was because she expected intercourse.

Quoting a number of authors, Thornhill and Palmer say that "there is no evidence of a truly rape-free society" (2000, p. 142). By this they mean that there is no evidence of any society in which rape is wholly absent. Once again, they twist my words. My rape-free code was based on reporting by ethnographers that rape is rare or absent. I did not take the ethnographers to mean that rape was literally absent, only that they found no evidence that rape was commonplace. I assume that an instance of sexually coercive behavior can be found in any society. Not admitting this would be like saying that there is absolutely no stealing in even the most crime-free society. Such a conclusion, however, does not impute a genetic basis either to rape or stealing.

Thornhill and Palmer come close to my conclusions regarding variation in the incidence of rape when they say that "[t]he ethnographic evidence indicates that *some frequency* of rape is typical of *Homo sapiens* . . . (2000, p. 142; emphasis mine). However, I disagree with their conclusion that "human males in all societies so far examined in the ethnographic record possess genes that can lead, by way of ontogeny, to raping behavior . . ." (ibid.). If this were the case, we would expect a much higher incidence of rape in societies like the United States where the necessary environmental facts are present in the adolescent male peer culture. Yet, my research demonstrates that not all adolescent males take advantage of a vulnerable woman nor are they always able to perform sexually in environments marked by group male sexual coercion (see discussion in section "Denigrating Feminist Social Science," to follow).

4. These variables, listed in table 3 of Sanday (1981, p. 23), include (1) presence of war ($p = .03$); (2) distant proximity of father to care of infants ($p = .08$); (3) no evidence of female power and authority ($p = .03$); (4) sexual segregation such as seen in presence of special places for men ($p = .01$); and (5) presence of special places for women ($p = .08$). All of these associations fit my general conclusions regarding the sociocultural context of rape that follows.

5. I could find no evidence (see Sanday 1981, p. 25) for the popular belief that sexual repression explains the incidence of rape. Rape is not an instinct triggered by celibacy, enforced for whatever reason.

6. In support of the first argument regarding why men rape, noted earlier in this chapter, Thornhill and Palmer say it is necessary to identify "mechanisms involved in rape that were designed by selection in the past specifically for reproduction by means of rape" (2000, p. 62). Because such mechanisms exist in the morphology of certain insects, they conclude that they must also exist in humans. To make this case, the authors draw parallels with scorpion flies, an insect studied by Thornhill. Male scorpion flies, it seems, have a physical adaptation for rape. This adaptation consists of a specific organ they describe as "a pair of clamp-like structures, one on either side of the penis," that serves to keep unwilling females in a mating position (ibid., p. 63). According to Thornhill and Palmer, this organ "functions to secure a mating with an unwilling female to retain her in copulation for the period needed for full insemination." They view it as a "rape adaptation," designed for increasing "the mating and the reproductive success of males that raped relative to those that did not rape" (ibid., p. 64). Admitting that there is no "conspicuous morphology that might be a rape adaptation" in human males, Thornhill and Palmer (ibid., pp. 64–65) look "to the male psyche for candidates for rape adaptations." They propose (ibid., pp. 65–66) a number of "psychological mechanisms" as "adaptations" that can be viewed as "analogous" to the rape adaptations observed in "male insects." They define an "analogous adaptation" as a product of the same selection pressure, but one that "molds different phenotypic features to accomplish the same function." Thus, the clamplike structures designed for rape in the scorpion fly becomes a "psychological adaptation" for rape in human males. In the human as well as the insect case, the ultimate benefit of these different adaptations is the same, namely reproductive success in the "production of offspring" (ibid., pp. 64–65).

References

Boeringer, S. G. (1996). Influences of fraternity membership, athletics, and male living arrangements on sexual aggression. *Violence against Women* 2(2): 134–147.

Broude, G. J. and S. J. Greene (1976). Cross-cultural codes on twenty sexual attitudes and practices. *Ethnology* 15(4): 409–430.

Caplan, Pat, ed. (1987). *The Cultural Construction of Sexuality.* London: Tavistock.

Degler, Carl N. (1991). *In Search of Human Nature: The Decline and Revival of Darwinism in American Social Thought.* New York: Oxford University Press.

Geertz, C. (1973). *The Interpretation of Cultures: Selected Essays.* New York: Basic Books.

Koss, M. P. and K. E. Leonard (1984). Sexually aggressive men: Empirical findings and theoretical implications. In N. M. Malamuth and E. Donnerstein, eds., *Pornography and Sexual Aggression,* pp. 213–232. New York: Academic Press.

Malinowski, B. (1929). *The Sexual Life of Savages in North-western Melanesia.* London: G. Routledge and Sons.

Michael, R. T., J. H. Gagnon, E. O. Laumann, and Gina Kolata (1994). *Sex in America: A Definitive Survey.* Boston: Little, Brown.

Murdock, George P. and Douglas White (1969). Standard cross-cultural sample. *Ethnology* 8: 329–369.

Murphy, Yolanda and Robert Murphy (1974). *Women of the Forest.* New York: Columbia University Press.

Nuwer, Hank (1990). *Broken Pledges: The Deadly Rite of Hazing.* Georgia: Longstreet.

Nuwer, Hank (1999). *Wrongs of Passage: Fraternities, Sororities, Hazing, and Binge Drinking.* Bloomington: Indiana University Press.

Sanday, Peggy Reeves (1981). The socio-cultural context of rape: A cross-cultural study. *Journal of Social Issues* 37(4): 5–27.

Sanday, Peggy Reeves (1990). *Fraternity Gang Rape: Sex, Brotherhood, and Privilege on Campus.* New York: New York University Press.

Sanday, Peggy Reeves (1996). *A Woman Scorned: Acquaintance Rape on Trial.* Berkeley: University of California Press.

Sanday, Peggy Reeves (2002). *Women at the Center: Life in a Modern Matriarchy.* Ithaca: Cornell University Press.

Tanner, Nancy (1981). *On Becoming Human.* Cambridge: Cambridge University Press.

Thornhill, R. and C. T. Palmer (2000). *A Natural History of Rape: Biological Bases of Sexual Coercion.* Cambridge: The MIT Press.

Vance, Carol S. (1984). Pleasure and danger. In Carol Vance, ed., *Pleasure and Danger,* pp. 1–28. London: Routledge and Kegan Paul.

15

What Is "Rape"?—Toward a Historical, Ethnographic Approach

Emily Martin

> Since Hobbes, at least, the competitive and acquisitive characteristics of Western man have been confounded with Nature, and the Nature thus fashioned in the human image has been in turn reapplied to the explanation of Western man. The effect of this dialectic has been to anchor the properties of human social action, as we conceive them, in Nature, and the laws of Nature in our conceptions of human social action. Human society is natural, and natural societies are curiously human.
>
> —Marshall Sahlins, *The Use and Abuse of Biology*

As a cultural anthropologist, I found the most stunning thing about reading Thornhill and Palmer's *A Natural History of Rape* is how little the authors engage with the large number of previously published critiques of the assumptions on which their sociobiological (evolutionary psychological) view of human behavior is based.[1] The book contains a chapter called "Why Have Social Scientists Failed to Darwinize?" but for the most part, the authors dismiss opposing points of view as ideological, and they engage in little substantive discussion of their claims (pp. 105–122). Faced with the task of critiquing a view of human behavior espoused by authors who are evidently not much interested in reexamination of any of their basic assumptions, my heart nearly went out of the effort. Surely, I thought, further argument would be as futile as trying to argue a religious person into discarding the tenets of his or her faith.[2] So, to open a psychological space where there is at least the possibility that some reader might listen, I have not written this essay with the goal of dissuading Thornhill, Palmer, and their colleagues in mind. Instead, my imagined audience is composed of college or high school teachers and members of the general public, who hear many stories constructed on sociobiological principles, from newspaper accounts in the *New York Times'* "Science Times," through standard textbooks, to the Discovery channel, but who listen with a degree of unease and wonder how it would be possible (for the sake of themselves, their students, or their children) to question the closed world of sociobiological principles.

I will attempt this discussion by arguing that human acts involving intentionality—rape as well as all others—can be understood only through categories used to make sense of them in the cultural setting in which they occur. This means that understanding what people do is complex, context-dependant, and often changes through time and across space. This also means that intentional actions cannot be separated from the contexts in which they occur (rich and multifaceted as these may be) without losing what gives them sense in the first place. I argue that Thornhill and Palmer, assuming that there are "acts" out there in the world and also separate descriptions that can be applied to them from a completely different context, such as sociobiology, have, in making this move, lost exactly the qualities that make acts like "rape" human actions in the first place. Ignoring the way human actions are constituted by cultural meaning, their argument is thus founded on fundamental mistakes about what sort of thing human actions are.

Victorian Science

The principles animating the sociobiological view of the world arose out of the specific historical context of Victorian England. On one side stood the commitment to progressive reforms, the power of technology and the "naturalizing of morals and man" displayed in the Crystal Palace (Desmond and Moore 1991, p. 392). On the other stood the brutality of the struggle in the Crimean War. Darwin, himself a heavy investor in industry and the railway companies that made industrial growth possible, accomplished an elaborate metaphoric extension from the dynamics of the Victorian economy and Nature: "Nature was a self-improving 'workshop,' evolution the dynamic economy of life. The creation of wealth and the production of species obeyed similar laws. Division of labor was nature's way as well as man's" (ibid., pp. 420–421).

At about the same time, but in places outside Victorian England, images of biological organisms (or their genetic components) as self-promoting individuals acting on utilitarian economic principles, engaged in all-out struggle for reproductive survival have not held sway.[3] Daniel Todes has shown how in the late nineteenth and early twentieth centuries Russian biologists rejected Darwin's major metaphor, the struggle for existence, especially when it appeared in connection with Malthusian ideas about overpopulation. In developing an alternative theory of mutual aid, Russian naturalists argued four tenets:

the central aspect of the struggle for existence is the organism's struggle with abiotic conditions; organisms join forces to wage this struggle more effectively, and such mutual aid is favored by natural selection; since cooperation, not competition, dominates intraspecific relations, Darwin's Malthusian characterization of those relations is false; and cooperation so vitiates intraspecific competition that the latter cannot be the chief cause of the divergence of characters and the origin of new species. (Todes 1989, p. 545)

In rejecting Darwin's assumptions, Russians identified the idea of individualized competitive struggle as a product of English culture and society. Darwin's use of this assumption was "the same as if Adam Smith had taken it upon himself to write a course in zoology" (quoted in Todes 1987, p. 541); a Russian expert on fisheries and population dynamics wrote that the English "national type accepts [struggle] with all its consequences, demands it as his right, tolerates no limits upon it" (quoted in Todes 1989, p. 41).

This response to Darwin's theory, common to Russian intellectuals of a variety of philosophical and political viewpoints, derived, as Todes persuasively argues, from several factors:

Russia's political economy lacked a dynamic, pro–laissez faire bourgeoisie and was dominated by landowners and peasants. The leading political tendencies, monarchism and a socialist-oriented populism, shared a cooperative social ethos and a distaste for the competitive individualism widely associated with Malthus and Great Britain. Furthermore, Russia was an expansive, sparsely populated land with a swiftly changing and often severe climate. It is difficult to imagine a setting less consonant with Malthus's notion that organisms were pressed constantly into mutual conflict by population pressures on limited space and resources. (Todes 1989, p. 168)

Comparative historical material such as this allows us to begin to question the universal applicability of the competitive, individualistic world sociobiology imagines.

The cultural backdrop for the theories that fascinated Darwin, and puzzled the Russians, continues to serve today as a backdrop for the theories that fascinate Thornhill and Palmer. As Robert Young puts it, "we find that levels and concepts intermingle and that it is from society that we derive our conceptions of nature. These conceptions are in turn inextricably intermingled with our conceptions of human nature" (1985, p. 626). Young goes on to catalog the terms that are the basic "working vocabulary" of the bible of modern sociobiology, E. O. Wilson's *Sociobiology: The New Synthesis:* "division of labor (sexual and task), hierarchy, competitiveness, domination and submission, peck order, aggression, harem, promiscuous, mob, combat, spite, bachelor, jealously, territoriality, leadership, indoctrinability, élites" (p. 626). Similarly, in a somewhat more popularly accessible presentation of sociobiology, Richard Dawkins's *The Selfish Gene,* the basic terms include "cheat, sucker, grudger" (p. 626) and of course by the time we reach Thornhill and Palmer, we add "rape." Young comments, "What possible source except a society such as ours can we consider for a conceptual vocabulary such as that? What possible significance except the scientific underpinning of a competitive, fatalistic, individualistic élitist, patriarchal, sexist society can be attached to the following titles that have appeared recently around these questions: *On Aggression, The Naked Ape, The Territorial Imperative, The Imperial Animal, The Dominant Man, The Inevitability of Patriarchy, The Biological Imperative . . . The Selfish Gene"* (p. 626)?

How Sociobiologists Look at "Rape"

Moving to the specifics of *A Natural History of Rape,* how do Thornhill and Palmer define rape? It is

copulation resisted to the best of the victim's ability unless such resistance would probably result in death or serious injury to the victim or in death or injury to individuals the victim commonly protects. (p. 1)

They argue that this behavior occurs because in the course of human evolution, it gave a selective advantage to those males who practiced it. These males gained in the competition for sexual partners and hence in their sexual fitness. Psychological mechanisms that promote male rape developed in the human species that both enabled and ensured that the behavior would continue to occur (pp. 65–66).

It is important to this argument that a behavior called rape exists, like a thing, in the world, so that it can be observed, described, and then counted and mapped. If it turned out that on investigation the thing called rape was not found very often around the world, Thornhill and Palmer's argument would be greatly weakened, because presumably traits that arise as a result of evolutionary processes would be found in all human populations.

> The ethnographic evidence indicates that some frequency of rape is typical of *Homo Sapiens* and that there is no evidence of a truly rape-free society. . . . [T]his does not mean, of course, that rape is a genetically determined act unaffected by learning and culture. It means only that human males in all societies so far examined in the ethnographic record possess genes that can lead, by way of ontogeny, to raping behavior when the necessary environmental factors are present, and that the necessary environmental factors are sometimes present in all societies studied to date. (p. 142)

So everything hinges on there being a sense in which something called rape can be found universally, and that things counted as rape meet the minimum definition: "copulation resisted to the best of the victim's ability unless such resistance would probably result in death or serious injury to the victim or in death or injury to individuals the victim commonly protects" (p. 142). The first problem we run into is that the minimum definition of the act depends on how the act is understood by those who are engaging in it. Was I forced? Did I intend to force? Did I want to? Did she (or he) want to? If questions like these cannot be answered unambiguously and in ways that are exactly comparable across cultures and across settings within them, our ability to count acts as rape is profoundly thwarted.

How Cultural Actions Are Constituted by Their Contextual Meaning

Let me give some examples of how tricky the answer to these deceptively simple questions is in practice. In many forms of Chinese marriage, on a traditional model, marital relationships gave the husband access to sexual relations with his wife.[4] No social or legal support (at least from the dominant institutions in Chinese society) would be forthcoming if a wife attempted to resist sex with her husband. More important, the institution of marriage was traditionally one in which the consent of the wife, to the marriage itself, let alone to sexual relations within it, was quite irrelevant. Marriage was a contract between two families, involving exchange of goods and the assumption of new kin obligations. The woman's consent as a choosing, deciding person with a will of her own was by and large irrelevant. Within such a context (in its broad outlines not an uncommon one worldwide), to segregate some acts as with the woman's consent and others without seems a crude misreading of what these acts mean in context. We would be introducing elements into a cultural system that did not belong there, much as if we tried to understand a game we were unfamiliar with and thought mistakenly that a strike was called on a batter in baseball only when he did not *want* to hit the ball. Whatever the batter's state of mind, his act only counts as a strike if certain socially determined conditions are met. To introduce issues of volition into the definition of a strike would be to make a category mistake of large proportions.

The difficulty knowing whether to categorize acts as "rape" exists just as acutely in places such as the United States where individual will is almost always considered to be involved in the understanding of social acts. In the United States, a woman's consent is considered legally and socially central to the classification of an act as rape, consistently outside marriage and increasingly inside marriage. The United States is certainly one place where Thornhill and Palmer's definition of "rape" comes close to generally accepted common sense understandings. Yet consider the complexities involved in categorizing rape nonetheless. Thornhill and Palmer cite the following case as a clear example of rape:

A friend of ours once told us that after a movie she returned with her date to his car in an isolated parking lot. Then, instead of taking her home, the man locked the doors and physically forced her to have sexual intercourse with him. (p. 3)

But only slight contextualization of this scenario would make it much more difficult to categorize: What if the couple had been engaged in heavy making out just before entering the car? What if the couple mutually agreed to have intercourse but, although the woman insisted and the man agreed to withdraw before ejaculating, he ejaculates inside her? What if the woman resists, but playfully, or momentarily in order to insert a diaphragm? What if the woman does not actively resist, as in the encounters in Coetzee's recent novel, *Disgrace,* between a 52-year-old university professor and a 20-year-old student in his literature class:

Not rape, not quite that, but undesired nevertheless, undesired to the core. As though she had decided to go slack, die within herself for the duration, like a rabbit when the jaws of the fox close on its neck. So that everything done to her might be done, as it were, far away. (1999, p. 25)

And so on ad infinitum. In practice, intent and consent are more often than not anything but crystal clear: For this reason, a legal finding of rape, especially when the couple are acquainted, is complex and problematic (Temkin 1986; Cowling 1998, pp. 81ff; Edwards 1987; MacKinnon 1989). This is not to say that a finding of rape is impossible to establish beyond a reasonable doubt. It is only to say that such a finding depends on examining a whole, complex social and cultural context in which intent is situated.

So one might ask whether the solution to this situation is to make the definition of rape clearer, add conditions, clarify where they apply. Such a move will only push the problem back a step. If we add the condition that the woman must show a physical gesture of resistance, we are only further led to the problem of what physical gestures count as meaning resistance. As with the intent to rape, the intent to resist can be known only from examination of the complexities of the context. The problem is not one of inadequate definition; the problem is that Thornhill and Palmer have made a category mistake.

They treat "rape" as if it were a thing in the world whose significance were self-evident. They make an analogy between the eye and rape: Just as the eye evolved "by natural selection because it increased our ancestors' ability to detect light" (p. 5), so rape behavior evolved to increase "male reproductive success by way of increasing mate number" (p. 59).[5] In their view, vision has a proximal cause and an distal cause: Its proximal cause is the action of rods and cones in relaying visual information to the brain; its distal cause is evolution through selection. Similarly, according to Thornhill and Palmer, rape behavior has both proximal and distal causes: Its proximal causes include such things as hormonal levels and learning; its distal cause is evolution through selection (pp. 6–7). My point is that in this analogy they are comparing things that belong in different categories. The eye is a physical structure with a relatively clearly definable function. In a great variety of different organisms, it would make sense to say the eye is an organ whose function is to communicate visual information to the brain. But "rape" is not a physical structure with a clearly definable function. It is a behavior whose very existence depends on the intentions and reactions of at least two complex social beings in some particular cultural context. It would be impossible to know from a description of behavior alone whether the act amounted to rape.

The absurdity of the comparison between the eye and a rape is plain. A better comparison would be between "insight" and "rape" because in both cases, no simple description of a "thing" in the world could tell us whether they were present.

Throughout the book, Thornhill and Palmer are astonishingly tone deaf to the nature of cultural meaning. Basic insights taught to undergraduates in any introductory course in cultural anthropology seem to have passed them by. The sense in which human acts are imbued with meaning through layers of intentionality and complexly interrelated contexts—thereby making simple descriptions of observed behavior inadequate to attribute meaning—is missing. Clifford Geertz called the kind of description that would be adequate "thick description," and turned to Ryle's account of how intricate human intentionality is to get the point across. Ryle's account is worth quoting at length to convey the irreducibility of human acts to a single behavioral description:

Two boys fairly swiftly contract the eyelids of their right eyes. In the first boy this is only an involuntary twitch; but the other is winking conspiratorially to an accomplice. At the lowest or the thinnest level of description the two contractions of the eyelids may be exactly alike. From a cinematograph-film of the two faces there might be no telling which contraction, if either, was a wink, or which, if either, were a mere twitch. Yet there remains the immense but unphotographable difference between a twitch and a wink. For to wink is to try to signal to someone in particular, without the cognisance of others, a definite message according to an already understood code. It has very complex success-versus-failure conditions. The wink is a failure if its intended recipient does not see it; or sees it but does not know or forgets the code; or misconstrues it; or disobeys or disbelieves it; or if any one else spots it. A mere twitch, on the other hand, is neither a failure nor a success; it has no intended recipient; it is not meant to be unwitnessed by anybody; it carries no message. It may be a symptom but it is not a signal. The winker could not not know that he was winking; but the victim of the twitch might be quite unaware of his twitch. The winker can tell what he was trying to do; the twitcher will deny that he was trying to do anything. So far we are on familiar ground. We are just drawing the familiar distinction between a voluntary, intentional, and, in this case, collusive and code-governed contraction of the eyelids from an involuntary twitch. But already there is one element in the contrast that needs to be brought out. The signaler himself, while acknowledging that he had not had an involuntary twitch but (1) had deliberately winked, (2) to someone in particular, (3) in order to impart a particular message, (4) according to an understood code, (5) without the cognisance of the rest of the company, will rightly deny that he had thereby done or tried to do five separately do-able things. He had not both tried to contract his eyelids and also tried to do a second, synchronous thing or several synchronous things. Unlike a person who both coughs and sneezes, or both greets his aunt and pats her dog, he had not both contracted his eyelids and also done a piece of synchronous signaling to his accomplice. True, he had contracted them not involuntarily but on purpose, but this feature of being on purpose is not an extra deed; he had contracted them at the moment when his accomplice was looking in his direction, but its being at this chosen moment is not an extra deed; he had contracted them in accordance with an understood code, but this accordance is not an extra deed. He had tried to do much more than contract his eyelids, but he had not tried to do more things. He had done one thing the report of which embodies a lot of subordinate clauses; he had not done what the report of would embody several main verbs conjoined by "ands." There are five or more ways in which his winking attempt might have been a failure, but he was not attempting to do five things. If he is successful, he has not got five successes to put on a list, but only one. . . .

Come back to our winker. Perhaps, being new to the art, he winks rather slowly, contortedly and conspicuously. A third boy, to give malicious amusement to his cronies, parodies this clumsy wink. How does he do this? Well, by contracting his right eyelids in the ways in which the clumsy winker had winked. But the parodist is not himself clumsily trying covertly to signal a message to an accomplice. He is deftly trying conspicuously to exhibit something, and he fails if his cronies are not looking, or are not amused, or mistakenly suppose him to be trying covertly to signal to an accomplice. There is only one thing that he is trying to do, namely to take off the winker, and he does this just by contracting his right eyelids. Yet there is now a threefold internal complexity in his own report of what he has been trying to do. For he may say, "I was trying (1) to look like Tommy trying (2) to signal to his accomplice by trying (3) to contract his right eyelids." There is, so to speak, the beginning of a Chinese box of internal subordinate clauses in the parodist's report of what he was trying to do—for all that there was only one thing that he was trying to do, namely to parody the winker; and for all that the cinematograph-film records only the one eyelid-contraction. We can easily add to this nest of Chinese boxes. For our parodist, to make sure of getting his parody pat, may in solitude practise his facial mimicry. In so practising he is not yet trying to amuse anyone, for he is alone. He is rehearsing for a subsequent public performance. So he could report what he is now doing by, "I am trying (1) to get myself ready to try (2) to amuse my cronies by grimacing like Tommy trying (3) to signal covertly to his accomplice by trying (4) to contract his eyelids." Another box can easily be added. For our winker himself might report that he had not, on this occasion, really been trying covertly to signal something to his accomplice, but had been trying to gull the grown-ups into the false belief that he was trying to do so. So now our parodist, in practising his parody of this, would have to be described with the help of five verbs of trying—and still there is only one thing he is trying to do, and still there is only the one contraction of the eyelids that, at a given moment, the cinematograph film records. The thinnest description of what the rehearsing parodist is doing is, roughly, the same as for the involuntary eyelid twitch; but its thick description is a many-layered sandwich, of which only the bottom slice is catered for by that the thinnest description. (Ryle 1971, pp. 480–482)

As Geertz summarizes the point and brings home its relevance to culture:

The point is that between what Ryle calls the "thin description" of what the rehearser (parodist, winker, twitcher . . .) is doing ("rapidly contracting his right eyelids") and the "thick description" of what he is doing ("practicing a burlesque of a friend faking a wink to deceive an innocent into thinking a conspiracy is in motion") lies the object of ethnography: a stratified hierarchy of meaningful structures in terms of which twitches, winks, fake-winks, parodies, rehearsals of parodies are produced, perceived, and interpreted, and without which they would not . . . in fact exist, no matter what anyone did or didn't do with his eyelids. (Geertz 1973, p. 6)

The intentions of the people involved determine what description the action should be given. One act is "rape" and another is not, even though as recorded by video or audio means they might look and sound indistinguishable. This is *not* because the cultural meaning of behavior lies in a hidden domain within the mind:[6] The meaning of the behaviors lies in the context (what are the social norms governing sexuality in this place and time, what are the rights of women, the obligations of men, what is proper conduct for women during sex, how is force exerted or resisted, and so on). One could think of the acts, thoughts, utterances, explanations, facial expressions, clothing, and so on as interrelated elements of a linguistic system: The meaning of any one of them resides in how it is combined with all the others.

Changes in Cultural Meaning of "Rape" Over Time

Apart from problems interpreting behavior in different cultural settings, what rape consists in has changed profoundly over time, even within Western history.

From Old Testament Jewish codes up to feudalism, rape was treated primarily as theft, as a property offence, but one perpetuated against *men*. The crime was principally that of stealing or abducting a woman from her rightful proprietors, normally her father or husband. (Porter 1986, p. 217)

Nor was the transition to the modern concept of rape sudden and clear. In the early modern period, rape contained both the notion of property theft and of violation of the woman's will. "'Rape' descends from the Latin 'rapere,' which signifies theft or, if its object is a woman, abduction. This definition of 'rape' as 'abduction' is still available in the early modern period. Yet it also carries the meaning 'violation' which it signifies today. The coexistence of these two definitions of the word accounts for much of the complexity surrounding the issue of rape" (Catty 1999, p. 12). Some historians of the early modern period suggest that "rape is the overpowering of the female body by male force while seduction is its overpowering by desire. Both scenarios are located in the physical. . . . the destruction of the woman's (physical) chastity is often of greatest weight, rather than the role of her (mental) volition in the sexual act" (ibid., p. 19). Subsequently,

Very gradually the law came round to its more modern form. Statutes and commentators alike reiterated its gravity . . . , but opinion gradually came to stress that the true injured party was the woman. Once abduction was made a distinct felony in the sixteenth century, the crime of rape came to be seen essentially as that of sexual ravishment, which in turn was viewed as the theft of chastity and virtue, rather than of body and chattels. Yet since the law still saw wives and children as patriarchal property, court room practice continued [into the 18th century] to treat rape as a crime to be settled man-to-man. (ibid., p. 217)[7]

But Thornhill and Palmer's failure to grasp what kind of phenomenon human culture is goes far beyond being tone deaf to the complexities of how actions are imbued with meaning. Their understanding of culture is so profoundly oversimplified as to be unbelievable. For them, understanding culture is a matter of understanding how particular traits are *copied* intact over the generations. From conception, genetic instructions allow individuals to develop in interaction with the environment:

Genetic and environmental influences also construct the emotional and cognitive adaptions of the brain, including those involved in the *copying* of behavior and the highly specialized mechanisms designed to *copy* language. If the social learning (*copying*) involves English in parent and offspring generations, there will be parent-offspring resemblance and the behavior of speaking English can be said to have been inherited. (p. 26; emphasis added)

With this astonishingly impoverished view of cultural processes in place, they can go on to argue that

There is no fundamental difference in the mechanisms of inheritance of cultural and non-cultural behavior, nor is there a difference between the mechanisms of inheritance of cultural behavior and the mechanisms of inheritance of physiology and morphology. Inheritance occurs—like begets like, traits breed true—when and only when both genetic and environmental influences are repeated between generations. (pp. 26–27)

As Tim Ingold recently expressed it, reading this kind of thing is like stepping into a time machine to return to the 1920s to 1950s when "analogies and comparisons between cultural and biological evolution were commonplace" (2000, p. 1):

Over the last quarter of a century, sociocultural anthropologists have advanced way beyond these rather elementary formulations. Where once they thought of culture as a kind of content—whether conceived as clusters of traits, bundles of instructions, or compendia of rules and representations—which filled the capacities of the human mind, they are nowadays much more conscious of culture as *process*. This process is an unfolding of relations among people and between people and non-human components of the environment, out of which knowledge and understanding is continually being generated or produced. Even within those situations we might label as "learning," it is recognized that knowledge is not so much transmitted ready-made as produced anew—that is, it is being *reproduced* rather than *replicated*. And we now understand much better, too, how persons come into being as centres of intentionality and awareness within fields of social relationships, which are in turn carried forward and transformed through their own actions.

The picture Thornhill and Palmer wish to draw of rape as a definable object in the world that could be selected for and then replicated over the generations begins to fall apart at the seams. Ingold makes clear how misguided is the supposition that culture is made up of traits that are passed on like genes:

The idea of culture as consisting in transmissible and diffusible bundles of instructions is based on the false assumptions, firstly, that the meaning of each instruction can be specified independently of the particular environmental contexts of its application, and secondly, stemming from this, that information is tantamount to knowledge. For another thing, no known form of learning in human society can reasonably be described as a simple process of replication. Moreover, what people do is embedded in lifelong histories of engagement, as whole beings, with their surroundings, and is not the mechanical output of interaction between pre-replicated instructions (whether genetic or cultural) and prespecified environmental conditions, as selectionists would have us believe. (p. 2)[8]

Unexamined Assumptions in Sociobiology

Another approach to seeing what is wrong headed about Thornhill and Palmer is to consider how unexamined their own cultural assumptions are. Since these assumptions are unacknowledged and unexamined, they can exist submerged in the subconscious and thence arise to inform explanations of behavior in other cultures, times, and places (and even other species) as if they were objective facts about the world rather than products of a particular, historically produced viewpoint. As Thornhill and Palmer, as well as most who espouse the tenets of sociobiology, see the world, it is made up of highly individualized agents bent on maximizing their own advantage, defined as increasing their genetic stake in the next generation. Any means to that end, however ruthless, violent or aggressive, will be looked for and justified as necessary to increasing fitness, so defined. It may be that the strong resemblance to the kind of conduct that seems to denizens of late capitalist social systems necessary for survival in the ruthless employment and stock markets on every side is an accident, or it may be that the resemblance is a result of unconscious cultural projection.

As we have come to expect since the day of early sociobiologists like Edmund Wilson (1975), other species are written in the same language of conquest and aggression that has been the hallmark of Western myth and culture for millennia. Female dung flies

typically shake and struggle when grasped by a male. . . . The shaking and struggling occur only at this time and in this context. In mating attempts, a male grasps a female with elaborately modified forelegs that clamp the female's wings at their bases and allow the male to hold the struggling female. Struggling females sometimes prevent copulation, as do resisting female scorpionflies and waterstriders. Thus female struggling acts to select mates that are capable of holding onto them. . . . [F]emale struggling, and the resultant rape when their resistance is overcome by certain males, may be a female adaptation that helps females mate with males of superior phenotypic and genetic quality. (Thornhill and Palmer 2000, pp. 82–83)

Males use force to overcome females; males rape when female resistance can be overcome: Where does the license to interpret the insects' behavior this way come from? Is it not possible that the female is writhing from pleasure or squirming from being tickled when having their wings held just so? Is there any way to know for sure whether these flies are enacting a rape scene, displaying helpless ticklishness, or enduring an agony of passion?

In another depiction of insect life, Thornhill and Palmer describe an organ in scorpion flies they see as "designed specifically for rape" (p. 63). The "notal organ" is a clamp used by the male to grasp the female fly by force when he does not have a "nuptial gift" to present to the female, which can be either a "hardened mass of saliva that he has produced, or a dead insect" (ibid.). Although Thornhill and Palmer claim that experiments have ruled out all other explanations of the function of the notal organ other than rape, one must wonder whether, if the scientists explaining this behavior lived in a society governed by different principles, different insect scenarios would have been envisioned.

For example, in a human society governed on principles of reciprocity, where individuals and institutions were organized around the desirability of social ties built by exchanging objects and services as evenly as possible over time, men and women might prefer to mate when a gift exchange could be made. Thornhill and Palmer note that among dung flies, females do prefer males with gifts. If a male fly had no food offering and clasped the female by her wing, would he be attempting to rape her? Or would he be requesting her to engage in a social act in the absence of a gift, a request that the female denies, according to Thornhill and Palmer, the vast majority of the time (p. 79)? What Thornhill and Palmer see as a forceful grip preparatory to rape might equally well be an effort to get her attention by grasping her shoulder, a plea expressed by a gesture. If the grip is followed by mating, is this "rape"? Do the movements of the female fly signify "Rape!" or "You lousy bum!" (which would be a statement about his inappropriate preamble to sex)?

The matrilineal society described by Peggy Sanday as "rape-free," the Minangkabau of West Sumatra, value vulnerability, passivity, and kindheartedness. "All human behaviour should be non-aggressive and polite, thinking first about the feelings of others. . . . There is an air of graciousness that suffuses all human interaction" (1986, p. 95). A respected leader of customary law (*adat*) in West Sumatra explained their ideals:

The main core of *adat* philosophy is good deeds and kindheartedness. Democracy and thoughtfulness for the feelings of others is very important. *Adat* teaching is orientated to human morals, the principle of which is kindheartedness. You do not accuse someone directly. You do not criticize directly. You do so with proverbs. It is very rude to point out mistakes directly. There should be no force in decision-making. There should be mutual understanding. In Minangkabau democracy there is no room for rivalries. Differences of opinion are regarded as normal—consensus is arrived at through discussion. About differences of opinion there is a proverb: Crossing wood in the hearth makes the fire glow. (ibid., p. 96)

Would a Minangkabau science of scorpion flies see them as doing their best to express differences and resolve them according to appropriate social conventions?

Seeing the notal organ as a specific adaptation for rape in flies plays a crucial role in the argument of Thornhill and Palmer's book. By analogy, just as selection pressures molded the notal organ in ancestral populations of flies, increasing the "reproductive success of males that raped relative to those that did not rape" (p. 64), so selection pressures on human ancestral populations molded adaptations that "influenced males in ancestral populations to rape when the ultimate benefit (production of offspring) outweighed the ultimate costs (negative fitness consequences resulting from injury, punishment, etc.)" (p. 65):

> Men obviously don't have a clamp designed specifically for rape, nor do they have any other conspicuous morphology that might be a rape adaptation. We must therefore look to the male psyche for candidates for rape adaptation. If found such adaptations would be analogous to those in the male insects. (pp. 64–65)

If rape is a part of the natural history of flies, Thornhill and Palmer argue, then surely it is also part of the natural history of humans. But if we can dislodge the assumptions that make rape seem obvious and natural among flies, perhaps we would be less inclined to see the role of rape among humans as obvious and natural.

Are Thornhill and Palmer Sad Bearers of the Bad News?

At this point my imaginary audience might begin to wonder about Thornhill and Palmer's motivation in writing such a book. There can be little doubt that Thornhill and Palmer do not wish to increase the misery women experience at the hands of raping men. Instead they present themselves as the sad but implacable bearers of the bad news: If we do not realize rape is really the biological imperative of sexual competition, we will continue to fail to stamp rape out and to alleviate the suffering of the raped person. In this stance, I find them both disingenuous and insidious. They are disingenuous because they elide to an astonishing degree the extent to which efforts of feminists and others have had a major impact in the United States on the legal system's definition of rape, making it less acceptable to blame the victim for causing rape and more acceptable to acknowledge that rape can occur within a marriage (*Harvard Law Review* 1986) and intimate relationships (Estrich 1987). They also elide the extensive system of support facilities (in the form of housing for abused women, educational programs for police, special training for officers who attend rape victims, and the development of more available technology to detect evidence of a rape), much of which has resulted from energetic political activism on the part of feminists in many quarters. Further, they misunderstand, willfully or out of ignorance, the claim often made by feminists that rape involves an act of exerting power over the victim (p. 124).

Thornhill and Palmer are at pains to say that rape is *not* a matter of as-
serting superior power; rather it flows out of deep sexual urges to spread
one's seed. How did Thornhill and Palmer miss the fact that feminists
have been arguing for over 100 years that in Euro-American cultures,
sexual interactions are always imbued with relations of power? To say that
power is involved is by no means to say that rape is not sexual in any way,
as much as it is to say that sexuality in Euro-America is virtually always
part and parcel of a relationship involving disparate power (Griffin 1975;
Bourque 1989, p. 286; Bell 1991; Cowling 1998, pp. 18–19).

Their stance is insidious because, their protestations to the contrary,
their account actually amounts to an incitement to rape. Thornhill and
Palmer take pains to avoid the naturalistic fallacy, to avoid implying that
because something happens "in nature" it is a *good* thing. But the naturalistic fallacy is the least of our worries. The important worry is that whenever a form of human behavior appears to us to be written in nature, it
comes to seem among those behaviors that are most unchangeable. Even
though Thornhill and Palmer make numerous (and far from novel) suggestions for changes in education, criminology, and psychiatry to reduce
the incidence of rape, they do not seriously consider the probable social effects of their message itself.

Notes

1. These are some classic and more recent critiques: Sahlins (1976); Travis and
White (2000); Ingold (2000); Hubbard (1990); Gould (1997); Dusek (1999);
Lewontin (1991); Kitcher (1987); Rose and Rose (2000).

2. Nelkin (2000) discusses at length the religious character of evolutionary
psychology.

3. Sahlins (1976) characterizes sociobiology as resting on utilitarian economic
principles enacted according to possessive individualism (pp. 73, 97–98).

4. For analyses of the position of women in Chinese marriage, see M. Wolf (1972);
A. Wolf and Huang (1980); Wolf and Witke (1975).

5. In the context of this statement, the authors introduce a controversy over
whether rape behavior is an adaptation that was directly favored by selection or a
by-product of other psychological adaptations (pp. 57–58).

6. Thornhill and Palmer make unnecessarily simple-minded divisions between
mental states and behavior (p. 25).

7. See also Paxton (1999), pp. 8–9.

8. See also Ingold (2000).

References

Bell, V. (1991). Beyond the "thorny question": Feminism, Foucault, and the desexualisation of rape. *International Journal of the Sociology of Law* 19: 83–100.

Bourque, L. (1989). *Defining Rape*. Durham, N.C.: Duke University Press.

Catty, J. (1999). *Writing Rape, Writing Women in Early Modern England: Unbridled Speech*. New York: St. Martin's Press.

Coetzee, J. M. (1999). *Disgrace*. London: Secker and Warburg.

Cowling, M. (1998). *Date Rape and Consent*. Aldershot: Ashgate Publishing.

D'Cruze, S. (1992). Approaching the history of rape and sexual violence: Notes towards research. *Women's History Review* 1(3): 377–396.

Davis, D. and S. E. Harrell (1993). *Chinese Families in the Post-Mao Era*. Berkeley: University of California Press.

Dawkins, R. (1976). *The Selfish Gene*. New York: Oxford University Press.

Desmond, A. J. and J. Moore (1991). *Darwin*. New York: Norton.

Dusek, V. (1999). Sociobiology sanitized: The evolutionary psychology and genic selectionism debates. *Science As Culture* 8 (2): 129–169.

Edwards, A. (1987). Male violence in feminist theory: An analysis of the changing conceptions of sex/gender violence and male dominance. In J. and M. M. Hanmer, eds., *Women, Violence, and Social Control*, pp. 13–29. Atlantic Highlands, N.J.: Humanities Press International.

Estrich, S. (1987). *Real Rape*. Cambridge, MA: Harvard University Press.

Ferguson, F. (1987). Rape and the rise of the novel. *Representations* 20: 88–112.

Geertz, C. (1973). Thick description: Towards an interpretive theory of culture. In *The Interpretation of Cultures*, pp. 3–30. New York: Basic Books.

Gould, S. J. (1997). Darwinian fundamentalism. *New York Review of Books,* June 12, 34–37.

Griffin, S. (1975). Rape: The all-American crime. In J. Freeman, ed., *Women: A Feminist Perspective*, 1st ed., pp. 24–39. Palo Alto, Calif.: Mayfield Publishing.

Harvard Law Review (1986). To have and to hold: The marital rape exemption and the fourteenth amendment. *Harvard Law Review* 99: 1255–1273.

Horney, J. and C. Spohn (1991). Rape law reform and instrumental change in six urban jurisdictions. *Law and Society Review* 25: 117–53.

Hubbard, R. (1990). *The Politics of Women's Biology*. New Brunswick, N.J.: Rutgers University Press.

Ingold, T. (2000). Evolving skills. In H. Rose and S. Rose, eds., *Alas, Poor Darwin: Arguments against Evolutionary Psychology*, pp. 273–297. New York: Harmony Books/Random House.

Ingold, T. (2000). The poverty of selectionism. *Anthropology Today* 16(3): 1–2.

Kitcher, P. (1987). Precis of vaulting ambition: Sociobiology and the quest for human nature. *Behavioral and Brain Sciences* 10: 61–100.

Lewontin, R. C. (1991). *Biology as Ideology: The Doctrine of DNA*. New York: Harper-Collins.

Lewontin, R. C. (1979). Sociobiology as an adaptationist program. *Behavioral Science* 24: 5–14.

MacKinnon, C. (1989). *Toward a Feminist Theory of the State*. Cambridge, MA: Harvard University Press.

Nelkin, D. (2000). Less selfish than sacred? Genes and the religious impulse in evolutionary psychology. In H. Rose and S. Rose, eds., *Alas, Poor Darwin: Arguments against Evolutionary Psychology*, pp. 17–32. New York: Harmony Books/ Random House.

Paxton, N. L. (1999). *Writing under the Raj: Gender, Race, and Rape in the British Colonial Imagination, 1830–1947*. New Brunswick, N.J.: Rutgers University Press.

Porter, R. (1986). Rape—Does it have a historical meaning? In Sylvana Tomaselli and Roy Porter, eds., *Rape*, pp. 216–236. Oxford and New York: Basil Blackwell.

Rose, H. and S. E. Rose (2000). *Alas, Poor Darwin: Arguments against Evolutionary Psychology*. New York: Harmony Books/Random House.

Ryle, G. (1971). The thinking of thoughts. What is "le penseur" doing? In G. Ryle, *Collected papers* (vol. II, *Collected Essays* 1929–1968), pp. 480–496. New York: Barnes and Noble.

Sahlins, M. D. (1976). *The Use and Abuse of Biology: An Anthropological Critique of Sociobiology*. Ann Arbor: University of Michigan Press.

Sanday, P. R. (1986). Rape and the silencing of the feminine. In Sylvana Tomaselli and Roy Porter, eds., *Rape*, pp. 84–101. Oxford and New York: Basil Blackwell.

Temkin, J. (1984). Regulating sexual history evidence—The limits of discretionary legislation. *International and Comparative Law Quarterly* 33: 942–978.

Temkin, J. (1986). Women, rape, and law reform. In Sylvana Tomaselli and Roy Porter, eds., *Rape*, pp. 16–40. Oxford and New York: Basil Blackwell.

Thornhill, R. and C. T. Palmer. (2000). *A Natural History of Rape: Biological Bases of Sexual Coercion*. Cambridge, MA: MIT Press.

Todes, D. P. (1989). *Darwin without Malthus: The Struggle for Existence in Russian Evolutionary Thought*. New York: Oxford University Press.

Travis, C. B. and J. W. E. White (2000). *Sexuality, Society, and Feminism*. Washington, D.C.: American Psychological Association.

Watson, R. S. and P. B. E. Ebrey (1991). *Marriage and Inequality in Chinese Society*. Berkeley: University of California Press.

Wilson, E. O. (1975). *Sociobiology: The New Synthesis*. Cambridge, Mass.: Harvard University Press.

Wolf, A. P. and Chieh-shan Huang. (1980). *Marriage and Adoption in China, 1854–1945*. Stanford, Calif.: Stanford University Press.

Wolf, M. (1972). *Women and the Family in Northern Taiwan.* Stanford, Calif.: Stanford University Press.

Wolf, M. and R. E. Witke (1975). *Women in Chinese Society.* Stanford, Calif.: Stanford University Press.

Young, R. (1985). Darwinism *Is* Social. In D. Kohn, ed., *The Darwinian Heritage,* pp. 609–638. Princeton, N.J.: Princeton University Press.

16

Understanding Rape: A Metatheoretical Framework

Jacquelyn W. White and Lori A. Post

Until the women's movement of the 1960s, rape was perceived to be a rare and marginalized event and thus did not gain the attention of policymakers and academics. Rape was seen as a sexual deviance (Amir 1971), and research was conducted primarily by biologists, doctors, and therapists. Hence, we see early explanations of sexual behavior from a Darwinian, Freudian, or Kinseyian perspective (Tiefer 1988). In 1973, in response to the growing concern over rape, Senator Charles Mathias introduced a bill to establish the National Center for the Prevention and Control of Rape (Largen 1985). Shortly thereafter, Susan Brownmiller published her groundbreaking book *Against Our Will* (1975), which was one of the first attempts to address rape as a nonbiological event. She conceptualized rape as a cultural phenomenon with a political agenda. With the addition of Koss's important contribution on the pervasiveness of rape in American society, the issue was exposed as a significant social problem (Koss, Gidycz, and Wisniewski 1987). The etiology and prevalence of sexual violence have since been heavily debated topics with little consensus.

Theoretical development regarding violence against women evolved within multiple disciplines. However, within each discipline, theory development took the form of singular explanations with strong disciplinary biases (Hiese 1998). More recent studies on violence against women acknowledge the need to address gendered violence at multiple levels (Crowell and Burgess 1996; Hiese 1998; Koss 2000; Miller 1994; White and Kowalski 1998). Hiese (1998) noted that:

The task of theory building has been severely hampered by the narrowness of traditional academic disciplines and by the tendency of both academics and activists to advance single-factor theories rather than explanations that reflect the full complexity and messiness of real life. (p. 262)

One such single-factor theory of rape was published by Thornhill and Palmer (2000). They argue that rape can be understood in an evolutionary framework as a behavioral adaptation molded by sexual selection. In sum, Thornhill and Palmer see rape as a biological phenomenon with a reproductive agenda. Other authors in this book respond to the merits (or lack thereof) of Thornhill and Palmer's work from a Darwinian or sociobiological basis. Although it is possible to consider rape as having some biological foundation, Thornhill and Palmer present more of an ideological basis for their theory rather than one grounded in empirical evidence. Additionally, their work neglects the past 25 years of literature in the nascent field of evolutionary psychology, as well as in social psychology and sociology. Because critiques of Thornhill and Palmer's work from biological and evolutionary perspectives are addressed in other chapters in this book, this chapter will focus on rape as a complex multifactor phenomenon and argue for a theoretical approach and research methods that are sophisticated enough to accommodate the complexities. Instead of conceptualizing rape within a singular theoretical framework, we posit rape should be understood within a metatheoretical model that recognizes and integrates factors across several levels of analysis.

This chapter will discuss empirical research on rape in the context of the integrated contextual developmental model of violence against women (White and Kowalski 1998). This approach provides a more comprehensive account of rape than any account that relies on just one level of analysis (Koss 2000). The model recognizes commonalities across various forms of violence against women, argues for the multiply determined nature of rape, and can readily account for variability in rape proclivity among men. Prior to the discussion of the integrated contextual model, a brief overview of current issues and findings in rape research is presented. This is followed by a brief overview and critique of the traditional accounts of rape. The inadequacies of these single-factor theories to account for rape serve as a basis for the development of the integrated contextual model.

A Complex Phenomenon Requires Complex Theorizing

A number of factors suggest the need for a theory of rape that recognizes it as a complex phenomenon. As we discuss below, variations in definitions of sexual coercion and rape and variations in incidence and prevalence rates, as well as differences among those more and less likely to be involved in sexual assault, attest to the need for a theory that can account for these variations.

Defining Sexual Assault

Recognizing the complexities associated with defining sexual assault and rape underscores the need for a theoretical model that acknowledges and accounts for these complexities. There are clear incongruities between legal and social definitions of what constitutes "real rape" (see Martin, this volume). Susan Brownmiller (1975) noted that

the question of "What is a rape?" is not answered by a powerful legal litmus test but through a system of beliefs that drive from a misogynistic social context, the "rape culture." (p. 436)

Defining rape is difficult both legally and socially. The legal definition is problematic as it varies from state to state. Furthermore, state definitions are not consistent with federal definitions and vary over time. The FBI legal definition of rape differs from state police agencies in that they do not include same-sex rape and forms of sexual penetration outside of penile/vaginal penetration (Kuecker 1999). Also, in many states consensual sex between males is still considered a sexual crime. Many states such as Michigan have updated their rape laws and are moving toward degrees of criminal sexual conduct (Tomaselli and Porter 1986). On a positive note, the new Criminal Sexual Conduct (CSC) codes are much improved; however, they place a hierarchy on crimes whereas murder trumps rape or CSC first degree. The FBI's indexing of serious crimes (also known as Uniform Crime Reports) records crime and not motivation of crime; therefore, sexually motivated homicides are solely recorded as homicides. Other crimes trump lesser CSC degrees, that is, armed robbery trumps CSC third degree. So, in defining the crime, many cases of sexual violence are "lost" by definition.

Sexual assault, sexual coercion, and sexual aggression are all terms used to refer to instances in which one person engages in sexual behavior against another's will. These terms encompass acts that range from unwanted sexual contact, such as forced kissing or the fondling of breasts and/or genitals, to attempted rape and rape. Coercive tactics may range from psychological pressure (i.e., threatening to end the relationship, saying things he does not mean, such as falsely professing love), verbal persuasion ("if you loved me, you'd let me"; "you owe it to me"), verbal threats of harm, use of alcohol and drugs, physical intimidation, mild physical force (pushing, slapping, holding down), severe physical force (beating, choking), to displaying or using a weapon.

The term rape has been shown to have different meanings for women and men, as well as different segments of the community such as police officers and mental health counselors (see White and Humphrey 1991 for a review). Some people are hesitant to label forced sex between acquaintances as rape, particularly if any of the following circumstances are present: The man initiated the date; he spent a great deal of money; the couple went to his place; there had been drinking, kissing, and petting; the couple had been sexually intimate on previous occasions; the woman had sex with other men (Goodchilds et al. 1989; Muehlenhard and Linton 1987); or "no" was not explicitly verbalized (Sawyer, Pinciaro, and Jessell 1998). College students in general, and sexually aggressive men in particular, believe that sexual precedence (i.e., a past history of sexual intercourse) reduces the legitimacy of sexual refusal (Shotland and Goodstein 1992).

The reluctance to use the label rape is apparent in recent criticisms appearing in the popular press (i.e., trade books, such as Roiphe 1993; newspaper articles and magazine features, see Collison 1992) questioning the veracity of rape statistics. These critics suggest that if young women do not label their experiences as rape, then they are not victims (Gilbert 1993). Of course, this is illogical. Although a woman may not realize that forced sexual intercourse by an acquaintance during a date is rape, this does not change the legal definition of the act as rape, nor does it reduce the culpability of the perpetrator (Koss 1994). Furthermore, whether or not a sexual assault is labeled rape, it has serious consequences.

Variations in the Frequency of Sexual Assault

Estimates of the frequency of sexual assault vary across cultures (Rozee 1993), across ethnic groups (Marsh 1993; Sorenson and Siegel 1991), regions (George, Winfield, and Blazer 1992; Wyatt 1992), and across definitions and research methods (Fisher 2000; Koss 1992), as well as being affected by who reports assaults and under what circumstances. These variations, in conjunction with different definitions of sexual assault and rape, call for a theoretical perspective that can account for such complexities.

Rape is the crime least likely to be reported and, if reported, the least likely to result in a conviction, particularly if committed by an acquaintance. Not only do many women not report their assault to the authorities, many never tell anyone. Thus, crime statistics greatly underestimate the frequency of rape by as much as 50 to 90 percent (Gise and Paddison 1988). Researchers must rely on large-scale surveys of women to obtain more accurate estimates of victimization rates. Women are asked about a number of sexual experiences that may have involved force or threat of force, some of which meet the legal criteria for rape, rather than being asked directly "Have you ever been raped?" This is important because many victimized women (73 percent) never label forced sexual intercourse as rape. This approach has suggested that the actual rape victimization rate is 10 to 15 times greater than corresponding FBI estimates (Koss 1992). Because most of these unlabeled, unreported rape experiences are perpetrated by acquaintances, acquaintance rape has been labeled a "hidden" crime (Koss 1985, 1989).

A comprehensive survey asked over 3,000 college women from 32 institutions of higher education across the United States about sexual experiences since the age of 14 (Koss et al. 1987). Of those surveyed, over half (53.7 percent) had experienced some form of sexual victimization; 15.4 percent had experienced acts by a man that met the legal definition of rape (though only 27 percent labeled the experience rape), and 12.1 percent, attempted rape. An additional 11.9 percent had been verbally pressured into sexual intercourse, and the remaining 14.4 percent had experienced some other form of unwanted sexual contact, such as forced kissing or fondling with no attempted penetration. More recent studies confirm these high numbers among Canadians (DeKeseredy 1997), as well as among a probability sample of 8,000 women in the United States (Tjaden and Thoennes 1998). Community-based surveys have found that 25 percent of African-American women, 20 percent white women (Wyatt 1985), and 8 percent Hispanic women (Sorenson and Siegel 1991) reported at least one sexual assault experience in their lifetime. High school women also appear to be at greater risk for rape than previously thought. A recent survey of 1569 entering college students found that 13 percent reported being raped between the ages of 14 and 18, and an additional 16 percent reported being victims of an attempted rape (Humphrey and White 2000).

Who Is at Risk?

Research confirms that not all women are equally likely to be sexually victimized. Numerous studies have been conducted to identify risk factors for sexual victimization, most with little success. The greatest risk factor is being female. Although men are also sexually victimized, the likelihood is less than for women. Age is also a risk factor, with adolescence being the period of greatest vulnerability; during adolescence the risk of first being victimized increases steadily from age 14 to 18 and declines thereafter (Humphrey and White 2000). Another risk factor is being a college student; sexual victimization rates are about three times higher among college students than in the general population (Aizenman and Kelley 1988; Koss et al. 1987), although recently the opposite has been found (Zweig, Barber, and Eccles 1997). Other risk factors have been difficult to determine. Several researchers have confirmed that the best predictor of victimization is past victimization; typically childhood victimization increases the risk of adolescent victimization, which in turn increases the risk of victimization as a young adult (Collins 1998; Gidycz et al. 1993; Mills and Granoff 1992; Humphrey and White 2000; Wyatt, Guthrie, and Notgrass 1992). Additionally, childhood victimization has been related to earlier age of menarche and sexual activity (Vicary, Klingman, and Harkness 1995), as well as alcohol use. It is likely that alcohol is implicated in several ways. Women with a history of victimization may turn to alcohol as a means of coping. Unfortunately, alcohol and other substance abuse put women at increased risks of sexual victimization (Norris, Nurius, and Graham 1999; Richardson and Hammock 1990).

Who Does This?

Not only are all women not equally likely to be victims of sexual assault, all men are not prone to sexual assault and rape. The survey (Koss et al. 1987) described above also examined the sexual experiences of over 2900 college men. Of this group, 4.4 percent admitted to behaviors meeting the legal definition of rape, 3.3 percent admitted to attempted rape, 7.2 percent to sexual coercion, and 10.2 percent to forced or coerced sexual contact, indicated that 25.1 percent of the college men admit to some form of sexual aggression. Similar rates have been reported in community samples (Calhoun et al. 1997) and in a community college sample (Lowdermilk, Holland, Cameron, and White 1998).

The typical acquaintance rapist appears to be a "normal" guy. He is not a crazed psychopath, although he may display psychopathy-related traits (Kosson, Kelly, and White 1997). Among college students, alcohol use (Koss and Gaines 1993; White and Humphrey 1994), athletic affiliation (Jackson 1991; Frintner and Rubinson 1993; Koss and Gaines 1993), and fraternity membership (Frintner and Rubinson 1993, but cf. Koss and Gaines 1993) have been associated with sexual aggression toward women. Other significant correlates of sexual assault include a history of family violence; an early and varied sexual history, including many sexual partners; a history of delinquency; acceptance of rape myths; sexual promiscuity; hostility toward women; self-centeredness; low empathy; an impulsive personality; hedonistic and dominance motives for sex; lower than average sense of self-worth; and lower religiosity; as well as peers who condone and encourage sexual conquests (see White and Koss 1991 for a review). Finally, sexually aggressive men are more likely to perceive a wider range of behaviors as indicative of sexual interest than do non–sexually aggressive men (Bondurant and Donat 1999) and are attracted to sexual aggression (Calhoun et al. 1997).

Theories of Aggression Applied to Rape

Ideally, a theory should address and be able to account for variation in definition, incidence, and prevalence, as well as variation in characteristics of victims and perpetrators. Unfortunately, most traditional theories do not do this. These theories tend to address aggression and violence only at the individual level and do not address gender as a central construct (White and Kowalski 1998). Empirically, we have substantiated the pervasiveness and variability of rape as well as risk factors. Singular explanations do not suffice to explain rape. To this end, we will first discuss single-factor theories and then integrate them into a metatheoretical model to better capture the complexities of rape.

Popular belief regarding aggression assumed that men have always been aggressive because of God's design and/or biological determinants; men's aggressiveness was seen as universal and natural (Lerner 1986). Lerner's historical analysis of the origins of patriarchy argues that male aggression is rooted in a warrior culture. However, we must first consider human behavior across time. Humans have existed as the species genus *Homo sapiens* for tens of thousands of years. Human activities have been recorded for less than 1 percent of that time; therefore, it is difficult to accurately assess the presence and circumstances of violence, rape, and warrior cultures in prerecorded history. Thus, it is not prudent to assess male aggression as natural or universal with less than a 1 percent accounting of human history and significant evidence to the contrary on the remaining time spent as foragers.

Anthropologists turn to modern day hunter-gatherers to shed light on ancient humans as well as examine archeological findings for evidence of ancient warring societies (Carman and Harding 1999). Hunter-gatherers or foragers can be meaningfully referred to as the "human state of nature" as humans have lived in this state for 99.5 percent of their existence (Gat 2000). "Available evidence contradicts the assumption that warfare was a regular part of our ancestral environment of evolutionary adaptation" (Ferguson 2000, p. 167). In modern-day hunter-gatherer groups, there is evidence of more egalitarian male-female relationships, although there exist gendered divisions of labor (Mascia-Lees and Black 2000; Shostak 1981; and Ward 1999). "It is generally agreed that the sexual division of labor in foraging groups was relatively equalitarian" (Ward 1999; p. 25). Women did not wait around the camp while the men were out hunting; rather, foraging for food required the participation of all members of the social group, whose structure neared equality (Friedl 1975; Mascia-Lees and Black 2000). Inequality appears to increase when resources are stressed or nomads are forced into settlement (Gat 2000; Shostak 1981) but not in all cases (Ferguson 2000). Focusing on gender inequality and theories of aggression sheds light on the etiologies of rape; however, we cannot infer that warring cultures or rape are inherent in the "human state of nature."

After early humans turned to land possession and agriculture, Blumberg (1978) suggests the division of labor became more pronounced in these horticultural societies. According to Vannoy (2001), gender stratification became more severe over time as populations increased and economic/political systems evolved into more complex forms with industrialism leading to the most pronounced forms of inequality between social groups. Agrarian and industrial societies comprises less than 1 percent of human history. Most social theories connect the origins of gender stratification with the sexual division of labor and ownership of the means of production (Chafetz 1988).

Theories regarding gender inequality have been cataloged variously as biological, social, cultural, anthropological, political, and psychological. Although it is beyond the scope of this chapter to review fully all the various theories, several exemplars will be described.

Biological theories of aggression proposed that men are more aggressive than women because of higher testosterone levels (Johnson 1972). Thus, male violence is associated with their biologically based gender identity (Balkan et al. 1980; see Salzman 1979 for a critique of the biologically based accounts of gender differences in aggression). Sociobiological theories also suggest genetic or hormonal paths to sexual aggression (see Ellis 1991). Freud (1901) melded biological and instinctual factors with unconscious psychological processes to posit an early "modern" personality theory of aggression. Male aggression was rooted in resolution of the Oedipal complex. Aggression directed toward others was seen as normal and a compensation for the frustration of childhood sexual instincts. Some contemporary psychoanalysts have suggested that women and men possess the same drives and impulses, but "differ exclusively in how drives and aggressive impulses are worked through and expressed . . . [and] may to a large extent be explained on the basis of forms and practices of child rearing" (Mitscherlich 1987, p. 224). This results in men turning aggression outward and women turning aggression inward. Reinterpretation of Freudian theory into learning terms led Dollard et al. (1939) to posit the frustration-aggression hypothesis. In contrast, social learning theories (Bandura 1973) stress the differential socialization experiences of men and women. Gender socialization theories explain rape as rooted in the dominant culture with its emphasis on masculinity and learned patterns of aggression and domination (Andersen 1997). The mechanisms of social learning (including rewards, punishments, and modeling) result in different gender-related expectations and in different behavioral outcomes for women and men.

Social disorganization theory is an exemplar of a sociological approach to crime and deviancy. Emanating from Shaw and McKay's research out of the Chicago School (1942), Shaw and McKay hypothesized violence and crime as symptomatic of communities disrupted by disorganizing factors such as migration, divorce, and cultural heterogeneity. Baron extrapolates crime and deviance to include rape: "To the extent that marital disruption and migration are disorganizing factors, such conditions may reduce social constraints against rape" (Baron and Straus 1989, p. 10). Hirschi (1969) further developed the social disorganizing theory to include "control" as a function of the connection an individual has to the greater social structure. Control theory addresses linkages between the individual and friends and family; time and energy invested in a future goal such as education, a career or reputation; involvement in community activities such as school or work; and commitment to the existing culture's mores and values. When extrapolating macrosociological theories to rape, control theory explains why men rape whereas social disorganization theory explains why some communities have more rape than other communities. Social disorganization, control, and psychological theories are based on deviances from mainstream society, whereas gender socialization theory poses rape as an exaggeration of traditional gender roles. In sum, men rape because they have learned that rape is acceptable and normal behavior (Andersen 1997).

Currently, feminist models are being developed that acknowledge explicitly the socially constructed meanings of aggression, violence, and rape (Bourque 1989; White and Humphrey 1991; White, Donat, and Bondurant 2001). These meanings affect how and when forced sexual intercourse is acknowledged and under what circumstances it is labeled rape (Donat and White 2000). Feminist analyses of power relations indicate that men have defined what constitutes rape, effectively silencing women with regard to their experiences. Mitscherlich (1987) stated, "those who dominate define what constitutes violence . . . those in power can alone stipulate whose job it is to be maternal and gentle and when" (p. 10). What remains is an androcentric rational means-ends analysis that fails to account fully for the contextualized nature of women's experiences.

Feminist theories also emphasize the need to understand rape in terms of the status of women in society—to reveal, acknowledge, and define it from the woman's perspective. The intersection of race, class, and gender is of central importance to these theories. Feminists agree with the assertions of social learning theorists regarding the effects of social arrangements on the likelihood of rape. However, feminists push the analysis further to bring to center stage patriarchy, with its attendant differential status and power. The power differences between women and men, along with women's restricted opportunities and resources, contribute to an increased likelihood of female victimization, especially in interpersonal relationships rather than in other contexts.

An Integrated Contextual Developmental Model

White and Kowalski (1998) proposed a model to integrate a wide range of factors across various forms of gendered violence (see figure 16.1). The model provides a metatheoretical framework within which to think about violence against women. It is intended to guide researchers in the generation of substantive hypotheses derived from various theoretical perspectives and argues for systematic research across levels of analysis. It is derived from the ecological model of Bronfenbrenner (1979) (see also Dutton 1988; Lerner 1991; Williams, Guerra, and Elliott 1999). The model describes five levels of interacting factors: sociocultural (including historical, cultural, and community traditions and values), social networks, dyadic, situational, and intrapersonal. This perspective examines individual behavior in context.

Time is a critical component of the model, based on the assumption that effects change across time and are cumulative. The most distal influences

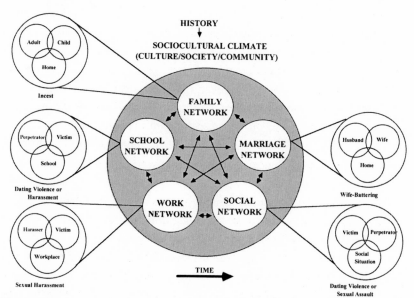

Figure 16.1
An integrative contextual developmental model of violence against women.

are historical and sociocultural. Embedded in these are a number of inter-connected relationships a person has (or may have at different points across the lifespan) and includes family, social life, school, and work. Within each network is embedded a relationship between two individuals, the potential perpetrator and potential victim. These two individuals have an interaction history that will influence their behaviors in any given situation; the situation provides the proximal cues for aggression and violence. All these factors coalesce to determine the particular behavioral manifestation of aggression (i.e., direct, indirect; verbal, physical, sexual). Certain situational factors will increase the likelihood of an aggressive encounter.

This integrative contextual developmental perspective suggests that intrapersonal variables are expressed within a cultural and social context, while also reflecting the influences of personality, attitudes and beliefs, cognitive processes, and learning history. Thus, certain intrapersonal variables predict violence, but only in specific situations (White and Humphrey 1997).

The model assumes that patriarchy operating at the historical/sociocultural level affects the power dynamics of all relationships. Shared patterns of ideas and beliefs passed down from generation to generation define one's social networks. Historical and sociocultural factors create an environment in which the growing child learns rules and expectations, first in the family network, and later in peer, intimate, and work relationships. Early experiences define the context for later experiences (Huesmann and Eron 1992; Olweus 1993; White and Bondurant 1996). Embedded in these social networks are characteristics of the personal relationships in which individuals act violently. Power dynamics become enacted in social networks and result in the internalization of gendered values, expectations, and behaviors. Thus, cultural norms governing the use of aggression as a tool of the more powerful to subdue the weaker combine with gender inequalities to create a climate conducive to violence. Violence is inextricably bound to the social context of male domination and control. Rape represents an extreme behavioral manifestation on the continuum of dominance and control. The patriarchal view of society gives men a higher value than women. Patriarchy takes it for granted that men should dominate in politics, economics, and the social world including family life and interpersonal relationships. This model can be applied specifically to an understanding of rape as a particular type of violence against women.

Sociocultural Level

The sociocultural level of analysis examines historical, cultural, social, institutional, and community influences on behavior at the macrolevel of analysis. In this context, history serves as a means of transmitting sociocultural attitudes and beliefs regarding gender and rape. Sexual violence is perpetuated insofar as cultural traditions are reproduced and transmitted from generation to generation (see Wyatt 1992 for a discussion of how rape stories have been transmitted among African Americans from the time of slavery to the present).

Modern histories tend to be ethnocentric, plagued with Western bias and devoid of the histories of Asia, Africa, precolonial Americas, and Australia. This Western bias extends to studies of feminism as well as violence (Samarasinghe 1994; Young and Dickerson 1994). Additionally, historical accounts of rape have been minimal until recently. It is only the recent women's movement and activism that has given rape a place in history (Lerner 1986; Porter 1986). However, there are accounts of rape, patriarchy, and the devaluation of females in ancient Hebrew, Greek, Roman, and Christian societies (Holmes 1991).

A great deal of macrolevel research, especially in the sociological tradition, has documented the role that sociocultural factors play in rape (Baron and Straus 1989; Rozee 1993; Sanday 1981). Baron and Straus (1989) suggest that cultures with pervasive legitimate violence are more conducive to sexual violence. Legitimate violence may be reflected in a variety of cultural activities such as mass media violence saturation, and government-sanctioned violence as in the death penalty, violent sports, hunting, and so on. In sum, cultural support for rape is not limited to beliefs and attitudes regarding rape; various cultural elements also indirectly support rape. This would be expected in cultures where violence is the norm and where legitimate violence spills over to sexual expression.

Other sociocultural factors implicated in rape include sexual inequalities, gender role prescriptions (including dating and sexual scripts), and cultural norms and myths about women, men, children, family, sex, and violence, as well as scripts for enacting relationships. Expectations about the appropriate roles for men and women are communicated through various institutionalized practices of a society, including those of the legal system, the church, schools, media, politics, and the military. All set the stage for the evolution of cultural myths that perpetuate male violence against women. During adolescence, young men and women experience extreme pressure to conform to traditional gender role expectations. It appears that violence in adolescence is so prevalent, in part, because of the overall structure and meaning of maleness in our culture that encourages boys to feel entitled to power at any cost. Scripts for being male or female are fairly well defined and have not changed much over several decades. A script is a set of rules to be followed. Dating and sexual scripts in particular afford men greater power relative to women (Breines and Gordon 1983; La-Plante, McCormick, and Brannigan 1990; Rose and Frieze 1993). Women are assumed to be responsible for "how far things go," and if things "get out of hand," it is their fault. Men who endorse traditional scripts are more likely than men who do not to perceive force and coercion as acceptable means of obtaining desired outcomes regardless of the circumstances (Goodchilds et al. 1989).

Cultures in which less traditional gender roles are prescribed and in which male dominance and female subordination are not encouraged show fewer instances of male violence against women, supporting the idea of sociocultural contributions to such violence (Rozee 1993). However, although all men within a given culture are typically exposed to similar sociocultural pressures to behave in accordance with their assigned gender roles, not all men are violent, nor do they rape. One reason not all men are violent lies in the multiply determined nature of violence. Embedded within one's culture are social, dyadic, situational, and individual influences that may either increase the likelihood of violence or mitigate against it.

Social Network Level

The social network level of analysis focuses on one's history of personal experiences within various social institutions (family, peers, school, faith community, and work settings). The gendered norms and expectations that contribute to violence are transmitted through these institutions. Witnessing and experiencing violence in the family of origin alters the likelihood of later involvement in violent episodes. Men who either witnessed or experienced violence as a child show a higher likelihood of delinquency, as well as being sexually (Koss and Dinero 1989) and physically aggressive in dating situations (Kalmuss 1984; Straus, Gelles, and Steinmetz 1980). As with the family unit, other social networks may promote a system of values that reflects sociocultural understandings of gender inequality.

Within these networks, the acceptance of interpersonal violence may be encouraged and rewarded. For example, exposure to delinquent peer groups, whether at school, work, or in the community at large, has been shown to be related to delinquency in general (Ellickson and McGuigan 2000), as well as dating violence and sexual assault (Ageton 1983; Gwartney-Gibbs, Stockard, and Brohmer 1983; White and Koss 1991).

The gender-related patterns learned in childhood are played out in adolescent dating and committed relationships. Young people usually begin dating in high school, although children as young as kindergartners talk about having boyfriends and girlfriends. The idea of being paired with a member of the other sex is pervasive in our society. Traditionally, it has been assumed that children's "playing house," and later, dating provide a context for socialization into later roles, including husband, wife, lover, and confidante (Rice 1984). Dating also offers opportunities for companionship, status, sexual experimentation, and conflict resolution. However, courtship has different meanings for young women and men (Lloyd 1991). Whereas for men courtship involves themes of "staying in control," for women themes involve "dependence on the relationship." Violence is one of the tactics used to gain control in a relationship, as is discussed further in the next section.

Dyadic Level

Whereas social networks focus attention on a perpetrator and victim's history of interpersonal relationships, particularly within the family and peer groups, the dyadic level focuses on the nature of one specific relationship, the one between the perpetrator and victim. Crime statistics tell us that individuals are more likely to be victimized by someone they know than by a stranger; this is particularly true for women. Approximately 85 percent of all sexual assaults are perpetrated by someone at least casually known to the victim. Romantic partners commit as many as 57 percent of all assaults (Koss 1990). Several researchers have found that violence is more likely to occur in serious than in casual relationships (Pedersen and Thomas 1992), suggesting that violence in more committed relationships may reflect the acceptance of violence as a legitimate mode of conflict resolution (Billingham 1983). On the other hand, violence in a developing relationship may be a way of "testing the relative safety of a relationship before movement to greater commitment is risked" (Billingham 1987,

p. 288). Shotland (1992) has suggested that rape serves different functions at different stages in a relationship. In the early stages of dating, rape may actually be a strategy some men use to obtain sex. These men are more likely to have antisocial tendencies and hold misogynist and rape-supportive attitudes. However, during the later stages of dating, Shotland suggests that a couples' sexual ground rules have probably been established; however, if they do not allow for the level of sexual intimacy desired by the male he may experience anger, which, combined with his sexual arousal, may contribute to the likelihood of rape. Finally, Shotland suggests that some men may see sexual intimacy as a sign of a more intense relationship and resort to force if his partner does not share that view.

Sexual and dating violence are more likely in relationships plagued by problems, including jealousy, fighting, interference from friends, lack of time together, breakdown of the relationship, and problems outside the relationship (Riggs 1993), as well as disagreements about drinking and sexual denial (Roscoe and Kelsey 1986). These are the conflicts young people report most frequently leading to feelings of confusion and anger and resulting in violence (Sugarman and Hotaling 1989). Malamuth et al. (1995) have shown that relationship distress predicts verbal and physical violence.

Nonverbal and verbal communication patterns between the members of the dyad may set the stage for violent interactions. More specifically, men and women do not always perceive behaviors in exactly the same way. Some men interpret women's behavior in more sexualized ways than it was intended (Abbey 1991; Kowalski 1992, 1993), do not take her verbal protestations seriously (Check and Malamuth 1983), and perceive the woman's rejection of sexual advances as a threat to their manhood (Beneke 1982). According to Kowalski (1993), men who endorse adversarial sexual beliefs and interpersonal violence are more likely to misinterpret a woman's behavior as sexually connotative than men who do not hold such beliefs. Similarly, women may enter dating relationships with a cognitive set toward trust, companionship, and having a good time, and hence be less alert to the warning signs of assault (Nurius and Norris 1996).

According to Thornhill and Palmer, when access to women via looks, wealth, or status is not available, men are more likely to rape. However, there are no data to support such a claim. In fact, Makepeace (1987) has presented evidence that some men are more likely to assault women of lower status than themselves. Furthermore, sexually aggressive men typically have more consensual sexual partners than nonsexually aggressive men (Koss and Dinero 1989; Makepeace 1989; White and Humphrey 1995).

Situational Level

The situational level of analysis focuses on situational variables that increase or decrease the likelihood of interpersonal violence (Craig 1990). For violence to occur, the situation must be conducive to the violence. Features of the situation influence the likelihood that violence will occur by affecting the opportunity for violent acts (i.e., times when privacy is available and detection minimal) and/or by contributing to the ambiguity of the situation (White and Koss 1991). The routine activities model of crime emphasizes the role of opportunity (Cohen and Felson 1979, 1981). Situations that include violent cues are likely to promote violence, especially for men (Bettencourt and Kernahan 1997). A number of situational variables, including time of day, location, and the presence of social inhibitors or disinhibitors, such as alcohol and drugs, are known to affect the likelihood of crime differentially for women and men. According to the U.S. Department of Justice (1997), women are more likely to be the victim of crime during daylight hours (54 percent) than at dark, the more likely time for men (47 percent). A private home is the most likely site of victimization for women, or a private vehicle if they are traveling. Not surprisingly then, courtship violence is most likely to occur in private settings (Laner 1983; Roscoe and Kelsey 1986) and on weekends (Olday and Wesley 1983). Alcohol and drugs are also related to incidents of rape (Pagelow 1984). Alcohol acts as a disinhibitor for the man, as an excuse for the rape after it has occurred, and as a means of reducing the victim's resistance (Richardson and Hammock 1991). In cases of dating violence, alcohol use is common (LeJeune and Follette 1994; Williams and Smith 1994). In cases of acquaintance rape, alcohol may enhance ambiguity by increasing the likelihood that men may misinterpret a woman's friendly behaviors as sexual (Abbey 1991). Some men may interpret a woman's consumption of alcohol as an indication that she is "loose."

Individual Level

The most developed theories of violence occur at the individual level of analysis. The focus at the individual level is on attitudinal, motivational, and characterological features of the individual. However, it is recognized that individual attributes typically emerge as the result of experiences in various social networks. Thus, there is a dynamic interplay between factors operating at these various levels. For example, the attitudinal underpinnings of rape, in particular, the endorsement of traditional sex-role stereotypes and cultural myths about rape, often stem from being reared in households where violence was considered normative. The extent to which these specific individual variables influence the incidence of rape depends on the degree to which cultural norms and the influence of social groups affect individual mental representations of the situation and the relationship with the victim.

Certain personality and behavioral variables have been identified in individuals with a history of rape and include antisocial tendencies (Malamuth 1986), nonconformity (Rapaport and Burkhart 1984), impulsivity (Calhoun 1990), low socialization and responsibility (Barnett and Hamberger 1992; Rapaport and Burkhart 1984), hypermasculinity, delinquent behavior, affective dysregulation (Hall and Hirschman 1991; Murphy, Meyer, and O'Leary 1993) and self-centeredness coupled with insensitivity to others (Dean and Malamuth 1997).

Violence in intimate relationships has been associated with the endorsement of traditional sex-role stereotypes and cultural myths about violence. Relative to non–sexually aggressive men, sexually aggressive men more strongly subscribe to traditional gender stereotypes (Burt 1980; Malamuth 1988; Mosher and Anderson 1986; Rapaport and Burkhart 1984). Similar findings have been obtained in studies examining the characteristics of men who abuse their dating partners or spouses (Dutton 1988). A history of promiscuous-impersonal sex and hostile masculinity (distrust of women combined with gratification from dominating women) represent factors associated with sexual violence toward a female partner (Malamuth et al. 1995; Malamuth 1996).

Furthermore, a man's need for power, dominance, and control appears to play a role in violent behavior. A man who feels threatened by a loss of control, such as by being rejected, may attempt to regain that control by behaving aggressively. A consideration of the components of the violent acts perpetrated against women (i.e., intimidation, coercion, belittlement) suggests that motives for power and dominance bear some relationship to the incidence of violence. Men who are quick to react to anger, believe that violence will aid in winning an argument, and have successfully used violence in other situations are likely to do so again (Riggs and Caufield 1997;

White, Koss, and Kissling 1991). Similarities between men who engage in courtship violence and wife-batterers have been found (Ryan 1995).

Conclusions

To understand violence we must first recognize that culturally based socialization practices encourage men to be aggressors and women to be victims (Andersen 1997). In societies where there is no formal hierarchy that privileges one group over another and in which women and men exercise relatively equal power, general levels of aggression, male violence against women, and rape are low (Lepowsky 1994; see also Sanday, this volume). Gendered violence is learned early in life and continues across the lifespan (Kaufman 1995). Data from numerous sources reveal the social influences and overall patterns of gendered violence found in society (Andersen 1997). They reveal that women are the victims of intimate violence more often than men at every stage of development, with the exception of early childhood physical abuse. The data also demonstrate that not all women are victims of violence nor are all men perpetrators (Andersen 1997). These same patterns hold for rape as well.

Inequality in relationships, coupled with cultural values that embrace domination of the weaker by the stronger, creates the potential for rape. Both men and women learn that violence is a method people use to get their way. When individuals use force and are successful, they are reinforced and thus more likely to use it in the future; however, men have historically received greater rewards for aggression and violence than have women.

In this chapter we argue that the integrative contextual developmental model (White and Kowalski 1998) is useful for accounting for the complexities associated with sexual assault and rape. The model can better account for why some men rape and why some women are raped than a singular explanation, such as that of Thornhill and Palmer. The model suggests that a fuller understanding of rape can be achieved by examining it systematically at several levels, cultural, social, interpersonal, situational, and intrapersonal. Dynamic factors at each level operate to affect the likelihood of who will rape, who will be raped, and when rape is most likely. The proposed metatheoretical model can also help understand the various factors that affect when the term rape will and will not be used to label acts of forced sexual intercourse.

References

Abbey, A. (1991). Misperceptions as an antecedent of acquaintance rape: A consequence of ambiguity in communication between men and women. In A. Parrott and L. Bechhofer, eds., *Acquaintance Rape: The Hidden Crime*, pp. 96–112. New York: Wiley.

Ageton, S. S. (1983). *Sexual Assault among Adolescents*. Lexington, Mass.: D. C. Heath.

Aizenman, M. and G. Kelley (1988). The incidence of violence and acquaintance rape in dating relationships among college men and women. *Journal of College Student Development* 29: 305–311.

Amir, M. (1971). *Patterns in Forcible Rape*. Chicago: University of Chicago Press.

Andersen, Margaret L. (1997). *Thinking about Women: Sociological Perspectives on Sex and Gender*, fourth ed. New York: Allyn and Bacon.

Balkan, S., R. J. Berger, and J. Schmidt (1980). *Crime and Deviance in America: A Critical Approach*. Belmont, Calif.: Wadsworth Publishing.

Bandura, A. (1973). *Aggression: A Social Learning Process*. Englewood Cliffs, N.J.: Prentice-Hall.

Barnett, O. and L. K. Hamberger (1992). The assessment of martially violent men on the California Psychological Inventory. *Violence and Victims* 7: 15–22.

Baron, L. and M. A. Straus (1989). *Four Theories of Rape in American Society: A State-level Analysis*. New Haven: Yale University Press.

Beneke, T. (1982). *Men Who Rape*. New York: St. Martin's Press.

Bettencourt, B. A. and C. Kernahan (1997). A meta-analysis of aggression in the presence of violent cues: Effects of gender differences and aversive provocation. *Aggressive Behavior* 23: 447–456.

Billingham, R. E. (1987). Courtship violence: The patterns of conflict resolution strategies across seven levels of emotional commitment. *Family Relations* 36: 283–289.

Blumberg, R. L. (1984). A general theory of gender stratification. *Sociological Theory* 2: 23–101.

Bondurant, B. and P. L. N. Donat (1999). Perceptions of women's sexual interest and acquaintance rape: The role of sexual overperception and affective attitudes. *Psychology of Women Quarterly* 23: 691–705.

Bourque, L. (1989). *Defining Rape*. Durham, N.C.: Duke University Press.

Breines, W. and L. Gordon (1983). The new scholarship on family violence. *Signs* 8: 490–531.

Bronfenbrenner, U. (1979). *The Ecology of Human Development*. Cambridge, Mass.: Harvard University Press.

Brownmiller, S. (1975). *Against Our Will: Men, Women, and Rape*. New York: Simon and Schuster.

Burt, M. R. (1980). Cultural myths and supports for rape. *Journal of Personality and Social Psychology* 38: 217–230.

Calhoun, K. (1990). *Lies, Sex, and Videotapes: Studies in Sexual Aggression.* Presidential address to the Southeastern Psychological Association, Atlanta, Ga., March.

Calhoun, K. S., J. A. Bernat, G. A. Clum, and C. L. Frame (1997). Sexual coercion and attraction to sexual aggression in a community sample of young men. *Journal of Interpersonal Violence* 12 (1): 392–406.

Carlson, C. (1990). *Perspectives on the Family: History, Class, and Feminism.* Wadsworth Publishing Company.

Carman, J. and A. Harding (1999). *Ancient Warfare: Archaeological Perspectives.* Trowbridge, Wiltshire: Sutton Publishing.

Chafetz, J. S. (1988). *Feminist Sociology: An Overview of Contemporary Theories.* Itasca, Ill.: F. E. Peacock Publishers.

Check, J. V. P. and N. M. Malamuth (1983). Sex role stereotyping and reactions to depictions of stranger versus acquaintance rape. *Journal of Personality and Social Psychology* 45: 344–356.

Cohen, L. E. and M. Felson (1979). Social change and crime rate trends: A routine activity approach. *American Sociological Review* 44: 588–608.

Collins, M. E. (1998). Factors influencing sexual victimization and revictimization in a sample of adolescent mothers. *Journal of Interpersonal Violence* 3: 3–24.

Collison, M. N.-K. (1992). Scholar clashes with feminists over date rape data. *Chronicle of Higher Education,* Feb. 26.

Craig, M. (1990). Coercive sexuality in dating relationships: A situational model. *Clinical Psychology Review* 10: 395–423.

Crowell, N. A. and A. W. Burgess (1996). *Understanding Violence against Women.* Washington, D.C.: National Academy Press.

Dean, K. E. and N. Malamuth (1997). Characteristics of men who aggress sexually and of men who imagine aggressing: Risk and moderating variables. *Journal of Personality and Social Psychology* 72: 449–455.

DeKeseredy, W. S. (1997). Measuring sexual abuse in Canadian university/college dating relationships: The contribution of a national representative sample survey. In M. D. Schwartz, ed., *Researching Sexual Violence against Women: Methodological and Personal Perspectives,* pp. 43–53. Thousand Oaks, Calif.: Sage.

Dollard, J., L. Doob, N. Miller, O. Mowrer, and R. Sears (1939). *Frustration and Aggression.* New Haven: Yale University Press.

Donat, P. L. N. and J. W. White (2000). The social construction of consent: Sexual scripts and acquaintance rape. In C. T. Travis and J. W. White, eds., *Sex, Culture, and Feminism: Psychological Perspectives on Women,* pp. 355–376. Washington, D.C.: American Psychological Association.

Dutton, D. (1988). *The Domestic Assault of Women: Psychological and Criminal Justice Perspectives.* New York: Allyn and Bacon.

Ellickson, P. L. and K. A. McGuigan (2000). Early predictors of adolescent violence. *American Journal of Public Health* 90: 566–572.

Ellis, L. (1991). A synthesized (biosocial) theory of rape. Special Section: Theories of sexual aggression. *Journal of Consulting and Clinical Psychology* 59: 631–642.

Ferguson, B. R. (2000). The causes and origins of "primitive warfare" on evolved motivations for war. *Anthropological Quarterly,* July, pp. 159–164.

Finkelhor, D. (1983). Common features of family abuse. In D. Finkelhor, R. J. Gelles, G. T. Hotaling, and M. A. Straus, eds., *The Dark Side of Families,* pp. 17–18. Beverly Hills, Calif.: Sage.

Fisher, B. (2000). Measuring sexual victimization against women: Identifying differences between survey questions. Presented at National Institute of Justice's Research Conference on Violence Against Women and Family Violence, Washington, D.C., October 2.

Frayser, S. G. (1989). Sexual and reproductive relationships: Cross-cultural evidence and biosocial implications. *Medical Anthropology* 11: 385–407.

Freud, S. (1901). *The Psychopathology of Everyday Life.* New York: W. W. Norton.

Friedl, E. (1975). *Women and Men: An Anthropologist's View.* New York: Holt, Rinehart and Winston.

Frintner, M. P. and L. Rubinson (1993). Acquaintance rape: The influence of alcohol, fraternity membership, and sports team membership. *Journal of Sex Education and Therapy* 19: 272–284.

Gat, Azar (2000). The human motivational complex: Evolutionary theory and the causes of hunter-gatherer fighting. Part I. Primary somatic and reproductive causes. *Anthropological Quarterly,* January, pp. 20–34y.

George, L. K., I. Winfield, and D. G. Blazer (1992). Sociocultural factors in sexual assault: Comparison of two representative samples of women. *Journal of Social Issues* 48: 105–126.

Gidycz, C. A., C. N. Coble, L. Latham, and M. J. Layman (1993). Relation of a sexual assault experience in adulthood to prior victimization experiences: A prospective analysis. *Psychology of Women Quarterly* 17: 151–168.

Gilbert, N. (1993). Examining the facts: Advocacy research overstates the incidence of date and acquaintance rape. In Richard Gelles and Donileen R. Loseke, eds., *Current Controversies on Family Violence.* Beverly Hills, Calif.: Sage.

Gise, L. H. and P. Paddison (1988). Rape, sexual abuse, and its victims. *The Violent Patient II* 4: 629–648.

Goodchilds, J. D., G. L. Zellman, P. B. Johnson, and R. Giarrusso (1989). Adolescents and their perceptions of sexual interactions. In A. W. Burgess, ed., *Rape and Sexual Assault,* vol. II, pp. 245–270. Garland: New York.

Gwartney-Gibbs, P. A., J. Stockard and S. Brohmer (1983). Learning courtship violence: The influence of parents, peers, and personal experiences. *Family Relations* 36: 276–282.

Hall, G. C. N. and R. Hirschman (1991). Toward a theory of sexual aggression: A quadripartite model. *Journal of Consulting and Clinical Psychology* 59: 662–669.

Hiese, L. L. (1998). Violence against women: An integrated, ecological framework. *Violence against Women* 4: 262–290.

Hirschi, T. (1969). *The Causes of Delinquency.* Berkeley: University of California Press.

Holmes, Ronald M. (1991). *Sex Crimes.* Thousand Oaks, Calif.: Sage.

Huesmann, L. R. and L. Eron (1992). Childhood aggression and adult criminality. In J. McCord, ed., *Facts, Frameworks, and Forecasts: Advances in Criminological Theory,* vol. 3, pp. 137–156. New Brunswick, N.J.: Transaction Publishers.

Humphrey, J. A. and J. W. White (2000). Women's vulnerability to sexual assault from adolescence to young adulthood. *Journal of Adolescent Health* 27: 419–424.

Jackson, T. L. (1991). A university athletic department's rape and assault experiences. *Journal of College Student Development* 32: 77–78.

Johnson, R. N. (1972). *Aggression in Man and Animals.* Philadelphia, Penn.: W. B. Sanders.

Kalmuss, D. S. (1984). The intergenerational transmission of marital aggression. *Journal of Marriage and the Family* 46: 11–19.

Kaufman, M. (1995). The construction of masculinity and the triad of men's violence. In Michael S. Kimmel and Michael A. Messner, eds., *Men's Lives,* 3rd edition, pp. 30–51. New York: Simon and Schuster.

Koss, M. P. (1985). The hidden rape victim: Personality, attitudinal, and situational characteristics. *Psychology of Women Quarterly* 9: 193–212.

Koss, M. P. (1989). Hidden rape: Sexual aggression and victimization in a national sample of students in higher education. In M. A. Pirog-Good and J. E. Stets, eds., *Violence in Dating Relationships: Emerging Social Issues,* pp. 145–168. New York: Praeger.

Koss, M. P. (1990). The women's mental health research agenda: Violence against women. *American Psychologist* 45: 374–380.

Koss, M. P. (1992). The underdetection of rape: Methodological choices influence incidence estimates. *Journal of Social Issues* 48: 61–75.

Koss, M. P. (1994). The negative impact of crime victimization on women's health and medical use. In A. J. Dan, ed., *Reframing Women's Health: Multidisciplinary Research and Practice,* pp. 189–200. Thousand Oaks, CA: Sage Publications.

Koss, M. P. (2000). Evolutionary models of why men rape: Acknowledging the complexities. *Trauma, Violence, and Abuse* 1: 182–190.

Koss, M. P. and T. E. Dinero (1989). Discriminant analysis of risk factors for sexual victimization among a national sample of college women. *Journal of Consulting and Clinical Psychology* 57: 242–250.

Koss, M. P. and J. A. Gaines (1993). The prediction of sexual aggression by alcohol use, athletic participation, and fraternity affiliation. *Journal of Interpersonal Violence* 8: 94–108.

Koss, M. P., C. A. Gidycz, and N. Wisniewski (1987). The scope of rape: Incidence and prevalence of sexual aggression and victimization in a national sample of higher education students. *Journal of Consulting and Clinical Psychology* 55: 162–170.

Kosson, D. S., J. C. Kelly, and J. W. White (1997). Psychopathy-related traits predict self-reported sexual aggression among college men. *Journal of Interpersonal Violence* 12: 241–254.

Kowalski, R. M. (1992). Nonverbal behaviors and perceptions of sexual intentions: Effects of sexual connotativeness, verbal response, and rape outcome. *Basic and Applied social Psychology* 13: 427–445.

Kowalski, R. M. (1993). Inferring sexual interest from behavioral cues: Effects of gender and sexually-relevant attitudes. *Sex Roles* 29: 13–31.

Kramer, L. (2001). *The Sociology of Gender.* Roxbury Publishing Company.

Kuecker, T. (1999). Uniform crime reports data on reported forcible rapes in Michigan. *Violence and Intentional Injury Prevention Program, Institute for Children, Youth, and Families,* Michigan State University. Volume 2, issue 2 (May).

Laner, M. R. (1983). Courtship abuse and aggression: Contextual aspects. *Sociological Spectrum* 3: 69–83.

LaPlante, M. N., N. McCormick, and G. G. Brannigan (1990). Living the sexual script: College students' views of influence in sexual encounters. *Journal of Sex Research* 16: 338–355.

Largen, M. A. (1985). The anti-rape movement past and present. In A. W. Burgess, ed., *Rape and Sexual Assault: A Research Handbook,* pp. 1–13.

LeJeune, C. and V. Follette (1994). Taking responsibility: Sex differences in reporting dating violence. *Journal of Interpersonal Violence* 9: 133–140.

Lepowsky, M. (1994). Women, men, and aggression in an egalitarian society. *Sex Roles* 30: 199–211.

Lerner, G. (1986). *The Creation of Patriarchy.* New York: Oxford University Press.

Lerner, R. M. (1991). Changing organism-context relations as the basic process of development: A developmental-contextual perspective. *Developmental Psychology* 27: 27–32.

Lloyd, S. A. (1991). The dark side of courtship. *Family Relations* 40: 14–20.

Lowdermilk, L., L. Holland, K. Cameron, and J. W. White (1998). Prevalence of sexual perpetration among community college males. Paper presented at Southeastern Psychological Association, Mobile, Ala., March.

Makepeace, J. (1981). Courtship violence among college students. *Family Relations* 30: 97–102.

Makepeace, J. M. (1987). Social factors and victim-offender differences in courtship violence. *Family Relations* 36: 87–91.

Makepeace, J. (1989). Dating, living together, and courtship violence. In M. A. Pirog-Good and J. E. Stets, eds., *Violence in Dating Relationships,* pp. 94–107. Praeger: New York.

Malamuth, N. M. (1986). Predictors of naturalistic aggression. *Journal of Personality and Social Psychology* 50: 953–962.

Malamuth, N. M. (1988). A multidimensional approach to sexual aggression: Combining measures of past behavior and present likelihood. *Human Sexual*

Aggression: Current Perspectives, Annals of the New York Academy of Science 528: 113–146.

Malamuth, N. M. (1996). The confluence model of sexual aggression: Feminist and evolutionary perspectives. In D. M. Buss and N. M. Malamuth, eds., *Sex, Power, Conflict: Evolutionary and Feminist Perspectives*, pp. 269–295. New York: Oxford University Press.

Malamuth, N. M. (1998). The confluence model as an organizing framework for research on sexually aggressive men: Risk moderators, imagined aggression, and pornography consumption. In R. G. Geen and E. Donnerstein, eds., *Human Aggression: Theories, Research, and Implications for Social Policy*, pp. 229–245. San Diego: Academic Press.

Malamuth, N. M. and N. W. Thornhill (1994). Hostile masculinity, sexual aggression, and gender-biased domineeringness in conversations. *Aggressive Behavior* 20: 185–194.

Malamuth, N. M., D. Linz, C. L. Heavey, G. Barnes, and M. Acker (1995). Using the confluence model of sexual aggression to predict men's conflict with women: A 10-year follow-up study. *Journal of Personality and Social Psychology* 69: 353–369.

Malamuth, N. M., R. J. Sockloskie, M. P. Koss, and J. S. Tanaka (1991). Characteristics of aggressors against women: Testing a model using a national sample of college students. *Journal of Consulting and Clinical Psychology* 59: 670–681.

Marsh, C. E. (1993). Sexual assault and domestic violence in the African American community. *Western Journal of Black Studies* 17: 149–155.

Mascia-Lees, F. E. and N. J. Black (2000). *Gender and Anthropology*. Prospect Heights, IL: Waveland Press.

Miller, S. L. (1994). Expanding the boundaries: Toward a more inclusive and integrated study of intimate violence. *Violence and Victims* 9: 183–199.

Mitscherlich, M. (1987). *The Peaceable Sex: On Aggression in Women and Men*. New York: Fromm International Publishing.

Mosher, D. L. and R. D. Anderson (1986). Macho personality, sexual aggression, and reactions to guided imagery of realistic rape. *Journal of Research in Personality* 20: 77–94.

Mills, C. S. and B. J. Granoff (1992). Date and acquaintance rape among a sample of college students. *Social Work* 37: 504–509.

Muehlenhard, C. L. and M. A. Linton (1987). Date rape and sexual aggression in dating situations: Incidence and risk factors. *Journal of Counseling Psychology* 34: 186–196.

Murphy, C. M., S. Meyer, and K. D. O'Leary (1993). Family of origin violence and MCMI-II psychopathology among partner assaultive men. *Violence and Victims* 8: 165–176.

Norris, J., P. S. Nurius, and T. L. Graham (1999). When a date changes from fun to dangerous: Factors affecting women's ability to distinguish. *Violence against Women* 5: 230–250.

Nurius, P. S. and J. Norris (1996). A cognitive ecological model of women's response to male sexual coercion in dating. *Journal of Psychology and Human Sexuality* 8: 117–139.

Olday, D. and B. Wesley (1983). Premarital courtship violence: A summary report. Moorehead State University, Moorehead, KY. Unpublished.

Olweus, D. (1993). Victimization by peers: Antecedents and longterm outcomes. In K. H. Rubin and J. B. Asendorpf, eds., *Social Withdrawal, Inhibition, and Shyness in Childhood*, pp. 315–341. Hillsdale, N.J.: Erlbaum.

Pagelow, M. D. (1984). *Family Violence*. New York: Praeger.

Pedersen, P. and C. D. Thomas (1992). Prevalence and correlates of dating violence in a Canadian university sample. *Canadian Journal of Behavioural Science* 24: 490–501.

Porter, R. (1986). Rape—Does it have a historical meaning? In Sylvana Tomaselli and Roy Porter, eds., *Rape: An Historical and Social Enquiry*, pp. 216–263. London: Basil Blackwell.

Rapaport, K. R. and B. R. Burkhart (1984). Personality and attitudinal characteristics of sexually coercive college males. *Journal of Abnormal Psychology* 93: 216–221.

Renzetti, C. (1992). *Violent Betrayal: Partner Abuse in Lesbian Relationships*. Newbury Park, Calif.: Sage.

Rice, F. P. (1984). *The Adolescent: Development, Relations, and Culture*. Boston: Allyn and Bacon.

Richardson, D. and G. Hammock (1991). The role of alcohol in acquaintance rape. In A. Parrott and L. Bechhofer, eds., *Acquaintance Rape: The Hidden Crime*, pp. 83–95. New York: Wiley.

Riggs, D. S. (1993). Relationship problems and dating aggression: A potential treatment target. *Journal of Interpersonal Violence* 8: 18–35.

Riggs, D. S. and M. B. Caulfield (1997). Expected consequences of male violence against their female dating partners. *Journal of Interpersonal Violence* 12: 229–240.

Roiphe, K. (1993). *The Morning After: Sex, Fear, and Feminism on Campus*. New York: Little, Brown.

Roscoe, B. and T. Kelsey (1986). Dating violence among high school students. *Psychology* 23: 53–59.

Rose, S. and I. H. Frieze (1993). Young singles' contemporary dating scripts. *Sex Roles* 28: 499–509.

Rozee, P. D. (1993). Forbidden or forgiven? Rape in cross-cultural perspective. *Psychology of Women Quarterly* 17: 499–514.

Ryan, K. M. (1995). Do courtship-violent men have characteristics associated with a battering personality? *Journal of Family Violence* 10: 99–120.

Salzman, F. (1979). Aggression and gender: A critique of the nature-nurture question for humans. In R. Hubbard and M. Lowe eds., *Genes and Gender II: Pitfalls in Research on Sex and Gender*, pp. 71–89. New York: Gordian Press.

Samarasinghe, V. (1994). The place of the WID discourse in global feminist analysis: The potential for a "reverse flow." In Gay Young and Bette J. Dickerson, eds., *Color, Class, and Country: Experiences of Gender*, pp. 218–231. N.J.: Zed Books.

Sampson, R. J. and W. B. Groves (1989). Community structure and crime: Testing social-disorganization theory. *American Journal of Sociology* 94: 774–802.

Sanday, P. R. (1981). The socio-cultural context of rape: A cross-cultural study. *The Journal of Social Issues* 37: 5–27.

Sawyer, R. G., P. J. Pinciaro, and J. K. Jessell (1998). Effects of coercion and verbal consent on university students' perception of date rape. *American Journal of Health Behavior* 22: 46–53.

Schlegal, A. (1989). Gender issues and cross-cultural research. *Behavior Science Research* 23: 265–280.

Shaw, C. and H. McKay (1942). *Juvenile Delinquency and Urban Areas*. Chicago: University of Chicago Press.

Shostak, M. (1981). *Nisa, the Life and Words of a Kung Woman*. Cambridge, Mass.: Harvard University Press.

Shotland, R. L. (1989). A model of the causes of date rape in developing and close relationships. In C. Hendrick, ed., *Close Relationships*, pp. 247–270. Thousand Oaks, Calif.: Sage.

Shotland, R. L. (1992). A theory of the causes of courtship rape: Part 2. *Journal of Social Issues* 48: 127–143.

Shotland, R. L. and L. Goodstein (1992). Sexual precedence reduces the perceived legitimacy of sexual refusal: An examination of attributions concerning date rape and consensual sex. *Personality and Social Psychology Bulletin* 18: 756–764.

Sorenson, S. B. and J. M. Siegel (1991). Gender, ethnicity, and sexual assault: Findings from the Los Angeles Epidemiological catchment area study. *Journal of Social Issues* 48: 93–104.

Straus, M. A., R. J. Gelles, and S. Steinmetz (1980). *Behind Closed Doors: Violence in the American Family*. Garden City, N.Y.: Anchor Press.

Sugarman, D. B. and G. T. Hotaling (1989). Dating violence: Prevalence, context, and risk markers. In M. A. Pirog-Good and J. E. Stets, eds., *Violence in Dating Relationships*, pp. 3–32. New York: Praeger.

Thornhill, R. and C. T. Palmer (2000). *A Natural History of Rape: Biological Basis of Sexual Coercion*. Cambridge, Mass.: MIT Press.

Tiefer, L. (1988). A feminist perspective on sexology and sexuality. In M. M. Gergen, ed., *Feminist Thought and the Structure of Knowledge*, pp. 16–26. New York: New York Univ. Press.

Tjaden, P. and N. Thoennes (1998). *Stalking in America: Findings from the National Violence against Women Survey*. Denver, Colo.: Center for Policy Research.

Tomaselli, S. and R. Porter (1986). *Rape: An Historical and Social Enquiry*. London: Basil Blackwell.

U.S. Department of Justice, Federal Bureau of Investigation (1997). *Uniform Crime Reports*. Washington, D.C.: Government Printing Office.

Vannoy, Dana (2001). *Gender Mosaics: Social Perspectives.* Roxbury Publishing.

Vicary, J. R., L. R. Klingman, and W. L. Harkness (1995). Risk factors associated with date rape and sexual assault of adolescent girls. *Journal of Adolescence* 18: 289–306.

Ward, M. C. (1999). *A World Full of Women,* 2d ed. Boston: Allyn and Bacon.

White, J. W. and B. Bondurant (1996). Gendered violence. In J. T. Wood, ed., *Gendered Relationships,* pp. 197–210. Mountain View, Calif.: Mayfield Press.

White, J. W., P. L. N. Donat, and B. Bondurant (2001). A developmental examination of violence against girls and women. In R. Unger, ed., *Handbook of Feminist Psychology,* pp. 343–356. New York: Academic Press.

White, J. W. and J. A. Humphrey (1991). Young people's attitudes toward acquaintance rape. In A. Parrott and L. Bechhofer, eds., *Acquaintance Rape,* pp. 43–56. New York: Wiley and Sons.

White, J. W. and J. A. Humphrey (1994). Alcohol/drug use and sexual aggression: Distal and proximal influences. Paper presented at XI World Meeting: International Society for Research on Aggression. Delray Beach, Florida, July.

White, J. W. and J. A. Humphrey (1995). Sexual assault perpetration and re-perpetration: From adolescence to young adulthood. Paper presented at National Violence Prevention Conference, Des Moines, Iowa, October.

White, J. W. and J. A. Humphrey (1997). A longitudinal approach to the study of sexual aggression: Theoretical and methodological considerations. In M. D. Schwartz, ed., *Researching Sexual Violence against Women: Methodological and Personal Perspectives,* pp. 22–42. Thousand Oaks, Calif.: Sage.

White, J. W. and J. A. Humphrey (1990). A Theoretical Model of Sexual Assault: An Empirical Test. Paper presented at the symposium on Sexual Assault: Research, Treatment, and Education. Southeastern Psychological Association meeting, Atlanta, Ga., March.

White, J. W. and M. P. Koss (1991). Adolescent sexual aggression within heterosexual relationships: Prevalence, characteristics, and causes. In H. E. Barbarbee, W. L. Marshall, and D. R. Laws, eds., *The Juvenile Sexual Offender,* pp. 182–202. New York: Guilford Press.

White, J. W., M. P. Koss, and G. Kissling (1991). Gender differences in structural models of courtship violence. Poster presented at American Psychological Society, Washington, D.C., June.

White, J. W. and R. M. Kowalski (1998). Male violence toward women: An integrated perspective. In Russell Geen and Edward Donnerstein, eds., *Human Aggression: Theories, Research, and Implications for Social Policy,* pp. 205–229. New York: Academic Press.

Williams, K. R., N. G. Guerra, and D. S. Elliott (1999). *Supporting Youth by Strengthening Communities: Helping Children Grow and Preventing Problem Behaviors: The DART Model: Linking Development and Risk Together.* Boulder, Colo.: Center for the Study and Prevention of Violence, Institute of Behavioral Science, University of Colorado at Boulder.

Williams, J. G. and J. P. Smith (1994). Drinking patterns and dating violence among college students. *Psychology of Addictive Behaviors* 8: 51–53.

Wyatt, G. E. (1985). The sexual abuse of Afro-American and White-American women in childhood. *Child Abuse and Neglect* 9: 507–519.

Wyatt, G. E. (1992). Sociocultural context of African American and White American women's rape. *Journal of Social Issues* 48: 77–92.

Wyatt, G. E., G. Guthrie, and C. M. Notgrass (1992). Differential effects of women's child sexual abuse and subsequent sexual revictimization. *Journal of Consulting and Clinical Psychology* 60: 167–173.

Young, G. and B. J. Dickerson (1994). Introduction. In Gay Young and B. J. Dickerson, eds., *Color, Class, and Country: Experiences of Gender*, pp. 1–14. N.J.: Zed Books.

Zweig, J. M., B. L. Barber, and J. S. Eccles (1997). Sexual coercion and well-being in young adulthood: Comparisons by gender and college status. *Journal of Interpersonal Violence* 12: 291–230.

Coming Full Circle: Refuting Biological Determinism

Sue V. Rosser

In *Evolution, Gender, and Rape* anthropologists, evolutionary biologists, ecologists, philosophers, primatologists, psychologists, sociologists, and women's studies scholars respond to Randy Thornhill and Craig Palmer's book, *A Natural History of Rape: Biological Bases of Sexual Coercion,* published in 2000. Although chapter authors express varying disciplinary, professional, and personal reasons for laying aside their own significant research agendas and pressing scholarly obligations to refute Thornhill and Palmer, Michael Kimmel gives a most succinct answer to the question of why scholars should respond to *A Natural History of Rape.* Kimmel's answer, that it must be addressed because the Thornhill and Palmer book represents bad science, bad politics, and bad writing, is echoed by all respondents from their different disciplinary or interdisciplinary perspectives.

A Natural History of Rape stands as a recent addition to the lengthy tradition of biological determinism, in which biological differences among races, sexes, classes, and species in anatomy, hormones, and genes are studied to provide biological justifications for social, behavioral, and psychological inequalities. The biological determinism tradition predates the nineteenth century, and works by Gould (1981), Keller (1985), Rose (1982), and Sayers (1982) elegantly trace the roots connecting the nineteenth-century tradition to its pre-nineteenth-century antecedents, as well as its successors in the twentieth century.

Modern evolutionary biology is based on and has its roots in the nineteenth-century theory proposed by Charles Darwin ([1859] 1967). Although this theory seemed revolutionary at the time, scholars have suggested that natural selection, as described by Darwin, was ultimately accepted by his contemporaries because it was a paradigm laden with the values of nineteenth-century England. Rose and Rose (1980) underline the congruence between the values expressed in Darwin's theory and those of the upper classes of Victorian England: "Its central metaphors drawn from society and in their turn interacting with society were of the competition of the species, the struggle for existence, the ecological niche, and the survival of the fittest" (p. 28). These metaphors reflect Victorian society and were acceptable to it because they, and the "social Darwinism" quickly derived from it, seemed to ground its norms solidly in a biological foundation. When Darwin depicts the fittest as the individuals who pass on their genes to the greatest number of offspring, one thinks of the importance of passing on property in that society.

The upper class of Victorian England had self-serving reasons for finding Darwin's theory attractive: It gave a biological rationale for their position in society. Nor was Darwin's own position a matter unrelated to the acceptability of his theory. Even though Darwin himself was not aggressive in advancing it, he had wealthy and influential friends such as Thomas Henry Huxley, Sir Charles Lyell, and Sir Joseph Dalton Hooker who championed the theory for him. Aside from noting its statement in terms of upper-class Victorian values and decrying the misuse of his theory of natural selection by social Darwinists, feminist scientists by and large have not critiqued the theory of natural selection. As scientists, they have recognized the significance of the theory for the foundations of modern biology.

In contrast to accepting his theory of natural selection, many feminist scientists have critiqued Darwin's theory of sexual selection for its androcentric bias. The theory of sexual selection reflected and reinforced Victorian social norms regarding the sexes. By this theory Darwin set out to explain a phenomenon still not fully understood, that of the existence of secondary sex characteristics. He claimed that "when the males and females of any animal have the same general habits of life, but differ in structure, color, or ornament, such differences have been mainly caused by sexual selection" (Darwin 1967, p. 89). Expanding considerably on the theory first presented in the *Origin,* Darwin specified, in the *Descent of Man,* how the process functions and what roles males and females play in it: "The sexual struggle is of two kinds: in the one it is between the individuals of the same sex, generally the males, in order to drive away or kill their rivals, the females remaining passive; whilst in the other, the struggle is likewise between the individuals of the same sex, in order to excite or charm those of the opposite sex, generally the females, which no longer remain passive, but select the more agreeable partners" (Darwin 1871, p. 64). According to the theory, the males who triumph over their rivals will win the more desirable females and will leave the most progeny, thereby perpetuating and increasing, over numerous generations, those qualities that afforded them victory. The females who succeed, by the seductive means they employ, in being chosen will also procreate best and pass on their characteristics. As a result, by the time evolution has produced modern man and modern woman, the two are considerably different, men being superior to women both physically and mentally. Not only are they "taller, heavier, and stronger than women, with squarer shoulders and more plainly pronounced muscles," but also they attain to a "higher eminence" in whatever they take up (Darwin 1871, p. 564). The theory reflects the Victorian age, with its depiction of active males competing and struggling with each other for passive females. That depiction of male-female interaction would have seemed quite obvious to most segments of Victorian society and its grounding in scientific fact most reassuring.

The process of selection involved in the theory of sexual selection encountered considerable resistance. Why, then, one wonders, did Darwin insist on the theory so much? What role did it play in his total conception of change in nature? Initially in the *Origin,* Darwin used the theory as a secondary agent to explain the means by which evolution takes place: "Amongst many animals, sexual selection will give its aid to ordinary selection, by assuring to the most vigorous and best adapted males the greatest number of offspring" (1967, p. 127). The reader understands readily that sexual selection is a minor support to natural selection. But the reader may be surprised to see that only males are mentioned as the bearers of the desirable characteristics that are sexually selected. At this point in the text Darwin adds a second benefit of sexual selection: "Sexual selection will also give characters useful to the males alone, in their struggles with other males." Again, the focus is entirely on the male half of the species. The only activity envisioned in this expression is bound up in a masculine world.

What seems to have struck Darwin most when he observed males and females of species throughout the natural world was the tremendous difference between them: "How enormously these sometimes differ in the most important characters is known to every naturalist" (1967, p. 424).

What amazed him was the fact that such different beings belong to the same species. When viewing the human world in the light of other natural realms, he was even surprised that even greater differences had not been evolved. "It is, indeed, fortunate that the law of the equal transmission of characters to both sexes prevails with mammals; otherwise it is probable that man would have become as superior in mental endowment to woman, as the peacock is in ornamental plumage to the peahen" (1871, p. 565).

At first view it may seem strange that Darwin stresses the differences between the sexes. In the *Origin* he depicts the struggle for existence as a mainly interspecific conflict, claiming that competition is fiercest among those closest in the scale of nature (1967, p. 76). Yet when he comes to those beings most closely related, namely the males and females of a given species, he does not speak of competition at all but rather of an entirely masculine struggle for females. Indeed, as he depicts male-female interaction, it seems that the males constitute something like a separate group, interacting mainly with each other in relation to another quite separate group, the members of which have relatively fewer secondary sex characteristics. To make the differentiation between males and females as strong as possible, the theory of sexual selection is needed. The theory is the agent of differentiation, that which assures an ever-increasing separation between the sexes and their operation in two quite distinct realms that touch only for the purpose of procreation.

Social Darwinism, the nineteenth-century form of biological determinism, used Darwin's work on evolutionary biology to provide a biological justification for social inequalities between people of different classes (Rose and Rose 1980); like the nineteenth-century Social Darwinists (Spencer 1892); Thornhill and Palmer rely on evolutionary biology as the basis for their arguments about rape. In her chapter in this volume, "What Is Rape?" Emily Martin underlines the significance of the cultural context of Victorian England for Darwin's theory and suggests that particular aspects of the twentieth century provide the context for Thornhill and Palmer's work to gain a foothold.

When sociobiology, the scholarly tradition with which *A Natural History of Rape* overtly connects itself, emerged, critics (e.g., Lowe and Hubbard 1979; Bleier 1979, 1984; Lewontin, Rose, and Kamin 1984) immediately stamped it as a new form of biological determinism. Sociobiology added genes to the nineteenth-century factors of anatomical and hormonal differences that might justify social inequalities between human sexes, races, and classes.

In reviewing critiques of sociobiology literature in 1992, I wrote the following:

Some sociobiologists, such as Barash (1977), Dawkins (1976), and Wilson (1975) have based their new discipline on biological determinism in stating that behavior is genetically determined and that differences between males and females in role, status, and performance are biologically based. Sociobiology is the study of the biological basis of behavior. It attempts to show that human social institutions and social behavior are the results of biological forces acting through prehuman and human evolution. The theory is based on Darwin's theory of evolution through natural selection, which sociobiologists claim to extend and amplify (Lowe & Hubbard, 1979). Sociobiologists describe human sex roles and behaviors as innate and programmed into the genes. They base these roles and behaviors on examples of social interaction in lower animals, which, not coincidentally, remind us in their turn of the human world: "Aggression," "selfishness," "male dominance" (Wilson, 1975).

Feminist critiques of sociobiology have centered around criticisms of the assumption that behaviors such as aggression, homosexuality, promiscuity, selfishness, and altruism are biologically determined and the problems involved with anthropomorphism in animal behavior studies. The anthropomorphism occurs in at least two forms: (1) the use of human language and frameworks to describe animal behavior that is then used to "prove" that certain human behaviors are innate as they are also found in animals; and (2) the selective choice of species for study that mirror human society. The data from those selected species are then assumed to be the universal behavior of all species. Some scientists have suggested that these feminist critiques are obvious. However, the most renowned sociobiologists (Dawkins, 1976; Trivers, 1972; Wilson, 1978) have continued to assume that genes do determine behavior and that the behaviors described as aggression, homosexuality, rape, selfishness, and altruism in animals are equivalent to those behaviors in humans, even though more than one decade of criticism by feminists (Bleier, 1976; Hubbard, 1990; Lowe, 1978; Lowe & Hubbard, 1983) has been leveled against the "obvious" flaws in the sociobiological theories and assumptions. (Rosser, 1992, p. 60)

Some critiques raised by authors of *Evolution, Gender, and Rape* to *A Natural History of Rape* point out the continuing use of anthropomorphic language and selective choice of species. Although many authors underline faulty use of language, particularly regarding the definition of rape, Tobach and Reed detail the logical fallacies surrounding Thornhill and Palmer's use of rape, including the redefinition of rape in war. In his detailed refutation of the scientific basis for Thornhill and Palmer's claim that human rape is an evolved adaptation, Jerry Coyne also points out that the evolutionarily based social reforms proposed by Thornhill and Palmer are easily derived from nonevolutionary views of rape.

In that same 1992 book where I reviewed sociobiology critiques, I wrote the following:

Similarly, it was clear in the early primatology work (Yerkes, 1943) that particular primate species, such as the baboon and chimpanzee, were chosen for study primarily because their social organization was seen by the observers as closely resembling that of human primates. However, subsequent researchers forgot the "obvious" limitations imposed by such selection of species and proceeded to generalize the data to universal behavior patterns for all primates. It was not until a significant number of women entered primatology that the concepts of the universality and male leadership of dominance hierarchies among primates (Lancaster, 1975; Leavitt, 1975; Leibowitz, 1975; Rowell, 1974) were questioned and shown to be inaccurate for many primate species. The "evident" problems discussed by feminist critics (Bleier, 1984) of studying nonhuman primates in an attempt to discover what the true nature of humans would be without the overlay of culture, have been largely ignored by many of the sociobiologists and scientists studying animal behavior. Feminist critiques of animal behavior and sociobiology attack the assumption of biological determinism: that biology (genes) determines behavior and that those biological effects may be measured separately from those of culture. (Rosser 1992, pp. 60–61)

In their respective chapters in this volume, both Drea and Wallen and Gowaty provide numerous examples of variations among mammalian species in rape behaviors and female control over male sexual behavior. These many examples underline the fallacy of drawing conclusions as Thornhill and Palmer have done based on selective choice of species. Gowaty also brings attention to the significant role of variance *within* the female population of the same species. Some females possess greater physical strength or more effective behavioral strategies for avoiding male sexual coercion. Both among- and within-species variation among nonhuman primates and other mammals emphasize the importance of using extreme caution in drawing universal conclusions about behaviors such as rape in humans by extrapolating data from behaviors that may be inappropriately anthropomorphized in species that may have been selectively chosen because they reflect human society.

As Sanday reports in her chapter, her research on ninety-five band and tribal societies documents that the incidence of rape varies considerably cross-culturally and depends on a variety of social factors, particularly the status of women within that society. Thus, human rape varies tremendously across cultures within the species, thereby refuting the notion of Thornhill and Palmer that rape is universal and adaptive. The same critiques made of Thornhill and Palmer's research—selective use of species, anthropomorphic and vague language, universalizing and extrapolating beyond the limits of data, and failure adequately to study female behavior—represent recurrent arguments leveled by numerous scholars to reveal flaws in some sociobiology claims in the 1970s and 1980s.

In 1984, Dagg outlined six ways in which bias, especially sexual bias, entered the literature of social behavior of animals:

1. internal contradictions in reports, with generalizations contradicting primary data;

2. inadequate experimental design in behavioural studies so that female behaviour was largely ignored;

3. biased collection of data so that information showing females as sometimes dominant, often aggressive, and active in mating (anti-stereotypes for women) was not adequately collected;

4. misinterpretation of observations, with females seen as possessions of and inferior to males;

5. misleading presentation of data in popular works and textbooks so that males are seen as preeminent to females; and

6. misinformation, with sociobiologists actually changing observed field data so that they would fit in with their theories of sociobiology. (p. 118)

In *Evolution, Gender,* and *Rape,* chapter authors uncover similar biases in Thornhill and Palmer's 2000 work to those outlined by Dagg for sociobiology in 1984:

1.   Generalizations contradicting primary data   Although virtually all chapter authors critique Thornhill and Palmer for drawing inappropriate generalizations from primary data, Shields and Steinke directly confront Thornhill and Palmer's assertion of "identifying ultimate causes" (p. 4) because "an ultimate explanation of a biological phenomenon can account for all proximate causes influencing the phenomenon, whether the phenomenon is an adaptation or an incidental effect of an adaptation" (p. 12). Shields and Steinke painstakingly uncover problems in using self-report data on which Thornhill and Palmer's arguments are based, as well as the logical inconsistencies these introduce in the conclusions Thornhill and Palmer draw about rape.

In his chapter, "The Evolutionary Value of the Man (to) Child Affiliative Bond," Mackey underlines that rape is not an adaptive behavior for males because rape often precludes the biological father from becoming the social father. Because rape produces offspring that are disadvantaged adults, this contradicts the generalization drawn by Thornhill and Palmer that rape is an effective evolutionary strategy.

2. Ignoring female behavior   Several authors, particularly Gowaty, as well as Drea and Wallen, underline Thornhill and Palmer's failure to include experimental data, based on women's behavior in primates and other species, that contradicts their conclusions. Lloyd reveals additional ignorance or overlooking by Thornhill and Palmer. Lloyd points out that the main arguments for the evolutionary explanations for rape given by Thornhill and Palmer rest on their "hypothesis about the evolution of sex differences: that because women bear the brunt of the effort in reproduction—through pregnancy, nursing, and infant care—they have evolved to be very selective about their mates" (this vol. p. xx). Although selection is important, it is not the only mechanism accounting for evolution. Drift, mutation, recombination, and gene flow, in addition to selection, all cause evolution. As Lloyd underlines, not only do Thornhill and Palmer ignore the contributions of these four factors, but they also fail to demonstrate that rape is inheritable or adaptive.

3, 4. Data on females biased or misinterpreted   As their chapter titles, "Female Sexuality and the Myth of Male Control" and "Power Asymmetries between the Sexes, Mate Preferences, and Components of Fitness," announce, both Drea and Wallen and Gowaty in their respective chapters document examples from animal behavior where females are dominant, aggressive, and active in mating. These contradict the universal behaviors and generalizations drawn by Randy Thornhill and Craig Palmer. These two chapters also provide counterevidence for the misinterpretation of evidence where Thornhill and Palmer interpret females as inferior to males because of evolutionary dispositions. In "The Origins of Sex Differences in Human Behavior," Eagly and Wood compare and contrast the arguments for sex differences based on the evolutionary dispositions with those based on social roles. They demonstrate that social structures provide equally effective explanations to those of evolutionary psychology for sex-differentiated social behaviors. Thornhill and Palmer have interpreted data to privilege the evolutionary psychology explanations and ignore the social structural causes for rape.

5. Misleading presentation in popular works *A Natural History of Rape* itself targets a popular audience. In that sense, the entire volume becomes a misleading presentation of data in popular works and textbooks so that males are seen as preeminent to females as documented by the chapter authors in this volume. As their chapter title, "Pop Sociobiology Reborn: The Evolutionary Psychology of Sex and Violence," suggests, Vickers and Kitcher carefully uncover the leaps in logic and scant solid science, compounded by outright mistakes, that underpin the evidence Thornhill and Palmer marshal for their evolutionary basis for rape.

6. Misinformation As Vickers and Kitcher spell out, the new pop sociobiology, known as evolutionary psychology, is very appealing to popular audiences because it provides a simple, pseudoscientific explanation for the complex phenomenon of sex and violence known as rape. Almost all authors in *Evolution, Gender, and Rape* but most especially Kimmel, Lloyd, Shields, and Steinke have uncovered the ways in which Thornhill and Palmer's work represents bad science and/or pseudoscience. In their respective chapters, Travis, Koss, and White and Post demonstrate why a unicausal, biological explanation is too simple for a complex psychological, social, behavioral, and cultural phenomenon such as rape.

The reason the simple, pseudo-scientific biological explanation appeals to the general public is understandable. First, it is simple. Social structural explanations analyzing power, economic inequalities, stratification of the labor market, and other social factors, as well as biological variance, are complicated. Not only is it difficult to sort out the contribution of each, it becomes almost impossible to convey the complex explanations simplistically with sound bites that appeal to the general public. Second, if rape is based solely in biology, it removes guilt and responsibility. No one can be said to cause it (and thus be blamed) and no one can do much to fix it (pay for it with expensive social, educational programs to level inequalities). Finally, it explains why this latest contribution to the lengthy tradition of biological determinism, from its nineteenth-century antecedents, through Social Darwinism, to animal behavior to sociobiology to evolutionary psychology, receives attention.

A Natural History of Rape receives attention from the general public because it meshes with people's desire to find a simple explanation for a troubling, complex phenomenon. It draws the attention of part of the scientific community, who are understandably excited about the promise of evolutionary psychology because of the recent, fundamental advances from the Human Genome Project.

Some good research in evolutionary psychology occurs when properly designed experiments are used in a particular species to answer a focused question. In the earlier work in sociobiology in the 1970s and 1980s, excellent animal behavior research carried out by well-known scientists on insects, birds, and lower mammals, became problematic only when the results were extrapolated beyond what the data warranted and when inappropriate generalizations were made to human beings. For example, no one questions the validity of E. O. Wilson's entymological work on insect behavior. The controversy arose when he extrapolated results from data on insect behavior to mammals, particularly to human beings. To distinguish the well-grounded excellent animal behavior research based on genetics in insects or birds from the less-documented, over-generalized leap to human behavior, the former began to be referred to as sociobiology (small "s"), while the latter extrapolation to humans was designated as Sociobiology. The capital letter distinction provides an immediate marker to distinguish the well-done research from the pseudo-scientific extrapolations and conclusions for humans.

The reason *A Natural History of Rape* merits the attention of a refutation response from some of the most eminent anthropologists, evolutionary biologists, ecologists, philosophers, primatologists, psychologists, sociologists, and women's studies scholars is that the argument for the evolutionary psychology of rape presented by Thornhill and Palmer represents the latest contribution to Sociobiology. All of the flaws and biases identified as problems with Social Darwinism in the nineteenth century and Sociobiology in the twentieth century, including anthropomorphic use of language, selective use of species, ignoring female contributions, assuming male dominance, misinformation and misleading presentations of data, apply to Thornhill and Palmer's twenty-first-century version of biological determinism focused on the evolutionary psychology of rape.

References

Barash, D. (1977). *Sociobiology and Behavior.* New York: Elsevier.

Bleier, R. (1979). Social and political bias in science: An examination of animal studies and their generalizations to human behavior and evolution. In R. Hubbard and M. Lowe, eds., *Genes and Gender II,* pp. 49–70. Staten Island, NY: Gordian Press.

Bleier, R. (1984). *Science and Gender: A Critique of Biology and Its Theories on Women.* New York: Pergamon Press.

Dagg, A. I. (1984). Sexual bias in the literature of social behaviour of mammals and birds. *International Journal of Women's Studies* 7(2): 118–135.

Darwin, C. (1871). *Descent of Man.* London: Murray.

Darwin, C. (1859 [1967]). *On the Origin of Species: A Facsimile of the First Edition.* New York: Atheneum.

Dawkins, R. (1976). *The Selfish Gene.* New York: Oxford University Press.

Gould, S. J. (1981). *The Mismeasure of Man.* New York: W. W. Norton.

Hubbard, R. (1990). *Politics of Women's Biology.* New Brunswick, NJ: Rutgers University Press.

Keller, E. F. (1985). *Reflections on Gender and Science.* New Haven, CT: Yale University Press.

Lancaster, J. (1975). *Primate Behavior and the Emergence of Human Culture.* New York: Holt, Rinehart, and Winston.

Leavitt, R. R. (1975). *Peaceable Primates and Gentle People: Anthropological Approaches to Women's Studies.* New York: Harper and Row.

Leibowitz, L. (1975). Perspectives in the evolution of sex differences. In R. R. Reiter, ed., *Toward an Anthropology of Women.* New York: Monthly Review Press.

Lewontin, R. C., S. Rose, and L. Kamin (1984). *Not in Our Genes: Biology, Ideology, and Human Nature.* New York: Pantheon Books.

Lowe, M. (1978). Sociobiology and sex differences. *Signs: Journal of Women in Culture and Society* 4(1), 118–125.

Lowe, M. and R. Hubbard (1983) *Women's Nature: Rationalizations of Inequality.* New York: Pergamon Press.

Rose, H. and S. Rose (1980). The myth of the neutrality of science. In R. Arditti, P. Brennan, and S. Cavrak, eds., *Science and Liberation.* Boston: South End Press.

Rose, S. (1982). *Against Biological Determinism.* London: Allison and Busby.

Rosser, S. (1992). *Biology and Feminism: A Dynamic Interaction.* New York: Twayne.

Rowell, T. (1974). The concept of social dominance. *Behavioral Biology* 11: 131–154.

Sayers, J. (1982). *Biological Politics: Feminist and Anti-feminist Perspectives.* London: Tavistock.

Spencer, H. (1892). *The Principles of Ethics.* New York: D. Appleton.

Trivers, R. L. (1972). Parental investment and sexual selection. In B. Campbell, ed., *Sexual Selection and the Descent of Man.* Chicago, IL: Aldine.

Wilson, E. O. (1975). *Sociobiology: The New Synthesis.* Cambridge, MA: Harvard University Press.

Yerkes, R. M. (1943). *Chimpanzees.* New Haven: Yale University Press.

Index